Democracy, Inequality and C

In this comparative, historical survey of three East-Asian democracies, Jong-sung You explores the correlation between inequality and corruption in the countries of South Korea, Taiwan and the Philippines. Drawing on a wealth of rich empirical research, he illustrates the ways in which economic inequality can undermine democratic accountability, thereby increasing the risk of clientelism and capture. Transcending the scope of corruption research beyond economic growth, this book surveys why some countries, like the Philippines, have failed to curb corruption and develop, whilst others such as South Korea and Taiwan have been more successful. Taking into account factors such as the success and failure of land reform, variations in social structure and industrial policy, Jong-sung You provides a sound example of how comparative analysis can be employed to identify causal direction and mechanisms in political science.

JONG-SUNG YOU is Senior Lecturer at the Department of Political and Social Change, School of International, Political and Strategic Studies, ANU College of Asia and the Pacific, The Australian National University.

Democracy, Inequality and Corruption

Korea, Taiwan and the Philippines Compared

Jong-sung You

CAMBRIDGE
UNIVERSITY PRESS

CAMBRIDGE
UNIVERSITY PRESS

University Printing House, Cambridge CB2 8BS, United Kingdom

Cambridge University Press is part of the University of Cambridge.

It furthers the University's mission by disseminating knowledge in the pursuit of education, learning and research at the highest international levels of excellence.

www.cambridge.org
Information on this title: www.cambridge.org/9781107435322

© Jong-sung You 2015

First published 2015
First paperback edition 2016

A catalogue record for this publication is available from the British Library

ISBN 978-1-107-07840-6 Hardback
ISBN 978-1-107-43532-2 Paperback

Contents

Figures

Tables

Acknowledgments

As an activist-turned-scholar, I have to confess that the themes of this book – democracy, inequality and corruption – are the same issues that I focused on during my activist career. I fought for democracy under military dictatorships, and then fought against inequality and corruption in South Korea before pursuing an academic career. I was actively involved in the student movement for democracy to end the authoritarian regimes of Park Chung-hee and Chun Doo-hwan. I was pursued and investigated numerous times and even tortured several times by the police, Korean Central Intelligence Agency and the military. I was expelled twice from Seoul National University, convicted by the civilian and military courts in violation of the presidential Emergency Measure No. 9 and the Martial Law three times, and spent more than two years in prison. After the democratic transition, I fought for social and economic justice at a newly created civil advocacy group, Citizens' Coalition for Economic Justice, first as Director of Policy Research and later as General Secretary. The main work of this organization was advocating for reform of the *chaebol*-dominated polarized economy and anti-corruption reforms such as implementation of the real-name financial transaction system, fair taxation, greater transparency in corporate governance, political financing and government policy-making. It may not be coincidence that democracy, inequality and corruption thus became my central topics for intellectual inquiry.

This book project originated from a chapter in my dissertation entitled *A Comparative Study of Corruption, Inequality and Social Trust* for the fulfillment of Ph.D. in Public Policy at Harvard University in 2006. Central to this dissertation was a cross-national quantitative study on the causal effect of economic inequality on corruption. During the writing process, my advisor Professor Robert Putnam urged me to include a case study as a supplementary chapter. After struggling for a while, I wrote a comparative case study of Korea, Taiwan and the Philippines on inequality and corruption. That supplementary chapter eventually developed into this book. Without his advice, my intellectual journey for this book would not have even begun. His seminal work, *Making Democracy Work: Civic Traditions in Modern Italy*, provided the methodological inspiration for my own book. He was not only a great researcher, but also a wonderful instructor and mentor, and I was very lucky to have him as my academic advisor.

My study of the causal relationship between inequality and corruption was motivated by my frustration with previously available empirical studies. For me, corruption is normatively objectionable even before considering its consequences on economic development. This led me to write a chapter on "Corruption as Injustice." I did not agree with some early literature on corruption that argued for functionality of corruption, and was relieved by the empirical findings of later studies demonstrating that corruption is not only harmful for economic and social development, but that it also tends to increase inequality. However, I was disturbed by the previous empirical findings that economic development was by far the most important predictor, if not determinant, of corruption, while inequality was not deemed a significant factor for levels of corruption. Identifying some flaws in the methodologies and data from these studies, I worked on a more reliable and expanded model, using instrumental variables, and found a significant and important causal effect of inequality on corruption. Professor Sanjeev Khagram recognized the importance of this empirical finding and encouraged and helped me, as a second author, to develop my paper into a publishable piece. This paper was eventually published in a prestigious journal, *American Sociological Review*, in 2005. As for why inequality should increase corruption, we proposed a political economy explanation based on elite capture of the policy-making process.

When I worked on the case study for a supplementary chapter of the dissertation, I relied on secondary sources only, without any field study. I did not imagine that I would develop this chapter into a book at that time. My training at Harvard's Kennedy School of Government was centered on quantitative methods, and I tended to value quantitative studies more than qualitative studies. Since beginning work in the Korea-Pacific program at the Graduate School of International Relations and Pacific Studies (IR/PS), UC San Diego in 2006, I have become increasingly interested in the study of corruption and development in South Korea and East Asia. A large research grant provided by the Academy of Korean Studies for the study of the political economy of contemporary Korea encouraged me to embark on a comparative historical investigation of Korea, Taiwan and the Philippines to better explore the causal mechanisms between inequality and corruption. In addition to acknowledging that this work was supported by the Academy of Korean Studies

Grant funded by the Korean Government (MEST) (AKS-2007-CB-2001), I would like to note the energetic and enthusiastic support and push from Professor Do-hyun Han, then Director of Strategic Initiative for Korean Studies at the AKS. The support from the Korean Studies Promotion Service (formerly SIKS) at the AKS, under the directorship of Dr. Han and his successor Professor Hee-young Kwon, has not only helped me and my colleague Stephan Haggard to work on our own book projects, but enabled us to support many scholars' book projects as well. This has directly led to the publication of five books thus far and four ongoing projects on various subjects relating to the political economy of Korea.

I would also like to acknowledge the East Asia Institute's fellowship that supported my initial short field trip to Taiwan and provided me with opportunities to present my dissertation chapter on the comparative case study and discuss it with scholars in Korea, Taiwan and Japan in May and June 2008. This experience became the starting point of this book project. I thank Professor Sook-jong Lee and Ms. Ha-jeong Kim, Director and Managing Director of the EAI, Professor Yun-han Chu at National Taiwan University, and Professor Yoshihide Soeya at Keio University for these opportunities. Shortly afterward I made a research trip to the Philippines, supported by a UCSD Academic Senate grant in the summer of 2008. I am grateful to Professor Bong Mendoza at the University of the Philippines for arranging many interviews and library privileges for me. The Rising Stars in Political Science Conference at the University of Southern California in October 2009, hosted by Professor David Kang, gave me another opportunity to present my early work and interact with many junior and senior scholars. However, various issues hindered me from starting on major field research until the Fall of 2010, when I was a visiting scholar for four months at the Asiatic Research Institute, Korea University, under the leadership of Professor Nae-young Lee, and support from the Korea Foundation's field research fellowship. From the archives of the Korea University Library and the National Assembly Library, I found a great deal of valuable and interesting materials, especially for the first few decades of post-independence Korea. In particular, I found evidence for gradual development of a meritocratic bureaucracy during the Syngman Rhee and Chang Myon governments, which were completely unrecognized or ignored by the previous literature on Korea's developmental state. I also spent several months in Korea in the subsequent years as a visiting scholar at Yonsei University and Hansung University thanks to generous arrangements by Professors Jae-jin Yang and Sam-yol Lee at Yonsei University and Professor Sang-jo Kim at Hansung University.

Although I began to accumulate a large amount of primary- as well as secondary-source materials for Korea, and a substantial amount of primary- and secondary-source materials for Taiwan and the Philippines, I found it hard to write a book. I later realized that it was primarily because of theoretical weaknesses. Capture theory alone was not sufficient to explain the various sequential events across the three countries. I also found it very challenging to compare three cases, not just one or two cases, and moreover historically, not just at a given time. I sometimes wondered if I was too ambitious and considered scaling down to a single case study of Korea, supplemented by a cross-national quantitative chapter. I finally began to think about clientelism as another important causal channel. With an expanded theoretical framework for causal mechanisms, incorporating both capture and clientelism, I began to reorganize and rewrite the chapters. I myself found my arguments much more convincing, and completed the first full draft, except for the concluding chapter, in the early Fall of 2012.

For the continuous intellectual support throughout this process, I am in debt to my former colleague and mentor, Professor Stephan Haggard, Director of the Korea-Pacific Program at IR/PS. He read several versions of my manuscript, from an initial incomplete draft to the final versions, and provided many useful comments and suggestions. I also benefited substantially from a manuscript conference in November 2012, which was supported by IR/PS. Professors John Lie and Gabriella Montinola flew to San Diego to participate in the day-long conference, in addition to Professors Susan Shirk, Krislert Samphantharak and Stephan Haggard at IR/PS, and visiting scholar Professor Jaeun Shin. In addition, Professor Shelley Rigger participated in the conference via Skype, and Professor T. J. Cheng sent me his feedback by email. Several graduate students, including Brigitte Zimmerman, who were collectively writing a dissertation about corruption in Africa, also participated in the conference. In particular, the feedback from area specialists such as John Lie (Korea), Gabriella Montinola (the Philippines), and Shelley Rigger and T. J. Cheng (Taiwan) helped to make sure that I did not err in any details regarding these countries. But the more important feedback was about the organization of the chapters. Several months after the conference, I was able to complete the full manuscript after making substantial revisions.

As I recollect my long journey for this book, I want to further acknowledge a number of people who provided me with various kinds of help and support. Besides the scholars I have mentioned above, Professors Susan Rose-Ackerman, Eric Uslaner, Bo Rothstein and Chung-in Moon have given me much intellectual support in various forms. I am fortunate to have rich intellectual interactions with these prominent scholars. Professors Carlos Waisman, Jacque Hymans, Eui-young Kim, Jae-jin Yang and Elieen Baviera also read my earlier paper and gave me very good comments at various seminars. Professors Herbert Kitschelt and Yuko Kasuya kindly provided me with their data set. I also wish to thank three anonymous reviewers for Cambridge University Press. I have been helped by many able research assistants for the last several years, including Ji-myoung Moon, Jia Jung, Pai Chen, Kwang-seok Yeon and Yoon-jung Ku. Brigitte Zimmerman and Shannon Colin helped to polish my English for the entire manuscript, and Geoffrey Fattig helped me with editing at the final stage. In particular, I want to express my deep thanks to Lucy Rhymer, editor of Cambridge University Press, who opened my eyes to the important role an editor plays in the book publication process.

Last, but not least, I want to thank the members of two groups who have given me broad moral support for my intellectual journey. The Korean studies faculty in Humanities at UCSD, in particular Professors Jin-kyung Lee and Todd Henry, have supported me with respect to various aspects of my academic career. My wife Seung-hee, brothers Jong-soue, Jong-keun and Jong-il, and sisters Soon-ja and Myung-sook have been long-time supporters of my activist and academic careers. In particular, Seung-hee and Jong-il, who were my comrades in the anti-dictatorship student movement, are still playing important roles in promoting democracy, equality and anti-corruption in South Korea's politics and academia. Long before I began to work on this book, we all shared a belief that democracy should be able to address the problems of inequality and corruption, and that inequality and corruption inhibit the proper functioning of democracy. Amazingly, my daughter Soosun, who is doing graduate work in public policy, has been increasingly showing her interest in the issues of democracy, inequality and corruption. Finally, the greatest debt I owe is to my loving, deceased parents to whom it gave great pain to see their son in prison and under constant surveillance during my years as a student activist. I dedicate this book to them.

1 Introduction

The puzzles, arguments and methodology

In the World Economic Forum's annual Executive Opinion Survey (2003–11), three young democracies in East Asia – the Philippines, Taiwan, South Korea (hereafter Korea) – performed very differently. In the Philippines, 22.9 percent of businessmen defined corruption as the largest obstacle to business. Corruption surpassed inefficient bureaucracy (16.3 percent), inadequate infrastructure (14.9 percent) and policy instability (12.7 percent). In contrast, only 2.4 percent of Taiwanese businessmen and 5.5 percent of South Korean businessmen regarded corruption as the largest obstacle to business. A similar pattern emerges when considering Transparency International's Corruption Perceptions Index (CPI) or the World Bank's Control of Corruption Index. The CPI scores in 2011 were 2.6 for the Philippines, 5.4 for Korea and 6.1 for Taiwan. The CPI scores can range between zero (most corrupt) and ten (least corrupt), and a higher value counterintuitively represents a lower level of corruption. The Control of Corruption scores (and percentile ranks in parentheses) in 2011 were as follows: −0.78 (23rd percentile) for the Philippines, 0.45 (70th percentile) for Korea and 0.90 (78th percentile) for Taiwan. The Control of Corruption scores have a mean of zero and a standard deviation of one; a higher value represents a lower level of corruption. The Philippines has a level of corruption 0.78 standard deviation higher than the world mean. Korea and Taiwan, in comparison, have levels of corruption that are 0.45 and 0.90 standard deviation lower than the world mean.

These observational data paint a clear picture: of these three countries, the Philippines is most corrupt, Taiwan is least corrupt and Korea is in between the other two countries, closer to Taiwan's end of the spectrum. What led to this vast difference between these three countries' experiences with corruption? More generally, what explains cross-national variations in the levels of corruption, especially among young democracies?

In this book, I argue that economic inequality increases the risk of clientelism and elite capture, thereby limiting the effectiveness of democratic accountability mechanisms such as elections, and corrupting "policy implementing" and "policy implementation" processes. Thus, inequality becomes the primary factor in determining cross-country variations in corruption, particularly among democracies. I will present empirical evidence supporting this argument both by conducting a comparative historical investigation of Korea, Taiwan and the Philippines, and by providing cross-national quantitative analysis.

Corruption and development

One seemingly obvious explanation for different levels of corruption in Korea, Taiwan and the Philippines is the level of economic development. It is commonly known that poor countries tend to be corrupt. Thus, there might be nothing puzzling between a high level of corruption in the Philippines and relatively low levels of corruption in Korea and Taiwan. However, one should be aware of the issue of causal direction. Is the Philippines' higher level of corruption caused by the poorer state of economic development? Or is the Philippines poorer as a result of greater state corruption? Answering this question requires a rigorous analysis of the historical trends of both corruption and economic growth.

The issue of causal direction between corruption and development is critical in the study of the Philippines, Korea and Taiwan. When the three countries were liberated from colonial rule after World War II, the Philippines was ahead of the other two countries in terms of per capita income. The Philippines continued to have higher per capita income than both Korea and Taiwan until the late 1960s. If the level of economic development had determined the level of corruption, the Philippines should have been less corrupt than Korea and Taiwan. Empirical evidence demonstrates, however, that the Philippines has suffered from a much greater level of corruption than have Korea and Taiwan since at least 1980, and most likely since the 1950s or 1960s (see Chapter 3). Considering that the effect of economic development on corruption is likely to occur over time, economic development cannot explain the higher level of corruption in the Philippines. It is more likely that corruption would have the causal effect on economic development. While the highly corrupt Philippine economy stagnated, the less corrupt Korean and Taiwanese economies took off in the 1960s and continued to grow, far surpassing the Philippines in the decades that followed.

Since Paolo Mauro's (1995) cross-national study on the negative effect of corruption on economic growth, numerous studies have reconfirmed the robustness of this finding (Bentzen 2012; Halkos and Tzeremes 2010; Johnson, LaFountain and Yamarik 2011; Kaufmann and Kraay 2002;

Keefer and Knack 1997; Mo 2001; Wei 2000). Although some studies have failed to find a significant effect of corruption on growth (Glaeser and Saks 2006; Svensson 2005), no cross-country studies have found positive effects of corruption on growth. On the other hand, corruption has been found to negatively influence education, health care, income distribution and subjective well-being (Lambsdorrf 2005). Furthermore, corruption has also been found to adversely affect social trust, or generalized interpersonal trust, which past research has shown to have a positive effect on economic growth (You 2012a; Zak and Knack 2001). Before cross-national measures of corruption became publicly available, debates about the functionality of corruption had been influential, but not fully resolved. Samuel Huntington (1968) and Nathaniel Leff (1964) represented the functional views of corruption. They argued that corruption might promote economic growth by enabling firms to avoid cumbersome regulations and bureaucratic delay, especially in developing countries. However, functional arguments in favor of corruption were largely dismissed as quantitative cross-national studies found mounting evidence for the predominantly negative effects of corruption on economic and social development.

Bolstered by the empirical findings that corruption is harmful for economic growth, the international development community, including the World Bank, United Nations, OECD, and numerous international organizations and NGOs such as Transparency International, has intensified the fight against corruption since the mid-1990s. It should be noted, however, that there is no firm consensus about the causal direction among scholars. A number of studies suggest that the level of economic development is an independent predictor for corruption (Ades and Di Tella 1999; La Porta et al. 1999; Pellegrini and Gerlagh 2004; Treisman 2007). There may be a reciprocal causal relationship under which corruption deters economic development and also under which societies with greater economic development are more likely to successfully mitigate corruption. Studies of corruption and development have been plagued by endogeneity problems in the absence of sufficient longitudinal data and convincing instruments. That being said, the historical experience of the three East Asian countries – Korea, Taiwan and the Philippines – supports the view that corruption affects economic growth. Kaufmann and Kraay's (2002) sophisticated empirical study also provides quite convincing evidence that the causal direction runs primarily from corruption to development rather than the reverse.

Considering the consensus of the international development community about the negative effect of corruption on economic and social development, the considerable cross-national evidence and the historical experience of the three East Asian countries supporting this view, it thus becomes paramount to identify the causes of corruption. In order to design effective anti-corruption strategies and programs, we need to understand what causes or helps to increase or reduce corruption. The problem of corruption has been gaining increased attention in recent years because many young democracies in the developing world are suffering from and struggling with this issue. Apart from being an obstacle for economic development, corruption is also a vital political concern because it poses a significant challenge to new democracies by undermining the legitimacy of democratic government and eroding public confidence in elected leaders (Seligson 2006).

Corruption and development in East Asia

While most of the developmental state literature has assumed that the high-growth economies of East Asia such as Korea and Taiwan were relatively free from corruption and capture due to a Weberian type of meritocratic and professional bureaucracy (Amsden 1989; Evans 1995; Johnson 1987; Wade 1990), some scholars such as David Kang (2002), Andrew Wedeman (1997; 2012) and Mushtaq Khan (2000; 2006) have argued that these countries actually achieved high economic growth in spite of high corruption, and have attempted to explain the different effects of corruption on economic performance in various East Asian nations. Kang (2002) argued in his comparative study of crony capitalism in Korea and the Philippines that Korea neither had a more autonomous and coherent state, nor was subject to any less corruption than the Philippines. Rather, it was different types as opposed to different levels of corruption that led to varying effects on economic development in each country. He further claimed that a *mutual-hostage* type of corruption could be efficient, while *rent-seeking* and *predatory state* types of corruption would be harmful for economic development. During the authoritarian regimes of Park Chung-hee and Chun Doo-hwan, Korea had a situation of mutual-hostage corruption between the coherent state and the concentrated business community, and this cronyism helped to reduce transaction costs. By contrast, in the Philippines corruption deterred economic growth because it fostered both rent-seeking activities from the business sector (pre-Marcos) and predatory behavior on the part of the state (under Marcos).

Wedeman (1997) argued that Korea's corruption represented an efficient type of *dividend collection*, or transfer of a percentage of the profits earned by privately owned enterprises to government officials, whereas the Philippines represented an example of inefficient *rent scraping*, or conscious manipulation of macroeconomic parameters to produce rents, and the subsequent scraping off of these rents by public officials. Wedeman (2012) distinguishes between *degenerative* corruption and *developmental* corruption in the form of coalition-building machine politics, with the latter being represented by the developmental states of Korea and Taiwan. In the same vein, Michael Johnston (2008) proposes four syndromes of corruption in Asia, suggesting that Korea's *elite cartel* type of corruption characterized by collusion between political and business elites may have aided economic growth by providing a measure of predictability and political security. The Philippines is characterized by *oligarchs and clans*, with powerful families and their entourages plundering a weak state and thereby inhibiting growth, while Japan and China represent *influence markets* and *official mogul* corruption, respectively. Khan (2000; 2006) has also argued that certain types of rent-seeking and corruption can be efficient, as in the case of high-growth developing countries such as South Korea in the 1960s, or in contemporary China.

These critics of the developmental state literature's portrayal of Korea and Taiwan as autonomous and relatively uncorrupt states not only challenge my assumption that corruption is harmful for economic development, but also raise doubts about the relative cleanness of the Korean and Taiwanese political systems as compared to the Philippines. While I acknowledge that different types of corruption could have somewhat different effects on economic and social development, I argue that it was not just the *types* of corruption but the *levels* of corruption that distinguished the high-growth economies of Korea and Taiwan from the low-growth economies of the developing world, including the Philippines. With regard to the relative levels of corruption in Korea, Taiwan and the Philippines, I have introduced some stark examples at the beginning of this introductory chapter that clearly show that the Philippines has had much higher levels of corruption than the other two countries. I will provide a more thorough examination of relative levels of corruption in these countries in Chapter 3.

To take this point a step further, there is considerable empirical evidence that corruption has a negative effect on growth even in the countries of East Asia. Jae-Hyung Lee (2006) shows that business and public sector corruption had detrimental effects on the real per capita growth rate in South Korea, using annual data from 1986 to 2001. Wu and Zhu's (2011) empirical study of inter-county income disparity in China shows that counties with a higher degree of anti-corruption measures also tend to have higher levels of income as measured by county-level per capita GDP. Although Wedeman (2012) focuses on the coexistence of high corruption and high growth in China, he acknowledges that China's continuous high growth has been possible not because of high corruption, but because of the regime's ability to push back against the problem. In addition, numerous studies have shown the detrimental effects of corruption on growth in the Philippines and other countries in Southeast and South Asia (Hutchcroft 1998; Montinola 2012).

Corruption and democracy

There is evidence that the three countries were all very corrupt during the early years of independence. Examination of various available data on the first few decades of post-independence suggests that corruption decreased considerably in Taiwan and somewhat in Korea, but that it increased in the Philippines. This gives rise to an additional puzzle considered in this book: why have Korea and Taiwan become increasingly less corrupt than the Philippines post-independence? And why has the Philippines become more corrupt than both Korea and Taiwan even though the Philippines was initially more developed? More generally, what countries or regime types are better at combatting corruption?

Some people might be tempted to argue for the virtue of authoritarian rule in curbing corruption, citing Lee Kwan Yew, Singapore's former Prime Minister. Lee used to argue that authoritarian rule was necessary for control of corruption as well as for economic development (Zakaria 1994). While all three countries had democratic transitions in the late 1980s, democratic experience during the earlier post-independence period was most extensive and far ranging in the Philippines, shallow and short in Korea, and nil in Taiwan. The Philippines had enjoyed democracy until 1972 before it fell to Marcos's dictatorship. Taiwan was under a hard authoritarian regime until the late 1980s. Korea had some formal democracy in the early years of post-independence, but it was mostly under soft authoritarianism until 1972 and hard-authoritarian rule from 1972 to 1987. However, Marcos's authoritarian government further increased corruption instead of reducing it. Also, corruption did not increase after democratization in these countries. In fact, a variety of evidence shows that corruption declined particularly in Korea and also in Taiwan (see Chapter 3).

This leads us to turn to an opposite theory, i.e. that democracy is associated with less corruption. Indeed, there are many plausible reasons why democracies should be less corrupt than dictatorships, and there is a strong negative correlation between democracy and corruption across countries. In democracies, competitive elections, as a vertical accountability mechanism, enable the public to hold politicians responsible. In dictatorships, people can hold the regime accountable only through popular revolts, which are very difficult because of collective action problems and very costly because of the risks of repression. In addition, democracies have an elaborate system of checks and balances as a horizontal accountability mechanism, while in dictatorships power is concentrated on the ruler. Therefore, it is not surprising that democracies are on average less corrupt than dictatorships. However, democratic advantage cannot explain variations in corruption across the three countries. The most democratic country among them in the early period of post-independence was the Philippines, but it became the most corrupt. In addition, the three countries have had varying degrees of improvement since the democratic transition. In particular, the Philippines has experienced further deterioration since the mid-1990s, when the other two countries have made progress in battling corruption.

Thus, the relationship between democracy and corruption is not simple. In order to explain the differences in corruption among the three countries, we need a deeper understanding of the relationship between democracy and corruption. Why was the Philippine democracy unable to combat corruption both during the early post-independence period and the later post-Marcos era? Why is democracy working better in terms of producing more ethical governments in Korea and Taiwan than in the Philippines? More generally, we are confronted with the question, why are some democracies better at controlling corruption than others?

Cross-national studies have demonstrated variation in the effects of democratic institutional features on levels of corruption. Some studies have found that presidential systems are more corrupt than parliamentary systems (Gerring and Thacker 2004; Lederman *et al.* 2005; Kunicová and Rose-Ackerman 2005; Panizza 2001). Others have found that closed list proportional representation is associated with higher corruption than is the plurality electoral system (Kunicová and Rose-Ackerman 2005; Persson, Tabellini and Trebbi 2003), and that district magnitude also has an effect on corruption (Chang and Golden 2007). However, these findings are often insignificant and not robust once controls are introduced (Lambsdorff 2005; Treisman 2007). There is robust correlation between freedom of the press and lower corruption across countries (Adsera *et al.* 2003; Brunetti and Weder 2003; Chang *et al.* 2010), but the causal direction is ambiguous due to censorship by corrupt politicians. Some studies find non-linear effects of democracy with regard to the level or age of democracy; full or mature democracies are significantly less corrupt than dictatorships, but partial or young democracies are not significantly different from autocracies in terms of corruption (Bäck and Hadenius 2008; Manow 2005; Montinola and Jackman 2002; Sung 2004;

Treisman 2007). On the other hand, Charron and Lapuente (2010) present some cross-country evidence that the relationship between democracy and corruption, or the quality of government more broadly, is conditional on economic development.

Existing cross-national studies have, however, only a limited ability to explain the large democratic variations in control of corruption. There still remain large variations in corruption even after accounting for the duration of democracy, as well as other factors which have been suggested to explain democratic variations. For the purposes of this book, these factors can hardly be used to explain the differences among the three countries. These countries are all presidential systems with a plurality electoral system predominating. They also have similar ages of their respective democracies, in terms of continuous experience of democratic government. If we count the earlier episode of democracy as well, then the Philippines should be less corrupt than Korea and Taiwan. While the level of economic development may partly explain the different performances of democratic institutions in these countries, its explanatory power is doubtful for the earlier period of democracy in Korea and the Philippines, when the latter was more developed but less successful in controlling corruption than the former.

Given that corruption is considered one of the biggest challenges for many young democracies, it is important to determine which factors impact the effectiveness of democratic control over corruption. Hence, we need to consider theoretical reasons why democratic mechanisms for controlling corruption will work better or worse under certain conditions.

Corruption, clientelism and capture

Corruption can be defined in numerous ways, but in this book I follow the most commonly used definition as "misuse of public office for private gain" (Rose-Ackerman 2008; Treisman 2007). Corruption can be defined narrowly to mean illegal acts only, or one can consider some legal acts and practices corrupt such as political influence of big money and conflicts of interest. I adopt the narrow definition, while recognizing that these legal forms of inappropriate influence and behavior often lead to illegal forms of corruption. Corruption takes various forms such as bribery, embezzlement and extortion, and certain acts of nepotism and favoritism can also fall under this heading. Corruption can be classified into political, bureaucratic, judicial and corporate corruption, depending on the types of actors involved, and petty and grand corruption, depending on the magnitude of the transactions. I will consider both petty and grand corruption involving various sectors, such as political, bureaucratic and corporate corruption.

When we consider the effectiveness of democratic control of corruption, we can think of two main problems that can hinder the functioning of democratic accountability mechanisms such as elections and checks and balances. These problems are clientelism and capture, either of which may render democratic institutions for accountability ineffective. By clientelism, I mean clientelistic politics, in which politicians and voters exchange votes for particularistic benefits. In theory, clientelism is not necessarily illegal or corrupt; indeed, it may involve only legitimate constituency services such as providing information, attending funerals and weddings, and writing letters of recommendation for job applicants. However, clientelism in young democracies usually involves illegal acts of corruption such as vote-buying in cash, gifts, entertainment, free tours, etc. In the context of young democracies, clientelism typically represents a form of electoral corruption. By capture, I mean that the state or a specific government agency has lost autonomy and now serves the interests of the elite rather than regulating them. Although state capture can occur without illegal corruption (i.e. through connections and legal campaign contributions), capture by the private interests typically involves illegal exchange of government favors, illegal campaign contributions or bribery. Capture represents a high level of political corruption that deprives the autonomy of the government or a government agency.

Elections in younger democracies tend to be characterized by clientelistic competition (Keefer 2007; Keefer and Vlaicu 2008). Thus, clientelism may partly explain why young democracies tend to be more corrupt than mature democracies. Clientelism can seriously jeopardize the democratic control of corruption. When elections are characterized by clientelistic mobilization of voters, or the exchange of votes for particularistic benefits between voters and politicians, the voters will likely lose the ability to punish corrupt politicians at the polls. Moreover, clientelism often involves electoral corruption such as vote-buying. Clientelism likely increases political corruption during the policy-making process because politicians need clientelistic resources from government funds or private sources, and these funds often come from corrupt means (Hicken 2011; Stokes 2007). Moreover, clientelistic politicians lack the genuine political will to combat corruption; therefore, many anti-corruption reforms are merely rhetorical. In addition, clientelism often involves the exchange of public sector jobs for votes. This exchange increases patronage jobs in the bureaucracy, which will encourage bureaucratic corruption (Calvo and Murillo 2004).

The capture of policy processes by powerful private interests is another reason for the failure of democratic control of corruption. Citizens in democracies should be able to exert more power than those in dictatorships in the policy-making process, and they should be able to do this through their elected representatives. Citizens in democracies should also be able to better monitor both the policy implementation process in the legislature and policy implementation process in the bureaucracy. Various mechanisms for checks and balances among the branches of government and oversight agencies should reduce the opportunities for abuse of power. However, the democratic policy process is not immune from capture. While capture can occur through legal lobbying, it often involves corrupt means such as bribery. Hence, capture is an important component in explaining why some democracies are more corrupt than others. The role of clientelism and capture in increasing democratic corruption is illuminating, but we are still left with the task of explaining why some democracies have a greater incidence of clientelism and capture.

Causes of corruption in East Asia

Regarding the causes of corruption in East Asia, there are relatively few comparative studies, and early literature tended to focus on the role of cultural or social norms. Confucianism's authoritarian features, Asian culture's emphasis on extended family and gift-giving, or Chinese emphasis on *guanxi* (personal connections or particularistic ties) has often been suggested as breeding nepotism, favoritism and corruption (Gold 1986; Kim 1999; Lande 1965; Pye 1985). Cultural explanation for corruption has often been popular not just for East Asia, but for other parts of the world as well, such as Edward Banfield's (1958) discussion of amoral familism in Italy. A major weakness with cultural explanation is that it is close to tautology ("a country has more corruption because its norms are more favorable to corruption"), as Pranab Bardhan (2005: 152–3) noted. A better explanation would require finding out how otherwise similar countries (or regions in the same country, like northern and southern Italy) may settle with different social norms in equilibrium or how a society may move from one equilibrium to another (as developed Western countries, and to a certain extent Korea and Taiwan, have experienced).

Based on Leslie Palmier's (1985) comparative case studies of corruption in Hong Kong, India and Indonesia, Jon S. T. Quah (1999) examined three factors as important causes of corruption: opportunities or red-tape, bureaucratic salaries and policing, or probability of detection and punishment. After examining the anti-corruption efforts of Mongolia, India, the Philippines, Singapore, Hong Kong and South Korea, he argued for the critical importance of political will in combatting systemic corruption (Quah 2003). Obviously, the commitment of political leadership is crucial for effective control of corruption, but the question then becomes: what kinds of political institutions and social conditions will engender such political commitment?

This is where the significance of clientelism and capture come into play. Clientelistic politicians are likely to lack genuine political will to fight against corruption because a large part of their clientelistic resources may come through corrupt means. Similarly, captured politicians are by definition likely to serve the interests of the captor even when it involves some forms of corruption. In this regard, Carl Lande's (1965) classic study of clientelism in the Philippines shows how the prevalence of clientelism hinders the development of programmatic politics, and James Scott's (1972) study of political corruption cites the Philippines as a model case of electoral corruption dominated by clientelistic competition. Further buttressing the case is the running theme found in developmental state literature emphasizing the crucial importance of state autonomy, or freedom from elite capture, in both Korea and Taiwan (Amsden 1989; Cheng *et al.* 1998; Evans 1995; Johnson 1987; Wade 1990). Thus, clientelism and capture seem to be the critical components in the study of corruption in East Asia. Existing research, however, has not rigorously explored what explains the varying degrees of these features across countries in East Asia, instead focusing largely on the role played by social and cultural forces in determining patterns of corruption.

Point of departure: inequality and corruption in democracies

I argue that economic inequality increases the likelihood of both clientelism and capture, and thereby increases corruption in democracies. In other words, there is an interaction effect between inequality and democracy on the level of corruption. Democratization will positively contribute to corruption control at low levels of inequality. Conversely, there is the potential that democratization will negatively contribute to corruption control at high levels of inequality because of increased clientelism and capture.

First, high inequality will increase and intensify clientelism. The literature on clientelism has found that the poor are more prone to clientelism than the middle class (Brusco *et al.* 2004; Calvo and Murillo 2004; Hicken 2011; Kitschelt and Wilkinson 2007; Scott 1972; Stokes 2007). Since higher inequality means a higher proportion of the poor at a given level of economic development, it follows that there will be a larger sector of the population prone to clientelism in countries with higher levels of inequality. At the same time, high inequality will encourage the wealthy to prevent the development of programmatic competition and to rely on clientelism to secure support. At higher levels of inequality, the median voter with presumably the median income will support larger redistribution. This is because the gap between the mean income and the median income becomes larger as inequality increases under a typically right-skewed income distribution (Meltzer and Richard 1981). Hence, programmatic competition under high levels of inequality is likely to strengthen leftist parties that pursue significant redistribution of income and wealth. The rich will have incentives to buy votes from the poor in order to prevent programmatic politics from developing. Thus, both the supply side (the wealthy elite) and the demand side (the poor) of clientelistic politics indicate that economic inequality will likely encourage clientelism and deter the development of programmatic politics. I do not mean to say that clientelism will not occur under low levels of inequality; simply that higher inequality will likely increase both the prevalence and the persistence of clientelism and delay the development of programmatic parties.

Second, inequality increases the probability of state capture by powerful private interests. Capture is more likely at higher levels of inequality because of higher stakes and greater expected returns for the elite. Higher inequality will increase redistributive pressures, and hence the rich will have more incentives as well as ability to corrupt and capture the government (You 2006; You and Khagram 2005). The wealthy will try to buy political influence to reduce taxes and costly regulations during the law-making process and to bribe bureaucrats to get preferential treatment during the policy implementation process. At high levels of inequality, there are a small number of the extremely wealthy. Hence, the wealthy are more likely than the poor and middle classes to overcome collective action problems because they are relatively smaller in number and have more abundant resources.

In summary, high economic inequality is likely to increase the prevalence and persistence of clientelistic politics and the risks of capture by powerful private interests. Clientelism typically involves petty electoral corruption and provision of patronage jobs that violate merit rules, and it encourages political and bureaucratic corruption. Capture represents a high level of corporate and political corruption that facilitates the government or a government agency in serving the sole interests of the elite. High inequality is likely to render anti-corruption reforms ineffective because of resistance from clientelistic politicians, bureaucrats and the private interests that benefit from the corrupt system. Thus,

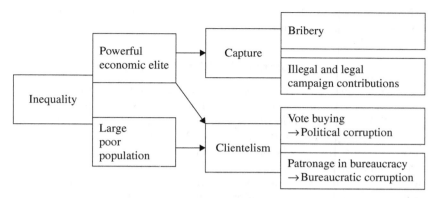

Figure 1.1 Causal mechanisms linking inequality to corruption in democracies

democratic control of corruption is not only ineffective under high levels of inequality; democratization may even increase corruption in highly unequal societies. Figure 1.1 graphically depicts the causal mechanisms delineated above.

What will be the effect of inequality on corruption in authoritarian regimes? Since power is concentrated in the ruler or the ruling party, the preferences of the ruler or the ruling party will be very important in determining the amount of high-level political corruption (Hollyer and Wantchekon 2012). Defining capture within authoritarian regimes is challenging because the authoritarian ruler or ruling party often makes dominant coalitions with the elite, and this is not considered to be corruption. Hence, the effect of inequality on corruption under dictatorships is likely to be weaker than that under democracies. However, many authoritarian regimes employ elections at the national or subnational level for various purposes. When competitive elections are held, clientelism will likely develop. Likewise, inequality may potentially exert an effect on the prevalence of clientelism. Thus, inequality likely has an effect on clientelism and corruption in authoritarian countries with elections.

Based on the above discussion, I propose that the effect of democratic institutions on reducing corruption is negatively associated with the level of economic inequality. That is to say, corruption will increase with inequality in democracies and authoritarian countries with elections. In addition, I also propose the following sub-hypotheses on causal mechanisms. High inequality increases clientelistic politics (electoral corruption), patronage appointments in bureaucracy, capture by the powerful private interests, and thereby leads to greater prevalence of political, bureaucratic and corporate corruption.

The case for comparative historical analysis

My earlier cross-national studies using instrumental variables show that inequality significantly increases corruption (You 2006; You and Khagram 2005). Other studies have found a significant effect of corruption on inequality (Dincer and Gunalp 2012; Gupta *et al.* 2002; Li *et al.* 2000). Chong and Gradstein (2007) and Apergis *et al.* (2010) suggest a mutually reinforcing relationship between inequality and institutional quality. Eric Uslaner (2008) and Bo Rothstein (2011) demonstrate the existence of a low trust-corruption-inequality trap. There does, however, exist a gap in the literature; it is not entirely clear whether inequality increases corruption, corruption increases inequality, or if both have a mutual effect on each other. While most existing studies of causes of corruption rely on cross-national analysis and other quantitative methods, these studies have all suffered from the difficult problem of endogeneity. While some studies have employed the instrumental variable method, the validity of instruments is often subject to controversy. Some studies conducted panel analysis, but the quality and reliability of the longitudinal data on corruption is doubtful (See the discussion on measuring corruption in Chapter 3.)

It is even more challenging to identify and/or test causal mechanisms with cross-national study. My earlier studies also found that the correlation between inequality and corruption is much higher among more democratic countries than among less democratic countries. However, these studies were unable to identify the reasons why inequality was more strongly associated with corruption in democracies. I will test the causal mechanism hypotheses as best as I can through cross-country analysis using available data on electoral clientelism, bureaucratic patronage and elite capture, but it will be difficult to claim robustness for these findings due to the lack of convincing instrumental variables.

In order to overcome the shortcomings of cross-national analysis, my main methodology for this research will be a comparative historical analysis of three East Asian countries: Korea, Taiwan and the Philippines. Comparative historical analysis has rarely been used to explore the causes of corruption, but it can be a powerful tool for causal studies (Mahoney and Rueschemeyer 2003). Systematic and contextualized comparisons of similar and contrasting cases paired with explicit analysis of historical sequences can help reveal not only the causal direction between the factors of interest, but also the causal mechanisms. Thus, comparative historical investigation can overcome or supplement the weaknesses of cross-national quantitative research results in studying the causes of corruption.

For example, J. S. Mill's "method of agreement" and "method of difference" can be used for causal analysis in comparative historical studies (Mahoney 2003). I employ the method of difference to eliminate potential causes of corruption by comparing both the dependent variable and potential causal factors in my three countries of focus. I also employ "process tracing" within each of the three countries to examine the causal processes. Process tracing can not only help to avoid mistaking a spurious correlation for a causal association, but can also help to identify the causal mechanisms. By combining cross-case comparisons and within-case process tracing, I will attempt to provide a convincing causal narrative.

Although my primary approach in this book is a comparative historical investigation, I will supplement it with cross-national analysis. While comparative historical analysis can be useful for identifying causal mechanisms, it is hard to generalize the findings from this approach beyond the cases under study. Presentation of cross-national analysis will bolster my claim for generalizability.

Case selection: why Korea, Taiwan and the Philippines?

Some readers may be curious about my case selection of Korea, Taiwan and the Philippines, because they look so different today. The three countries were chosen to satisfy the requirements of the "most similar cases." Ideally, the selection of the most similar cases requires that the chosen cases are similar in all respects except the variables of interest, i.e. the dependent variable (corruption) and the key explanatory variables (democracy and inequality) (Gerring 2007: 131–134). This will enable the researcher to utilize the method of difference to discern causal mechanisms.

The three countries are ideal comparison cases because they share a number of similar initial conditions. Robert Lucas (1993) and David Kang (2002) note striking similarities in many of the socio-economic conditions during the early period of post-independence between South Korea and the Philippines. This applies to Taiwan as well. The three countries were all similarly poor at the time of independence. The Philippines had a somewhat higher level of economic development and educational attainment, as Table 1.1 indicates. Korea and Taiwan were trailing

Table 1.1 *Similar initial conditions of the three countries*

	Korea	Taiwan	Philippines
GDP per capita 1953 (2005 constant PPP $)	1,586	1,243	1,730
Primary enrollment 1950 (%)	83	79	91
Secondary enrollment 1950 (%)	16	11	27
Tertiary enrollment 1950 (per 10,000 population)	18	9	88
Urban population 1950s (%)	18	–	15
Non-agricultural population 1950s (%)	30	–	29
Population 1950 (thousands)	20,846	7,981	21,131

Sources: Heston *et al.* (2009); McGinn *et al.* (1980: 150–1); Vanhanen (2003).

behind the Philippines in terms of per capita income until 1968, according to the data from Heston *et al.* (2009). By 1960, Korea and Taiwan achieved near universal enrollment for primary education, but they were still behind the Philippines in secondary and tertiary enrollments (McGinn *et al.* 1980: 150–1). This initial advantage to the Phillipines only enhances the puzzle of the country's subsequent high levels of corruption. There were no major differences in urbanization and industrialization among these countries during the 1950s. They all experienced colonial rule until the end of World War II. They had all been occupied by the Japanese, and were all heavily supported and influenced by the United States during the Cold War era.

With respect to the dependent variable, corruption, the three countries show wide variation, both between each other and over time. The Philippines is regarded as a very corrupt country, while Taiwan is relatively corruption free, and Korea's level of corruption is in the middle, but closer to Taiwan's end of the spectrum. There is cross-national evidence that this rank order of corruption traces back to the early 1980s, and probably much earlier, but initially, Korea and Taiwan also suffered from endemic corruption during the early period of independence. This means that corruption decreased slightly in Korea and considerably in Taiwan during the first few decades after independence, while it increased in the Philippines during the same period. The Philippines has faltered greatly in attempts to reduce corruption after its democratic transition during the late 1980s. Korea and Taiwan, on the other hand, have shown substantial improvement in corruption reduction. Thus, there is variation in both the levels and trends of corruption in these countries both during the pre- and post-democratic transition periods.

There are two main independent variables in this study: democracy and inequality. Each country had democratic transition in the late 1980s, but there were substantial differences in regime characteristics in the earlier period. Although Taiwan operated under hard authoritarian rule throughout this time, the regime held local elections periodically. Both Korea and the Philippines were officially "electoral democracies" until 1972, but the Korean political system was conducted in a more authoritarian way than the Filipino system. There were free and competitive elections at both national and local levels in the Philippines, although the left was excluded in both cases. In Korea, competitive national elections were regularly held, with the exclusion of the left, but local elections were held only for a short period. Thus, with regard to regime type (democracy, soft or hard authoritarianism) and the scope of elections (local level only, national level only, or both), there have been considerable variations both across the three countries and across time within each country.

Finally, the countries had similar levels of inequality at the time of independence, but have diverged over time. The distribution of income has been considerably less equal in the Philippines than in Korea and Taiwan. However, there is evidence that Korea and Taiwan also had high levels of income inequality at the time of independence. Sweeping land reform around 1950 made the distribution of wealth and income unusually equal in Korea and Taiwan. The Philippines, on the other hand, maintained a high inequality of wealth and income due to the repeated failure of land reform during this time. Additionally, Korea's *chaebol*-centered (family-controlled large conglomerates) industrialization led to more industrial concentration and income inequality over time than Taiwan's small and medium-sized enterprise (SME) based economy. This has resulted in variations in both the levels and trends of inequality across these countries.

With these substantial variations in both the dependent variable and the two explanatory variables in spite of similar initial conditions, these countries offer an ideal set of cases for a comparative historical investigation of the causal mechanisms linking inequality to corruption in democracies and authoritarian regimes with elections. However, without being able to show that inequality is exogenous to corruption trends, the direction of causality would still be uncertain. My comparative historical analysis of Korea, Taiwan and the Philippines rests on the following argument regarding the exogeneity of levels of inequality in the country after independence: Success and failure of land reform was primarily determined by exogenous factors such as external communist threat and US pressures. In turn, this land reform produced different levels of inequality, which in turn influenced subsequent levels of corruption. I will also show that Korea's initial choice of *chaebol*-centered industrial policy and Taiwan's SME-centered strategy were largely exogenous to business lobbying or corruption, and that these different industrial policies have produced diverging levels of inequality and corruption over time.

Organization of the book

In Chapter 2, I present my theoretical arguments, based on the principal-agent-client model, as to why economic inequality increases corruption in democracies and authoritarian countries with elections. The principal-agent-client model will help the reader understand why clientelism and capture are major challenges to democratic accountability mechanism. I will also further elaborate my arguments about the effects of inequality on clientelism and capture laid out in the introduction, and propose three mechanism hypotheses: inequality increases corruption in democracies through clientelistic politics, bureaucratic patronage and elite capture.

In Chapter 3, I examine the relative levels and trends of corruption in these countries, and then conduct simple tests of the plausibility of alternative explanations using Mill's method of difference. Since no single measure of corruption is adequate, I examine various cross-national measures of perceived and experienced corruption. This chapter shows that each of the three countries had a high level of corruption in the early years of independence, but Taiwan and Korea were able to reduce corruption over time both during the first few decades after independence and after their democratic transitions. This chapter demonstrates that Korea has been somewhat more corrupt than Taiwan and that corruption has worsened throughout the post-war history in the Philippines. Examination of simple correlations between corruption and its various possible causes shows that inequality is positively correlated with corruption across the three countries, while other factors that have been suggested previously as causes of corruption by the literature are not. I then present my tentative arguments about how different levels of inequality have affected electoral clientelism, bureaucratic patronage and elite capture in industrial policy in the three countries.

In Chapter 4, I demonstrate that, while the three countries all had high levels of inequality and corruption in the early years of independence, the success and failure of land reform policies created divergence in inequality across these countries. Sweeping land reform in Korea and Taiwan dissolved the landed elite and produced an unusually equal distribution of income and wealth. In the Philippines, on the other hand, land reform failed. I find that the success (in Korea and Taiwan) and failure (in the Philippines) of land reform was primarily determined by exogenous factors such as the communist threat from North Korea and mainland

China, as well as US pressures for reform. Success and failure of reform not only produced starkly different levels of inequality, but also had a profound effect on the broader political economy of these countries.

In the following three chapters, I examine how the three causal mechanisms – clientelistic politics, bureaucratic patronage and elite capture – have worked in these countries. In Chapter 5, I explore how inequality has influenced clientelism and political corruption in the context of democratic and authoritarian elections. Political clientelism has been more prevalent and persistent in the highly unequal Philippines than in Korea and Taiwan, where programmatic politics have developed and anti-corruption efforts have been more effective. In the Philippines, the need to mobilize clientelistic resources has encouraged political corruption and weakened the political will to fight against it, making the numerous anti-corruption agencies ineffective. Moreover, Filipino voters have been unable to punish corrupt politicians at the polls because of prevalent practices of vote buying and clientelism, unlike Korean and Taiwanese voters who held corrupt politicians accountable through elections.

Chapter 6 addresses how inequality influenced bureaucratic structure and corruption. In the highly unequal Philippines, the bureaucractic system was continuously corrupted by patronage through clientelistic provision of jobs in the bureaucracy, as well as penetration by powerful private interests. In Korea and Taiwan, low levels of inequality and rapid expansion of education contributed to the gradual development of meritocratic bureaucracies, by increasing bureaucratic recruitment via competitive civil service examinations. There is evidence that the gradual evolution of meritocracy has been accompanied by the gradual decline in bureaucratic corruption.

Chapter 7 traces the ways in which economic concentration interacted with industrial policy, government-business relations, rent-seeking and capture. Creating and implementing industrial policy in the Philippines was heavily influenced by the powerful landed-industrial oligarchy throughout the post-war history, and it was incoherent and prone to rent-seeking. In Korea and Taiwan, however, industrial policy was more coherent and less influenced by business; furthermore, export-oriented industrialization mandated that international markets discipline firms. Whereas the success and failure of land reform determined the crucial differences in the degree of economic concentration and elite capture between the Philippines on the one hand and Korea and Taiwan on the other, substantial divergence also occurred between Korea and Taiwan due to industrial policy differences: Korea's *chaebol*-centered policy versus Taiwan's SME-centered policy. Park Chung-hee's *chaebol*-favored strategy led to increasing economic concentration and collusion between government and business in Korea until significant corporate and financial sector reforms were implemented in the aftermath of the East Asian financial crisis.

Although the above three chapters provide convincing evidence supporting my theoretical arguments about the effect of inequality on corruption through electoral clientelism, bureaucratic patronage and elite capture, it is hard to generalize the findings beyond the three East Asian countries. In Chapter 8, I will present the results of various cross-national analyses in order to strengthen the case for the generalizability of this study. The instrumental variable regressions and other analyses provide strong cross-national evidence in support of the main hypothesis that the effect of democracy on reducing corruption is negatively associated with the level of economic inequality. Interestingly, both the effect of inequality on corruption and the interaction effect between democracy and inequality are estimated to be much larger by instrumental variable regressions than by ordinary least squares (OLS) regressions. However, both the effect of economic development and the interaction effect between democracy and economic development become insignificant in instrumental variable (IV) regressions, while they are strong and significant in OLS regressions. This implies that the effect of democracy on corruption control depends on the degree of economic inequality rather than on the level of economic development. I also test the mechanisms hypotheses, although my test does not fully address the problem of endogeneity due to a lack of convincing instrumental variables. I provide evidence that economic inequality is significantly associated with electoral clientelism and bureaucratic patronage, which in turn are significantly associated with political and bureaucratic corruption, respectively, in democracies. I also find that inequality is associated with elite capture in a sample of transition economies, which in turn is associated with corporate corruption.

Finally, Chapter 9 will conclude with a summary of key findings, prospects for control of corruption in these countries, and a discussion of the theoretical and policy implications of this work.

2 Democracy, inequality and corruption
Theory and hypotheses

One of the world's puzzling challenges is why many countries with democratic accountability mechanisms would suffer from rampant corruption and why democratic countries, especially young democracies, experience different levels of effectiveness in controlling corruption. I argue that inequality increases the risk of clientelism and elite capture, thereby isolating democratized countries that are plagued by corruption from those that manage to control it.

Corruption is increasingly recognized as an important obstacle for development, and many studies have explored its causes, mostly using cross-national quantitative analyses. Despite numerous cross-national studies, however, our understanding of the causes of corruption is still very limited. The direction of causal effects is often unclear, and causal mechanisms are even more ambiguous. In particular, with regard to the causal effects of democracy and economic inequality on corruption, which is the focus of this study, previous cross-national studies have not clearly established causal directions and mechanisms. In order to overcome the weaknesses of previous studies in sorting out causal directions and mechanisms, it is important to clearly present a plausible theory and theory-based hypotheses before testing them empirically.

In this book, I pay special attention to the effect of economic inequality on corruption in the context of democratic institutions. Political institutions can affect the incentives and opportunities for corruption on the part of politicians and bureaucrats, as well as the ability of the public to select, monitor and sanction corrupt officials. Democratic institutions, such as competitive elections and checks and balances, should in principle reduce corruption compared to autocratic institutions. However, existing cross-national studies do not indicate any simple relationship between democracy and corruption. I argue that the effect of democracy on corruption is tempered by economic inequality, because high inequality can inhibit proper functioning of democratic institutions of accountability. At low levels of inequality, democratic institutions should reduce corruption. At high levels of inequality, however, the effect of democratic institutions on corruption may be nil or even negative.

I propose two major causal mechanisms linking inequality to corruption through democratic institutions. First, I argue that inequality increases the probability of powerful private interests capturing the policy-making and policy-implementing processes. Capture of legislative and bureaucratic processes and erosion of state autonomy can be achieved through influence (i.e. legal lobbying and connections) or corruption (i.e. illegal means such as bribery). Second, I argue that inequality increases the prevalence and persistence of clientelistic politics, inhibiting the development of programmatic politics. Clientelism typically involves various forms of electoral corruption, such as vote-buying. Clientelistic politicians are more likely to engage in corruption during the policy-making process in order to recoup large campaign expenses and to further mobilize clientelistic resources for subsequent elections. Clientelism also involves the provision of patronage jobs in the public sector in exchange for electoral support. Patronage appointment is a form of corruption in breach of the meritocratic recruitment principle. It further increases corruption during the policy implementation process because clientelistic bureaucrats are more likely to seek promotion via patronage than via merit.

Furthermore, the effect of economic inequality on corruption will be more pronounced in democracies than in dictatorships. This is because democratic elections are more prone to clientelism, and democratic policy processes are more vulnerable to capture by special interests than their authoritarian counterparts are. Since authoritarian regimes typically avoid holding competitive elections or only permit elections within manipulative scope, there are weaker grounds for clientelistic politics. Then, since authoritarian policy processes are centralized in the dictator, there is less scope for capture. In other words, the effect of democracy on reducing corruption depends on inequality because inequality increases the likelihood and degree of clientelism and capture.

In order to rigorously consider the effects of economic inequality on clientelism and capture in democracies, I will elaborate my theoretical arguments using the principal-agent-client model of corruption. The literature on corruption has typically understood corruption as a principal-agent problem. While this model is important in understanding corruption, considering perversion of the principal-agent relationship into patron-client relationship and the role of third-party clients in the principal-agent framework will shed important insights on clientelism and capture. I will first examine why clientelism and capture are major threats to democratic accountability mechanisms, as based on the principal-agent-client model of corruption. I will then explain why economic inequality increases the likelihood of capture and clientelism. It is important to note that the effect of inequality on corruption in democracies might demonstrate a vicious cycle of mutual reinforcement wherein high levels of corruption are likely to maintain high inequality.

Principal-agent-client model of corruption

Corruption is commonly defined as "misuse of public office for private gain" (Rose-Ackerman 2008; Treisman 2007). The principal-agent model is often used to explain the phenomenon of corruption, where the principal is the public and the agent is the public official, who betrays the principal by serving her own interests at the expense of the public interests (Klitgaard 1988; Rose-Ackerman 1978). This perversion occurs because in the principal-agent relationship, there is a problem of informational asymmetry. The agent may abuse her discretionary power and exploit her informational advantage vis-à-vis the principal, and it is costly for the principal to monitor the behavior of the agent. An extension of the model is a principal-agent-client model, wherein the agent interacts on the principal's behalf with a client (Klitgaard 1988). The agent may betray the principal (or the public interest) and collude with a client for her own private interests. For example, a tax official may abuse her discretionary power to reduce taxable income for a taxpayer in return for a bribe.

Corruption as an agency problem

There are multiple layers of principal-agent relationships in the political system. In a democracy, these can be thought of as a chain that runs from voters to politicians to bureaucrats. The president can be viewed as the agent of the people or of his coalition. Ministers are agents of the president. Bureaucrats in each ministry are agents of the minister. In each layer of the principal-agent relationship, the principal delegates her power to the agent, but the agent can abuse her discretionary power, exploiting her informational advantage vis-à-vis the principal. Corruption is understood as an agency loss problem, in which politicians or bureaucrats betray their principal in order to reap private gain at the expense of public interest. Furthermore, two distinct types of corruption result from the many layers of principal-agent relationships: political corruption during the policy-making process; and bureaucratic corruption during the policy implementation process.

Scholars have extensively analyzed the conditions under which agency loss is most common. This will depend on the extent of information asymmetry and the incentive structures of the principal-agent relationship. Lack of transparency in political and administrative procedures will increase the problem of information asymmetry and opportunities for corruption. Wide discretionary power on the part of public officials may increase opportunities for corruption. Furthermore, the probability of detection and the degree of punishment will affect the expected cost of corruption. Hence, the degree of corruption will be determined not only by incentives and opportunities for corruption by the agent, but also by the ability of the principal to monitor and sanction the corrupt behavior of the agent.

Clientelism, adverse selection and corruption

While the problem of agency loss is important in understanding corruption, I argue that the problem of adverse selection is equally significant. If corrupt or corruption-prone individuals are selected into public office in the first place, they are much more likely to incur agency loss once in office. Given the same opportunity and incentive structures – such as the expected material benefit and cost of corruption – psychological and reputational costs may be lower for corrupt or corruption-prone officials than for honest officials. In order to control corruption effectively, it is important to both select high-quality agents for office and provide monitoring mechanisms for those in office. In other words, reducing both adverse selection and agency loss will reduce corruption.

Democracies and dictatorships differ in how they select politicians. In democracies, competitive elections, as a vertical accountability mechanism, enable the public to select candidates and hold politicians accountable. In dictatorships, people can hold the regime accountable only through popular revolts, which are very difficult because of collective action problems and very costly because of the risk of repression. Therefore, it is not surprising that democracies are less corrupt than dictatorships on average.

Nonetheless, there are large variations in the level of corruption both among democracies and dictatorships. Although many dictatorships are corrupt, not all are. Some scholars and politicians, notably Lee Kuan Yew, former Prime Minister of Singapore, argue that authoritarian regimes are superior to democracies in controlling corruption and achieving economic growth (Zakaria 1994). Singapore is an often-cited case of an authoritarian regime with a reputation of non-corruption, but it is really an exceptional case, as a vast majority of dictatorships have high levels of corruption. In dictatorships, the preferences of the dictator seem to be crucial in determining the political will for curbing corruption. Perhaps external constraints could considerably influence the preferences of dictators, although dictators might be less constrained by domestic politics than democratic leaders.

There are much larger variations in corruption among democracies than among dictatorships. A large part of the democratic variation in corruption may be explained by the mode of electoral competition (i.e. whether elections are contested via programmatic competition or clientelistic competition). In many democracies, endemic clientelism undermines programmatic politics and therefore inhibits elections as an accountability mechanism. Clientelism is contrasted with programmatic redistributive politics, which "redistribute resources from classes of non-beneficiaries to classes of beneficiaries, but within a class of beneficiaries, any people who qualify cannot be excluded." Clientelistic benefits are "only available on condition that the client complies by providing political support" (Stokes 2007).

The selection of politicians in democratic elections can be complicated through the corrupt act of clientelism during the electoral process. The *principal-agent* relationship between the public (voters) and the politicians is converted into a *patron-client* relationship based on clientelism. In the principal-agent relationship, politicians are supposed to represent the public interest or broad interests of their coalitions, and the voters are supposed to hold them accountable through elections. In clientelistic politics, however, the voters become clients of the politicians, who act as the patron. The voters support their patron in elections, and the patron rewards the clientele with particularistic benefits, such as cash, gifts and the promise of jobs in the public sector. Thus, clientelism corrupts both the voters and politicians. The voters, who are supposed to be the principal but have turned into clients, and the politicians, who are supposedly the agent of their constituents but have become their patron, are engaging in corrupt exchanges. Hence, corrupt politicians are more likely to be elected through a corrupt electoral process.

Clientelism undoubtedly increases adverse selection, but it can also increase agency loss. The demand for clientelistic resources will increase the incentives for politicians to divert state resources or raise funds through illicit means (Chang and Golden 2007; Kitschelt 2007; Magaloni 2006; Singer 2009). Singer (2009) finds that clientelism is significantly associated with illegal fundraising and high-level corruption, although clientelism is not significantly associated with petty bureaucratic corruption. Clientelism also undermines the ability of citizens to hold corrupt public officials accountable and fosters a culture of impunity. Since the voters' primary concerns are particularistic benefits rather than universal or broad benefits (such as provision of public goods or policies that help broad constituency), voters may continue to support corrupt politicians only if the latter continue to provide the former with various particularistic benefits. Corrupt politicians are therefore more likely to survive subsequent elections under clientelistic competition than under programmatic competition. Corrupt incumbents can maintain public support by buying off voters. Likewise, political reform candidates will find it hard to garner sufficient support when clientelistic mobilization dominates elections (Manzetti and Wilson 2007).

Beyond the link between clientelism and adverse selection of politicians, clientelism creates adverse selection problems not only for politicians, but also for bureaucrats. Clientelism encourages politicians to provide patronage jobs in the public sector in exchange for support. In the chain of principal-agent relationships, politicians work simultaneously as the agent of the voters and the principal of the bureaucrats. The voters do not select the bureaucrats, but the politicians do. In a presidential system, the president typically appoints ministers and high-level officials. Ministers appoint other officials in the central government, and governors and mayors appoint officials in provincial and local governments. Although many countries have established a system of career civil service to ensure meritocratic recruitment of civil servants, this is not always the result. The appointment authorities of the president, ministers, governors and mayors are often abused to make patronage appointments. Whether these politicians have been elected through clientelistic or programmatic competition will have important consequences on the mode of bureaucratic recruitment and promotion. Those who have been elected via clientelistic competition are more likely to use bureaucratic appointments for clientelistic purposes. In addition, other politicians, such as members of the parliament, have a variety of means to influence those who have appointment authorities. Hence, clientelistic politicians may try to influence bureaucratic recruitment and promotion for clientelistic purposes even when they do not directly have appointment power.

Under clientelism, it has been observed that patronage jobs in the public sector are often exchanged for votes. The concept of patronage is closely related to clientelism, but the two concepts are distinct from each other. Patronage can be defined narrowly as the "exchange of a public sector job for political support," while clientelism includes not only jobs, but also other benefits (Robinson and Verdier 2013). Patronage can be more broadly defined as the "use of resources and benefits that flow from public office," while clientelism includes the additional use of private resources (Hicken 2011). Robinson and Verdier (2013) explain why patronage often takes the form of employment in the public sector. A job is selective and reversible and thus ties the utility of a voter to the political success of a particular politician over time. When politicians find it difficult to make credible commitments to voters with broad public policies, patronage employment will be an attractive means of redistributing targeted goods to their supporters. Where clientelism is prevalent, meritocratic recruitment of bureaucrats is hindered by political pressure for patronage jobs. Thus, clientelism creates adverse selection problems not only for elected offices, but also for appointed offices.

The adverse selection of bureaucrats will also increase agency loss. Politicians are required to monitor and sanction bureaucrats in order to effectively counteract corruption. However, clientelistic politicians are unlikely to perform these jobs effectively and in an impartial manner. Corrupt politicians may demand kickbacks from government employees given patronage jobs or even develop corruption networks with them (Rose-Ackerman 1999: 137). Bureaucrats who have acquired their jobs through patronage are also likely to seek promotion via patronage and thus have incentives to engage in corruption to support and reward their patrons (Hodder 2009). Weberian bureaucracy, and in particular meritocratic recruitment, is found to be closely associated with lower corruption and higher economic growth (Evans and Rauch 1999; Rauch and Evans 2000; Dahlström et al. 2012). It is evident that bureaucracies with rampant patronage appointments will have high levels of corruption because patronage itself is considered a kind of corruption, and it encourages further bureaucratic corruption.

The problem of the corrupt client and elite capture

Another neglected issue in the existing corruption literature is the problem of the corrupt 'client', or the 'supply' side of corruption (Wu 2005). The literature has mostly focused on the "demand" side of corruption, or corrupt behavior of the public officials as "agents" of the public. Although the client can be a victim of extortion by public officials, corruption often takes place as a mutually beneficial transaction between corrupt public officials and their clients. Typically, a favor and a bribe are exchanged between them; the exchanges can be initiated by the official or the client. Recent research on corruption in Nigeria, based on the in-depth interviews of thirty-two founders/CEOs of entrepreneurial firms, however, found that entrepreneurs were active perpetrators of bribery more frequently than they were victims of corrupt government agents (Ufere et al. 2012). Also, studies of Russia and other transition economies found that many firms were actively engaging in corruption "to shape the rules of the game to their own advantage" (Hellman *et al.* 2000; Iwasaki and Suzuki 2007). This finding illustrates the need for more attention on the supply side of corruption.

There are diverse kinds of clients for politicians and bureaucrats. The clients of bureaucrats include individual citizens, groups and firms who: receive various benefits and subsidies from the government; pay taxes, fees and tariffs to the government; and are regulated by the government. Private actors may offer bribes to bureaucrats to receive preferential treatment, avoid or reduce taxes, or circumvent regulations. The clients of politicians are usually those individuals, organizations and businesses who want to exert influence on the formulation and implementation of government policies. The bulk of these clients seek to enhance their own private interests, although there can be public interest groups and individuals, as well. Some clients may attempt to exert influence purely by providing the politicians with relevant information about the policy issue of interest. Other clients may attempt to buy influence by providing the politicians with legal campaign contributions or even illegal contributions or bribes.

Incentives for private sector clients to engage in corruption are often associated with rent-seeking opportunities with regard to the government's economic policies. Entrepreneurs may seek rents in various forms of licenses and subsidies, such as tax expenditures, underpriced credit and foreign exchange that are associated with industrial policies. They may lobby for protection from foreign and domestic competition in order to continue enjoying monopoly rents.

Corrupt transactions can turn into collusive relationships over time. This implies that corruption may result in the systematic capture of a public agency. A regulatory agency may be captured by an industry that the agency is supposed to regulate. Legislators, the legislature, bureaucrats and bureaucratic agencies may be captured by powerful private interests. The most concerning form of capture is the risk of "elite capture" or state capture by the wealthy elite. This is what Hellman *et al.* (2000) call a "capture economy." Under elite capture, policy-making and policy-implementing processes are significantly distorted by powerful private interests. The wealthy elite can employ two means of capture: influence and corruption. Hellman *et al.* (2000) distinguish between influence and state capture with regard to firm behavior. According to their definition, *state capture* addresses firms shaping and affecting the rules of the game through private payments to public officials and politicians, while *influence* means taking the same action without recourse to payments. My definition combines what Hellman, Jones and Kaufmann call state capture, or capture by corrupt means, and what they call influence, or capture by legal means. Thus, state capture is defined as "powerful private interests shaping and affecting formulation of the rules of the game through legal (influence) and illegal (corruption) means." State autonomy means the absence of state capture.

While state capture typically involves high-level political corruption (i.e. the capture of politicians or legislative process) and bureaucratic corruption (i.e. the capture of a bureaucratic agency or bureaucratic process), it can take place without corruption and purely through influence. Indeed, the most powerful players in the private sector are more likely to be able to capture the policy process using their influence, while the less powerful players will be compelled to rely more on corruption in order to compensate for smaller influence. Hence, capture by the powerful interests will spread corruption among the entire private sector. The businesses will not only engage in political and bureaucratic corruption to buy favors from politicians and bureaucrats, but also in corporate corruption. Corporate governance and accounting will likely become opaque and irregular with more frequent signs of illicit political contributions, bribes, illegal profits and tax evasion. State capture, in turn, will benefit the elite, maintaining or even further increasing inequality.

In summary, in the principal (voters) – agent (politicians and bureaucrats) – client (the private sector) relationship, corruption can be thought of as a betrayal of the principal by the agent, who abuses her power for private gain by exploiting informational asymmetry. Controlling corruption requires the effective monitoring and sanctioning of politicians and bureaucrats, as the existing literature has recognized. However, the principal should prevent corrupt agents from being selected ex ante, and then monitor and sanction them ex post. While it is important to structure incentives in a way that minimizes the agent's conflict of interest and effectively monitors the behavior of the agent, it is perhaps even more important to select honest agents in the first place. Unfortunately, democratic election processes dominated by clientelism encourage adverse selection of politicians and bureaucrats. Clientelism converts the principal-agent relationship between voters and politicians into a patron-client relationship. Clientelism corrupts both voters and politicians during the electoral process. Then, corrupt politicians corrupt not only the politics (i.e. policy-making process), but also the bureaucracy (i.e. policy-implementing process). Thus, clientelism will not only lead to electoral corruption, but also high-level political corruption and rampant bureaucratic corruption. Also, we need to consider the supply side of corruption, and in particular the capture by powerful private interests. The capture of politics and bureaucracy by powerful interests not only involves influence (i.e. legal lobbying and connections), but also high-level political and bureaucratic corruption. It further increases the incentives of the entire corporate sector to engage in corruption, thus increasing corporate corruption, as well. Clientelism and capture are two major risks for corruption in democracies.

Furthermore, clientelism and capture may reinforce each other. Clientelistic politicians and bureaucrats are likely to be more vulnerable to capture than programmatic politicians and bureaucrats recruited via meritocratic means because of the former's need for clientelistic resources. Furthermore, captured politicians are more likely to rely on clientelism than non-captured politicians are because the former will find it difficult to promote the interests of the captor with programmatic politics.

Democracy, inequality and corruption

The principal-agent-client model of corruption suggests that clientelism and capture are major threats to democratic accountability mechanisms. I argue that economic inequality increases corruption in democracies by fostering clientelism and capture. Let me first begin with a brief review of literature on clientelism and capture.

Inequality as a cause of clientelism

Above, I considered the link between clientelism and corruption, demonstrating that clientelistic politics leads to corruption through both adverse selection and agency loss. Here, I consider what causes clientelism to thrive instead of programmatic politics, introducing inequality as the previously overlooked explanatory variable.

Scholars have considered a variety of factors that cause clientelism. First, Keefer (2007) and Keefer and Vlaicu (2008) argue that younger democracies are more prone to clientelism because it takes time for political parties to build policy reputations. Politicians in younger democracies will find it hard to make credible pre-electoral commitments to voters. Hence, they are likely to rely on patron-client relationships to mobilize support rather than to engage in programmatic competition. It is notable that young democracies are substantially more corrupt on average than mature democracies. Cross-national studies have found that long-established democracies are significantly less corrupt, but young democracies are not (Treisman 2007; You and Khagram 2005). An important reason why young democracies suffer from high levels of corruption is probably the tendency of widespread clientelism, or the difficulty in developing programmatic politics.

Second, some scholars have argued that political institutions, such as electoral systems, can influence clientelism. Candidate-centered electoral systems tend to encourage cultivation of a personal vote and thereby clientelistic competition, compared to party-centered electoral systems, such as closed-list proportional representation (Carey and Shugart 1995; Hicken 2007). In particular, electoral rules that encourage intraparty competition will create great incentives for clientelistic competition. Many cross-national studies have examined the relationship between electoral systems and corruption, and some studies have found that district magnitude is associated with lower corruption (Panizza 2001; Persson *et al.* 2003). This is perhaps because smaller districts are more prone to clientelistic mobilization. It is easier for candidates to build and maintain clientelistic networks and to buy off voters in smaller districts.

Third, the level of socioeconomic development – including variables such as income, urbanization and education – may explain the differences in clientelism. Students of clientelism agree that poor, rural and uneducated voters are more prone to clientelism than middle-class, urban and educated voters. In particular, the demand for and susceptibility to vote-buying and other forms of clientelism is fueled by poverty (Brusco *et al.* 2004; Calvo and Murillo 2004; Hicken 2011; Kitschelt and Wilkinson 2007; Scott 1972; Stokes 2007; Weitz-Shapiro 2012). As incomes rise, the cost of vote-buying will rise, while the marginal benefit to a voter will decline. Charron and Lapuente (2010) suggest that lower-income societies are likely to over-value immediate consumption, such as patronage jobs and direct cash, through clientelistic exchange. Likewise, lower-income societies will more likely under-value long-term investments in administrative capacity, such as developing a meritocratic recruitment system and fighting favoritism and corruption. Charron and Lapuente further argue that the relationship between democracy and the quality of government is conditional on economic development. Democratization of rich countries will produce better quality of government, including lower corruption, but democratization of poor countries will lead to worse quality of government, including higher corruption. Urbanization may have an impact on candidate strategy independent of the income effects (Ramseyer and Rosenbluth 1993; Nielson and Shugart 1999; Bloom *et al.* 2001). Traditional patron-client networks, largely based on landlord-tenant relationship, are strong in rural areas, but it is difficult to create patron-client relationships in urban areas. Educational attainment may also influence electoral strategies because more educated voters are less prone to clientelism and vote-buying. Uneducated and poor citizens may discount the future and therefore prefer direct, clientelistic exchanges over indirect, programmatic linkages (Kitschelt 2000: 857).

Although the literature on clientelism generally agrees that the poor are prone to clientelism, it does not have to be that way. If the poor are well informed and well organized, and if there is a strong political party that represents the interests of the poor, the poor will support that party, allowing programmatic competition to develop. Hence, poverty or low levels of economic development should not necessarily produce clientelistic politics. In the real world, however, the poor are typically ill informed and disorganized. These challenges make it hard for the poor to overcome the collective action problem. Individuals will more likely make the rational choice to seek particularistic benefits in return for their political support (i.e. vote-selling) instead of supporting the collective benefit for the public at large. This is especially true in the absence of a powerful political party that not only advocates for the interests of the poor, but also has realistic chances of taking power or participating in the governing coalition.

In this regard, poverty is not the only challenge to collective action problems; high inequality is a major obstacle. Higher inequality means that a larger proportion of the population will be poor, and hence the poor will face more difficult problems of collective action due to the larger number of group members. Higher inequality also means greater relative poverty, and hence the poor will lack resources to invest in collective action. The historical experiences of social democracy in Europe show that it typically requires a large size of middle class to develop a powerful social democratic party. The poor alone cannot make a powerful political party, and they need to make a coalition with the middle class. Economic inequality leads to political inequality because all but the most affluent citizens lose subjective sense of efficacy at high levels of inequality. Without the sense of efficacy, the vast majority of the poor do not actively participate in politics (Solt 2008). For poor individuals at high levels of inequality, it is rational to pursue particularistic benefits from politicians in return for their votes.

In addition, at higher levels of inequality, the elite will have greater incentives to prevent the development of programmatic politics and to rely on clientelistic mobilization to secure support. At high levels of inequality, programmatic competition is likely to strengthen leftist parties that will jeopardize the elite interests. Hence, the rich have incentives to buy votes from the poor and to curb programmatic competition. Clientelism thus becomes an attractive political strategy for the elite in situations of high inequality, as Robinson and Verdier (2013) argued. This strategy signifies an attempt to make the vote of the large poor population meaningless in order to maintain the status quo of elite domination (Solt 2008). In an empirical study of electoral fortunes of the left in Latin America, Debs and Helmket (2010) find that the probability of the left candidate to be elected was lower at higher levels of inequality, using data on 110 elections in eighteen Latin American countries from 1978 to 2008. This is presumably because the rich bribed poor voters to avoid redistribution. Thomas Markussen's (2011) empirical study of South India shows evidence for a strong association between economic inequality and political clientelism.

Inequality also increases the prevalence of patronage in bureaucratic recruitment and promotion because clientelism typically involves the provision of patronage jobs in the public sector (Calvo and Murillo 2004). Once meritocratic principles are violated by patronage appointments, bureaucratic promotion is also likely to be affected by patronage and political interference. In addition, the rich may also directly participate in politics and penetrate the bureaucracy through political appointments. The relative value of elected and appointed offices for the rich will be higher as inequality increases because the importance of political influence and discretionary bureaucratic power increases as their stake in redistributive politics increases. It is not just the political market, but also bureaucratic recruitment and promotion that are corrupt. Bureaucratic penetration by the rich, in turn, will further increase patronage appointments and promotions. For example, Ziblatt (2009) finds evidence that land inequality led to penetration of local institutions by landed elites in late nineteenth-century Germany. Thus, inequality will increase adverse selection of both politicians and civil servants.

Inequality as a cause of capture

In addition to clientelism, capture is another major threat to democratic accountability mechanisms, and capture can also be caused by inequality. Inequality increases the probability of state capture by powerful private interests. Capture of the legislature, the judiciary and the administration by powerful private interests has the power to render democratic control mechanisms powerless.

Acemoglu and Robinson (2008) proposed a model of "captured democracy," in which de jure political power of citizens is offset by de facto political power of the elite based on lobbying, bribery and the use of extralegal force. "Captured democracy" is more likely at higher levels of inequality because of higher stakes and greater expected returns for the elite from controlling politics. Also, higher inequality will increase redistributive pressures, and politicians will promise more redistribution even when programmatic competition is limited and clientelistic practices are prevalent. In such circumstances, the rich have more incentives to corrupt and capture government, as You and Khagram (2005) suggest. The wealthy will try to bribe politicians in order to reduce taxes and costly regulations; they will also try to bribe bureaucrats to obtain preferential treatment. At high levels of inequality, the extremely wealthy people are very few in society. They are more likely to overcome collective action problems because of their relatively small number and abundance of resources. The capture by the powerful private interests may explain why higher inequality does not lead to higher redistribution, even among rich countries.

Todd Mitton (2008) suggests that higher economic concentration is associated with greater monopoly power and that those monopolistic firms exert greater political power to induce distortionary policies favorable to their own interests. He finds that countries with higher economic concentration had higher entry costs for new firms and weaker anti-trust policy, which is presumably evidence for capture. Economic concentration was also associated with more burdensome regulation and weaker rule of law, which suggests that only the powerful firms are able to circumvent costly regulation. Other firms have to make side payments in order to circumvent regulation. Kathy Fogel (2006) finds that higher inequality was associated with greater oligarchic family control of the economy, lower shareholder rights and less strict accounting disclosure rules. This is evidence that powerful family-controlled business groups in high-inequality economies exert their political influence to shape rules of the game in their favor, weakening investor protection and maintaining opaque corporate governance. Another interesting finding by Xun Wu (2005) is the significant effect of corporate governance on the level of corruption, with standard controls including democracy and economic development. Both the efficacy of corporate boards in representing outside shareholders and the quality of accounting practices were found to be significantly associated with the level of corruption. Taking Kathy Fogel's (2006) and Xun Wu's (2005) findings together, it can be inferred that higher inequality is associated with greater oligarchic family control and worse corporate governance, which in turn is associated with higher corruption.

Inequality and corruption in democracies and dictatorships

The above review of literature on clientelism and capture suggests that high inequality will increase clientelism and capture in democracies. Clientelism will directly increase petty electoral corruption and encourage political corruption. Clientelism will also increase patronage in bureaucratic recruitment, which will increase bureaucratic corruption.

Capture will involve high-level political and bureaucratic corruption, and it will spread corporate corruption.

In addition, the effectiveness of anti-corruption agencies and various reform measures in democracies is likely to be weaker as inequality increases. In democracies, politicians should show responsiveness to popular demand for anti-corruption reform, but the reforms could be rhetorical or genuine depending on the political will of the top leadership and the strength of civil society. Effectiveness of the prosecution and of various oversight agencies may also depend on the political will and civil society. Anti-corruption measures will be more effective when the monitoring capacity of the civil society is higher, but that capacity is likely to be lower at higher levels of inequality. The middle class is more likely than the poor to actively organize and monitor the malfeasance of politicians and high-level public officials. The relative size of the middle class tends to be larger in lower-inequality countries. Also, clientelism and capture will make it difficult to carry out and maintain genuine anti-corruption reform. Clientelism creates incentives for politicians to resist genuine anti-corruption reforms, and clientelistic politicians may try to make anti-corruption measures toothless and ineffective (Geddes 1994; Singer 2009). Powerful private interests may also resist anti-corruption reforms if these reforms jeopardize their ability to capture the state.

This discussion begs the question: What is the effect of economic inequality on corruption in dictatorships? Inequality may not be a significant factor for corruption in dictatorships because the causal mechanisms proposed above are more relevant for democracies. Since authoritarian regimes typically do not hold competitive elections, there is less scope for clientelistic politics. Since authoritarian policy processes are centralized in the authoritarian ruler or ruling party, there is less scope for capture. However, many dictatorships often hold elections – even if they are not truly competitive – as a mechanism to legitimize their rule. Authoritarian regimes usually manipulate electoral rules, limit the abilities of opposition candidates to campaign, and rely on coercion, intimidation and fraud in elections. But many soft authoritarian regimes or illiberal electoral democracies combine clientelistic mobilization, or "competitive clientelism," with intimidation and fraud (Gandhi and Lust-Okar 2009). To the extent that authoritarian regimes hold some degree of competitive elections, inequality could increase the clientelism employed during elections in these regimes as well. Considering all things together, we can expect that the effect of inequality on corruption in *liberal democracies* will be higher than that in *illiberal electoral democracies*, which in turn will be higher than that in *dictatorships*.

General hypotheses

Based on the above discussion, I will explore the following main hypothesis (H1) about the effect of democracy and economic inequality on corruption and three sub-hypotheses (MH1–MH3) about causal pathways through which inequality increases corruption in democracies.

H1: Corruption increases with inequality in democracies and authoritarian countries with elections. In other words, the effect of democratic institutions on reducing corruption is negatively associated with the level of economic inequality.

Mechanism hypothesis 1 (MH1): High inequality increases clientelism (electoral corruption) and thereby political corruption (corruption during the policy-making process).

Mechanism hypothesis 2 (MH2): High inequality increases patronage appointments in bureaucracy and thereby bureaucratic corruption (corruption during the policy implementation process).

Mechanism hypothesis 3 (MH3): High inequality increases state capture by the powerful private interests and thereby corporate corruption.

In addition, the following hypothesis (H2) is a corollary to the main hypothesis (H1). The two hypotheses (H1 and H2) are like two sides of the same coin.

H2: The effect of economic inequality on corruption in *liberal democracies* will be higher than that in *illiberal electoral democracies*, which in turn will be higher than that in *dictatorships*.

In the remainder of the book, I will test the above hypotheses through both comparative historical analysis of Korea, Taiwan and the Philippines, and cross-national analysis. The starting point of the comparative historical study will be a rigorous examination of the dependent variable, i.e. corruption in these countries, followed by a discussion of how the general hypotheses can be applied to the three East Asian countries. This will be the task of the next chapter.

3　Corruption in Korea, Taiwan and the Philippines
Relative levels, trends and possible explanations

I will now provide an overview of the relative levels and trends of corruption in Korea, Taiwan and the Philippines. Delineating the levels and trends across these countries is especially important considering the inherent difficulty of measuring corruption and different views among scholars about the relative levels of corruption across these countries. Hence, this chapter will present a thorough examination of various available cross-national measures of corruption for the three countries.

As discussed in the introduction, the Philippines has been more corrupt than Korea and Taiwan, at least since 1980 and arguably from a much earlier period. I also stated that, between Korea and Taiwan, Korea has been perceived to be somewhat more corrupt than Taiwan. Some may be skeptical about my assessment. Although there is a general consensus that the level of corruption has been very high in the Philippines and relatively low in Taiwan, there is no such agreement on the relative level of corruption in Korea. On the one hand, Korea, like Taiwan, is considered a model *developmental state* with a competent and relatively uncorrupt bureaucracy (Amsden 1989; Evans 1995; Haggard 1990a; Johnson 1987; Rodrik 1995). While these scholars found substantial corruption in Korea, they argue that corruption and rent-seeking did not develop to the extent that would jeopardize the autonomy and coherence of the developmental state. On the other hand, Korea is often cited as a case of successful development in spite of high corruption (Kang 2002; Khan 2006; Wedeman 1997).[1] Indeed, Korea, like the Philippines, was often labeled a country of *crony capitalism*, especially in the aftermath of the East Asian financial crisis of 1997 (Kang 2002). Hence, an important empirical question is whether Korea has been as corrupt as the Philippines or relatively clean like Taiwan. It is important to assess the relative

[1] Andrew Wedeman argues that Taiwan as well as Korea represents what he calls *developmental corruption*. However, he acknowledges that high-level corruption was relatively contained in Taiwan, although it remained widespread at the subnational and local levels (Wedeman 2012: 34–5).

levels and trends of corruption in Korea, Taiwan and the Philippines as correctly as possible before attempting to explain them.

The lack of consensus about the relative level of corruption in Korea stems largely from the inherent difficulty of measuring corruption. Therefore, I will first discuss the pros and cons of various measures of corruption. I will show that various cross-national measures of perceived and experienced corruption provide reasonably good estimates of levels of corruption, but we should not attach too much meaning to small differences across countries and yearly fluctuations within countries. In particular, short-run changes are likely to reflect changes in media exposures and economic performance more than changes in actual levels of corruption. Fortunately, if we triangulate many sources, we can get a picture of both cross-sectional differences and trends. This study will use a variety of available data, including both cross-national and unique country-level data.

Unfortunately, no cross-national measures of corruption are available for the period before 1980. Although it is hard to accurately present the relative levels of corruption across the three countries for the earlier period, available evidence suggests that corruption was rampant in all three countries in the late 1940s immediately after liberation from colonial rule. During the early 1980s, when all three countries were under authoritarian regimes, the available cross-national measures of corruption indicate a clear rank order of corruption among the three countries. The Philippines under Ferdinand Marcos was more corrupt than Korea under Chun Doo-hwan, which was more corrupt than Taiwan under Chiang Ching-kuo. This rank order has been maintained until today, a quarter century after democratic transition in these countries, according to various cross-national data on corruption. There is also evidence that Korea and Taiwan have been making improvement at least since the mid-1990s, while the Philippines has shown deterioration during the same period.

After examining various data on the relative levels and trends of corruption in these countries, I will conduct a simple test for possible causes of corruption, applying Mill's "method of difference." Finally, I will discuss how the general hypotheses delineated in the previous chapter apply in these three cases. These hypotheses will be explored in subsequent chapters.

Measuring corruption

It is inherently difficult to measure corruption because most corrupt acts are conducted secretly. Objective measures of corruption, such as the number or proportion of corruption convictions or newspaper articles on corruption, may reflect the rigor and effectiveness of the judicial system or the freedom of the press rather than the actual level of corruption. Hence, it is often argued that measures of perceived corruption are actually more reliable than objective measures of corruption for cross-national comparison. Perceived measures of corruption, however, are subjective by definition and are hence prone to bias and errors.

Much empirical research on the causes and consequences of corruption has been facilitated by the availability of the cross-national measures of perceived corruption, such as Transparency International's Corruption Perceptions Index (CPI) and Kaufmann, Kraay and Mastruzzi's (2010) Control of Corruption Indicator (CCI) as one of six Worldwide Governance Indicators. Both CPI and CCI are composite indexes of perceived corruption, aggregated from multiple sources and based on expert assessments or surveys of business people and households. Proponents of these measures note that there are high inter-correlations among the sources and argue that aggregation can help to reduce measurement error. Another perceived measure of corruption widely used by scholars is the Political Risk Service Group's International Country Risk Guide (ICRG) index of corruption. The ICRG index of corruption is one of many indicators of investment risks that are commercially provided to international investors. One advantage of this index is that the data has been available for a relatively long period of time since 1984, and there have been attempts to conduct panel data regressions using the data. However, Johanne Lambsdorff (2006), architect of the CPI, raised doubt about the reliability of the ICRG index. He noted that it measures *political risks* rather than *degrees* of corruption. The CPI has not included the ICRG measure as a source because of this concern.

The reduction of measurement error due to the aggregation of multiple sources of data may not be as robust as expected because the sources are not perfectly independent (Knack 2006). Since the CPI is widely publicized, it is likely to influence the ratings by other agencies, which, in turn, become the sources of the CPI in subsequent years. Knack (2006) found some evidence that the ICRG index was readjusted to conform more closely to the CPI. The correlation between the ICRG and CPI in June 2001 was only 0.72, but it rose to 0.91 with the massive recalibration by ICRG in November 2001. This evidence of interdependence between CPI and ICRG implies a circularity problem for CCI, which uses ICRG as a source. This also raises a problem with longitudinal data analysis using the ICRG data.

Measurement error is a particularly serious concern for the purpose of trend analysis. Although the correlation between CPI and CCI for any given year is close to one (typically, r = 0.97 or 0.98) and the correlations between their source data are also generally very high, the correlation between change in CPI and change in CCI is not very high. When I correlated the change in the CPI and CCI over the one-year or two-year period, I found that the correlation was usually insignificant and that the sign was even negative in some cases. When I compared changes in CPI and CCI over longer time spans of three years or more, the correlations became modestly higher and statistically significant. The extremely high correlations between various years of CPI and CCI within countries, together with the low correlations between yearly changes in CPI and CCI, imply that yearly changes in these indexes contain substantial measurement errors rather than real changes in corruption. Although both CPI and CCI are constructed based on various surveys and country ratings by experts, there are some differences in their selection of sources and countries in the data. Each year, different sources of data can be used for the same country, and the addition of new source data or the removal of previously used source data can change the CPI score of a particular country. This can happen even when all the common sources of data do not change their ratings of that country. Also, TI has strived for methodological improvement each year. As Lambsdorff (2006) noted, year-to-year changes of a country score may not only result from the changing perception of a country, but also from a changing sample and methodology.

Moreover, people's perceptions can be volatile. Even when a country's real level of corruption remains the same, the media exposure of corruption scandals can fluctuate and public perceptions will be affected accordingly. In this case, yearly variation will reflect the fluctuation in perceptions rather than the true change in corruption levels. In addition, the CPI, as well as its source data, may be affected by economic performance (Donchev and Ujhelyi 2009). For example, the CPI for Argentina was 5.2 in 1995 when its economy performed well. By 2002, however, the Argentine economy was in ruins and its CPI score plummeted to 2.8. The CPI on Argentina might have declined not because corruption increased, but because the poor performance of the economy convinced the observers that corruption must be higher than they thought it had been (Seligson 2006). There is a concern that systemic bias in favor of rich countries in the cross-national measures of corruption may lead to overestimation of the effect economic development has on corruption in OLS regressions (You and Khagram 2005).

This discussion reveals some pitfalls in the cross-national "perceived" measures of corruption such as the CPI and the CCI. In order to solve the potential biases in the perceived measures of corruption, a promising method of measuring "experience" of corruption has been developed. For example, TI's annual Global Corruption Barometer (GCB) surveys have asked the respondents about their experience of bribery since 2004. The new approach has been partly inspired by crime-victimization surveys. Criminologists have long recognized the unreliability of official crime rates and developed crime-victimization surveys, which are widely believed to provide a more accurate tally of crime rates (Seligson 2006). Micro-surveys of the experience of corruption were also successfully used to elicit information about firms' extra payment or bribery payment (Reinikka and Svensson 2003).

One concern about experience surveys is the possibility of under-reporting. Individuals may not honestly report their experiences of corruption out of the fear of possible legal trouble. Focus-group research, however, has shown that an under-reporting problem exists but is surprisingly limited, according to Seligson (2006). Another critique of this survey approach is that it measures only low-level corruption and misses high-level corruption. Special caution is required about the survey methodology and the exact wording of the questionnaire because different methodology (i.e. face-to-face survey versus phone survey) and different question wordings can produce different results with different degrees of under-reporting. In fact, experience survey data also suffers from large measurement errors. The GCB surveys of bribery experience show substantial yearly fluctuations within countries, which are likely largely due to measurement errors rather than actual yearly changes in bribery.

Measures of perceived and experienced corruption have different characteristics. Cross-national measures of perceived corruption, such as the CPI and CCI, largely represent the views of experts and business people. These views are not necessarily based on their direct experience and can be influenced by media reports and other information. The CPI and CCI are likely to reflect high-level corruption rather than petty corruption. On the other hand, data from the experience of bribery surveys are likely to reflect the petty corruption experienced by ordinary people rather than high-level corruption. Fortunately, the two measures correlate highly. The correlation between the GCB data on the public experience of petty bribery and the CPI or CCI is quite strong, with $r = 0.62$ or $r = 0.63$. The correlation becomes even higher if the logarithm of GCB bribery is used, with $r = 0.8$ for both CPI and CCI. Such high correlations confirm that the perceived measures of corruption, such as CPI and CCI, substantially reflect the actual levels of corruption experienced by the people.

These correlations also imply that there is a very high correlation between petty corruption and grand corruption. Political systems that are very corrupt at the level of day-to-day transactions are also highly corrupt at the top level (Seligson 2006). Therefore, both the measures of perceived corruption and experienced corruption are useful and reliable if we pay close attention to the small differences across countries and small variations over time within countries. Various measures of perceived and experienced corruption can also be supplementary. However, substantial noise in the yearly variations within countries of both perceived and experienced measures of corruption requires special caution in regard to longitudinal data analysis. The correlation between CPI 1995 and CPI 2012 is 0.94, and that between CCI 1996 and CCI 2011 is 0.89, which indicates that perceived corruption is variable and changes very slowly over time in most countries.

Another problem presented by using composite indexes such as CPI and CCI is that they lack a precise definition of the corruption they measure. The source data used for these indexes lack conceptual precision, and the aggregation of multiple sources further compounds the conceptual problem. Hence, if researchers need measures for different types of corruption, they should look at individual indicators of corruption or survey data on responses to specific questions. For example, the GCB experience of bribery may largely reflect petty bureaucratic corruption. If one is interested in cross-national measures for political, judicial and corporate corruption, World Economic Forum's annual surveys of business people provide useful data. These surveys include some questions on different types of corruption and have found that the perceived levels of different corruption types are closely correlated with CPI and CCI. In particular, corporate corruption is very highly correlated with both CPI and CCI at more than 0.9, while the correlation between perceived political corruption and CPI or CCI is around 0.8.

Some researchers have used the official statistics of corruption convicts for the study of corruption in the United States (Alt and Lassen 2003). Perhaps official statistics on prosecution or conviction of corruption can be better used for cross-time comparison within a country than for cross-national comparison. There is too much variation across countries in the rigor and effectiveness of judicial systems, as well as the legal definition of corruption, to compare official statistics on corruption. This problem is largely solved in regard to within-country analysis, and there is usually substantial information on over-time changes in the efforts and effectiveness of the anti-corruption agencies, as well as the political will to fight corruption.

In summary, both perceived and experienced measures of corruption contain a large measurement error. Yearly variations are likely to contain a more significant degree of measurement error than real changes in actual levels of corruption. Short-run changes in perceived corruption are likely to correlate with other determinants such as economic performance, and thus are less likely to be useful, but high correlations between measures for perceived corruption and those for experienced corruption suggest that both kinds of measures are reliable to a considerable extent. Since no single measure of corruption is perfect, this study will use a variety of available data, including measures of both perceived and experienced corruption, prosecution data and some proxy indicators of corruption. Sufficient caution will be given to not misinterpret various kinds of data, but to best exploit the merits of them.

Relative levels and trends of corruption in Korea, Taiwan and the Philippines

From the early period of post-liberation (late 1940s) to the early 1980s

For the period before 1980, it is impossible to present relative levels and trends of corruption with high precision. But it is possible to roughly describe the degree and trend of corruption in each country with some anecdotal evidence and secondary sources. In brief, corruption was rampant in all three countries in the early period of post-independence. Apparently, corruption declined in Taiwan but increased in the Philippines between the early years of post-liberation and the early 1980s. However, it is rather difficult to discern the trend of corruption in Korea for the same period.

Students of Korean politics and political economy generally agree that there was rampant corruption during the periods of the first president, Syngman Rhee (1948 to 1960), and the military dictator, Chun Doo-hwan (1980 to 1987). Rhee himself was not corrupt, but his regime was corrupt. Corruption scandals that involved the ruling party and business took place in every election year. "The dynamic of graft reverberated down the bureaucratic hierarchy and penetrated the country" (Lie 1998: 32). Official corruption reached both high and low levels. Rural police often collected and pocketed "taxes," and members of Rhee's own political machine exacted "voluntary assessments" (Gayn 1954: 215). Rhee had to resign as president in 1960 owing to the pressure of large student demonstrations against the election rigging and corruption of the regime. While Chun displayed individual acts of corruption, his family, relatives and ruling party were also implicated in numerous scandals of corruption. It is hard to tell if corruption increased or decreased between Rhee's presidency and Chun's.

There is a disagreement about the extent of corruption in Korea under the military dictator, Park Chung-hee (1961 to 1979), who is credited with uplifting Korea to the path of rapid industrialization and growth. The developmental state literature on Korea tends to contrast between Rhee's corrupt and inefficient rule and Park's relatively uncorrupt and efficient rule (Amsden 1989; Campos and Root 1996; Evans 1995; Haggard 1990a; Hutchcroft 2011). However, some scholars argue that both regimes were similarly corrupt (Kang 2002; Wedeman 1997, 2012).

Corruption was an important issue for every government during this period in Korea. After the student revolution of April 1960, which overthrew Rhee's regime, anti-corruption was a salient political agenda under the democratic Chang Myon government (1960 to 1961). Both Park Chung-hee and Chun Doo-hwan justified their coup d'état in 1961 and in 1980, respectively, with a slogan of anti-corruption. The recurrent emphasis of anti-corruption reform at the onset of each regime suggests that every previous regime could not control corruption satisfactorily in the eyes of most people. However, bureaucratic corruption seems to have declined over time with the gradual development of a meritocratic bureaucracy. Even David Kang acknowledges that agency slack in Korea's bureaucracy was low, while political corruption continued to be high (2002: 74).

Taiwan also suffered from rampant corruption during the early years after liberation from Japanese rule in 1945, but Taiwan experienced a steeper decline in corruption after the declaration of martial law in 1949. With Japanese surrender at the end of World War II, Taiwan reverted back to control of the Chinese government under Chiang Kai-shek's Kuomintang. Most Taiwanese welcomed the reinstitution of Chinese rule, but the military government headed by Chen Yi, the first governor-general, was infamous for its widespread corruption, nepotism and looting. The Taiwanese people commonly complained, "Dogs go and pigs come!" (Kerr 1965: 97). Many of the high-ranking public officials held lucrative private management positions at the same time. They often abused their power to create shortages in goods and services under the government's monopoly and sell them on the black market for a handsome profit. Many mainlanders in powerful positions embezzled the former Japanese properties confiscated by the Chinese government. There were countless incidents of police corruption and collusion between the police and criminal gangs (Roy 2003: 61–65). Taiwanese resentment over corruption and oppression led to the February 28 uprising in 1947. During the popular uprising, about a thousand mainlanders were killed or injured. Subsequently, a massacre of thousands of Taiwanese was carried out by

Chiang Kai-shek's reinforced troops and armed police during the recapture of the cities (Roy 2003: 67–73).

After the Republic of China relocated to Taiwan and declared martial law in 1949, the formerly corrupt Koumintang (KMT) transformed itself into a clean and coherent party. Taiwan enjoyed a relatively good reputation with regard to corruption (Taylor 2009: 487–8). Although corrupt practices were relatively rare at high levels in the central administration, they were more widespread at the local level. A Western observer noticed that "Taiwanese enterprisers became fully as adept as mainlanders in cultivating and passing 'the red envelope' to officials" (Cole 1967: 651–2). Corruption was never a big political issue during the authoritarian period, although repression of the freedom of the press might have led to under-reporting of high-level corruption. Scholars generally agree that there was substantial improvement in the control of corruption during the early period of independence in Taiwan.

The Philippines offers a bleaker picture of curbing corruption over time. Students of Philippine politics generally agree that corruption was not only high, but worsened over time during the early democratic period (1946 to 1972), and that corruption increased further during the martial law period (1972 to 1986). James Scott (1972: 96–7) called the Philippines a "model electoral corruption." Congressmen commonly engaged in brokering the allocation of government favors to the private businesses in return for kickbacks. The bureaucracy was increasingly occupied by patronage appointments, and corruption increased over time. In a survey of bureaucrats in 1971, two-thirds of the respondents complained about the prevalence of corruption in the Philippine government (Montinola 1999). State resources were plundered in various forms by politicians and powerful oligarchs. The landed oligarchy expanded their wealth and power relying on government-created rents and privileges (Hutchcroft 2011). Corruption was a recurrent political issue, and every incoming president pledged to fight against it. However, anti-corruption measures were ineffective and the scope and extent of corruption increased over time. When Marcos declared martial law in September 1972, he promised to clean up the government and transform the corrupt oligarchic democracy. There seemed to be some improvement in bureaucratic corruption in the first few years of martial law regime. However, Marcos turned out to be one of the most corrupt presidents in the world.

From the historical narratives of the three countries, it is evident that all of them suffered from high levels of corruption in the early years of independence. However, the three countries seem to have had diverging experiences in the control of corruption during the first few decades of post-independence. The above narratives suggest that corruption increased

Table 3.1 *Perceived levels of corruption in the early 1980s*

	BI 1980–83	CPI 1980–85
Taiwan	6.75	6.0
Korea	5.75	3.9
Philippines	4.50	1.0

Source: BI ratings from Mauro (1995); Historical CPI for 1980–85 from Transparency International (www.transparency.org/).

considerably in the Philippines, decreased considerably in Taiwan, and might have decreased somewhat in Korea between the early period of post-independence and the late years of authoritarianism. These trends become more evident when we compare these countries' corruption ratings in the 1980s.

The early 1980s is the earliest period for which cross-national data on perceived corruption are available for the three countries. During that time, all three countries were under authoritarian regimes. Korea was ruled by Chun Doo-hwan, Taiwan by Chiang Ching-kuo and the Philippines by Ferdinand Marcos. Note that Chun and Marcos are known as the most corrupt presidents in the history of South Korea and the Philippines, respectively. Table 3.1 presents two cross-national measures of corruption for the period covering the early 1980s. Both the Business International's ratings of corruption for 1980 to 1983 and the Transparency International's "historical CPI" for 1980 to 1985 can range between 0 (totally corrupt) and 10 (totally clean). The two measures show somewhat different scores, but they present the same rank order of corruption among the three countries: the Philippines is the most corrupt, Taiwan is the least corrupt, and Korea is in between Taiwan and the Philippines.

This rank order corroborates with the relative magnitude of corruption committed by the authoritarian rulers of the time in these countries. In Korea, President Chun Doo-hwan was later convicted of raising slush funds of $890 million and of receiving $273 million in bribes. The Philippines's Ferdinand Marcos was known to have accumulated $3 billion, and was found to have deposited around $550 million in Swiss banks and $250 million in Hong Kong banks (Wedeman 1997). Marcos's corruption was more severe than that of Chun, especially considering that the Philippine GDP was much smaller than that of Korea in the 1980s.

Table 3.2 *Trends of CPI scores and ranks out of fifty-four countries in the initial sample*

Country/Period	1980–85	1988–92	1995–2000	2001–05	2006–10
Taiwan	6.0 (25)	5.1 (29)	5.2 (24)	5.7 (24)	5.7 (24)
Korea	3.9 (38)	3.5 (37)	4.3 (32)	4.5 (30)	5.3 (25)
Philippines	1.0 (49)	2.0 (46)	3.0 (39)	2.6 (43)	2.4 (46)

Source: Transparency International (www.transparency.org/).

It is known that corruption was concentrated on the authoritarian ruler in both countries at that time, so comparison of the magnitude of the two presidents' corruption is likely to provide a good proxy of the relative degree of corruption in the two countries. In Taiwan, Chiang Ching-kuo was never implicated in corruption, and any corruption scandal in the early 1980s did not reach the magnitude of corruption scandals in Korea and the Philippines.

From the democratic transitions of 1986/87 to the present

The three countries all experienced democratization, starting in 1986 or 1987. The rank order of corruption among these countries has not changed until today, showing strong path dependence. However, there have been some notable changes. During the first few years of democratic transition, the Philippines seemed to be making progress in corruption control, Taiwan deteriorated and Korea experienced no significant change. But in a longer span of a quarter century after democratic transition, the Philippines has failed to make any improvement, even showing deterioration over the last fifteen years. Korea and Taiwan seem to have made some improvement in corruption control during the same period.

TI's Corruption Perceptions Index (CPI): Table 3.2 displays Transparency International's "historical CPIs" for the periods of 1980 to 1985 and 1988 to 1992 and the average values for annually published CPIs during the periods of 1995 to 2000, 2001 to 2005, and 2006 to 2010 for these countries. The TI has been publishing CPI annually since 1995, but it also provides historical CPI data for the two periods. Note that values of CPI from the historical data are not comparable to those from annually published data because of differences in the source data, so comparing rankings across the initial sample of fifty-four countries rather than evaluating absolute scores will be more compelling. I have averaged CPI for roughly five-year periods to minimize measurement errors contained in yearly variations.

The table shows that the Philippines has consistently been perceived as the most corrupt, Taiwan the least corrupt and Korea in between with a trend of substantial improvement. Comparison of the countries' worldwide ranks over time illuminates the trend of corruption in these countries. Taiwan seems to have suffered from increasing corruption in the early years of democratic transition. Its rank within the sample of fifty-four countries slipped from twenty-fifth in the 1980 to 1985 period to twenty-ninth in the 1988 to 1992 period. But the country has recovered and made some improvement since then, with its rank rising to twenty-fourth in the subsequent periods. Korea does not show significant change initially, with its rank rising just one step from thirty-eighth in the 1980 to 1985 period to thirty-seventh in the 1988 to 1992 period. But Korea has made substantial improvement since then, with its rank rising to thirty-second in the 1995 to 2000 period, to thirtieth in the 2001 to 2005 period and to twenty-fifth in the 2006 to 2010 period, right behind Taiwan. The Philippines made some improvement in the early years of democratic transition, with its rank rising from forty-ninth in the 1980 to 1985 period to forty-sixth in the 1988 to 1992 period and to thirty-ninth in the 1995 to 2000 period. However, the country has shown significant deterioration since then, with its rank falling to forty-third in the 2001 to 2005 period and further to forty-sixth in the 2006 to 2010 period.

We can examine the trends of CPI for these countries more in detail from 1995 to present, for which annual data are available. Figure 3.1 shows that Taiwan has made some improvement in CPI rather steadily, although there was a slight increase in 2001 after the election of Democratic Progressive PartyP's Chen Shui-bian as president in 2000 and a slight drop during his second term (2004 to 2008). Taiwan's CPI score started with around 5 in 1995 but surpassed 6 in 2011. Korea has also made some improvement, albeit with fluctuations, from about 4.3 in 1995 to about 5.4 in 2011. Korea's CPI score reached 5.6 in 2008 and almost caught up with Taiwan, but Korea's performance slightly declined under Lee Myung-bak's government (2008 to 2012). The Philippines seems to have made some improvement until 1999, from 2.8 in 1995 to 3.6 in 1999, but its CPI score has declined since then to around 2.5 in recent years.

In 1999, the CPI score for Korea fell to 3.8 and that for the Philippines rose to 3.6. They were very close to each other, and both were far below that for Taiwan (5.6). These levels seem to validate the view that Korea was closer to the Philippines than to Taiwan in terms of crony capitalism and corruption. However, yearly fluctuations in CPI could be

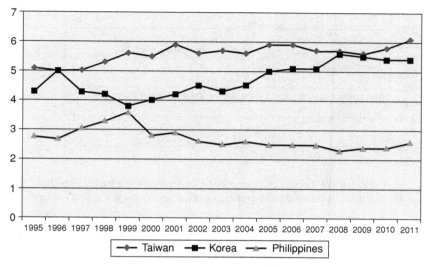

Figure 3.1 TI's Corruption Perceptions Index, 1995–2011
Source: Transparency International (www.transparency.org/).

from changes in composition of source data in addition to changes in perceptions rather than changes in actual corruption. A close examination of the CPI's source data reveals that Korea's jump in 1996 and fall in 1999 are partly due to changes in the composition of source data. In addition, the financial crisis of 1997 to 1998, which provoked a high number of discussions about crony capitalism in Korea, seems to have contributed to the fall of Korea's CPI in 1999, while the fact that the Philippines was less affected by the financial crisis helped to improve its CPI score. This displays how the economic performance of a country impacts perceptions of corruption. The notion of crony capitalism in Korea and Korea's CPI score in 1999 seemed to have reinforced each other.

KKM's Control of Corruption Indicator (CCI): Let us examine another popularly used cross-national measure: Kaufmann, Kraay and Mastruzzi's Control of Corruption Indicator (CCI), which has been published since 1996, every two years until 2002 and annually thereafter. Figure 3.2 shows the trends in CCI for Korea, Taiwan and the Philippines. The figure also indicates that Taiwan has been perceived to be the least corrupt, the Philippines the most corrupt and Korea in between, but gradually converging toward Taiwan. Thus, the trends of CCI for the three countries are similar to those of CPI, but there are some differences.

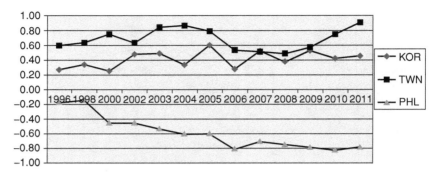

Figure 3.2 Trends of Control of Corruption Indicator, 1996–2011
Source: Worldwide Governance Indicators (www.govindicators.org).

It is easy to interpret CCI because it is a standardized score with the mean of 0 and the standard deviation of 1, and a higher CCI value represents a better control of corruption, or a lower level of corruption. Since the world mean is 0, it is easy to see that the Philippines has been consistently perceived as more corrupt than the world average, while Taiwan and Korea have been rated as less corrupt than the world average. The trend of corruption control (CCI) for the Philippines is a deteriorating one, starting from about 0.2 standard deviation below the world mean in 1996 and moving downward to about 0.8 standard deviation below the mean in recent years. In terms of percentile rank, the place of the Philippines plummeted from the fifty-first percentile in 1996 to the twenty-third percentile in 2011. Taiwan's CCI shows a slight improvement from 1996 to 2004, followed by some deterioration until 2008 and a rebound since then, indicating a trend from about 0.6 standard deviation above the world mean in 1996 to over 0.8 in 2004, to 0.5 in 2008, to 0.9 in 2011. In terms of percentile rank, Taiwan started at the sixty-fifth percentile in 1996, and with ups (the eightieth percentile in 2003) and downs (the seventy-second percentile in 2007–9) it has recently reached the seventy-eighth percentile in 2011. Overall, Taiwan has made a slight improvement during the fifteen years from 1996 to 2011, although its CCI score declined temporarily during the scandal-ridden second term of Chen Shui-bian's presidency (2004 to 2008). Korea's CCI score improved from about 0.2 in 1996 to 0.6 in 2005, but it has slightly declined to 0.45 in 2011. In terms of percentile rank, Korea's place rose from the sixty-fifth percentile in 1996 to the seventy-third percentile in 2007, followed by a slight fall to the seventieth percentile in 2011.

The trends of CCI for the three countries are roughly similar to those of CPI, with Korea and Taiwan making improvements, but with the Philippines showing deterioration in control of corruption. There are some differences as well. The Philippines's CCI score has not only steadily declined, but has been consistently far below that of Korea. Thus, the kind of convergence between the Philippines and Korea that was seen in CPI for 1999 is not observed in CCI. Also, Korea's yearly fluctuations in CCI are smaller than those in CPI.

World Economic Forum's Executive Opinion Survey: Looking at specific indicators of corruption that are comparable across countries and across time sheds light on corruption perception. The Executive Opinion Survey of the World Economic Forum has been asking businessmen to choose the biggest obstacle to conducting business from a list of fourteen (in 2003 to 2007) or fifteen factors (in 2008 to 2011) in each country since 2003.[2] The advantage of this question is that while both Filipinos and Koreans may answer that their country is very corrupt and that their government bureaucracy is very inefficient at the same time, they have to distinguish which is a more serious problem. Thus, the survey question reduces the problem of respondents having different standards of corruption, one of the major problems with previous surveys about perceived corruption.

Table 3.3 shows that in the Philippines, an average of 22.9 percent of businessmen interviewed between 2003 and 2011 chose corruption as the greatest problem affecting business. Indeed, corruption was considered a greater problem than inefficient government bureaucracy (16.3 percent), inadequate infrastructure (14.9 percent) and policy instability (12.7 percent). In contrast, only about 2.4 percent of Taiwanese businessmen and about 5.5 percent of Korean businessmen regarded corruption as the biggest problem for doing business during the same period. Taiwanese chose policy instability (22.4 percent) and inefficient bureaucracy (14.3 percent) as the biggest obstacles for business. Koreans also chose policy instability (17.3 percent) and inefficient bureaucracy (15.1 percent), followed by restrictive labor regulations (12.2 percent) and access to financing (12.0 percent).

---

[2] The list of other barriers to doing business includes inefficient government bureaucracy, policy instability, tax regulations, inadequate supply of infrastructure, access to financing, tax rates, poor work ethic in national labor force, inadequately educated workforce, inflation, foreign currency regulations, crime and theft, restrictive labor regulations, government instability/coups and poor public health (added in 2008). The survey asks the respondents to select the five most problematic in order, and the results were then tabulated and weighted according to the ranking assigned by respondents.

Table 3.3 *Percentage of businessmen who cite corruption as the biggest problem for doing business*

Country/Year	2003	2004	2005	2006	2007	2008	2009	2010	2011	Average
Singapore	0	0	0	0.3	0.3	0.1	0.8	0.1	0.3	0.2
Japan	1	0	1	1.8	1.1	0.7	0.2	0.1	0.1	0.7
Taiwan	**3**	**3**	**2**	**3.6**	**3.2**	**3.2**	**0.9**	**2.6**	**0.5**	**2.4**
Hong Kong	4	4	5	1.6	2.3	1.6	2.5	3.4	0.7	2.8
Korea	**6**	**5**	**8**	**4.6**	**4.0**	**4.7**	**5.9**	**5.9**	**5.6**	**5.5**
Malaysia	4	12	8	8.0	9.0	14.5	10.4	8.0	9.6	9.3
Sri Lanka	11	10	12	8.7	8.4	11.5	7.1	10.5	9.1	9.8
Timor-Leste	–	–	10	10.2	9.7	11.4	9.6	10.7	14.4	10.9
Indonesia	17	19	11	4.6	4.2	10.7	8.7	16.0	15.4	11.8
Mongolia	–	–	10	10.5	11.3	11.6	11.2	12.2	12.8	11.4
China	11	15	13	12.0	11.6	7.4	7.4	9.5	8.5	10.6
Nepal	–	–	–	12.2	10.3	11.9	10.8	12.1	10.0	11.2
India	16	16	14	10.5	11.9	10.1	11.0	17.3	16.7	13.7
Thailand	17	15	13	14.7	10.8	10.3	11.0	11.4	14.5	13.1
Pakistan	13	18	16	13.3	11.5	13.1	11.5	18.4	11.6	14.0
Vietnam	15	22	20	18.8	14.8	9.0	5.1	4.8	5.7	12.8
Bangladesh	26	25	25	22.8	23.7	18.5	16.0	14.5	18.5	21.1
Cambodia	–	–	24	19.6	21.2	24.5	23.9	21.5	16.8	21.6
Philippines	**22**	**22**	**23**	**21.5**	**22.3**	**23.9**	**24.3**	**22.7**	**24.4**	**22.9**

Source: World Economic Forum, *Global Competitiveness Report* (2003–11).

If we compare three-year averages for 2003 to 2005 and 2009 to 2011, the average percentage for Taiwan decreased from 2.7 to 1.3 percent, that for Korea slightly decreased from 6.3 to 5.8 percent, but that for the Philippines slightly increased from 22.3 to 23.8 percent. It may be too early to read trends from the rather short period of eight years, but at least we can see that there is no convergence between the Philippines and the other two countries. Among the Asian countries presented in Table 3.3, the Philippines (22.9 percent) is one of the top three countries, together with Cambodia (21.6 percent) and Bangladesh (21.1 percent), where corruption is cited by business people as the largest obstacle to business. In contrast, Taiwan (2.4 percent) and Korea (5.5 percent) were substantially below the Asian mean (10.8 percent), although they did not reach the very low levels of Singapore (0.2 percent), Japan (0.7 percent) or many advanced European nations, where typically less than 1 percent of business executives select corruption as the largest obstacle to business. This survey clearly indicates that corruption is considered the most serious problem in the Philippines, while it is less of a problem in Taiwan and Korea. It also distinguishes that Koreans perceive corruption to be a more serious problem than Taiwanese do.

TI's Global Corruption Barometer (GCB): We have thus far examined perceived measures of corruption. We will now examine survey data on people's experience with corruption. TI's Global Corruption Barometer (GCB) survey asks the general public if the respondents or their family members have ever paid a bribe in any form to public officials during the past year. This survey question captures the relative frequency of petty bribery. In the Philippines, 17.5 percent of the respondents on average (measured between 9 and 32 percent each year from 2004 to 2010) admitted paying a bribe to officials, while in Korea and Taiwan the averages were 2.9 and 3.3 percent respectively. Table 3.4 indicates that Korea and Taiwan are among the least corrupt in Asia in terms of petty bureaucratic corruption, together with Japan (2.5 percent), Hong Kong (3.7 percent) and Singapore (4.0 percent). The Philippines shares a similar level of petty corruption with Indonesia (19.9 percent) and India (21.2 percent), although it does not reach the extreme levels of Afghanistan (61 percent) and Cambodia (59.8 percent).

With experiential measures of corruption, respondents will inevitably offer different degrees of under-reporting, but this is not a large problem. Yearly variations are quite high for some countries, which may be due to the slightly different question wordings and the ways in which surveys were conducted. Hence, we should not give too much weight to small differences in these numbers. However, these data still give a broad picture of different degrees of petty corruption prevalence, and it seems

Table 3.4 *Percentage of people whose family members have bribed during the last twelve months*

Country/Year	2004	2005	2006	2007	2008/09	2010	Average
Japan	1	0	3	1	1	8.9	2.5
South Korea	6	4	2	1	2	2.4	2.9
Taiwan	1	3	2	–	–	7.1	3.3
Hong Kong	1	0	6	3	7	5.2	3.7
Singapore	1	4	1	–	5	8.8	4.0
Malaysia	3	6	3	6	8	9.1	5.8
China	–	–	–	–	–	9.3	9.3
Thailand	–	6	10	–	11	22.7	12.4
Philippines	21	9	16	32	11	16.1	17.5
Indonesia	13	11	18	31	28	18.2	19.9
India	16	12	12	25	8	54.2	21.2
Pakistan	19	13	15	44	18	49.4	26.4
Vietnam	–	–	–	14	–	43.9	29.0
Mongolia	–	–	–	–	28	47.6	37.8
Cambodia	–	36	–	72	47	84.0	59.8
Afghanistan	–	–	–	–	–	61.0	61.0

Source: Transparency International, *Global Corruption Barometer Survey* (2004–10).

to be safe to judge that petty corruption is much more prevalent in the Philippines than in Korea and Taiwan.

World Economic Forum's Measures of Corruption in Different Sectors: One important note is that the experience of petty bribery largely reflects petty *bureaucratic* corruption. Corruption occurs in different sectors. We need to therefore examine the differing measures of corruption forms. The World Economic Forum's surveys have asked questions regarding the different types of corruption (i.e. corporate, judicial and political). One question measuring corporate corruption asks the business executives to assess the corporate ethics (ethical behavior in interactions with public officials, politicians and other enterprises) of firms in their country on a scale of 1 to 7 (1 = among the worst in the world, 7 = among the best in the world). Taiwan, Korea and the Philippines scored 4.8, 4.5 and 3.4 respectively on average from 2006 to 2012. For the question measuring *judicial* corruption (irregular payments in judicial decisions), the average scores for Taiwan, Korea and the Philippines were 5.5, 4.8 and 2.7 respectively. There were three questions about *political* corruption (irregular payments in government policy-making, prevalence of illegal political donations and policy consequences of legal political donations). The average scores for these questions on political corruption were 4.5 for Taiwan, 4.0 for Korea and 2.5 for the Philippines. Regardless of which

Table 3.5 *Comparison of the three countries regarding different types of corruption*
(1 = worst, 7 = best in the world)

Country/Type	Corporate	Judicial	Political	Average
Taiwan	5.3	5.5	4.5	5.1
Korea	4.6	4.8	4.0	4.5
Philippines	3.6	2.7	2.5	2.9

Source: World Economic Forum, *Global Competitiveness Report* (2001–10).

type of corruption was addressed, the rank order was consistent among the three countries. The Philippines, together with Bangladesh, Nepal, Cambodia and Timor-Leste, was one of the most corrupt countries in Asia. Taiwan was among the least corrupt countries and Korea was slightly behind Taiwan.

Summary

I have presented a variety of historical evidence and cross-national measures on perceived and experienced corruption, including political, bureaucratic, judicial and corporate corruption. First, all three countries were highly corrupt in the early period of post-independence. There is no lack of evidence that shows rampant corruption in the Philippines in that period. The initial Chinese government of Taiwan after liberation from Japanese rule was notoriously corrupt. The rampant corruption even provoked a popular uprising in 1947. It is also notable that the KMT regime in mainland China before its relocation to Taiwan was infamous for rampant corruption. Corruption was prevalent under Korea's first president Syngman Rhee (1948 to 1960), who was forced to resign as president after large-scale student demonstrations against the election rigging and corruption of the regime.

Second, during the early 1980s when all of these countries were under authoritarian rule, the Philippines was the most corrupt, Taiwan the least corrupt and Korea in between. This suggests that there was substantial improvement in control of corruption in Taiwan and some improvement in Korea during the first few decades of the post-independence period. In the Philippines, corruption worsened over time both during the early democratic period (1946 to 1972) and during the authoritarian period (1972 to 1986).

The rank order of corruption among the three countries, which was set in the first few decades of post-independence, has not changed until the current time period. This indicates the strong tendency of path dependence, or stickiness of corruption, but there have also been some changes over time. In the early years after democratic transition, the Philippines and Korea displayed some improvement, but Taiwan experienced increasing corruption. However, the more long-term effect of democratization was not positive for the Philippines, while it was positive for both Taiwan and Korea. Both CPI and CCI indicate that the corruption gap between the Philippines and the other two countries has widened. While Korea and Taiwan have made progress in controlling corruption since at least the mid-1990s (or over the entire period during which both CPI and CCI have been published), the level of corruption in the Philippines has increased. Today, both surveys of business perceptions and public experience of corruption demonstrate that the Philippines is one of the most corrupt countries in Asia, while Korea and Taiwan are among the least corrupt countries.

Possible explanations

Having established the relative levels and trends of corruption in the three countries, it is time to explore the causes of the differences. The specific questions to address are as follows:
1. Why did Korea and Taiwan become much less corrupt than the Philippines during the first few decades of state building?
2. Between Korea and Taiwan, why was the former less successful in reducing corruption than the latter during the same period?
3. Why has the Philippines experienced further deterioration, while Korea and Taiwan have made improvements after the early years of democratic transition (at least since the mid-1990s, or over the entire period during which both CPI and CCI are available)?

I consider the various factors established by existing literature to be the causes of corruption in order to address all possible factors that could have shaped the levels of corruption across the three countries. I have conducted simple correlation tests, applying Mill's method of difference, regarding economic development, educational attainment, government intervention, religion and culture, and ethnic homogeneity in addition to democracy, bureaucratic structure and inequality.

As a preview, the rank order of the three countries in terms of corruption perfectly matches those in terms of economic inequality and meritocracy/patronage in bureaucracy. Inequality, patronage and corruption are highest in the Philippines, much lower in Korea and the

Table 3.6 *Predictive ability of possible causes of corruption*

Independent variables	Ranking of the independent variables	Predicted ranking of corruption	Match or not?
Economic development	KOR = TWN < = PHL (until late 1960s)	KOR = TWN > = PHL	No
Education	KOR = TWN < = PHL (until c. 1970)	KOR = TWN > = PHL	No
Government intervention	KOR = TWN > PHL	KOR = TWN > PHL	No
Ethno-linguistic diversity	PHL = TWN > KOR	PHL = TWN > KOR	No
Protestantism	KOR > TWN = PHL	KOR < = TWN = PHL	No
Confucianism	KOR = TWN > PHL	KOR = TWN > PHL	No
Democracy	KOR = PHL > = TWN	KOR = PHL < = TWN	No
Inequality	PHL > KOR > = TWN	PHL > KOR > = TWN	Yes
Meritocratic bureaucracy	TWN > = KOR > PHL	PHL > KOR > = TWN	Yes

lowest in Taiwan. However, as Table 3.6 shows, none of the rank orders for other potential causes of corruption is correctly correlated with that for corruption. Thus, no other factors besides economic inequality and bureaucratic structure appear to provide a convincing explanation for the three cases in question. There is no simple relationship between democracy and corruption, and the effect of democracy seems to depend on the level of inequality. Let me examine each of the potential causes of corruption in more detail.

First, many empirical studies have found that the level of economic development (per capita income) is negatively associated with corruption to a significant degree. In other words, more developed countries are generally less corrupt (Lambsdorff 2005; Treisman 2007). The direction of causality, however, may run exclusively from corruption to lower development rather than from underdevelopment to corruption (Kaufmann and Kraay 2002). The effect of economic development on corruption may have also been overestimated by OLS in previous empirical studies due to systemic bias in favor of rich countries in the cross-national measures of corruption (Donchev and Ujhelyi 2009; You and Khagram 2005).

Figure 3.3 indicates that the Philippines was initially more developed in terms of per capita GDP than either Korea or Taiwan; it was only surpassed by them in the late 1960s. Considering that Korea and Taiwan became much less corrupt than the Philippines during the first few decades of post-independence, it is more likely that different levels of

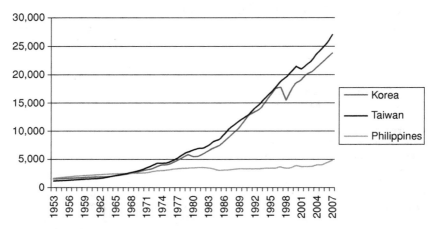

Figure 3.3 Real GDP per capita of Korea, Taiwan and the Philippines, 1953–2007 (in 2005 constant dollars)
Source: Heston *et al.* (2009).

corruption explain the variations in economic growth in these countries rather than the other way around. The large differences in the level of economic development in later periods, in particular after the democratic transition of the three countries in the late 1980s, may explain to a certain extent the continued differences and even further divergence in the level of corruption between the Philippines on the one hand and Korea and Taiwan on the other. This could be consistent with the argument made by Charron and Lapuente (2010) that the effect of democracy on corruption and quality of government should depend on the level of economic development. I will scrutinize this possibility more deeply in the subsequent chapters. It is important, however, that the level of economic development was not a robust predictor of corruption during the crucial period in which the basic rank order of corruption among the three countries was established.

Apart from the effect of economic development, it has been suggested by some scholars that educational attainment affects the degree of corruption (Botero, Ponce and Shleifer 2012; Svensson 2005; Uslaner and Rothstein 2012). At the time of independence, however, the Philippines was ahead of South Korea and Taiwan in terms of educational attainment. As Table 3.7 shows, the Philippines had higher enrollment rates in primary, secondary and tertiary education than South Korea and Taiwan in 1950. The average educational attainment (measured as average years of schooling for the population aged 25 and over) for Filipinos

Table 3.7 *Educational attainment in the three countries, 1950–2000*

	Year	Korea	Taiwan	Philippines
Primary enrollment (%)	1950	83	79	91
	1960	96	102	91
Secondary enrollment (%)	1950	16	11	27
	1960	29	29	29
Tertiary enrollment (per 10,000 population)	1950	18	9	88
	1960	41	33	108
Average years of schooling (for aged 25 or over)	1960	3.23	3.32	3.77
	1970	4.76	4.39	4.81
	1980	6.81	6.37	6.06
	1990	9.25	7.44	7.07
	2000	10.46	8.53	7.62

Sources: McGinn *et al.* (1980: 150–1); Barro and Lee (2001).

was higher than those for Koreans and Taiwanese until 1970. Thus, educational levels cannot explain the early trends of corruption across the three countries. Although the average schooling years for Filipinos fell behind Korea and Taiwan later on, the difference between Taiwan and the Philippines is still not large, and Korea is substantially ahead of both countries, according to data from Barro and Lee (2001). Expansion of education may have played some role in reducing corruption in Korea and Taiwan, but its direct impact does not seem to have been strong.

The degree of government intervention in the economy, which is often measured as the size of government or the proportion of government expenditure over GDP, is often regarded as a cause of corruption, because government intervention or red tape can create rents and encourage rent-seeking activities. Governments in Korea and Taiwan intervened in the economy very heavily, while the role of the Philippine state was not so large. The share of government in real GDP was lower in the Philippines, with an average of 12.7 percent between 1953 and 1970, than in the other two countries, with an average of 20.9 percent in Korea and 25.2 percent in Taiwan during the same period, according to data from Heston *et al.* (2009).[3] However, the level of corruption was not lower, but higher, in the Philippines.

Ethno-linguistic fractionalization has been found to be positively correlated with corruption, although its significance often disappears after

[3] One can certainly object to using the size of government as a measure of government intervention, but scholars generally agree that governments in Korea and Taiwan heavily intervened in the economy, while the role of the Philippine state was not large (Wurfel 1988: 56).

per capita income and latitude controls are added (Mauro 1995; La Porta *et al.* 1999). Ethno-linguistic diversity may partly explain high levels of corruption in the Philippines, considering that Chinese-Filipino businessmen tended to bribe government officials and provide politicians with illicit campaign contributions to avoid discriminatory treatment in doing business (Wurfel 1988: 57–8). However, it is common knowledge that corruption was not confined to Chinese-Filipinos, but was ubiquitous across ethnic lines. Korea has an extremely high level of homogeneity both ethnically and linguistically, but corruption used to be somewhat higher in Korea than in ethnically and linguistically heterogeneous Taiwan. Thus, the ethno-linguistic story does not seem to fit very well for the three countries overall.

Many cross-country empirical studies have found a significant link between Protestantism and less corruption (La Porta *et al.* 1999; Paldam 2001).[4] On the other hand, "Confucian familism" has often been accused of fostering patrimony, nepotism, social distrust and bribes or gift exchanges (Fukuyama 1995; Kim 1999). However, the role of religion and culture, and particularly Protestantism and Confucianism, does not explain the relative levels of corruption across these three countries. Korea has had a larger Protestant population than Taiwan, but Korea used to be slightly more corrupt than Taiwan. The Confucian tradition is very strong in Korea and Taiwan, while it is absent in the Philippines. Korea and Taiwan, however, are much less corrupt than the Philippines. In fact, the meritocratic bureaucracies in Korea and Taiwan actually have historical roots in Confucian tradition (Evans 1995; Woo-Cumings 1995).

Now, let us turn to our primary explanatory variables: democracy, bureaucratic structure and inequality. Figure 3.4 shows the trends of Polity IV scores for the three countries, a measure of the level of democracy. Both Korea and the Philippines initially had some degree of formal democracy until 1972 (pre-*Yushin* period except for the short period of direct military rule during 1961 to 1963 in Korea, and pre-martial law period in the Philippines), and had a dramatic democratic transition in 1986 (the Philippines) and 1987 (Korea) through "people power" movements. Taiwan had an authoritarian regime for a long time and experienced a gradual democratic transition starting in the late 1980s.

---

[4] One could suspect Catholicism, the main religion in the Philippines, as a factor, but Catholicism does not seem to have a significant effect on corruption. Although Protestantism is significantly associated with lower corruption, Catholicism is not significant according to cross-national studies. In addition, the Catholic Church in the Philippines often played an important role in democratization and anti-corruption movements that forced Marcos and Estrada to step down as president.

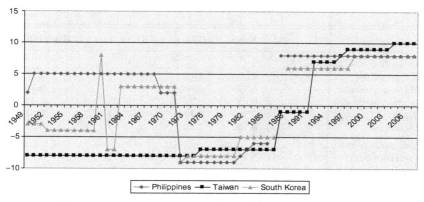

Figure 3.4 Trends of Polity IV scores
Source: Polity IV Project.

Interestingly, among the three countries, Taiwan used to be the least democratic until the early 1990s, but also the least corrupt. This seems to support the argument of Lee Kwan Yew (Zakaria 1994). However, corruption has indeed decreased since the democratic transition, especially since the mid-1990s, in Korea and Taiwan. Also, Ferdinando Marcos's martial law regime (1972 to 1986) and Chun Doo-hwan's authoritarian regime (1980 to 1987) are known as the periods of most egregious corruption in the history of the Philippines and Korea. Thus, there is no simple relationship between democracy and corruption among these countries. As we discussed in the earlier theoretical chapter, the effects of democracy on corruption in these countries might have varied depending on other factors, such as inequality, causing democratic accountability mechanisms to function better in Korea and Taiwan than in the Philippines.

Weberian bureaucracy, in particular meritocratic recruitment, is known to be closely associated with lower corruption as well as higher economic growth (Dahlström *et al.* 2012; Evans and Rauch 1999; Rauch and Evans 2000). According to Evans and Rauch's (1999) "Weberianness" scores data for thirty-five countries in the period of 1970 to 1990, Korea and Taiwan were among the top, with Weberianness scores of 13 and 12 respectively, while the Philippines had a low score of 6.[5] Their assessment, which is based on a survey of country experts, is largely consistent with the developmental state literature on Korea and

[5] See Evans and Rauch (1999) and Rauch and Evans (2000) for details about the data.

Table 3.8 *Bureaucratic structure in Korea, Taiwan and the Philippines*

	Korea	Taiwan	Philippines	Sample mean
Evans & Rauch data (N=35):				
Weberianness	13	12	6	7.2
Merit recruitment	0.72	0.96	0.67	0.58
Internal promotion	0.68	0.72	0.29	0.44
Salary	0.50	0.47	0.28	0.51
Meritocracy	0.70	0.84	0.48	0.51
QoG data (N=105):				
Professional	5.05	4.42	3.71	3.93
Impartial	0.71	0.61	−0.73	−0.11

Note: Meritocracy is the average value of meritocratic recruitment and internal promotion.
Sources: Evans and Rauch (1999); Rauch and Evans (2000); Teorell *et al.* (2011).

Taiwan (Amsden 1989; Campos and Root 1996; Cheng *et al.* 1998; Evans 1995; Haggard 1990a; Johnson 1987; Rodrik 1995; Wade 1990; World Bank 1993). When I created the meritocracy score by averaging "meritocratic recruitment" and "internal promotion and career stability," Taiwan had a score of 0.84, Korea 0.70 and the Philippines 0.48 as Table 3.8 indicates. Thus, meritocracy in bureaucratic recruitment and promotion is inversely correlated with corruption across the three countries. The Quality of Government's new survey data on bureaucratic structure (Teorell *et al.* 2011) also depicts the same picture: in terms of "professional bureaucracy": Korea, Taiwan and the Philippines score 5.05, 4.42 and 3.71 respectively. In terms of "impartial administration," the scores for Korea, Taiwan and the Philippines are 0.71, 0.61 and − 0.73 respectively. Whereas "professional bureaucracy" implies absence of patronage, "impartial administration" implies the absence of bureaucratic corruption.

Finally, inequality appears to have the strongest correlation with the relative levels of corruption among these three countries. Figure 3.5 presents the trends of income inequality (i.e. *Gini* Index) in the three countries. Income inequality in the Philippines has been much higher than that in Korea and Taiwan since at least the mid-1960s. This corresponds with the Philippines's much higher level of corruption. Between Korea and Taiwan, Korea seems to have had a slightly higher level of inequality, especially during the 1970s and 1980s. This corresponds with the earlier finding that Korea's levels of corruption have been slightly higher than those in Taiwan.

Interestingly, income inequality in Taiwan was high in the 1950s, but it dramatically declined between 1953 and 1965. Although Korea's income

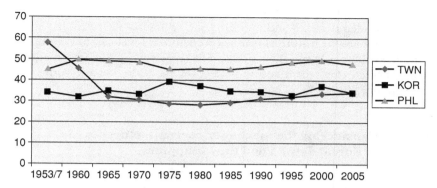

Figure 3.5 Trends of income inequality (*Gini* Index) in the three countries, 1953–2005
Source: UNU-WIDER World Income Inequality Database (version 2.0c).

inequality was lowest among the three countries in 1953, there is evidence that inequality was high at the time of liberation from Japanese rule in 1945 (Ban *et al.* 1980: 290–1). Thus, Korea and Taiwan reduced inequality in the early period of independence, while the Philippines maintained a high level of inequality throughout the post-independence period. We also know that corruption was high in all three countries during the late 1940s, that it declined in Korea and Taiwan, and that it sustained itself and may have even increased in the Philippines. The crucial question is about causal direction: did shifting levels of inequality cause changes in the levels of corruption or did corruption variation change inequality levels?

In summary, the only conventionally recognized causes of corruption that correlate as expected with the level of corruption in the three countries are inequality and bureaucratic structure. The levels of economic development in the three countries are correctly correlated with the degrees of corruption for the later period, but not for the earlier period during which the basic rank order of corruption across these countries was established. Although meritocratic bureaucracy is closely correlated with the levels of corruption, patronage itself is a kind of corruption which needs to be explained. Inequality is a relatively strong predictor of corruption levels across the three countries.

However, correlation does not mean causation. Reverse causality and spurious correlation are always possible. In order to clarify the causal direction and its mechanisms, it is necessary to trace how the three countries came to have different degrees of income inequality and how inequality and corruption affected each other over time. In order to test my three sub-hypotheses about causal pathways from inequality to corruption in democracies and authoritarian regimes with elections, a rigorous comparative historical analysis is required. I will carefully examine whether different levels of economic development – rather than inequality – affected clientelism and the effectiveness of democratic control of corruption.

Considering the inequality-corruption hypothesis in Korea, Taiwan and the Philippines

From the comparison of trends in corruption and its potential causes across the three countries, the most striking finding is the close correlation between trends of corruption and trends of inequality. The Philippines has maintained both a high level of inequality and a high level of corruption since the early period of post-independence until today. In Korea and Taiwan, inequality decreased dramatically and corruption also declined during the early post-independence period. Below are my tentative arguments about the causal relationship and mechanisms between inequality and corruption across these countries.

The success and failure of land reform in reducing inequality

I argue that the primary exogenous cause of the steep reduction of income inequality in Korea and Taiwan is land reform (Rodrik 1995; You 1998; You 2012b). It is well known that land reform was successful in Korea, Taiwan and Japan after World War II, but failed in the Philippines. I argue that success and failure of land reform produced different levels of inequality, which in turn affected corruption.

However, it is also theoretically possible that different levels of corruption determined the fate of land reform, and hence produced different levels of inequality. Although it is unlikely that corruption determined the fate of land reform, given that corruption was high in all three countries upon independence, it would be prudent to carefully examine this possibility. Therefore, in Chapter 4, I will show that success and failure of land reform was largely determined by exogenous factors such as external communist threat and US pressures and that it is therefore likely that inequality had an independent effect on corruption. The crucial question then addresses how different levels of inequality produced by success and failure of land reform have influenced corruption. I now consider the three mechanism hypotheses explaining the link between inequality and corruption in these three countries.

Democracy, elections and clientelism

MH1: High inequality increases clientelism (electoral corruption) and thereby political corruption (corruption during the policy-making process).

For democratic regimes, an important question is whether elections properly function as a mechanism of vertical accountability. While programmatic competition will enhance accountability, clientelistic competition is likely to increase adverse selection of politicians. High inequality and poverty are likely to increase clientelism, and thereby political corruption during the policy-making process. Hence, clientelism (electoral corruption) and political corruption should have been more prevalent and persistent in the highly unequal Philippines than in the relatively equal Korea and Taiwan.

Korea, Taiwan and the Philippines all had democratic transition in the late 1980s and have held competitive elections since then. Korea and the Philippines also held presidential and parliamentary elections until 1972 (except for 1961 to 1963 in Korea), although the elections in Korea were somewhat less free and competitive than those in the Philippines. Even the hard authoritarian regimes of Park (*Yushin* regime 1972 to 1979), Chun (1980 to 1987) and Marcos (1972 to 1986) held some national elections. In Taiwan, local-level elections were routinely held and national-level elections were gradually opened during the authoritarian period. To the extent that elections were held, clientelism might have developed even under authoritarian regimes. Chapter 5 will explore how clientelistic and programmatic politics has developed and been curtailed over time in these countries. In particular, I will try to identify whether it was underdevelopment or economic inequality that has affected the prevalence and persistence of clientelism. I will also address the development of programmatic politics.

Bureaucracy, patronage and corruption

MH2: High inequality increases patronage appointments in bureaucracy and thereby bureaucratic corruption (corruption during the policy implementation process).

Inequality will likely increase patronage in bureaucratic recruitment and promotion through clientelism and penetration by the powerful private sector. Hence, it is expected that the Philippines would suffer from more prevalent practices of patronage in bureaucratic recruitment and promotion than Korea and Taiwan. Also, bureaucratic corruption will be higher in the Philippines. As we have demonstrated in the earlier section, Evans and Rauch's (1999) data on bureaucratic structure for the period of 1970 to 1990 shows that meritocracy was better developed in Taiwan and Korea than in the Philippines. It is notable, however, that the Philippines inherited a better bureaucracy from the colonial period than Korean and Taiwan did. The Philippines established meritocratic principles early during the US colonial period, and the Filipino bureaucrats were highly educated, compared with their counterparts in Korea and Taiwan. Chapter 6 will explore how meritocracy developed in Korea and Taiwan and how patronage has increased in the Philippines, with a focus on how inequality has affected clientelistic provision of jobs in the bureaucracy. I will also examine whether it was just poverty and underdevelopment or economic inequality that has influenced the degree of patronage and meritocracy in these countries.

Industrial policy and government-business relations

MH3: High inequality increases state capture by the powerful private interests and thereby corporate corruption.

Powerful private interests can corrupt and capture politics and the bureaucracy, and high inequality and economic concentration will increase the probability of state capture. Hence, it is expected that the Philippines must have suffered more from state capture by private interests than Korea and Taiwan. Chapter 7 will examine this hypothesis, focusing on industrial policy and government-business relations.

All three countries initially pursued import-substitution industrialization (ISI) strategies, but later switched to export-oriented industrialization (EOI) policy. Industrial policy in the Philippines was heavily influenced by the family conglomerates, and was therefore less coherent and more prone to rent-seeking than those industrial policies in Korea and Taiwan. ISI policy encouraged rent-seeking and corruption, but the problem should have been especially great in the Philippines. EOI policy might have also been more coherent and less prone to rent-seeking in Korea and Taiwan than in the Philippines. It is well known that economic concentration by family conglomerates is high in Korea as well as in the Philippines. Economic concentration was low after the land reform in Korea, but President Park Chung-hee's *chaebol*-favored industrial policy led to increasing *chaebol* concentration over time. I argue that Park's policy of favoring the *chaebol* was not a result of capture, but that increasing *chaebol* concentration intensified the problem of capture over time. This may partly explain why corruption used to be higher in Korea than in Taiwan.

Rigor and effectiveness of anti-corruption reforms

An important policy implication of this book is that anti-corruption reforms are not always effective, especially under high levels of inequality. Anti-corruption reforms are more likely effective when a country has a well-organized and active civil society. The capacity of the civil society will be likely higher at lower levels of inequality. At higher levels of inequality, there will be more resistance to reform from powerful private interests, clientelistic politicians and bureaucrats. Hence, it is expected that anti-corruption reforms would be the least effective in the Philippines and the most effective in Taiwan. In Korea, anti-corruption reforms should have been ineffective as *chaebol* concentration increased until there was a breakthrough after the East Asian financial crisis of 1997 to 1998 when the political influence of *chaebol* weakened. Throughout Chapters 5 to 7, I examine where and when political, bureaucratic and economic reforms were more or less effective and how inequality (economic concentration and poverty) impacted the effectiveness of reform.

In summary, the subsequent narrative chapters will explore the following tentative arguments:

1. Successful land reform in Korea and Taiwan produced relatively equal distribution of wealth and income, while the failure of land reform in the Philippines maintained a high level of inequality (Chapter 4).
2. Political clientelism and political corruption developed to a greater extent in the highly unequal Philippines than in Korea and Taiwan (Chapter 5).
3. In Korea and Taiwan, meritocracy developed in bureaucratic recruitment and promotion, but in the Philippines patronage increased over time because of clientelistic provision of jobs in the bureaucracy (Chapter 6).
4. Industrial policy in the Philippines was influenced heavily by the family conglomerates from the early stage of ISI, and hence it was more incoherent and prone to rent-seeking than in Korea and Taiwan. Korea's industrialization strategy favored conglomerates, and economic concentration increased over time. As a result, Korea's industrial policy became increasingly more subject to capture by the *chaebol* (Chapter 7).
5. Anti-corruption reforms were the least effective in the Philippines. In Korea, anti-corruption reforms became ineffective as *chaebol* concentration increased until the East Asian financial crisis of 1997 (Chapters 5 to 7).

4 The genesis of inequality, land reforms and path dependence

It is well known that Korea and Taiwan have maintained much lower levels of inequality than the Philippines since at least the 1960s. But inequality was very high in both Korea and Taiwan at the time of liberation from Japanese rule. Thus, all three countries initially had very high levels of inequality in wealth and income, but subsequently Korea and Taiwan dramatically reduced inequality while the Philippines failed to do so. The different trajectories of inequality for these countries were critically determined by the contrasting experiences of land reform. The success or failure of land reform not only produced starkly different levels of inequality, but also had a long-lasting impact on the political economy of these countries.

In Korea, Taiwan and the Philippines, the landlord class was the foundation of traditional society, with considerable wealth, power and prestige. The landed elite dominated the countryside because their land ownership ensured dominance in major spheres of social life. Land ownership was highly skewed in all three countries at the time of independence. They then experienced vastly different rates of success of land reform after independence. The post-liberation land reform in Korea and Taiwan was the "crucial structural transformation that destroyed their [the landed elite's] power base and made later development possible" (Lie 1998: 5). The Philippines, however, failed to make any significant structural reform.

When Korea was liberated from Japanese colonial rule in 1945, it was primarily an agricultural economy with few landlords and a vast number of peasants. In the southern part of pre-reform Korea, the richest 2.7 percent of rural households owned two-thirds of all the cultivated lands, while 58 percent owned no land at all. By 1956, however, the top 6 percent owned only 18 percent of the cultivated lands. Tenancy dropped from 49 to 7 percent of all farming households, and the area of cultivated land under tenancy fell from 65 to 18 percent in South Korea (Ban *et al.* 1980; Lie 1998). Tenancy also dropped in Taiwan from 38 percent in 1950 to 15 percent in 1960, with the proportion of land under tenancy falling from 44 to 14 percent (Fei, Ranis and Kuo 1979: 42–3). While the landed class was effectively dissolved in Korea and Taiwan, the highly skewed land ownership pattern changed little in the post-independence Philippines. Tenancy increased from 37 percent in 1943 to 50 percent in 1961, and only 1.5 percent of rural families still owned 50 percent of total agricultural land as late as 1981 in the Philippines (Putzel 1992: 28–29; Simbulan 2005 [1965]: 58).

South Korean and Taiwanese land reforms are considered to be the most comprehensive and egalitarian reforms among those that took place in the twentieth century, while the Philippines is commonly cited as a case of failed land reform (Powelson and Stock 1990; Putzel 1992; Tai 1974). Many studies credit land reform with contributing to the rapid industrialization and "growth with equity" in Korea and Taiwan (Lie 1998; Rodrik 1995; World Bank 1993; You 1998; You 2012b). Failed land reform is considered an important cause of the poor economic performance of the Philippines (Bello et al. 2004; Montinola 2012). More importantly, however, the success or failure of land reform had a profound effect on the broader political economy of these countries. The success and failure of land reform not only resulted in differences in economic inequality and growth, but also political inequality and corruption. Hence, I start the explanation for the different levels of corruption in these countries with the stories of successful and failed land reform.

Land reform in South Korea was carried out first by the US Military Government (USMG), including the reduction of rent to one-third of crops in October 1945 and the sale of formerly Japanese-held lands to former tenants in the spring of 1948. After two separate governments were formally established in the Korean peninsula in 1948, the South Korean government began to implement agrarian land reform in 1950, just before the Korean War (1950 to 1953) broke out. In addition, many farmlands were sold directly by landlords to their tenants. Thus, 89 percent of the total land that had been cultivated by tenants was transferred to them by 1952, and the principle of land-to-the-tiller was realized (Hong 2001).

In Taiwan, land reform was also extensively carried out in three stages. First, in 1949, farm rents were reduced to 37.5 percent from the previous levels of 50 percent or above. Second, arable public lands were sold to tenant farmers starting in 1951. Third, in 1953, the land-to-the-tiller program, or the compulsory sale of land by landlords, was launched. Absentee ownership was abolished, and a low ceiling was imposed on land that could be retained by landlords. As a result, 25 percent of total cultivated area was redistributed to 48 percent of the total farm households, and the distribution of land holdings dramatically changed in Taiwan (Fei et al. 1979: 41; Lamba and Tomar 1986).

In the Philippines, however, land reform has been continuously stymied. Almost all Filipino presidential candidates since the 1950s have run on platforms offering promises of land reform, but reform has seldom been pursued with vigor (Kang 2002). The initial discussion of land reform under the Quirino government (1948 to 1953) collapsed, and President Magsaysay's (1953 to 1957) moderate proposal of land reform legislation was watered down by the landlord-dominated Congress. Congress also weakened the Macapagal administration's (1962 to 1965) land reform legislation, and the president did not put genuine effort into implementing the law (Putzel 1992: 113–7). Marcos's land reform during the martial law period (1972 to 1986) sounded ambitious at first, but implementation was slow and minimal. By 1985, only 4 percent of the country's cultivated lands were acquired by the cumulative achievements of Philippine land reform, and the number of beneficiary families was just 6 to 8 percent of those landless nationwide (Riedinger 1995: 97).

In this chapter, I will first describe the political process, content and implementation of land reform in each of the three countries. I will then discuss the causes and consequences of success and failure of reform. When I discuss the causes, I pay particular attention to potential reverse causation, or the possibility that different levels of corruption determined the success or failure of land reform a priori. As I will show, the fate of land reform in these countries was largely determined by exogenous factors such as communist threats from North Korea and mainland China. Subsequently, the success and failure of land reform had a wide-ranging impact on socio-economic structure and politics, including, but not limited to, corruption.

Successful land reform in Korea

When Korea was liberated from Japanese rule on August 15, 1945, one of the most pressing concerns for the Korean people was the extremely unequal land distribution. The Korean People's Republic was established on September 6 on the basis of People's Committees. It declared robust agrarian policies, including the rent ceiling of 30 percent for the year of 1945 and a call for redistribution of land. Although the Korean People's Republic established power in almost every county of the country, it was later denied any legitimacy by the US Military Government. The National League of Peasant Unions (NLPU) was established on December 8, 1945, with attendance of 670 representatives from 190 county peasant associations. They adopted a twenty-eight-point action program at the convention, and the first two points were as follows: "Confiscate the lands of Japanese imperialists and the national traitors and distribute them to the poor peasants," and "Reduce the rent on the lands of the Korean landlords who were not pro-Japanese collaborators nor national traitors to 30 percent of the harvest and in principle paid in cash." The NLPU claimed a membership of more than 3 million, including 2 million in the southern part of Korea (Lee 1990: 111–2). Although these numbers were apparently exaggerated, the peasant movement was strong and the landlords, who were tainted by their collaboration with the colonial rule, were on the defensive.

The initial land policies of the US Military Government (1945 to 1948), however, maintained the status quo. On September 22, the USMG declared that there would be no change of land ownership in the occupied area. Although opposed to a complete redistribution of land, American occupants were aware of the obvious peasant aspirations to reform the existing land tenure system. On October 5, 1945, the USMG issued an important Ordinance 9 that limited rents to a maximum of one-third of crop production and prohibited unilateral cancellation of tenancy contracts. Notably, the rent revolt already existed when the ordinance was declared. Tenants in the northern part of Korea and in areas where People's Committees were strong followed the KPR guideline of 30 percent of harvest. In a sense, the rent reduction ordinance was recognition of a fait accompli, obviously influenced by developments in the north (Lee 1990: 115–17). Finally, on March 5, 1946, in the Soviet-occupied north, the Provisional People's Committee announced a land reform based on uncompensated confiscation and free distribution. The reform was quickly implemented and completed by March 30. According to a North Korean source, 1,000,325 *chongbo* (one *chongbo* = 0.992 hectare) were confiscated and 981,390 *chongbo* were distributed to 724,522 households.

To the USMG, which was competing for legitimacy with the Soviets, the impact of North Korean land reform was enormous (Lee 1990: 117). On March 9, economic advisors to General Hodge, the Military Governor, announced the USMG's intention of ultimately transforming the tenant farmers into self-cultivators. On March 15, General Lerch, Chief of Civil Administration, disclosed a sale plan for the former Japanese-owned lands, which were then held by the New Korea Company (Lee 1990: 118). When the US army occupied South Korea in 1945, an immediate measure was to vest all Japanese-owned lands (280,000 hectares, 13.5 percent of the total arable area) in the Military Government under the New Korea Company (King 1977: 221). However, the planned sale of former Japanese-owned lands was thwarted on June 25, 1946, on the grounds that 80 percent of tenants wanted the planned sale postponed until the Korean government was established (Lee 1990: 118). In the end, the USMG implemented the distribution of formerly Japanese-held land in the spring of 1948, just before the South Korean government was established. The land was sold to the tenant-cultivators, who would pay three times the annual harvest in installments over fifteen years. By August 15, 1948, when South Korean government was established, 85 percent of the land designated for distribution had been distributed, according to Clyde Mitchell (1949).

Although there was confusion in the USMG's position on land reform, there is evidence that the United States switched from its initial conservative stance to supporting liberal land reform in 1946, while simultaneously stepping up repression of the left. In September 1946, the State Department announced that one of the USMG's major objectives was to implement land reform that would replace widespread tenancy with full ownership of the land by the individual farmer (Putzel 1992: 80). Discussion of redistribution of Korean landlord-held lands, however, was stalled under the USMG. The left-wing parties called for "uncompensated expropriation and free redistribution," the right-wing parties called for "government purchase of land from landlords and sale to tenants" and the moderates called for "conditional compensation to the owners and free distribution to the cultivators."

When the land reform bill was finally presented before the right-wing-dominated Interim National Assembly in December 1947, the Assemblymen sat on the bill and "killed" it largely on the grounds that the land dispute should be addressed by the Korean government (Lee 1990: 119–20, 122–3). However, the USMG had already begun to implement the redistribution of formerly Japanese-held land just before the May 1948 elections, and this action had raised tenant expectations. The US land redistribution is widely credited with having foiled a communist-led election boycott among the rural majority (Putzel 1992: 80).

Despite these de facto challenges, Article 86 in the Constitution of the Republic of Korea (promulgated on July 17, 1948) stipulated land redistribution. It read: "Farmland shall be distributed to farmers. The method of distribution, the extent of possession, and the nature of restricting ownership shall be determined by law." The Constitution showed the political will of the legislature for land reform. When the initial draft was presented to the plenary of the Assembly, it contained the words "in principle" in the clause on land reform so that it read: "Farmland shall *in principle* be distributed to farmers." However, the Assembly voted to remove the words "in principle" in spite of opposition from the Korean Democratic Party-affiliated law-makers, who largely represented landlords' interests (Seo 2007).

Shortly thereafter, the bill obtained a necessary ally. Syngman Rhee, who was elected President by the National Assembly, surprisingly appointed Cho Bong-am, an ex-communist, as Minister of Agriculture. Although Rhee had formed a conservative coalition with the KDP until the May elections, he began to distance himself from the KDP and demonstrated his political will for land reform by giving Cho the responsibility to draft a land reform bill. Although Cho's draft bill (2-*chongbo* retention limit, 150 percent of the standard output in compensation to landlords, 120 percent payment from beneficiaries) was somewhat weakened during the cabinet deliberation (3-*chongbo* retention limit, 200 percent of compensation, 200 percent payment), Cho played an important role in setting the tone for debate in the National Assembly. Although the KDP-dominated Industrial Committee of the Assembly proposed to increase both compensation and payment to 300 percent of annual produce, the "Farmland Reform Bill" that passed the Assembly in April 1949 stipulated 150 percent of compensation and 125 percent of payment. This was close to Cho's original proposal, with a 3-*chongbo* retention limit for landowners.

Although the bill became law in June 1949, President Syngman Rhee effectively vetoed the legislation and requested the Assembly to amend the law to balance the budget for compensation and payment. The National Assembly passed the amendment in February 1950, which stipulated 150 percent of average annual produce for both compensation and payment over five years. President Rhee signed it into law on March 10. The law provided for a redistribution of the excess farmland over 3 *chongbo* per household and all lands owned by absentee landlords. The landlord was issued a "land bond" with a designated amount of compensation, which the government was to reimburse at the official grain prices set each year over five years. The priority of distribution was as follows: (1) farmers currently cultivating the land in question; (2) farmers cultivating very small areas in relation to their households' capabilities; (3) bereaved families; (4) agricultural laborers; (5) farmers returning from abroad (King 1977: 222). In order to assist the implementation of reform, "farmland committees" were installed at each tier of public administration (from village to the center). These committees had equal numbers of landlords and tenants with the administrative chief as chairman ex officio.

The implementation of the reform at that point was expedient. The land redistribution was effectively completed before May 30, 1950, when the second National Assembly elections were held. President Rhee urged the administrators to quickly implement the redistribution of lands so that the tenants might know they would be farming their own lands immediately. One of his hidden motives might have been to weaken his main opposition, the landlord-dominated KDP, in the May 30 elections (Kim 1995). President Rhee's most dominant motivation for land reform was, however, to prevent communism by removing an effective propaganda mechanism of communist North Korea: its land reform. The United States also advised the Rhee government to quickly implement the reform to help cope with the North Korean threat.

Surprisingly, there was little deviation from the letter of the law during the implementation process, given the history of land reform in other countries. The land reform legislation itself allowed for certain exceptions to redistribution, such as reclaimed land and clan land, or land owned by educational institutions. According to the 1965 Farmland Survey, these legal exemptions constituted half the total rented area. The other half was privately owned and rented and hence illegally held under conditions of tenancy. Together, both types of land amounted to only 16 percent of the cultivated area in 1965 (Ban et al. 1980: 285–7).

An interesting pattern in Korean land reform involves the voluntary sale of private farmland to tenants. In December 1945, the total area of rented land was 1,447,000 chongbo, which represented 65 percent of the total cultivated land. 273,000 chongbo of "vested" land and 302,000 chongbo of private land were redistributed by the USMG and the Korean government respectively. Thus, the total area of redistributed land amounted to 575,000 chongbo, which represented only 40 percent of the total area of rented land as of December 1945. However, the area of rented land as of December 1951 was only 159,000 chongbo, or 11 percent of the total area of rented land as of December 1945. This huge gap between the official redistribution of farmland and the actual change in the farmland area under tenancy is explained by the vast amount of land sold out by landlords to tenants during the period. 713,000 chongbo of private farmland was transferred to tenants through voluntary sale, and this informal land reform represented a greater area than the formal land reform. Studies show that many landlords often sold their lands to their tenants at a below-market price when prospects of land reform became clear (Hong 2001).

Whatever the mechanism, land reform succeeded in turning most of Korea's cultivated land over to the households cultivating it. The proportion of families that owned all the land they farmed rose dramatically from 13.8 percent in 1945 to 71.6 percent in 1964. The proportion of tenants fell from 48.9 percent in 1949 to 5.2 percent in 1964 (Table 4.1). The area of rented land fell simultaneously from 65 percent in 1945 to 8 percent in 1951. Thus, South Korea fundamentally transformed rural

Table 4.1 *Owner-tenant distribution of farm households in South Korea, 1945–1965*

	1945	1947	1964	1965
Full owner	13.8	16.5	71.6	69.5
Owner-tenant	16.4	38.3	14.8	15.5
Tenant-owner	18.2		8.4	8.0
Tenant	48.9	42.1	5.2	7.0
Farm laborer and burnt-field farmers	2.7	3.1	–	–
Total	100.0	100.0	100.0	100.0

Source: Ban *et al.* (1980: 286).

class structure by implementing one of the most radical land reforms in the non-communist world.

Successful land reform in Taiwan

The Koumintang (KMT) government of Taiwan instituted the agrarian reform program in three phases: reduction of rent (1949), sale of public land (1951) and land-to-the-tiller program (1953). The rent-reduction program was implemented in April 1949, well before the Republic of China officially moved its capital to Taipei in December 1949. The provincial government released the "Regulations Governing the Lease of Private Farm Lands in Taiwan Province," which limited rent to a ceiling of 37.5 percent of the crop yield; this was a decrease from about 50 to 60 percent. Provided rent was paid, tenancy was made secure for six years (Tai 1974: 119).

General Chen Cheng was the primary advocate of the Taiwanese land reform policy. By late 1948, it was apparent that the ROC regime would have to evacuate to Taiwan and reinstitute the island as its new base. Chiang Kai-shek sent General Chen Cheng, his trusted ally, to Taiwan as governor-general in December 1948 (Roy 2003: 78). Upon becoming Governor of Taiwan, Chen was determined to implement the rent-reduction program quickly. The origin of this program can be traced back to the Chinese Land Law of 1930, which established the standard amount of rent to be 37.5 percent of the main crop's annual yield. The law was not well implemented in most provinces, but in the late 1930s, General Chen Cheng, then Governor of Hupeh Province, implemented the rent-reduction measure in this province. Having lost the peasantry to the communists on the mainland, the KMT leadership concerned itself primarily with avoiding the mistake of alienating the peasantry on the island once again. The KMT viewed rent reduction as a central move to ward off communist efforts to penetrate the rural areas (Tai 1974: 85, 119).

American advisors played a significant role in shaping Taiwan's land reform. In May 1948, US Ambassador to China J. L. Stuart presented a memorandum to President Chiang Kai-shek. The memorandum read: "If there is any single area where reform in deeds and not words is most necessary and most sought by the people, it is land reform" (Smith 1970: 17). The Joint Commission on Rural Reconstruction (JCRR), composed of two Americans and three Chinese, was established by the United States and Chiang Kai-shek's KMT in October 1948 in Nanking as a belated effort to introduce rural reform in China. In 1949, the JCRR requested Wolf Ladejinsky, who had played a critical role in the post-war Japanese land reform, to help with agrarian reform in Taiwan. Ladejinsky worked closely with KMT officials in Taiwan to implement a program of liberal agrarian reform (Putzel 1992: 72–3).

Upon Ladejinsky's recommendation, Farm Tenancy Committees were set up in all the counties, municipalities, townships and villages in 1951. Each committee consisted of five representatives for tenants, two for the local government, two for the landlords and two for owner-cultivators. The committees were originally assigned to deal with the tenancy disputes then arising during the enforcement of the rent-reduction program, but they were later assigned the job of assisting in the execution of the land-to-the-tiller program as well. Ladejinsky saw tenant participation as crucial not only to the land valuation and redistribution process, but also to developing democracy in the rural areas. From 1952 to 1956, when tenant-landlord conflicts were most intense and frequent, the committees settled a total of 62,645 disputes (Putzel 1992: 73–4; Tai 1974: 400–1).

In addition, the sale of public land, or formerly Japanese-held land, was announced in 1951. 71,663 *chia* (1 *chia* = 0.9699 hectares), which amounted to 8.1 percent of the island's arable land, were sold to existing tenants for 2.5 times the annual yield, payable in kind or in cash over ten years. Since total payments (purchase price plus land tax) were less than the 37.5 percent of yield previously paid in rent, the tenant was better off. The average amount purchased was 0.5 *chia*, which frequently supplemented other land already held. Thus, the average holding of the purchaser was 1.125 *chia* (Powelson and Stock 1990: 255).

Upon persistent recommendation by President Truman, the "land-to-the-tiller" program was conceived in 1951, when the JCRR conducted a detailed ownership classification survey. While the rent-reduction and sale-of-public-land programs were implemented by government regulations, the land-to-the-tiller program took the form of a legislative act before it was implemented. In 1952, the Land Bureau of the Taiwan Provincial Government submitted a draft of the program. When the Provincial Assembly, where landlords had some voice, tried to weaken the program by introducing a number of amendments to allow landlords the ability to retain more land and receive a greater compensation, President Chiang Kai-shek immediately called on the Central Reform Committee of the KMT in July 1952. The Committee concluded the following requirements: (1) the land-to-the-tiller program must be inaugurated in January 1953; and (2) all party members in both executive and legislative branches of the government must comply with the party's determination in this undertaking. The Provincial Assembly, whose concurrence was not required, dropped its amendments. Subsequently, after some minor changes by the Executive Yuan, the bill was referred to the Legislative Yuan in November 1952, which passed it on January 20, 1953; at that time, the bill was primarily preserved in its original status. President Chiang Kai-shek signed (and thus made effective) the Land-to-the-Tiller Act on January 26, 1953 (Powelson and Stock 1990: 255; Tai 1974: 120).

The law required every landlord with more than 3 *chia* to sell the excess to the government, which would resell it to the tenant. Both the compensation to the landlord and the price to the tenant were set at 2.5 times the annual yield. Landlords received 70 percent of their compensation in land bonds. The other 30 percent was given in shares of stock in four government enterprises. The former would be redeemable in twenty semi-annual installments at 4 percent interest. The new owners would also pay twenty semi-annual installments at 4 percent interest. The township government implemented the law, but farm tenancy committees checked that no land or landlords were overlooked. The total amounts of lands and farm households affected by all three programs (rent reduction, public land sale and land-to-the-tiller) are shown in 4.2 (Powelson and Stock 1990: 255).

As a result, the distribution of land holdings dramatically changed in Taiwan. The share of families owning medium-sized plots of land ranging from 0.5 to 3 *chia* increased from 46 percent in 1952 to 76 percent in 1960. The share of families owning less than 0.5 *chia* fell from 47.3 to 20.7 percent, and that of families owning more than 3 *chia* dropped from 7.3 to 3.3 percent during the same period. The proportion of families owning all the land they farmed rose from 36 percent in 1950 to 64 percent in 1960. During that same time, the proportion of tenant farmers fell from 38 percent in 1950 to 15 percent in 1960, and the proportion of land cultivated by tenants fell from 44 percent in 1948 to 14 percent in 1959 (Fei *et al.* 1979: 42–3).

Table 4.2 *Area and households affected by land reform in Taiwan*

	Reduction of farm rents	Sale of public land	Land-to-tiller program	Total redistribution
Area affected ('000 *chia*)	256.9	71.7	143.6	215.2
% of total area cultivated	29.2	8.1	16.4	24.6
Farm households affected (thousand)	302.3	139.7	194.9	334.3
% of total farm households	43.3	20	27.9	47.9

Source: Fei *et al.* (1979: 41).

Failure of land reform in the Philippines

In the Philippines, the politics of land reform were complex. There were repeated initiatives for land reform during the US colonial period (1898 to 1941) as well as after independence in 1946. All of these attempts were ineffective. The major enactments regarding Philippine land reform were the Friar Lands Act of 1903, the Agricultural Tenancy Act of 1954, the Land Reform Act of 1955, the Agricultural Land Reform Code of 1963, the Presidential Decree 27 of 1972 and the Comprehensive Agrarian Reform Law of 1988.

Introduced by the US colonial government in an attempt to diffuse rural unrest, the Friar Lands Act provided for the acquisition of approximately 166,000 hectares held by the Catholic Church. Although the original intention was to distribute the land to the tenants, most land ended up in the hands of wealthy landowners and American firms. Because the government paid a relatively high price for the land and wanted to recoup its costs, the land was sold at a price that poor farmers could not afford. That the tenancy rate increased from 18 percent in 1903 to 35 percent in 1933 reveals the failure of the US policy in the Philippines (Riedinger 1995: 86–7; Montinola 2012).

After the Philippines gained independence in 1946, the United States still exerted considerable political influence. Just as the State Department advised liberal land reform in Korea, Taiwan and Japan, it once did the same in the Philippines. In 1951, the US Mutual Security Agency commissioned Robert Hardie to study the tenancy problem in the Philippines. Growing concern over the rise of an armed and communist-led peasant movement called Huks, or the Hukbong Mapagpalaya ng Bayan (HMB – People's Liberation Army) caused this initiative. Hardie's report, released in December 1952, contained far-reaching, comprehensive land reform proposals, such as redistributing land to 70 percent of the tenants in the country (Putzel 1992: 84–5). The landlords and their representatives in Congress strongly resisted, however, and President Quirino called the Hardie Report a "national insult." Moreover, by 1953, the rise of McCarthyism in the United States had turned the tide against liberal reform advocates like Hardie and Ladejinsky. Future US representatives rejected Hardie's recommendations and advocated more conservative approaches (Putzel 1992: 91, 96–9). Once the US pressure for liberal land reform subsided, the landed oligarchy was easily able to preserve their economic base through their representatives in Congress (Doronila 1992: 102–4).

The push for comprehensive land reform was also mitigated by the collapse of the Huk rebellion. The movement collapsed because of the two-pronged strategy of co-optation of Huk members and massive military operations conducted by Ramon Magsaysay, who was appointed defense secretary in 1950, and then won the presidency in 1953 with promises of agrarian reform. Magsaysay initiated agrarian reform legislation, including the Agricultural Tenancy Act of 1954 and the Land Reform Act of 1955. However, as peasant unrest was at least temporarily defused, the landed elite felt confident in hamstringing Magsaysay's reform efforts. The original tenancy-reform proposal would have transformed share tenants into leasehold ("fixed" rent) tenants, but the 1954 legislation did not require a shift to leasehold tenancy. The law limited rent to 30 percent of the crop, but Congress allocated too few funds for enforcement of the new law. In the end, the program's modest aims went largely unrealized (Montinola 2012; Riedinger 1995: 88).

The Land Reform Act of 1955 was to provide for the expropriation of large estates and their redistribution to landless peasants. As introduced by Magsaysay, the law would have covered all private agricultural lands in excess of 144 hectares. Congress chose to limit the scope of the reform, however, to lands in excess of 300 contiguous hectares in the case of private rice farms, 600 hectares for corporations and 1,024 hectares for private farms devoted to crops other than rice. The high retention limits meant that less than 2 percent of the nation's cultivated land was even potentially subject to redistribution. What is more, land could be expropriated "only when a majority of tenants therein petition for such purchase." Given the superior economic and political power of the landlord, few tenants would have had the courage to initiate this petition. Faced with these various restrictions, the government acquired less than 20,000 hectares – less than 0.4 percent of total cultivated land – during the first six years of the program (Riedinger 1995: 88–91; Putzel 1992: 92).

President Macapagal appeared to serve as an unexpected advocate for land reform in the Philippines. Both President Garcia (1957 to 1961) and President Macapagal (1962 to 1965) were silent about land reform during their first few years in office. However, in 1963, Macapagal, who had opposed Hardie's recommendations a decade earlier, proposed surprising new legislation. The Presidential Land Reform Committee produced a draft legislation, which was bolder than any previous legislation, but timid in comparison to the programs introduced in Taiwan and South Korea. The draft legislation provided redistribution of rice and corn lands of 25 hectares and over, while exempting export crop lands. It also required that sharecropping be replaced with leasehold. The Congress ultimately passed the Agrarian Land Reform Code of 1963, but it subjected the Code to over 200 amendments, thus watering it down. The land retention limit was raised to 75 hectares, and the traditional definition of "just compensation" as payment at the land's market value was restored. Moreover, the Congress allotted less than 1 million pesos for the program, against an estimated cost of 200 million pesos for the first year and 300 million pesos for the next three years. By the end of Macapagal's administration it became clear that the president's legislative initiative was primarily "a ploy to win tenant support for his reelection in 1965." This was obvious because he failed to put genuine effort into implementing the law (Putzel 1992: 113–17).

Marcos's presidential decree failed to affect the trajectory of the Philippines land reform. By the late 1960s, the Communist Party of the Philippines (CPP) was re-established and its military wing, the New People's Army (NPA), was founded on the background of increasing peasant discontent. Shortly after President Marcos declared martial law in September 1972, he proclaimed a presidential decree (PD 27) to implement far-reaching land reform. PD 27 allowed tenants of rice and corn land whose landlords held more than 7 hectares to purchase the parcels they tilled, up to 3 hectares of irrigated land or 5 hectares of non-irrigated land. Valuation was set at 2.5 times the value of average annual production, with the beneficiary repaying the land costs to the government over fifteen years at 6 percent interest. This was an ambitious program, compared with previous ones, but the implementation was not rigorous. Prior to the Aquino administration, fewer than 315,000 hectares of private land had been acquired by the government, or only 4 percent of the country's 7.8 million cultivated hectares. Associated with this land were just over 168,000 beneficiary families, a figure equal to roughly 6 to 8 percent of those landless nationwide in 1985 (Riedinger 1995: 91–3, 97).

The land reform applied to rice and corn lands only, exempting a large portion of farmland area. Even in the areas affected by land reform, landlords converted their lands to exempted crops or subdivided them among relatives under the 7-hectare limit. The Department of Agrarian Reform (DAR) officials were sometimes bribed to declare the land exempt. Moreover, the pricing formula of PD 27, which would have resulted in a land value of approximately 68 percent of the current market price, was widely violated. The formula was suggestive; landlords were not required to accept it, but were allowed to directly negotiate the land price with tenants. For this reason, landlords pressured tenants to agree to overstated valuations, and they frequently delayed valuation agreements. DAR officials often sided with the landlords, and those who sided with the tenants found themselves harassed and subject to landlord-initiated legal actions. By 1977, tenant-beneficiaries were paying on average 44 percent higher than the valuations based on the formula (Powelson and Stock 1990: 375–6; Riedinger 1995: 93–4).

The degree of implementation was strongly influenced by political considerations. The priority of implementation was understandably given to areas of rural unrest, but more importantly, Marcos's political enemies were targeted first. For example, the Aquino family holdings were among the first to be expropriated (Riedinger 1995: 94). Moreover, Marcos was a large landowner and used the land reform to increase his own landholdings as well as those of his extended family. By the early 1980s, he and his immediate family were said to have acquired thousands of hectares (Putzel 1992: 146). PD 27 required share tenancies to be converted to fixed-rent leaseholds, with a rent ceiling of 25 percent of the average harvest. On paper, the program exceeded its goals. However, field surveys suggested that share tenancy continued to be practiced and rent levels often exceeded the ceiling (Powelson and Stock 1990: 376; Riedinger 1995: 96). Moreover, many landlords evicted tenants on rice and corn land in favor of hired laborers as one means of avoiding the application of PD 27. Wurfel suggests that by 1980 those deprived of land might well have outnumbered those who had received land titles under PD 27 (1988: 174). The rapid growth of the NPA in the late 1970s and early 1980s bears witness to the depth of peasant disenchantment with the reform (Riedinger 1995: 100–1).

A land registration program in 1988, which covered 80 percent of farm area, showed the extreme concentration of landownership. Only 5.8 percent of landowners, or 1.5 percent of rural families, with holdings of more than 12 hectares owned 3.8 million hectares of land, or 50 percent of total agricultural land reported. On the other hand, over 65 percent of all landowners owned only 16.4 percent of total farm area in holdings of less than 3 hectares. The *gini* coefficient of landownership inequality was 0.647, denoting a high degree of inequality (Putzel 1992: 28–9).

Causes of the success or failure of land reform

One of the central arguments of this book is that the success or failure of land reform influences income inequality, which in turn has an effect on corruption. However, testing this proposition would be impossible if corruption were responsible for the success or failure of land reform. It is therefore important to digress briefly on the causes of land reform. Why did South Korea and Taiwan implement sweeping land reform in the early period of independence, while the Philippines did not? Were the causes of land reform endogenous to corruption or was the success or failure of land reform largely exogenous to corruption? Let us examine various possible explanations for land reform such as the political system, strength of the peasant movement and rural unrest, landlords' political power, external communist threat and US influence in addition to corruption.

Tai's comparative study of the politics of land reform in eight countries finds that competitive political systems (i.e. Colombia, India and the Philippines) were less efficacious than non-competitive systems (i.e. Iran, Mexico, Pakistan, Egypt and Taiwan) in bringing about reform. The three countries with competitive systems generally carried out reform programs at a slower speed, with narrower scope and more limited results than did the five countries with non-competitive systems. He argues that this was because in a competitive system, the decentralization of authority affords the landed class opportunities to frustrate reform, whereas in a non-competitive system the centralization of power denies that class such an opportunity (Tai 1974: 469).

Tai's (1974) study includes Taiwan and the Philippines during the early democratic period (1946 to 1972), but does not include the South Korean or Filipino experience of land reform during the authoritarian period (1972 to 1986). Neither South Korean land reform during the formerly democratic period (1948 to 1952) nor that of the Philippines during the authoritarian period fit Tai's explanation. South Korea had a competitive political system, but implemented a far-reaching reform. Although the Syngman Rhee regime (1948 to 1960) is often classified as authoritarian, there were competitive elections and the land reform legislation was enacted through prolonged deliberations in the legislature, which was independent from the president. On the other hand, Marcos's land reform during the martial law period was ineffective. Interestingly, both South Korea under a competitive system and Taiwan under a non-competitive system successfully implemented sweeping land reform, while the Philippines failed to do so under both systems. The political system does not clearly explain the success and failure of land reform in these countries.

Strength of the peasant movement and rural unrest may be important factors influencing the success or failure of land reform. Tai (1974) found that rural unrest was a primary reason for the regimes to undertake land reform. In the case of the Philippines, the communist-led Huks rebellion during the 1940s and early 1950s motivated Magsaysay's land reform. Additionally, the NPA-initiated re-emergence of armed struggle from the late 1960s became the background of Marcos's land reform. However, both reform initiatives were ineffective, perhaps because Huks had been crushed by the military before Magsaysay's reform, and the newly emerging NPA did not pose a large enough threat to credibly compel the Marcos regime to introduce extensive reform.

In the case of South Korea, peasant movements were initially strong immediately after independence, but the US Military Government quickly repressed them (Lee 1990). The far-reaching land reform legislation was enacted after the leftist forces and peasant movements were repressed. It is puzzling how the Syngman Rhee government managed to introduce sweeping land reform despite the repression of the peasant movement, when in the Philippines the defeat of the peasant movement meant the dilution of land reform. In the case of Taiwan, a peasant movement calling for land reform was virtually absent. The KMT regime might have feared the possibility of future rural unrest due to communist propaganda of land reform in the mainland, but there was no visible rural unrest when the land reform was introduced in Taiwan (Tai 1974). Thus, peasant movement and rural unrest cannot explain the success and failure of land reform in these countries.

Landlord representation in government policy-making could be another explanatory variable for land reform. Clearly, the strong political power of landlords in the Philippines was a primary reason why land reform legislations were watered down (Putzel 1992). On the other hand, the landlords' weak voice in Taiwan made it possible for the KMT to implement sweeping reform. In this country, landlords had no representation in Executive Yuan and Legislative Yuan. Although they had their representatives in the Provincial Assembly, the Assembly did not have legislative authority – only consultative status. When they raised their voice in the Assembly, it was simply ignored by the regime (Powelson and Stock 1990).

However, it is puzzling that Korea was able to enact comprehensive and egalitarian land reform legislation in spite of substantial representation of landed interests in the National Assembly. Although the Korea Democratic Party, which represented the interests of landlords, had a larger number of seats than any other party or political group in the National Assembly, it did not overtly oppose land reform, and its efforts to increase compensation were largely ineffective. Recall that the KDP-affiliated National Assemblymen argued for landlord compensation to be 300 percent of annual yield, but the final bill that passed the National Assembly stipulated 150 percent of compensation. This is much lower than the 250 percent in Taiwan, where landlord representation was absent. Thus, landlord representation cannot explain the success and failure of land reform in these countries.

Another possible explanation for the success or failure of land reform is corruption. Where political corruption is high, comprehensive land reform is less likely to occur. This argument is of particular interest because of a classic endogeneity problem: corruption might be a determinant of the course of land reform rather than an effect of it. A high level of corruption might have made it difficult for the Philippine legislature to enact land reform legislation, and there is evidence that implementation of land reform was often circumvented by landlords through corruption in the Philippines.

In Taiwan, there was initially rampant corruption under the KMT's rule. The KMT regime in mainland China was also notoriously corrupt before it moved to Taiwan. However, the KMT regime in Taiwan launched both land reform and anti-corruption reform at the same time. The regime was not only successful in carrying out sweeping land reform, but also in transforming a formerly corrupt party into a well-disciplined one. Taiwan demonstrates that it is possible for a corrupt regime to conduct both land reform and anti-corruption reform.

South Korea's Syngman Rhee regime is also known to have suffered from endemic corruption, but it was able to legislate and implement extensive land reform. Detailed case studies (Chiang 1984, 1985; Ham 1991; Park 1987) have not found many instances of cheating in the implementation of land reform, although some landlords used the loopholes to evade the expropriation of their lands. It is puzzling why there was limited corruption during the implementation of land reform in South Korea, while there was rampant corruption in the distribution of other Japanese-held properties and of US aid (Woo 1991). Farmland committees had an equal number of landlords and tenants plus an administrative chief, and they were set up at villages and counties. Perhaps these committees played a role in minimizing cheating and evasion by landlords, but they were absent for the distribution of vested properties and US aid. Peasant expectations were high and they had watchful eyes because of their direct stakes, and the farmland committees gave them an avenue to raise their voice (Chiang 1984, 1985; Ham 1991; Park 1987). In addition, South Korean land reform encountered direct competition with North Korean land reform, which was declared at the early stage of Korean War in

1950. This was when the North Korean army was occupying a large part of South Korea, which further strengthened the position of tenants and minimized landlords' evasive tactics (Chung 2003; Kim 2005).

Thus, corruption might have contributed to the failure of land reform in the Philippines both during the legislative and implementation processes. Non-existent corruption does not, however, explain the introduction of land reform in Taiwan and South Korea. Taiwan represents a case of simultaneous reforms (land reform and anti-corruption reform), and South Korea represents a case of successful land reform in spite of high corruption. The South Korean case also shows that corruption could be minimized during the implementation of land reform while there was rampant corruption in other areas.

So far, I have considered plausible internal factors, but none of them explains the success or failure of land reform in these countries. Now, let us examine external factors. As the previous sections show, external communist threats played a decisive role in pushing for land reform in both South Korea and Taiwan, while the Philippines did not face such external threats.

In South Korea, the landed class had substantial representation in the National Assembly, but their representatives were unable to prevent or greatly weaken the land reform bill. The main reason for their lack of power was the communist threat from North Korea, which placed them in a weak position. Although radical peasant movements were violently suppressed and the Communist Party went underground in South Korea starting in the fall of 1946, the potential for rural unrest continued to exist through influence from North Korea, which carried out radical land reform in the spring of 1946. The establishment of two separate governments in the southern and northern parts of Korea sparked enormous tensions and heightened the possibility of civil war.

The following two episodes illustrate how the North Korean threat influenced South Korean policy-makers: When Dr. Yoo Jin-oh, a constitutional scholar, drafted a Constitution and presented it to Kim Seong-soo, leader of the Korea Democratic Party and a large landowner, Kim was initially reluctant to endorse the land reform clause. It read: "Farmland shall in principle be distributed to farmers." When Yoo persuaded Kim, however, that land reform would be the best way to prevent communism, Kim acquiesced (Seo 2007). President Rhee was not known to be a strong supporter of land reform before he was elected as the first president of South Korea. However, he showed strong political will for land reform by appointing ex-communist Cho Bong-am as Minister of Agriculture. He also urged the bureaucrats to quickly implement land redistribution even before he signed the Farmland Reform Bill to make it law in March 1950 (Kim 1995). When the implementation of land redistribution resumed after several months of interruption due to the Korean War, President Rhee told Yoon Young-sun, then Minister of Agriculture, to complete the land reform as soon as possible "if you want to prevail over communism" (Kim 2009).

In Taiwan, there was no visible rural unrest at the time of land reform, but the KMT regime was concerned about the potential for rural unrest due to communist influence from mainland China. Chen Cheng, the architect of land reform, wrote:

Traditional tenancy system created irreconcilable opposition between the landlord and the tenant. This provided the Communist agitators with an opportunity to infiltrate into the villages. It was one of the main reasons why the Chinese mainland fell into Communist hands. On the eve of rent reduction in Taiwan, the situation on the Chinese mainland was becoming critical and the villages on this island were showing signs of unrest and instability. It was feared that the Communists might take advantage of the rapidly deteriorating condition to fish in troubled waters. But with the implementation of rent reduction, the livelihood of the broad masses of the farming population was immediately improved. The Chinese Communists were effectively deprived of propagandistic weapons by a new social order that had arisen in the rural areas. (Cheng 1961: 47–8)

Thus, in Taiwan, land reform was a preventive measure and a show of resolve not to repeat the same mistake made by the KMT in the mainland. In both South Korea and Taiwan, the prime motivation of top political leaders for launching land reform was to cope with communist threats from North Korea and the Chinese mainland. In the Philippines, however, there was no such powerful external communist threat. The internal communist-led insurgency did not pose as great a threat to the Philippine regime as communist North Korea and China did to the South Korean and Taiwanese regimes, nor did it have ties to a competing power.

Lastly, the United States was exerting considerable political influence on these countries. Interestingly, it played a progressive role in pushing for sweeping land reform in South Korea, Taiwan and Japan, but not in the Philippines. In South Korea, the US Military Government initially took a conservative position regarding land reform. However, it switched its position to pursuing a liberal land reform in 1946 and redistributed formerly Japanese-held land in 1948 before the South Korean government was established. Moreover, the United States continued to advise the newly formed South Korean government to carry out a liberal land reform. In Taiwan, the Joint Commission on Rural Reconstruction (JCRR) and American advisors, such as Wolf Ladejinsky, played a significant role in shaping land reform. Americans encouraged the KMT

Table 4.3 *Possible explanations for success and failure of land reform*

	South Korea	Taiwan	Philippines
Period	1948–52	1949–53	1946–72/1972–86
Political system	Electoral democracy	Dictatorship	Democracy/dictatorship
Peasant movement	Strong, but crashed	Very weak	Strong, crashed, re-emerging
Landlord representation	Substantial	Weak	Strong
Corruption	Corrupt	Curbing corruption	Corrupt
External communist threat	Strong	Strong	Absent
US influence	Liberal	Liberal	Largely conservative

regime to introduce the land-to-the-tiller program and to set up the Farm Tenancy Committees.

In the Philippines, however, the US influence was largely conservative. The US colonial government was not particularly interested in transforming the tenancy system in the Philippines. After the United States granted independence to the Philippines in 1946, land reform was not a priority until 1951. This stands in contrast with South Korea and Taiwan, where the United States advised and pushed for land reform much earlier. After Robert Hardie released a report advocating a liberal land reform in 1952, he was soon recalled by the State Department. With the rise of McCarthyism, advocates of liberal land reform were purged and weakened in the United States, and future US representatives in the Philippines took a more conservative approach, advocating only minor reforms.

Thus, the success and failure of land reform in these countries is directly correlated with the US influence. Why did the United States play different roles in these countries? The answer again lies in the existence and absence of external communist threat to these countries. As the Cold War developed, US foreign policy was centered on preventing the spread of communism, and liberal land reform was considered an effective tool to fight it. Since South Korea and Taiwan faced grave threats from communist North Korea and China, the United States swiftly advocated land reform there. However, it did not demonstrate the same urgency in the Philippines: it did not call for land reform until 1951 when concern grew over the rise of communist-led peasant insurgency. As the Huks rebellion was quelled, US interest in Philippine land reform also disappeared.

Table 4.3 summarizes the above discussion. Examination of various possible explanations reveals that external factors, including a peripheral communist threat and US influence, were decisive in pushing South Korea and Taiwan to introduce comprehensive land reform, although this was not the case in the Philippines. Since the US position inherently depended on the urgency of an external communist threat, this is the ultimate factor that determined the fate of land reform in these countries. Internal factors (i.e. political system, peasant movement and rural unrest, landlord representation and corruption) might have partly influenced the process and content of land reform in these countries, but none of these factors comprehensively explains the success and failure of land reform.

This book demonstrates that exogenous factors – most notably an external communist threat and US pressures – determined the success and failure of land reform in South Korea, Taiwan and the Philippines more strongly than corruption did. Thus, land reform provides a sort of natural experiment that produced different levels of inequality in these countries, which in turn have influenced corruption.

Consequences of the success and failure of land reform

I find that the success of land reform in Korea and Taiwan along with the failure in the Philippines had an important impact on the political economy of these countries. Not surprisingly, land reform had a large equalizing effect on the distribution of land and income. Land reform also contributed to rapid expansion of education, as well as facilitation of industrialization. Land reform had the effect of partly breaking up the political power of the landed oligarchy, which had historically used corruption as a means of retaining power and influence. In the next chapters, I will explore the political consequences of land reform in more detail, but this section will briefly examine several major effects on economic, educational and political inequalities.

Success and failure of land reform made a huge difference in the distribution of land ownership in the three countries. While the rate of tenancy dropped from 49 percent (1945) to 7 percent (1965) in South Korea and from 38 percent (1950) to 15 percent (1960) in Taiwan, it increased from 37 percent (1943) to 50 percent (1961) in the Philippines (Simbulan 2005 [1965]: 58). Landless or near-landless families still accounted for 56 percent of agricultural families as of 1985 in the Philippines (Putzel 1992: 26). In South Korea and Taiwan, the landed class was completely dissolved. In the Philippines, however, landownership continued to be concentrated on a small number of large landlords. A 1955 study showed that 221 families, or 0.01 percent of all families, owned 9 percent of total farm area in the country, and that 0.36 percent of all families owned

Table 4.4 *Trends of land* gini

	Korea	Taiwan	Philippines
1945	0.73	–	–
c. 1950	–	0.58–0.62	0.58
c. 1960	0.38–0.39	0.39–0.46	0.52–0.53
c. 1990	0.37–0.39	–	0.55–0.65

Sources: Ban *et al.* (1980); Taylor and Jodice (1983); Putzel (1992); Frankema (2006).
Note: When there are multiple estimates, both the lower and higher estimates are included.

41.5 percent of total farm area. In 1988, less than 1 percent of all families, or 1.5 percent of rural families, still owned 50 percent of the total farm land (Montinola 2012; Putzel 1992: 28–9; Simbulan 2005 [1965]: 57). Table 4.4 shows the trends of land ownership inequality in these countries. While land *gini*, a measure of inequality in the distribution of land, fell sharply in South Korea and Taiwan, it did not in the Philippines. In South Korea, land *gini* dropped from 0.73 in 1945 to 0.38 to 0.39 around 1960. In Taiwan, land *gini* declined from 0.58 to 0.62 around 1950 to 0.39 to 0.46 around 1960. In the Philippines, however, land *gini* did not change much between 1950 (0.58) and 1988 (0.55 to 0.65). Note that different sources provide varying land *gini* coefficients, but the general trends are clear.

In South Korea and Taiwan, land reform helped to alleviate rural poverty and remarkably reduce overall income inequality. By the mid-1960s, income *gini* had fallen to roughly 0.33 in both South Korea and Taiwan, but it remained high, around 0.5, in the Philippines (see Figure 3.5). In South Korea, the Korean War further intensified the leveling effect of land reform (1950 to 1953). The war destroyed almost all industrial and commercial properties. In addition, inflation diminished the government bonds previously received by landlords as compensation for their dispossessed land into worthless pieces of paper. On the other hand, tenant-turned-owner-cultivators increased their income. According to an analysis by Ban *et al.* (1980: 290–1), the top 4 percent of the rural population (previous landlords) lost 80 percent of their income, while the bottom 80 percent (tenants and owner-tenants) increased their income by 20 to 30 percent; this was all because of land reform. Although income distribution data is unavailable for South Korea's pre-reform period, inequality must have been very high. After the land reform and the Korean War (1950 to 1953), however, South Korea had an unusually equal distribution of income with the *gini* of 0.34 in 1953 (Mason *et al.* 1980; You 1998). In Taiwan, a dramatic improvement in income distribution can be observed between 1953 and 1964. Income *gini* fell from 0.57 in 1953 to 0.33 in 1964 (see Figure 3.5). Ho (1978: 16) estimates that the combined redistributive effect of rent reduction and land-to-the-tiller was equivalent to about 13 percent of Taiwan's GDP of 1952. Lee (1971: 75) estimated that the percentage share of net farm income for tenants increased from 67 percent before the reform to 81 percent afterwards, while that for landlords decreased from 25 to 6 percent. The government share also increased from 8 to 12 percent (Powelson and Stock 1990: 257).

Land reform also facilitated the expansion of education, which in turn contributed to the development of professional bureaucracy, active civil society, industrialization and economic growth. In South Korea and Taiwan, land reform contributed to the rapid expansion of education by making it affordable for more people. In South Korea, primary school enrollment doubled between 1945 and 1955, even though the Korean War (1950 to 1953) led to destruction throughout the country. Secondary school enrollment increased more than eight times, and enrollment in colleges and universities increased ten times during the same period (Kwon 1984). A characteristic of post-war public education in Korea was an unusually large share of the financial burden imposed on private households relative to other countries with comparable enrollment (Mason *et al.* 1980). While the Education Law of 1949 established compulsory primary education, the limited resources and relatively small investment by government imposed significant burdens for families. Korea's 1960 public expenditure on education amounted to only 2 percent of GNP. This was less than the average of 2.2 percent for all developing countries as well as the East Asian average of 2.5 percent (World Bank 1993: 198). Without land reform, many peasants would have been unable to educate their children. Land reform also encouraged many large landowners to contribute their land to educational institutions, as these institutions were exempted from the expropriation of land. This led to the creation of many private universities and secondary schools (Oh 2004). Thus, land reform helped to increase both supply of and demand for education.

As we saw in the previous chapter, the Philippines surpassed South Korea and Taiwan in terms of educational attainment at the time of independence (Table 3.7). The Philippines had higher enrollment rates in primary, secondary and tertiary education than South Korea and Taiwan in 1950. However, enrollment rates in all levels of education increased very rapidly in South Korea and Taiwan, but only slightly in the Philippines. By 1960, South Korea and Taiwan had higher primary enrollment rates than the Philippines and the same secondary enrollment rate as the Philippines. Barro and Lee's (2001) data on the average years of schooling also indicates that, between 1960 and 2000, the average educational attainment increased much faster in South Korea and Taiwan than in the Philippines.

Expansion of education in Korea and Taiwan contributed to rapid industrialization by providing abundant labor with basic literacy and numeracy (Eichengreen 2010). Land reform also helped these countries to move capital resources from agriculture to industry – a transfer that is central to the industrialization process. Thus, land reform laid foundations for the subsequent industrial growth in Korea and Taiwan, while failed land reform impeded industrial growth in the Philippines. Furthermore, the preservation of the landed elite in the Philippines and the dissolution of the landed class in South Korea and Taiwan had a huge impact on the broader political economy.

In South Korea and Taiwan, land reform profoundly transformed the socio-economic and political structures. The dissolution of the landed class and conversion of former landless tenants to owner-cultivators produced unusually egalitarian societies. Land reform contributed to political stability, because farmers who own the land they cultivate tend to have more stakes in the existing political order. When North Korea, during the early months of the Korean War, initiated land reform in its occupied areas in South Korea, few peasants reacted with enthusiasm because most of them had already benefited from South Korean land reform (Kim 2009; Shin 1997). In both countries, the primary objective of preventing the rural population from being attracted to communism was successfully achieved.

Land reform also created an opportunity for state autonomy from the dominant class because there were no powerful economic interests in these countries for a considerable time after land reform. When South Korea and Taiwan launched an export-oriented industrialization drive in the 1960s, the governments' economic policy-making was mostly autonomous from the influence of the private sector. Both countries were able to establish meritocratic and autonomous bureaucracies, which were free from capture and penetration by special interests. Political clientelism and vote-buying practices existed in Korea and Taiwan, but their prevalence was less common than those practices in the Philippines.

In the Philippines, the failure of land reform helped the landed oligarchy to maintain and further expand their economic and political power. The landed elite expanded their economic power by diversifying to commerce, manufacturing and finance, and political and

Table 4.5 *Rankings of the political influence of community leaders in Tainan, Taiwan (1968) and Luzon, the Philippines (1969)*

	Tainan	Luzon
Local government officials	1	1
Party leaders	2	2
Teachers	3	5
Businessmen	4	8
Lawyers	5	4
Physicians	6	6
Landlords	7	3
Clergy	8	7

Source: Tai (1974: 335).

economic elites were closely intertwined (Wurfel 1988: 57). However, the political and economic dominance of the landed oligarchy was accompanied by continuous political instability, which was primarily caused by communist-led peasant insurgency.

The continuous dominance of the landed elite in the Philippines and the declining political and economic influence of landlords in South Korea and Taiwan can be confirmed by available evidence. Surveys of the rural population on the political influence of various types of community leaders in two rural towns in Taiwan and the Philippines in the late 1960s show that landlords were no longer regarded as having much influence in Taiwan, but they were still dominating forces in the Philippines. Table 4.5 shows that in Tainan, Taiwan, landlords ranked seventh out of eight categories, but in Luzon, the Philippines, landlords ranked third after local government officials (first) and party leaders (second). In the Philippines, many local government officials and party leaders were landlords or had landlord family members. In Taiwan, on the other hand, few local government officials and party leaders were landlords. In Taiwan, most landlords withdrew from local politics after land reform, and tenant farmers and owner-cultivators increased participation in local politics (Yang 1970).

Kim Young-mo's (1982) study of intergenerational mobility of the South Korean elites shows an interesting pattern that coincides with land reform. Unlike in the Philippines, a majority of business elites, along with bureaucratic and judicial elites, came from non-elite families in Korea. Table 4.6 presents fathers' jobs for Korean elites in the 1960s. While a majority of ministers (in 1962) and professors (in 1965) were from elite

Table 4.6 *Father's occupation for South Korean elites in the 1960s*

Father Elites (1960s)/	Landlord %	White collar %	Non-elite %	Survey year
Ministers	33.9	26.3	39.8	1962
Entrepreneurs	23	4	73	1966
Higher civil servants	6.1	25.0	68.5	1966
Judges	6.0	38.3	55.7	1970
Professors	29	32	39	1965
National average (1930)	3.0	0.6	96.4	1930

Source: Kim (1982).

(landlord or white collar) families, 73 percent of entrepreneurs (in 1966) as well as 68.5 percent of higher civil servants (in 1966) and 55.7 percent of judges (in 1970) were from non-elite families. While the landed oligarchy diversified into various industries and thus formed family conglomerates in the Philippines, Korean entrepreneurs were largely from humble social origin. As of 1985, about 38 percent of the top fifty *chaebol* owners came from poor farm families or small merchant families, and only one-quarter originated from the landlord or big-business families (Jones and Sakong 1980: 210–57; Koo 2007). Although South Korean *chaebols*, or family-controlled conglomerates, grew over time and their concentration of wealth rose, their political influence did not match that of their counterpart in the Philippines. It is also notable that many non-elite families educated their children to take higher civil service examinations or judicial examinations, which was a primary avenue of upward intergeneration mobility in South Korea.

The success and failure of land reform had an enduring impact on the social structure and political economy of these countries. While land reform confirmed state autonomy and helped to control corruption in Korea and Taiwan, it did not do so in the Philippines. The economic and political domination of the landed oligarchy and extensive rural poverty in the Philippines resulted in widespread and persistent practices of clientelism, such as vote-buying and provision of patronage jobs in the bureaucracy. These practices, as a result, increased political and bureaucratic corruption. Filipino politics were centered on "creating and dividing rents among the ruling elite" (Montinola 2012), and corruption increased over time. I will extrapolate on the detailed stories of how all these factors of corruption manifested in the subsequent chapters.

5   Elections, clientelism and political corruption

In the previous chapter, we saw how success and failure of land reform produced different levels of inequality in Korea, Taiwan and the Philippines. In this chapter, we will explore how inequality has influenced clientelism and political corruption under democratic and authoritarian regimes in these countries. Since all of these countries have alternated between dictatorship and democracy, there is an opportunity for both cross-sectional and time-series analyses. The three countries all went through a democratic transition in the late 1980s and have held competitive elections since then. Although Taiwan was continuously authoritarian until the late 1980s, Korea (except for 1961 to 1963) and the Philippines had formal institutions of democracy before 1972 in addition to the democratic transition in the later period.

The Philippines was initially the most democratic among the three countries, but it underwent an authoritarian martial law regime under Ferdinand Marcos (1972 to 1986). The Philippines during the 1946 to 1972 period was not fully democratic, with restrictions on the left, and could be categorized as "semi-democratic." The later period of the martial law regime (1978 to 1986) could be considered as a "soft authoritarian" regime, as Marcos introduced national legislative elections as a means to demonstrate his legitimacy (Haggard and Kaufman 2008: 117–20). Korea had electoral democracy during the presidencies of Syngman Rhee (1948 to 1960) and Park Chung-hee (1963 to 1972), but their regimes were quite authoritarian. Elections were often quite competitive, but intimidation and electoral fraud were common. The legislature did not function effectively as a check on the executive. Park Chung-hee's military junta rule (1961 to 1963) and so-called *Yushin* period (1972 to 1979) and Chun Doo-hwan's rule (1980 to 1987) were outright dictatorships. Taiwan had a long period of authoritarian one-party rule under Chiang Kai-shek (1949 to 1972) and Chiang Ching-kuo (1972 to 1986), after a short period of military rule (1945 to 1949).

I have proposed that the effect of democracy on corruption depends on inequality, partly because high levels of inequality increase the likelihood of clientelistic competition rather than programmatic competition. As inequality increases in democracies, the elite will fear programmatic competition in general and the development of leftist parties in particular, and hence they will have incentives to buy votes from the poor. On the other hand, the large size of poor population will be prone to clientelistic exchanges of votes for particularistic benefits. Thus, in highly unequal societies, electoral clientelism is more likely to develop and persist, while programmatic competition is difficult to develop. Without programmatic competition between political parties, elections cannot properly function as a mechanism of democratic accountability. Clientelism typically involves petty electoral corruption, such as vote-buying. It also increases large-scale political corruption due to the politicians' need for clientelistic resources, and makes it difficult for voters to punish corrupt politicians.

The purpose of this chapter is to explore the effect of inequality on electoral clientelism and political corruption in the three countries. Of course, electoral clientelism will be a particularly important problem in democracies, but high inequality may increase clientelism in dictatorships, too, especially when elections are introduced. The three cases discussed in this book provide an opportunity to explore clientelism under electoral authoritarianism. National or local elections were often held under various authoritarian regimes in the three countries. In Taiwan, the Koumintang (KMT) held local elections regularly, starting in 1946. National elections were frozen initially, but supplementary national elections were first held in 1969 and electoral opening expanded gradually under Chiang Ching-kuo's rule (1972 to 1986). In Korea, national elections (legislative and/or presidential elections) were often held even during the authoritarian periods. In the Philippines, both national and local elections were held for most of the time. Table 5.1 shows when various elections were held in these countries. Studying the variations in democratic elections and authoritarian elections, as well as the absence of both national- and local-level elections, allows us to explore how inequality affected clientelism.

I will not posit that clientelism develops only under conditions of high inequality. Clientelism is ubiquitous, especially in young democracies (Keefer 2007; Keefer and Vlaicu 2008; Kitschelt and Wilkinson 2007). My argument is that clientelism will be more prevalent and persistent at high levels of inequality and that this circumstance will make it harder to develop programmatic competition. Therefore, electoral clientelism and political corruption should be more widespread and programmatic competition more rare in the highly unequal Philippines than in the relatively equal Korea and Taiwan. The scope of clientelism will also

Table 5.1 *Comparison of electoral regimes*

	Philippines	Korea	Taiwan
Local elections	1946–present	1952–60, resumed in 1991 (councils) and in 1995 (executives)	1946–present
National legislative elections	1946–72, 1978–84 (limited competition), 1986–present	1948–60, 1963–71, 1973–85 (limited competition), 1988–present	Initially frozen, but limited opening, since 1969 (one party), fully opened since 1989
Presidential election	1946–69, 1986–present	1948 (indirect), 1952–60 (1960–61 parliamentary system), 1963–71, 1987–present	Since 1996

depend on whether elections are held at the local level, national level, or both.

The following three sections explore how inequality has affected electoral clientelism in authoritarian and democratic settings in the three countries. The historical case studies show that clientelism has been ubiquitous in all three countries, but there have been differences over time within countries as well as across the three countries. I then examine alternative explanations for the causes of clientelism and confirm that the role of inequality was critical in producing differences in the extent and persistence of clientelism across these countries. The final section explores how clientelism has affected political corruption and effectiveness of anti-corruption reforms in these countries.

The Philippines: persistent clientelism

The Philippines gained full independence from the United States in July 1946. Since the Japanese occupation had been brief and the United States voluntarily granted independence to the Philippines, American institutional legacy and influence was decisive. Thus, the Philippines inherited the political institutions of electoral democracy that had developed under the American colonial rule. Both during the early democratic period (1946 to 1972) and the post-Marcos democratic period (1986 to present), however, clientelistic competition such as vote-buying was prevalent, and programmatic competition had not developed. Oligarchic families dominated the politics as well as the economy, and political parties were nothing more than shifting coalitions of powerful families. The existence of powerful political-economic elite families and a large proportion of the poor population has facilitated clientelism and deterred the development of programmatic political parties.

Development of clientelism during the early democratic era (1946 to 1972)

The Philippines was regarded as a successful case of democracy in the third world during its early democratic era, unlike Korea and Taiwan. The presidential and legislative elections were both competitive, and two major parties, the Nacionalista Party and the Liberal Party, alternated in power regularly. The two rival parties were, however, virtually identical in terms of policies and social composition. Carl Lande's (1965) classic study of the Philippine political structure showed that both parties were loose coalitions of local and provincial factions, which were organized around a prominent family. The landed elite dominated local and provincial politics. Moreover, the nature of the patron-client relationship between landowners and tenants, which long antedated the introduction of national and local elections, translated directly into the political system. Typically, village leaders were prosperous peasants, municipal mayors were small landowners or professionals, provincial governors were members of the great landowning gentry and senators were the richest members of society. Clientelist networks extending from village leaders to local politicians to national politicians developed as local and national elections were held regularly.

Elite families, rather than political parties, were the real sources of power in Philippine politics, and these families developed into the parties that would ultimately shape democracy in the Philippines. In fact, political clans started to develop during the US colonial period, when members of the first Philippine Assembly were elected in 1907. Party alignments in the Philippines can be seen simply as an extension of the traditional rivalries of provincial and town factions (Lande 1965). After the war, a dissident branch of the Nacionalista Party broke away to form the Liberal Party, headed by Manuel Roxas. The Liberals successfully contested the presidency against Nacionalista Osmena in the new republic's first elections in 1946. The two parties vigorously competed for control, with power transfers occurring about every eight years until Marcos's declaration of martial law in 1972. However, both parties shared a common interest in suppressing leftist parties that tried to offer an alternative to the Liberals and Nacionalistas. The first of these was the Democratic Alliance formed by the Huk guerrillas, the Philippine Communist Party, and peasant, labor and professional groups. The Democratic Alliance won six congressional seats in 1946, but they were unseated by the two major parties on trumped-up election fraud charges. Facing military repression, the party disbanded in 1947 (Thompson 1995: 18). The Liberal and Nacionalista parties were so indistinguishable that politicians frequently switched sides. In 1953, Magsaysay changed his party affiliation from the Liberal Party to the Nacionalista Party and ran successfully for presidency. In 1965, Marcos also switched from the Liberal Party to the Nacionalista Party and was elected as president. Mass defections of legislators were more common. The defectors were switching to the incoming president's party to increase their share in the spoils (Montinola 2012).

All national politicians won their elections dependent upon the help of petty politicians at the grassroots level, who demanded material rewards for their help. National politicians also depended upon the outright purchase of votes from the electorate at large. As James Scott (1972: 96–7) writes, the Philippines was a "model of electoral corruption." Vote-buying practices became widespread and campaign costs rose rapidly. The major portion of a candidate's funds went to the village leaders, who kept a portion and used the rest to bribe voters. Although it was unlawful for a candidate to provide transportation, food or drinks during a public meeting, an invitation to a feast was a common practice to solicit support in the Philippines. In addition, vote-buying in cash was widespread, and it involved about a quarter of the electorate. The price of a vote varied depending on the affluence of the candidate and the closeness of the race, but it rose continuously, often reaching as much as the daily wage (Wurfel 1988: 99).

As a result of this system, by the early 1960s, Filipino elections were among the world's most costly. According to Heidenheimer's index of campaign expenditure, which is defined as per vote expenditure divided by average hourly wage of male industrial worker, the Philippines' index of 16 (in 1961) was much higher than those of Japan (1.36 in 1960), Italy (4.5 in 1958 to 1960, Thailand (3.3 in 1957), Malaya (5.4 in 1964) and Indonesia (12.0 in 1955) (Heidenheimer 1963; Milne 1968). According to one calculation, Korea's index of expenditure was 2.71 in 1963 (Lee and Kim 1964). Although Korea's index could be as high as 7 if a higher estimate of campaign spending was used, the Philippines clearly had the most expensive elections. High election costs were mainly due to high electoral corruption such as vote-buying, and these costs encouraged politicians to engage in corrupt deals after being elected. In the eight-year interval between the election of Magsaysay in 1953 and the victory of Macapagal in 1961, presidential campaign spending rose more than tenfold. Senatorial and congressional campaign expenses also rose steeply. The combined campaign spending amounted to 13 percent of the national budget in 1961. And in 1969, the total spending – including pork barrel (see explanation below) of 500 million pesos – for the presidential and congressional elections was estimated to be nearly 1 billion pesos, almost a quarter of the national budget for that year (Wurfel 1988: 100). Because the government was already burdened with the debt incurred during the non-election years, Marcos's heavy spending during the 1969 polls caused the Philippines' worst fiscal catastrophe up until that point (Thompson 1995: 35).

"Pork barrel" politics in the Philippines originated during the US colonial period, but they transformed into a more corrupt form to satisfy the clientelistic needs of politicians during the 1950s and 1960s. For the "community projects," otherwise known as "pork barrel," members of Congress had almost complete discretion over monetary allocation. Thus, congressmen and senators could select contractors and employees for the projects, which helped to maintain and expand their clientelistic networks (Kasuya 2009: 57). In the early 1960s, the average amount allocated to each representative was 300,000 pesos, and the amount allocated to each senator averaged 500,000 pesos. While the pork barrel budget was allocated to every congressman regardless of party affiliation, the president controlled the actual release of the funds. The ruling party members, as a result, received preferential treatment (Wurfel 1988: 86–7).

As clientelistic competition escalated between local and provincial factions, many provincial elite families created their own private armies, leading to an increase in political violence. Many warlords came to dominate provincial politics, and Filipinos complained that election results were determined by "guns, goons, and gold." Most candidates hired bodyguards for protection and intimidation of their opponents. Poll-related killings increased over time. When President Ferdinand E. Marcos, of the Nacionalista Party (NP), was elected to a second four-year term in 1969, the election was marred by terror as well as vote-buying and fraud. His opponent, Senator Osmena, bitterly complained that it was a case of winning the ballot, but being "out-gooned, out-gunned and out-gold [sic]" (Abueva 1970).

Authoritarian period (1972 to 1986)

By 1972, the Philippines was auspiciously an authoritarian regime. In September 1972, President Marcos declared martial law in order to "eliminate the threat of a violent overthrow of the Republic, to clean up government, and to encourage systematic development of the economy." It soon became clear that Marcos was undertaking pseudo reforms only to maintain his power indefinitely (Thompson 1995: 56–7). After several years of hard authoritarianism, Marcos had to promise a return to democracy in order to maintain US support. He resumed legislative elections in 1978 and officially lifted martial law in early 1981. In the 1978 legislative elections, however, the opposition was to be allowed no election inspectors, and the campaign period was shortened. The elections were totally fraudulent, and the opposition failed to win a single seat (Thompson 1995: 75–8).

At this point, the two parties diverged in their use of clientelism. Pressures for democratization increased both domestically and internationally, especially after the assassination of Benigno Aquino in August 1983. The Marcos regime had to reactively rely less on fraud and more on clientelistic mobilization. But the opposition relied less on clientelism and more on programmatic appeal for democratization. Unlike the 1978 elections, the 1984 legislative elections were hotly contested. Marcos's party, the Kilusang Bagong Lipunan (KBL, New Society Movement), had poured extensive money into its campaign. Warlords returned to politics, this time exclusively on the side of the ruling party, and election violence skyrocketed. Although the opposition candidates could not match the ruling party candidates in terms of clientelistic competition excluding a few provinces, they could draw on the popular outrage against the Marcos regime. Opposition parties won 60 of the 183 contested seats, including twenty-one of twenty-eight contests in urban areas. The opposition performed well in the cities. Massive vote-buying operations and government projects showered by the KBL on the cities proved ineffective. In addition, the opposition – armed with their own family-based political machines – prevailed in the eight provinces where powerful opposition clans were able to counter the KBL's financial advantage (Thompson 1995: 125–9).

Clientelism and electoral fraud came to a head under authoritarianism in the 1986 elections. In November 1985, Marcos declared snap elections for February 1986. He decisively bribed more voters in this crucial election, in which Corazon Aquino ran to compete with him for the presidency. According to some estimates, he allocated $500 million for vote-buying, which theoretically allowed party campaigners to pay off every voter in the country. The going rate offered between P50 and P100 (about $2.50 to $5) (Thompson 1995: 142). A provincial warlord boasted that Marcos sent him a check for 5 million pesos to be used for vote buying (Quirino and Peralta 1986: 139). Teofisto Guingona, the first Commission on Audit (COA) Chairman under the Aquino government, estimated that Marcos withdrew around $150 million from the national treasury for the 1986 polls (De Castro 1998). In addition to massive operations of vote-buying, disenfranchisement of voters, intimidation and violence, and vote-count cheating were pervasive. The Aquino-Laurel campaign spent a meager $6 million during the election, but moral appeals to restore democracy and establish honest government offset the financial disadvantage. When massive vote-count cheating was revealed, hundreds of thousands of people took to the streets to force the dictator to leave (Thompson 1995: 145–51).

The post-Marcos democratic period (1986 to present)

The dramatic democratic transition achieved by "People Power" failed to produce new politics of democratic accountability in the Philippines. After the dictator had gone, the traditional political-economic elite returned to dominate Philippine politics with the old style of political clientelism.

During the first legislative election after Marcos's fall, held in May 1987, the dominance of the traditional elite families was restored. Of the 200 representatives elected in 1987, 169 (nearly 85 percent) were classified as belonging to "traditional clans." Only thirty-one had no electoral record before 1972 and were not directly related to these old dominant families. Of the 169 congressmen from traditional political families, 102 were identified with the anti-Marcos forces, while sixty-seven were from pro-Marcos parties or families. Most of the twenty-four elected members of the Senate were also from prominent, pre-1972, political families (Mojares 1993). According to Julio Teehankee (2007), "For some 160 families, the two Houses of the Philippine Congress have practically been home for the last century."

The dominance of politically powerful clans, or political dynasties, also continued in later elections. According to Sheila Coronel (2004a), the percentage of House representatives with relatives in elective office remained almost constant from 62 percent in the 8th House (1987 to 1992) to 61 percent in the 12th House (2001 to 2004). Excluding party-list representatives, the percentage actually increased to 66 percent in the 12th House (Coronel 2004a). A study of the 15th Congress (2010 to 2013) shows that 70 percent of the members belong to political families (Mendoza *et al.* 2012). Political clans were traditionally from members of the wealthy landowning elite. Recently, celebrities have been building a number of new political clans. Most political families have multiple business interests (Coronel 2004b).

With the return of the traditional elite families, old politics of clientelistic competition were revived. While the opposition relied more on moral appeals than on clientelistic mobilization during the authoritarian era, all the politicians and parties relied on clientelistic competition after the democratic transition. Vote-buying practices continued. Political parties became increasingly meaningless. The pre-martial law two-party system broke down, various ideologically indistinguishable parties continuously surfaced and party-switching of elected officials all became the norm.

Clientelistic competition rather than programmatic competition defined politicians' main concerns after the democratic transition. In a 1999 to 2000 survey of House members and senators, Yuko Kasuya (2009) found that personal qualities and constituency service were most emphasized during their election campaigns, while the party's platform was least emphasized. The insignificance of the party platform during the campaign is understandable given the lack of distinction between the various platforms. The interesting result of Kasuya's study is the finding that "constituency service" refers mainly to the provision of favors and gifts. Attending the funerals, weddings or baptismal ceremonies of constituents, including an obligatory donation, is the most common form of constituency service in the Philippines. Korea and Taiwan, on the other hand, strictly ban politicians' donations to constituents as a form of implicit vote-buying.

Pork barrel politics were revived in a corrupt form to provide legislators with clientelistic resources. The Congress revived a pork barrel budget in 1990, and pork barrel allocations for legislators have increased over time. In the fiscal year 2002, the senators were given 150 million pesos each, while members of the House received 50 million pesos each. The pork barrel funds comprised 1.6 percent of the entire general appropriation. Moreover, 19.1 percent of the budget for the Department of Public Works and Highways was allocated to the members of Congress as pork barrel (Kawanaka 2007).

Pork barrel politics were not just used to finance various community projects, but to finance the legislators. Selection of contractors and even employees for the projects not only enabled the legislators to oil their clientelistic networks, but also gave them opportunities to receive a substantial portion of the budget in kickbacks. In 1998, newly appointed Finance Secretary Salvador Enriquez told reporters that kickbacks from public works projects make up, on average, 30 percent of the total project cost. He also held that up to 45 percent of funds might have been lost to "commissions" in the case of budget for school and other instruction materials (Parreno 1998). Thus, the total amount of kickbacks from pork

Table 5.2 *Pre-election expectations of election irregularities, 1992–2010 (%)*

	Apr. 1992	Apr. 2001	Apr. 2004	Feb. 2007	Apr. 2007	May 2007	Feb. 2010	Mar. 2010
Vote-buying	57	48	49	69	69	57	63	71
Cheating in vote-counting	48	30	36	53	53	45	49	51
Flying votes	41	27	29	48	46	41	39	48
Harassment of voters	36	17	22	39	39	30	34	45
Violence in campaign period	–	–	–	–	–	–	31	37

Source: Social Weather Stations (www.sws.org.ph/).

funds that each House member or senator acquires is likely to be substantial, and it will likely cover a good part of campaign costs. Kasuya's (2009: 63) interviews with a House representative and a senator's campaign manager confirm that the kickbacks are usually channeled to fund various constituency service activities and vote-buying.

As elections have remained as clientelistic contests between elite families, election irregularities of various forms have not declined either. Table 5.2 shows the trend of increasing perceptions of vote-buying and cheating in elections. The proportion of people who expect vote-buying in the upcoming elections decreased slightly from 57 percent in 1992 to 48 percent in 2001, but increased again to 71 percent in 2010. Furthermore, expectations of other election irregularities have also been increasing. In a post-election survey in June 2004, 19 percent of the respondents said that they had personally witnessed vote-buying in the May presidential election. During the 2007 elections, an NGO called Money and Politics Working Group found vote-buying practices occurring in three of the four districts they monitored. The only place where vote-buying was not observed was an uncontested district, with only one legislative candidate (PAP 2008). Vote-buying is often accompanied by other forms of irregularities, such as the violation of secret voting, and it often increases violence.

In these decades, the cost of election campaigns rose steadily in large part to fund clientelistic networks. Teehankee (2010) posits: "Traditionally, a well-oiled machinery was relied upon to deliver 75 percent of a [presidential] candidate's vote. The other 25 percent was delivered by provincial sorties, posters and propaganda materials". Although media expenses now account for more than half of the total "official" campaign spending for presidential and senatorial candidates, with lifting of the ban on political advertising in 2001, clientelisitc mobilization still seems to play a large role in national elections. While the presidential campaign spending, including media expenses, is limited to about 500 million pesos by law, political campaign specialists estimate that running a successful presidential campaign costs between 2.5 and 5 billion pesos ($125 million). Running a congressional campaign in a district of 500,000 registered voters costs 25 million pesos, or over 16 times the legal spending limit of 1.5 million pesos, even though congressional candidates seldom run TV or radio adverts (PAP 2008). These estimates imply that a huge amount of unofficial campaign spending is required to fund clientelistic mobilization.

Clientelism and programmatic competition are opposing forces. In the Philippines, the prevalence of political clientelism is closely connected with the absence of programmatic competition between political parties. A new development in post-Marcos Philippine politics is the emergence of a multi-party system, but it has nothing to do with programmatic politics. The single presidential term limit introduced in the post-Marcos era encouraged virtually every presidential hopeful to create a new political party. Thus, an unstable multi-party system replaced the stable two-party system of the pre-martial law era. However, the nature of district-level competition for House seats has remained largely the same. Kasuya states: "It is not the increased number of district-level candidates but the ways in which legislative candidates chose their party affiliation" that led to the advent of a multi-party system. It was the group of Nacionalista Party and Liberal Party candidates competing in most districts in the pre-martial law period. "In the post-Marcos period, a set of LAMP and Lakas candidates competed in some areas, while a set of LP and LAMP candidates competed in others." When aggregated at the national level, a multi-party system has emerged. Thus, the present multi-party system reflects the fragmentation of presidential competition rather than programmatic competition among parties of diverse ideological or policy positions (Kasuya 2009: 7–8).

In addition to clientelism and electoral fraud, the traditional practice of party-switching, or turncoatism, was revived soon after the democratic transition. With ample patronage at hand, pro-Aquino parties revived the pre-martial law practice of turncoatism. When Ramos won the presidential race in May 1992 with less than a quarter of the total votes, his Lakas-NUCD (National Union of Christian Democrats) was placed only third in races for both the Senate and the House. But free-flowing government patronage enabled his party to buy enough defectors to end a divided government (Thompson 1995: 178–9). As the number of programmatically indistinguishable political parties has increased, the frequency with which politicians engage in party-switching has also increased. While the percentage of House candidates who switched party affiliation in the next election during the pre-martial law era (1946 to 1971) was about 32 percent, it rose to 57 percent in the post-martial law era (1987 to 2004). Party-switching among senatorial candidates increased from 24 percent in the pre-martial law era to 42 percent in the post-martial law era (Kasuya 2009: 120).

As a number of ideologically indistinguishable political parties have emerged and died since 1986, and powerful families have frequently switched their party affiliation, it is difficult to establish personal continuity between the parties. Families, not parties, are the most enduring feature in Philippine politics (Coronel 2004a). Parties are essentially fragile coalitions of influential families, providing a clientelistic network that links local political bosses at the *barangay* (village) level to national politicians. The membership base of these parties is almost entirely drawn from the politically active elite clans, and parties do not have ordinary members. Candidate selection is determined informally between national and local politicians, which involves a non-transparent and undemocratic process of clientelistic horse-trading and bargaining (Hellmann 2011: 104–13). Not surprisingly, 67 percent of respondents in the 2004 and 2006 surveys conducted by the Social Weather Stations did not consider any political party as representing their welfare (Teehankee 2009).

There is one exception to these trends in the Philippines. Akbayan (Citizens' Action Party) primarily relies on programmatic appeals as a progressive membership-based party. Akbayan has won between one and three seats in the House through a party-list proportional representation system since 1998. After the electoral reform in 1998, political parties that represent a distinct sector are allowed to compete for the party-list seats up to the maximum of three seats. These parties are prohibited from fielding candidates for district seats, and parties competing in districts are not allowed to participate in the party-list seats. Hence, parties like Akbayan can have only limited influence (Hellmann 2011: 116–17; Teehankee 2009).

Korea: development of programmaticism

Although South Korea's Constitution introduced democratic political institutions, the actual running of the political institutions became authoritarian, with sporadic but increasingly popular struggles for democracy, until the democratic transition of 1987. During the largely authoritarian period (1948 to 1960 and 1961 to 1987), ruling parties relied heavily on clientelistic strategies as well as oppression to stay in power. Opposition parties primarily relied on programmatic strategies based on a pro-democracy platform, and enjoyed support among the growing population of urban, educated, middle-class voters. The scope and prevalence of clientelism was limited to a certain extent because political elites were largely separated from the economic elite as a result of land reform, meaning that the proportion of the clientelism-prone rural and poor population decreased over time. In addition, local elections were suspended after the military coup of 1961 and were not restored until the 1990s; this limited the scope and extent of clientelism. After the democratic transition, clientelistic competition initially intensified as elections became more competitive. However, programmatic competition between the two major conservative and liberal parties increased over time, and the effectiveness of clientelistic strategy diminished.

Early period of electoral democracy (1948 to 1972)

When the first nationwide elections for the National Assembly were held in May 1948, more than 40 percent of elected members were independents. The proportion of independents further increased to 60 percent in the second National Assembly (1950 to 1952), which indicates the weakness and under-institutionalization of political parties (Shim and Kim 2006: 344–6). Leftist parties were suppressed, and the best organized party was the Korea Democratic Party, which largely represented landlords and rightist intellectuals. Rhee created the Liberal Party in 1951, which he claimed to be "a national party based upon farmers and laborers" (Henderson 1968: 293). However, both the LP and the KDP were cadre parties, and there were initially no significant programmatic differences between them. Although land reform was a salient legislative issue and the KDP was on the conservative side in the first National Assembly (1948 to 1950), there were no salient socioeconomic issues that divided the LP and the KDP once the land reform issue was over.

Syngman Rhee was elected as the first president of the Republic of Korea by the National Assembly in 1948. President Rhee became increasingly authoritarian through constitutional amendments for direct presidential election and the exemption of a two-term limit for the first president. National elections became contests between the authoritarian ruling party and the pro-democracy opposition party. Thus, a two-party system was established and a voting pattern of "rural voters for the government party vs. urban voters for the opposition party" became apparent in the 1956 and 1958 elections. Elections were dominated by party politics, and the proportion of successful independent candidates in the 1958 elections decreased to 12 percent (Henderson 1968: 303; Shim and Kim 2006: 347).

Initially, there were many signs that clientelism in Korea would thrive. The Liberal Party's strong showing in rural areas was largely due to "conformity votes," and the police and the bureaucracy played an important role in increasing voter turnout and encouraging voters to support the ruling party candidates (Han 1974: 27). In addition, there were some forms of vote-buying through rice-wine parties and the provision of rubber shoes. Opposition candidates in rural areas were not only disadvantaged by the role of bureaucratic apparatus, but also by their weak position in terms of clientelistic competition. Although the KDP, or the predecessor of the opposition Democratic Party, was initially based on landlords, most landlords lost their wealth because of the land reform. Moreover, the Democrats were unable to mobilize enough clientelistic resources.

However, while the powers of bureaucracy and money were effective in intimidating and persuading rural voters to support the government party, they were ineffective in urban areas. Urbanization, expansion of education and an increase in newspaper circulation contributed to increasing support for the opposition Democratic Party among the more informed urban voters. In particular, the circulation of daily newspapers, primarily in urban areas, increased remarkably from 381,300 in 1946 to 1,980,000 in 1955 (Kim 1975: 145). This urban-rural divide along the political cleavage surrounding the issue of democratization continued to dominate Korean electoral politics until the democratic transition of 1987.

Rhee resigned as President when the student protest against massive electoral fraud during the 1960 presidential election escalated into the April 19 Student Revolution of 1960. But the Democratic Chang Myon government (1960 to 1961) was short-lived, as the military junta led by General Park Chung-hee seized power on May 16, 1961. Anti-corruption as well as anti-communism and economic development was a major rationale for the coup. But the military junta were soon faced with a dilemma due to the need for political financing.

Since the military junta promised to transfer power to a civilian government, largely due to US pressures, they had to prepare Park's running for presidential election. Kim Jong-pil, Park's nephew and a core member of the military coup, established the Korean Central Intelligence Agency, and then created the Democratic Republican Party, using the organizational base of the Korean Central Intelligence Agency (KCIA). Kim wanted to make the DRP a mass party, unlike cadre parties of the past, and established a large secretariat with 1,300 permanent-salaried staff members (Shim and Kim 2006: 318; Kim 1975: 236–7). As the presidential election of 1963 approached, Park distributed flour for free to rural villagers in an ostensible effort to help victims of the flood (Kim 1991). Although the permanent secretariat staff was reduced to 600, the running of the DRP and election campaigns cost a huge amount of money (Kim 1975: 250). Park won the 1963 presidential election, but only with a razor-thin margin in spite of huge operations by the DRP and the bureaucratic apparatus. During the National Assembly elections of the same year, the DRP provided each of its candidates with 2 to 3 million won (85 to 127 million won in 2000 constant prices) to help finance their campaigns (Park 1967). The DRP itself noted that the "timely and efficient distribution of campaign funds" contributed to the success in the 1963 elections (Kim 1975: 252–3).

The subsequent National Assembly elections of 1967 saw widespread irregularities such as intimidation, vote-buying and ballot stuffing because Park needed a two-thirds super-majority vote in the National Assembly to push for a constitutional amendment to the two-term limit for president. During the national referendum on constitutional amendment for three presidential terms, it was reported that local DRP officials openly passed out cash and bread to the rural villagers. Park ran for his third term and won in the 1971 presidential election, but there were charges of numerous irregularities. Park's opponent, Kim Dae-jung, made programmatic appeals for democracy and peaceful relations with the north, and carried the urban population (Kim 1975: 276, 282–3).

Authoritarian period (1972 to 1987)

Park relied more on the bureaucracy, the KCIA and the army than on the DRP as his primary control mechanism (Henderson 1968: 307). As Park found no constitutional path beyond his third term, he declared martial law, disbanded the National Assembly, and revoked the existing constitution in the name of *Yushin* (reformation) in October 1972. The *Yushin* Constitution abolished direct presidential election, effectively guaranteeing him a life-time presidency. It also gave him the authority to appoint a third of the National Assembly members.

Increasing concentration of power on the president meant increasing concentration of clientelistic resources. Unlike in the Philippines, where individual politicians created and maintained their own clientelistic networks, collection and distribution of clientelistic resources in Korea were concentrated on the president and the ruling party. Suspension of local elections by the military regime in 1961, which continued until the early 1990s, made it difficult for individual politicians, especially opposition politicians, to create and maintain extensive clientelistic networks that reached villages. Although the *Yushin* system eliminated costly presidential elections, the dictator still needed a large amount of money to run the DRP, National Assembly elections and national referendums, and even to bribe some opposition politicians. He made a customary practice of dispensing cash in white envelopes to his subordinates in order to secure their loyalty. The Park regime even tried to bribe US congressmen. In the so-called Koreagate, $850,000 was spent to bribe members of the US Congress (Clifford 1998: 88; Oberdorfer 2002: 50–1).

After Park's assassination by his KCIA chief in 1979, there was a short period of democratic opening, but the military junta led by General Chun Doo-hwan seized power through a two-stage coup and bloody suppression of the Kwangju uprising in May 1980. Chun created the Democratic Justice Party as a new ruling party. Plentiful funding was needed to recruit and train 1.6 million party members, or 6.5 percent of voters. Local party officials or candidates sponsored "membership training meetings," at which scores of people acquired instant ruling party membership and 100,000 won (US $150) each. Election campaigns were also expensive. Huge quantities of cash were needed to buy meals and token gifts for millions of ordinary voters during election campaigns. In rural areas, many of Chun's candidates arranged free tours or clandestinely doled out white envelopes containing cash to the voters (Schopf 2004: 64–5).

In spite of the vast patron-client networks of the DJP, the enormous diversion of funds, and the overarching power of police and bureaucracy, it became increasingly difficult to control the opposition parties and to manipulate elections, particularly in urban areas. In the 1985 National Assembly elections, the newly created opposition New Democratic Party prevailed in Seoul (Seo 2008: 214). With few clientelistic resources, the opposition was able to push the authoritarian ruling party on the defensive with its pro-democracy platform. Increasing urbanization, education and size of the middle class meant decreasing the effectiveness of the ruling party's clientelistic strategy.

Democratic era (1987 to present)

When hundreds of thousands of citizens, including students and white-collar workers, took to the streets of Seoul and all over the country in 1987, President Chun was forced to surrender to their key demands for democracy, including direct presidential election. In the December 1987 presidential election, Chun's hand-picked candidate of the DJP, Roh Tae-woo, won due to the split of opposition candidates. But in the April 1988 National Assembly elections, the combined seats obtained by three opposition parties exceeded the DJP's seats. The DJP candidates spent an unprecedented amount of funds on these elections, in large part for clientelistic mobilization of voters.

Apparently, democratization increased, not reduced, clientelism and illegal campaign funds. With competitive elections, stakes were much higher for the ruling party, but intimidation and electoral fraud became almost impossible. Hence, vote-buying became more important for the DJP candidates. Even the opposition candidates came to increase their reliance on clientelism. Although opposition parties during the authoritarian era typically appealed to voters with pro-democracy messages, they needed new appeals, and there was fierce competition between opposition candidates. An important part of new appeal came from regional mobilization based on regional sentiments, but clientelistic competition also increased, and regional ties were often utilized as clientelistic networks. Democratization also allowed opposition legislators the opportunity to receive political contributions from the business.

Roh says in his memoir (2011) that he received 140 billion won from Chun and spent 200 billion won in total on the 1987 presidential election, while Chun claimed that he gave 197.4 billion to Roh's campaign. Mo Jongryn (2009) estimates that Roh spent about 300 billion won ($375 million) and that the opposition candidates also raised and spent a substantial amount of money, since they had reasonable chances and the businesses needed to hedge. Considering that media expenses were almost negligible in 1987 and are still a relatively small portion of total campaign spending in Korea, the bulk of campaign expenditures was used for clientelistic mobilization.

Intense competition fueled the spread of clientelism during this period. The three-party merger in 1990 between Roh's DJP and two opposition parties led by Kim Young-sam and Kim Jong-pil created the new ruling Democratic Liberal Party and ended a divided government. Kim Young-sam, a long-time opposition leader, obtained the ruling party's nomination for presidential candidacy in 1992. Roh Tae-woo (2011) claims that he gave 300 billion won ($380 million) to Kim Young-sam in 1992. Roh is also known to have given 2 billion won ($2.5 million) to opposition candidate Kim Dae-jung, perhaps as insurance. The entrance of Hyundai founder and chairman Chung Joo-young's National Party in the 1992 National Assembly and presidential races further intensified competition, and the total spending in these elections was probably higher than that in the 1987 presidential and 1988 National Assembly elections. Various forms of vote-buying practices were widespread, but only a few unfortunate National Assembly members elected were prosecuted and lost their seats. In addition to Roh's generous contribution of 300 billion won, critics estimate that Kim Young-sam raised 200 to 300 billion won of presidential campaign funds. He raised so much money that the leftover funds from his lavish presidential campaign spending exceeded 100 billion won (Mo 2009).

Upon inauguration, however, Kim Young-sam launched an aggressive anti-corruption campaign in response to public criticism of electoral and political corruption. He declared that he would not receive any money from businesses during his presidency and introduced reforms in party and campaign finance. The 1995 local elections were largely regarded as relatively clean. During the National Assembly elections of 1996, however, the ruling party candidates were accused of lavish spending, including outright vote-buying in cash. It was discovered that the leftover funds were used to help the ruling party candidates in the 1996 elections. Kim Young-sam's political will for clean politics diminished after his losses in the local elections. Although he successfully pushed for prosecution of two former presidents, Chun Doo-hwan and Roh Tae-woo, for mutiny and corruption, he lost popularity because of several high profile corruption scandals that involved his aides and his own son. A long-time opposition leader Kim Dae-jung was elected as president in the midst of a financial crisis in December 1997, which represented the first transfer of power between parties through election. Five years later, another liberal presidential candidate, Roh Moo-hyun, was elected. Under the two liberal presidents, substantial political reforms were undertaken and clientelistic practices diminished.

Although President Kim Dae-jung was not entirely free from the old practices of clientelism, his reliance on clientelism was much less than that of his predecessors. In the 1997 presidential election, the ruling party candidate, Lee Hoi-chang, also ran as a reform candidate in response to popular demand for clean politics, openly breaking with the incumbent president Kim Young-sam. Although both candidates were found to have received illegal contributions, the total amount of illegally raised funds, as well as campaign spending, is likely to have fallen steeply (Mo 2009). In the post-election survey, the percentage of voters who admitted receiving cash, gifts, food or free tours declined to 3 percent from 12 percent in the 1992 presidential election.

Surprisingly, President Roh Moo-hyun encouraged the prosecution to conduct a thorough investigation of illegal campaign funds for both his camp and his opponent's camp for the first time in Korean history. The results were shocking. It was found that several *chaebol* delivered a truck-load(s) of cash to the conservative opposition candidate, Lee Hoi-chang. Lee's illegal fundraising totaled 82.3 billion won, while Roh's amounted to 12 billion won. Although Roh tried to rely on a large number of small

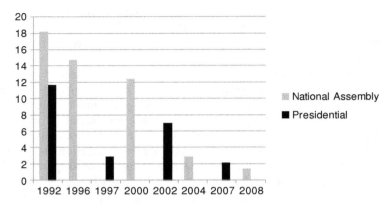

Figure 5.1 Voters given cash, gifts, food or tours during election campaigns (%)
Source: National Election Commission, various years.

contributions, he was still not free from *chaebol*'s illegal contributions. Both the total amount of campaign funds and the amounts of individual corporate contributions for the 2002 presidential election may be greater than those for 1997 election,[1] although they must be much smaller than those for the 1987 and 1992 elections.

The prosecution of illegal presidential campaign funds had a large impact on the behavior of political parties, politicians and *chaebol*. The conservative Grand National Party (successor of the Democratic Liberal Party) had to strive hard to change its image as the "corrupt party." In addition, there was further reform of political and campaign finance that required more transparent fundraising and expenditures. As a result, the National Assembly elections in 2004 were unusually clean, and the role of money and vote-buying in elections diminished. In post-election surveys, the percentage of respondents who admitted receiving cash, gifts, food or free tours during legislative elections declined to 3 percent in 2004, from double digit percentages in the past legislative elections. The percentage declined further to 2.1 percent in the 2007 presidential election and 1.4 percent in the 2008 legislative elections, as shown in Figure 5.1.

The gradual decline of clientelistic competition in Korea has been accompanied by the gradual development of programmatic competition

---

[1] Samsung's illicit donation to Lee's presidential campaign was 10 billion won in 1997, but it increased to 34 billion won in 2002, according to the investigation by the prosecutors. This indicates that the total amount of Lee's campaign funds for 2002 was probably higher than that for 1997.

and institutionalization of a party system, although clientelistic competition intensified during the early years of democratization. During the authoritarian era, the opposition parties primarily relied on programmatic mobilization of urban educated voters with the platform of pro-democracy, while the government parties relied heavily on clientelistic strategy such as vote-buying. During the early years of the post-democratization period, regional cleavages replaced the previous cleavage surrounding the issue of democratization (Kang 2003; Kim 2000a; Park 2003; Seong 2008). The major opposition parties were led by the three Kims: Kim Young-sam, Kim Dae-jung, and Kim Jong-pil; these politicians represented the Southern Youngnam, Honam and Choongcheong regions, while the government party led by Roh Tae-woo represented Northern Young-nam. The three-party merger among Roh Tae-woo, Kim Young-sam and Kim Jong-pil in 1990, together with the coalition between Kim Dae-jung and Kim Jong-pil in 1997 – which enabled Kim Young-sam and Kim Dae-jung to be elected president in 1992 and 1997 respectively – demonstrate the personal and regional characteristics of Korean politics during the 1990s. Because of frequent mergers and splits, as well as the creation of new parties by the three Kims, the party system was unstable and under-institutionalized. Most voters distinguished the political parties based on party leadership and regional base rather than ideological or policy differences. While charismatic mobilization and regional cleavages played important roles, clientelistic mobilization also became important (Kim 2000a; Nemoto 2009; Park 2008).

Programmatic competition began to develop noticeably in the 2002 presidential election, in which ideological and generational cleavages became as important as regional cleavages (Hellmann 2011: 41–6; Kim 2010; Kim et al. 2008; Kwon 2008; Moon 2005; Steinberg and Shin 2006; Wang 2012a). After Kim Dae-jung's liberal government introduced the "Sunshine Policy," or an engagement policy with North Korea which culminated in the first historical inter-Korean summit in 2000, the conservative Grand National Party criticized the policy, taking a more hard-lined stance toward the north. Thus, in the 2002 election, voters began to distinguish between a liberal candidate, Roh Moo-hyun, who promised to continue Kim Dae-jung's engagement policy, and a conservative GNP candidate, Lee Hoi-chang. The generational and ideological cleavages were even more salient in the 2004 National Assembly and subsequent elections. The development of programmatic competition was also reflected in the emergence of the leftist Democratic Labor Party as a significant party with ten seats in the National Assembly in 2004. Recently, socio-economic policies in addition to the North Korea policy are increasingly becoming important campaign issues between the liberal Democratic Party and conservative *Saenuri* Party (formerly the Grand National Party).

Although there were frequent mergers, splits and renaming of the parties, major conservative and liberal parties were clearly distinguishable at all times. There were cases of party-switching, but those politicians who changed their party affiliation from an opposition party to a ruling party for the sake of patronage usually suffered in the subsequent elections. Party-switchers therefore had to justify their decision in terms of ideological or programmatic conflict with the party leadership.

Political parties became increasingly institutionalized at the same time. For example, the selection of candidates for public office was largely determined by party leadership until the 1990s. Even the nomination of presidential candidates and election of party leaders were determined by a relatively small size of delegates, who were influenced by patron-client relationships with intraparty factional bosses. However, major parties began to introduce and increasingly rely on closed or open primaries and public opinion polls for the nomination of presidential candidates, as well as candidates for other offices (Hellmann 2011: 52–8). While regionalism still plays an important role in party competition and voting behavior, it is increasingly clear that Korean voters are choosing between two major parties, and conservatives and liberals have been alternating in power.

Taiwan: development of programmaticism

Taiwan had a long period of authoritarian one-party rule under martial law (1949 to 1987). Most landlords withdrew from local politics after the land reform, but local factions were formed spontaneously as local elections were held regularly. The KMT forged clientelistic relationships with local factions by doling out access to rents, and clientelism became widespread. With the democratization process and intensifying electoral competition at the national level, clientelistic practices, such as vote-buying, spread to national elections, and political corruption became an increasing concern to the public. Vote-buying did, however, become increasingly costly and ineffective, and the KMT's reliance on clientelistic strategies backfired. With the alternation of power between the KMT and the Democratic Progressive Party (DPP), anti-vote buying and anti-corruption prosecution intensified. Recently, local factions have been disintegrating and clientelistic competition has been declining, with the corresponding rise of programmatic party politics.

Authoritarian era (1949 to 1987)

The nationalist regime in Taiwan operated according to the Constitution of the Republic of China (ROC), adopted on the mainland in December 1947. The ROC's constitution outlined a democratic republic, but in May 1948 the National Assembly suspended the constitution and concentrated powers on the president. The ruling KMT, with 3,000 staff and vast assets, including many party-owned corporations, had a virtual monopoly of power on the island. Chiang Kai-shek ruled Taiwan as president and chairman of the party. Chiang Ching-kuo became premier in 1972, party chair after his father's death in 1975 and president in 1978. The KMT initially ensured its dominance of politics at the national level by forcing all Taiwanese people out of the national political offices. The party made a claim to be the government across all of China. In order to sustain this claim, the KMT regime maintained control through its representatives for the National Assembly, Legislative Yuan (legislature) and Control Yuan (supreme audit institution). These representatives had all been elected on the mainland in 1947. As more of the original members died, however, the government held supplementary elections starting in 1969 (Roy 2003: 84–5).

The regime was less reluctant to implement elections at the local level. Allowing the Taiwanese to compete for local positions did not pose much threat to the KMT's national agenda. Moreover, local elections enabled the KMT to neutralize or co-opt some of its potential opposition (Roy 2003: 85–6). In addition, elections helped Taiwan to retain international support during the Cold War. In order to maintain the "Free China" label, as opposed to "Red China," the ROC in Taiwan had to make some gestures in the direction of democracy (Rigger 1999: 81).

From the 1950s through much of the 1970s, the KMT dominated Taiwan's elections almost completely. Between 1951 and 1985, 88 percent of KMT nominees for municipal executive posts won the election, and 87 percent of the party's Provincial Assembly nominees were successful. The regime banned the formation of new parties, but allowed non-KMT members to compete in elections. Although the elections were largely open and competitive, independent candidates never threatened the KMT's ruling majority. Furthermore, most independents were easily co-opted by the regime. In the 1950s and 1960s, the KMT routinely recruited successful independent candidates after local elections (Rigger 1999: 82–3; Roy 2003: 85).

As local elections were held periodically, local factions were formed spontaneously. They arose from casual personal networks and competed against each other for party nomination and government office. Factions were organized at the two key administrative levels: township and county. Gallin's field research regarding a rural village in 1961 found village society in the midst of profound transformation. Traditional village leaders, mainly landlords, had lost the economic basis for their political power as a result of land reform. As most landlords withdrew from local politics, the leadership of newly created local factions was assumed by informal leaders, or "villagers who have more time and money than their fellows and who aspire to improve their status" (Gallin 1961: 116; Rigger 1999: 88).

Factions obtained votes on the basis of *guanxi*, or connections, between leaders and voters. Voting according to *guanxi* (and thus faction) was commonly accepted and indeed expected (Bosco 1994). The faction relied on the village and neighborhood *tiau-a-ka* (vote brokers) to mobilize votes on election day. Although factional mobilization primarily relies on informal networks such as locality, kinship, co-worker and classmate *guanxi*, vote-buying has been employed as a method for reinforcing pre-existing relationships between voters and the candidate. Gifts helped to reinforce personal relationships between candidates and voters (Rigger 1999: 88). "In general, the villagers consider elections unimportant, and candidates often buy votes. A few packs of cigarettes or some bath towels and soap may be all that is needed to secure someone's vote" (Gallin 1961: 116). Over time, vote-buying in cash, albeit on the basis of *guanxi*, became common (Rigger 1999: 94–9). Furthermore, it was observed that the Farmers Associations, the most important rural financial institution in Taiwan, played an important role in vote-buying.

The KMT relied heavily upon local factions to win local elections. From 1954 to 1994, 61.9 percent of the KMT nominees for Provincial Assembly seats had a local faction background, and 92.6 percent of those candidates were elected (Lin 1998: 164). The KMT had a weakness in connecting with local residents, because most KMT members were mainlanders who were working for the state sectors, including the military. The proportion of the Taiwanese in the KMT's Central Committee never exceeded 10 percent before 1976, even though they comprised more than 85 percent of the population (Kuo 1995: 37–41). Hence, local factions and their clientelistic vote mobilization abilities were critical to the KMT's electoral success.

Upon taking premiership in 1972, Chiang Ching-kuo introduced a Taiwanization policy that increased representation of the Taiwanese in both the party and the government. Chiang also sought to identify and nominate a new generation of native party-state loyalists, "who would be younger, better educated, and better qualified than the political bosses promoted by local factions" (Rigger 1999: 112). The anti-faction nomination strategy initially worked well. In the 1972 county executive elections, the KMT nominated non-factional candidates in twelve out of twenty counties, and they all won the election (Wang 2004a). As electoral competition intensified with increasing challenges from the opposition forces, however, the KMT's strategy of distancing itself from local factions backfired in the subsequent elections (Kuo 1995: 129–34).

The first significant effort of the opposition forces to field non-KMT candidates throughout the island came in 1977. They were called the Dangwai, or "outside-the-party." In the island-wide electoral contest, "a split between the ruling party leadership and local factions created an opening for the opposition to gain a foothold in electoral politics." The KMT suffered from an unprecedented loss of four municipal executiveships and twenty-one Provincial Assembly seats, fourteen of which went to Dangwai candidates. The KMT nominated candidates without factional connections for seventeen of twenty-one municipal executive posts. This time, the local factions did not acquiesce. In many municipal executive and Provincial Assembly races, the non-cooperation of local factions with the KMT helped Dangwai candidates to win. After 1977, the ruling party could not afford to alienate local factions, and the percentage of KMT nominees with factional backgrounds rose again (Rigger 1999: 114–16).

As the KMT faced increasing challenges from Dangwai candidates, its reliance on local factions and clientelistic mobilization strategy increased. Bribing was considered effective in mobilizing votes. It tended to be more effective in smaller and more rural districts, where voters, vote brokers and candidates were closely linked. It was more effective in electing councilors than in electing mayors or magistrates (Kuo 1995: 91–2). The fact that clientelistic mobilization works best in basic-level elections explains "an interesting paradox in Taiwan's election turn-out statistics": "Historically, turn-out for grassroots elections has been higher than turn-out for national elections" (Rigger 1999: 100).

The ruling party used the spoils of government to co-opt local leaders and their factions. Of the 518 faction-endorsed candidates during 1951 to 1986, 442 (85 percent) owned or shared at least one of the local monopolies, such as credit cooperatives, production cooperatives, Farmers' or Fishermen's Association credit bureaus, or transportation companies. In contrast, only 72 (9 percent) out of 846 candidates without factional support enjoyed such privileges. Except for public transportation, most local monopolies clustered around financing. It was often observed that during the two months before the voting date, huge loans were released for "electoral campaign purposes" from credit unions and credit departments of Farmers' Associations (Kuo 1995: 102–6).

While KMT candidates relied on clientelistic mobilization strategies, Dangwai candidates employed issue-based campaign strategies on the twin themes of democratization and ethnic justice. They did not have clientelistic resources, but their programmatic appeals were enough to solicit support from the growing size of urban, educated, middle-class Taiwanese. On September 28, 1986, Dangwai leaders meeting in Taipei voted to form the Democratic Progressive Party. This time, the regime did not suppress or prosecute the DPP leaders, as it did to the Democratic Party in 1960. On October 7, the president indicated that he would lift martial law and allow new parties to form (Rigger 1999: 126).

Democratic era (1987 to present)

With the formation of the DPP, the first formal opposition party, in 1986 and the lifting of martial law in 1987, a gradual process of democratization began in Taiwan. The initial period of democratic transition, however, saw increasing clientelism and political corruption. Electoral corruption spread to the national level, and recurrent scandals of money politics (gold politics) and political infiltration of organized crime (black politics) became salient political issues during the 1990s.

In the first democratic elections, KMT candidates invested heavily to mobilize their clientelistic networks. The first nationwide electoral contest between the newly formed opposition DPP and the ruling KMT took place for the Legislative, Executive and Provincial Assembly elections in December 1989. There were numerous reports of vote-buying. The price of a vote ranged from NT$200 for a legislative election in Taoyuan County to NT$2,000 for the Taipei County executive race. Candidates exerted enormous efforts to enlist vote brokers (Rigger 1999: 143). In spite of fierce mobilization of local factions and vote-buying, the KMT performed poorly. The DPP, with the powerful messages of democratic reform and "Taiwan for the Taiwanese," made substantial gains, capturing twenty-one seats in the legislature and six municipal executiveships.

Contrasting the KMT's electoral performances across different levels of elections demonstrated the different levels of effectiveness of local factions and clientelistic mobilization. Just six weeks after the December 1989 elections, the KMT was successful in the island-wide electoral contests for lower-level officials. The DPP secured only 5.6 percent of county assembly seats and 1.9 percent of the township executive positions (Bosco 1994). In the lower-level elections, clientelistic mobilization worked well. But, in the higher-level elections, the strategy posed a difficult dilemma for the KMT. On the one hand, clientelistic strategy was still effective, especially in rural districts. On the other hand, many people associated local factions with vote-buying and corruption, which damaged the image of the KMT, particularly among urban, middle-class voters. The KMT struggled to overcome this dilemma (Rigger 1999: 146).

Vote-buying practices continued in the 1992 and subsequent elections. According to surveys, 24 to 45 percent of voters admitted to vote-selling in the 1992 legislative elections and 27 percent of voters did so in 1999 (Wang and Kurzman 2007). As the price of vote-buying and other campaign spending expenses increased, total campaign spending skyrocketed. In the 1992 legislative elections, KMT candidates spent on average NT$150 million (Tien and Chu 1996). It was commonly believed that large portions of campaign spending were used for clientelistic mobilization relying on local factions. Clientelistic mobilization, including direct vote-buying, was a major component of campaign strategy for the majority of KMT candidates.

In a field study of a highly competitive election for a county executive in 1993, Chin-Shou Wang (2004a) found that the vote-buying system was very sophisticated. At the same time, he estimated that at least 45 percent of voters who sold their votes to the KMT did not, in fact, vote for the KMT candidate (Wang 2004a; Wang and Kurzman 2007). The effectiveness of vote-buying was declining, and the costs of clientelism were rising. With democratization, the intelligence apparatus became depoliticized, media exposure of vote-buying and corruption increased, and prosecutors were increasingly independent.

Clientelistic strategy increased the politicians' dependence on the wealthy businessmen and gangsters. Among the fifty KMT nominees with local factional backgrounds in the 1992 legislative elections, thirty-six were also identified as having business origins (Shiau 1996: 218f). In addition, gangsters increased their role and influence as effective vote brokers and enforcers of vote-buying contracts. Candidates often hired thugs to keep tabs on vote brokers and to keep rivals off their turf (Rigger 1994: 212). After these criminal figures became familiar with the election process, they ran for public office themselves. In 1996, Minister of Justice Liao Cheng-hao declared that out of the 858 city and county councilors across Taiwan, 286 had a gangster or criminal background. Liao also indicated that 25 percent of the Provincial Assembly members and 5 percent of the legislators and National Assembly deputies had shady backgrounds (Chin 2003: 14).

The KMT's increasing reliance on big businesses and gangsters, however, encouraged people to blame the ruling party for black-gold politics. The KMT was increasingly perceived as a corrupt party, and DPP presidential candidate Chen Shui-bian's electoral victory in 2000 was boosted by his anti-corruption agenda. Many scholars of Taiwanese politics agree that the prevalence and effectiveness of vote-buying has declined and anti-vote-buying measures have increased in strength since the change in ruling party in 2000 (Fell 2005a; Wang 2004b; Wang and Kurzman 2007). In the first post-turnover election of 2001, the DPP government's Minister of Justice, Chen Ting-nan, took a very strict enforcement approach, declaring any election gifts of a value greater than NT$6 as vote-buying. According to Wang and Kurzman (2007), some brokers panicked and gave up vote-buying campaigns after this announcement. Many local factions were disintegrating (Wang 2004a, 2004b).

Since 2000, all major parties have tried to keep their distance from local politicians with corrupt reputations. The KMT introduced a serious nomination reform after its defeat in 2000, disqualifying anyone "who has been convicted of a criminal offence or breaking the Election and Recall Law." This meant that a number of infamous and long-serving KMT politicians did not stand for election, and by the 2004 legislative elections, allegations of KMT "black-gold" candidates were rare (Fell 2005a).

Although local factions have weakened and vote-buying has declined, the old practices have not entirely disappeared. An international observation mission for Taiwan's legislative elections of 2004 observed that although vote-buying had existed in the past, most voters in Taichung City did not currently believe vote-buying was still taking place. Observers in the neighboring Taichung County, in contrast, were told that vote-buying was still common for some candidates of both camps and that it was especially effective against the older generation in rural areas, where local factions have a deeper penetration. The forms of vote-buying were reported to have become very sophisticated in order to evade detection. Most candidates conducted vote-buying as a dinner, a trip, etc. They also gave cash, but usually the candidates' agents were very careful (Hazri 2006). Bruce Jacobs (2008: 308–13) found that even some DPP candidates were employing vote-buying tactics in rural areas.

The trend of vote-buying prosecution shows a surge of vote-buying indictments in the early 2000s. This reflects intensified prosecution rather than increased incidents of vote-buying. Petty vote-buying practices, which were largely condoned in the past, are now facing rigorous investigation and punishment. The number of vote-buying cases was particularly high when municipal and provincial elections were held, suggesting that it is more important in local elections than in national elections. As a positive development, the Anti-Corruption Yearbook (MJIB 2011) notes that the number of indicted vote-buying cases and individuals during the 2010 local elections decreased by about 40 percent when compared with the statistics provided four years ago. This indicates the declining trend of vote-buying in spite of continuing rigorous prosecution.

Decreasing the effectiveness of vote-buying and clientelism tactics was accompanied by the increasing tendency of party-oriented and issue-based voting. During the early years of democratic transition, surveys of voting behavior found that most voters display weak party identification. However, party-oriented and issue-based voting increased over time (Rigger 1999: 182–3). At the same time, the party system has been solidly institutionalized, and programmatic competition has intensified between the major parties. The party system in Taiwan has been remarkably stable, compared to both systems in the Philippines and Korea. The KMT and the DPP have been the two major parties, with distinct platforms on the major issues as well as distinct support bases. Although Taiwan saw party splits and the creation of minor parties, broad coalitions were primarily built around the two major parties. As the splinter parties have become weaker and smaller over time, the two major parties have absorbed the support of most voters. The institutionalization of the two major parties is also reflected in their inclusive and institutionalized processes for candidate selection. Both parties experimented with some forms of closed primaries in the 1990s, and they both adopted a system that combines closed primary and public opinion surveys after 2000 (Fell 2006; Hellmann 2011: 84–8; Wu 2001).

The DPP has primarily relied on programmatic strategies since its foundation. While the KMT oscillated between more emphasis on clientelistic strategy and distancing itself from local factions until the presidential election of 2000, it has abandoned its traditional reliance on local factions since then. Unlike in the Philippines, Taiwan has seen increasingly critical attitudes by its large and educated middle-class voters, and this attitude has raised the costs and lowered the benefits of clienetelistic strategy. In addition, the separation between political and economic elites, together with the relatively weak influence of the latter, have made it less challenging for the KMT to abandon clientelism and adopt programmatic competition. Now both major parties primarily rely on programmatic rather than clientelistic strategy. The parties compete on the issues of national identity and relations with mainland China, although both the KMT and the DPP have moderated their positions over time (Fell 2005b; Hellmann 2011: 75–7; Wang 2012b). Still, the cross-strait relations issue, rather than the socioeconomic one, is the defining cleavage between the two major parties. Recently, the DPP has been paying increasing attention to the income disparities and class cleavages, and the salience of socioeconomic issues may gradually rise over time (Chen 2012; Wong 2010).

The causes of clientelism

Historical narratives of clientelism in the three countries show both commonalities and differences. In all three countries, political clientelism was prevalent for a long time. Primacy of clientelistic competition meant the lack of programmatic competition and the under-institutionalization of the party system, and these two factors reinforced each other. Authoritarian regimes were not immune from clientelism. When these regimes faced increasing challenges from the opposition, they displayed heavy reliance on clientelistic strategy, the use of state resources, intimidation and fraud.

While all three countries shared these commonalities, there were significant differences in the degree of political clientelism. If we compare Korea and the Philippines during the early electoral democracy before 1972 and the three countries after the democratic transition of the late 1980s, the Philippines appears to have had a more pervasive and extreme degree of clientelism than Korea and Taiwan. In Korea, clientelistic resources were concentrated in the president or ruling party leadership, and the ruling party distributed them to individual legislative candidates ahead of elections. In the Philippines, on the other hand, the presidents were not the only people in charge of clientelistic resources. Individual legislative candidates, including opposition candidates, mobilized and dispensed substantial amounts of clientelistic resources. In Taiwan, local factions mobilized clientelistic resources, and they were almost exclusively utilized by the ruling KMT candidates. In Korea and Taiwan, the opposition candidates mostly relied on programmatic appeals, but in the Philippines, the opposition politicians also commanded substantial amounts of clientelistic resources. Also, there was variation in the persistence of clientelism. Clientelism has noticeably declined in Korea and Taiwan, but it is hard to see such signs in the Philippines. On the other hand, there is an increasing trend of programmatic competition between major parties in Korea and Taiwan, but political parties are still unstable and programmatically indistinguishable in the Philippines.

These differences are roughly confirmed by the data on clientelism constructed by Herbert Kitschelt (2013). The average expert judgments on the politicians' and parties' clientelistic efforts on the scale of 1 (negligible or none) to 4 (a major effort) were 2.5 for Korea, 3.5 for Taiwan and 3.8 for the Philippines. Note that the average score of 3.8 indicates that most experts agree that Philippine politicians and parties make a major effort for clientelistic moblization. The average responses to the question on the change in clientelism over the past ten years from 1998 to 2008 (1 = much less now; 5 = much more now) were 2.5 for Korea, 3.4 for

Taiwan and 4.0 for the Philippines. This indicates that clientelism has declined in Korea, remained about the same in Taiwan and increased in the Philippines. While Kitschelt's data on clientelism in Taiwan is slightly different from my assessment of Taiwanese politics, it is completely consistent with my assessment of Korean and Philippine politics.[2] The data also shows that programmaticism is extremely low in the Philippines, but much higher in Korea and Taiwan.[3]

We will now examine the causation of these differences. I have indicated that a higher level of inequality in the Philippines led to more widespread and persistent clientelism. I have also suggested that clientelism may develop differently depending on the regime (whether elections are free and competitive or not) and the types of elections (whether elections are held at the local, national or both levels). But it will be prudent to consider other potential causes that clientelism literature has suggested, as well. Let us examine three other prominent explanations: the age of democracy, the electoral system and socioeconomic development such as per capita income, urbanization and education.

First, Keefer (2007) and Keefer and Vlaicu (2008) argued that younger democracies are more prone to clientelism because it takes time for political parties to build policy reputations. This explanation potentially applies to Korea and Taiwan. During the early episode of electoral democracy in Korea (1948 to 1972), it took some time for a two-party system to emerge, and for the main opposition to appeal to urban, educated voters with a pro-democracy message. During the early years after the democratic transition of the late 1980s, party identification was low and voting behavior was more influenced by regional sentiments (in Korea), ethnic identities (in Taiwan) and particularistic benefits provided by the candidates. Vote-buying was widespread in various forms. Over time, however, voters' party identification increased. The traditional ruling parties that heavily relied on clientelistic strategies in the past found the costs of clientelistic mobilization increasing, while the benefits were decreasing. Clientelistic strategies often backfired, because the majority

---

[2] The timing of the expert survey for Kitschelt's data may have caused experts' bias in the Taiwan case. Because of Chen Shui-bian's corruption scandal, many experts might have considered Taiwan politics to be very clientelistic, although clientelism and political corruption are conceptually different.

[3] Kitschelt's data on expert judgment on programmatic mobilization (between 0 and 1) indicates that programmatic mobilization is quite high in Korea (0.4) and Taiwan (0.54), but very low in the Philippines (0.12). However, Kitschelt's proposed measure for programmaticism that incorporates coherence, salience and polarization suggests that programmaticism is quite high in Korea (0.41), relatively low in Taiwan (0.14) and extremely low in the Philippines (0.07).

of the urban, educated population criticized the vote-buying and corruption of clientelistic parties and politicians.

In particular, the change of governing parties in Korea and Taiwan played an important role in promoting programmatic politics and reducing clientelism. Electoral victory of the opposition signified an important development in this regard because it demonstrated a victory of programmatic mobilization over clientelistic mobilization. This compelled the traditional ruling party, now without access to state resources, to employ programmatic strategies. These dynamics further increased the importance of programmatic politics, and people came to realize the significant policy differences between the major parties. Political parties clashed on policy issues such as the relationship with North Korea or mainland China. Although the new ruling party could not completely resist the temptation to use state resources for clientelistic purposes, it was constrained by the fear and possibility of a government transition, as well as the vigilant observation by the media and the opposition; these forces challenged the likelihood of clientelism. The prosecution of vote-buying also intensified. In fact, it is possible that the effect of the age of democracy is actually caused by the effects of changing governing parties.

However, the age of democracy cannot explain why the Philippines, with a slightly longer history of democracy than Korea or Taiwan, is still unable to develop programmatic competition and is stuck in clientelistic politics. It is notable that the change of ruling parties through elections took place regularly during the early democratic period, unlike in Korea at that time. Additionally, government changes have been more frequent in the Philippines than in Korea and Taiwan during the post-Marcos period. The reason why the change of governing parties did not increase programmatic politics or reduce clientelistic politics in the Philippines is that the electoral victory of the opposition did not represent a victory of programmatic mobilization. Since the changes of government took place as a result of clientelistic competition between programmatically indistinguishable parties, clientelistic politics persisted.

Second, many scholars have argued that political institutions such as the electoral system can influence clientelism. Candidate-centered electoral systems tend to encourage cultivation of a personal vote and thereby clientelistic competition, compared to party-centered electoral systems, such as closed-list proportional representation (Carey and Shugart 1995; Hicken 2007). In particular, electoral rules that encourage intraparty competition will create great incentives for clientelistic competition. In this regard, Taiwan's single non-transferable vote (SNTV) in the multi-member districts system – in which voters cast a single vote in multi-member districts and seats are awarded to candidates on the basis of the plurality rule – has been blamed for encouraging clientelistic mobilization strategies (Hicken 2007; Rigger 1999). Taiwan changed the electoral system for Legislative Yuan to a single-member district plurality in 2005, but the SNTV system has been maintained for lower-level assemblies. Also, other candidate-centered electoral systems such as the block-vote system for the Philippine Senate tend to encourage personalistic and clientelistic politics. The electoral system may partly explain the prevalence and persistence of clientelism and vote-buying in Taiwan. Although the role of local factions and vote-buying has declined, vote-buying still takes place and local factions are still active in many local elections. However, the electoral system cannot explain the higher prevalence and persistence of clientelism in the Philippines. The single-member district plurality system for the Philippine Congress should have been less supportive of clientelism than the SNTV system for Taiwan's legislature, but clientelism has been more prevalent and persistent in the Philippines.

Third, the level of socioeconomic development such as income, urbanization and education may explain the differences in clientelism. Students of clientelism agree that poor, rural and uneducated voters are more prone to clientelism than middle-class, urban and educated voters. In particular, the demand for and susceptibility to vote-buying and other forms of clientelism is fueled by poverty (Brusco *et al.* 2004; Calvo and Murillo 2004; Hicken 2011; Kitschelt and Wilkinson 2007; Scott 1972; Stokes 2007). As income rises, the cost of vote-buying will rise, while the marginal benefit to a voter will decline. Thus, widespread poverty due to low economic development may partly explain the prevalence and persistence of clientelism in the Philippines, compared to Korea and Taiwan. During the 1950s, however, Korea was poorer than the Philippines, and clientelism was still less prevalent as a certain degree of programmatic politics developed in Korea. Economic development can also not explain the rise of clientelism in the early 1990s or the decline of clientelism and the development of programmatic politics since the 1990s in Korea and Taiwan. Poverty might potentially interact with the age of democracy in influencing the persistence of clientelism. While the more developed Korea and Taiwan have expanded programmatic party politics over time, a less developed Philippines has been unable to do so. This theory, however, cannot explain the differences between the Philippines and Korea during the 1950s and 1960s.

Some scholars have suggested that urbanization has an impact on candidate strategy independent of the income effects (Bloom *et al.* 2001; Nielson and Shugart 1999; Ramseyer and Rosenbluth 1993). Traditional patron-client networks, largely based on the landlord-tenant relationship, are strong in rural areas, but it is difficult to create patron-client relationships in urban areas. Educational attainment may also influence electoral strategies because more educated voters are less prone to clientelism and vote-buying. Urbanization and education seem to explain, to a certain degree, the development of programmatic politics in Korea and Taiwan. In terms of urbanization and education, however, the differences between the Philippines and Taiwan are quite small, while Korea shows higher levels of urbanization and educational attainment. The proportion of the population that was urban in 1990 was 43 percent for the Philippines, 51 percent for Taiwan, and 72 percent for Korea, according to data from Vanhanen (2003). The average schooling years among the total population aged 15 and over in 2000 were 8.21 years for the Philippines, 8.76 years for Taiwan and 10.84 years for Korea. Moreover, the Philippines had a higher educational attainment than Korea during the 1950s, when clientelism was more prevalent in the former than the latter. Thus, urbanization and education can hardly explain the differences in clientelism across the three countries.

In summary, the duration of democracy, the electoral system and the level of socioeconomic development all partially explain variations in clientelism across the three countries or across time within countries. The explanatory power of these variables, however, is very limited. We shall now examine how the nature of the electoral regime (democratic versus authoritarian elections) and the types of elections (local, national or both) have affected clientelism. All of the authoritarian regimes in these countries relied heavily on clientelistic strategies in addition to intimidation and fraud when holding elections. Authoritarian ruling parties were able to use state resources, such as financial resources, intelligence and coercion, for electoral purposes. The strength of the opposition and international pressures for democracy appear to affect the relative significance of clientelism over tactics like intimidation and fraud. Opposition parties and politicians had no access to state resources and had to rely primarily on programmatic strategies with pro-democracy messages.

Whether an election was local or national also affected the scope and degree of clientelism. In Taiwan, national elections were mostly frozen during the authoritarian period, and electoral clientelism was largely confined to local levels. As competitive national elections were held with democratization, clientelistic practices expanded to the national level, and systemic vote-buying was conducted by local factions on a large scale. In the Philippines, both local and national elections were held regularly, and clientelist networks developed from the village level to the national level. In Korea, both local and national elections were held in the 1950s, but local elections were suspended for thirty years from 1961 to 1991. The absence of local elections made it difficult for legislative candidates in the opposition to create grassroots clientelistic networks. Even for the ruling party candidates, clientelistic networks at the village level were more poorly developed than their counterparts in Taiwan and the Philippines.

Instead, mobilization of the bureaucratic apparatus gave them significant advantages, especially in rural areas during the authoritarian period.

Finally, we will examine how inequality has affected the prevalence and persistence of clientelism. I have proposed that inequality increases clientelism via two channels: the incentives for the elite to employ clientelistic politics; and the large size of the poor population being susceptible to clientelism. Let us look at the supply side first. In the Philippines, political parties have been shifting coalitions of powerful families. Indeed, the central players in Philippine politics were elite families rather than political parties. Political clans were traditionally from members of the landed elite. As landlords diversified into commerce, industry and politics, the political and economic elites were closely connected through family ties. Even after the democratic transition in 1986, most politicians have been members of political clans and have had multiple business interests. An elite family helps a politician member of the family to mobilize clientelistic resources, and the politician is expected to reward not only his vote brokers, but also his clan members. This implies that even an opposition politician can command a considerable amount of clientelistic resources. Once elected, the politician has incentives to extract state resources as much as possible. One way of using state resources for clientelistic purposes was the "pork barrel" method. Although members of the ruling party have enjoyed advantages in the allocation of pork barrel, opposition members have also enjoyed considerable allocations because the presidents often need the opposition's help to pass certain bills through both houses of Congress. Thus, powerful elite families have had both incentives and abilities to maintain clientelism, and political parties have been no more than a tool for providing clientelistic networks. The historical strength of these political clans coupled with the weakness and instability of the party system has inhibited the development of programmatic politics.

Korea and Taiwan had no powerful economic elite after land reform. The opposition party in Korea was initially a party of landlords, but these people lost most of their wealth due to land reform and war. Although chaebol, or family-controlled conglomerates, grew over time, the political and economic elites were largely separated from each other. Traditionally, most opposition candidates were unable to mobilize a large amount of clientelistic resources, and without adequate resources, opposition parties primarily relied on programmatic competition with an anti-dictatorship platform. Although ruling parties primarily employed a clientelistic strategy, the use of state resources, as well as private donations, were concentrated on the top leadership. Thus, Korean legislators did not enjoy as many clientelistic resources as Philippine congressmen did. After the democratic transition in 1987, clientelistic competition initially intensified as the main issue of democratization disappeared. Unlike in the Philippines, however, political parties became stronger and institutionalized over time. Political parties were aligned along regional lines on the one hand and increasingly along ideological cleavages on the other. As party labels and platforms became increasingly important in electoral campaigns, the importance of clientelistic mobilization declined over time.

In Taiwan, most landlords withdrew from local politics after the land reform, and the ability of most local politicians to mobilize clientelistic resources was limited. Moreover, spoils from the elected local offices were limited because of strong central control over local governments, including fiscal and personnel matters (Kuo 1995: 116–17). The KMT was able to control local factions, utilizing them for electoral purposes only when they were strategically helpful; otherwise, the KMT abandoned them. When clientelistic strategy was found to be more of a liability than an asset, the KMT leadership was able to sever its ties with local factions and switch to a programmatic strategy. The KMT also recruited many business leaders into politics in the early period of democratization, but they soon quit this practice upon realizing that the negative costs to the party's image exceeded the benefits. Thus, the relative weakness of private sector players never enabled them to be main political actors. Also, most individual politicians were unable to command large amounts of clientelistic resources as successfully as the Philippine politicians who often have multiple business interests. As the KMT abstained from clientelistic strategies, programmatic competition between the two major parties intensified, and clientelistic networks and practices declined.

On the demand side, whether voters choose to support a candidate based on party identification and policy issues or based on particularistic interests determines the extent of clientelism. An important factor that affects voting behavior is poverty, as noted above. The persistence of clientelism in the Philippines may be in part caused by extreme poverty in the country. However, poverty is not just determined by economic development, but also by inequality.

In the Philippines, opinion pollsters and market researchers distinguish five classes: A (very rich); B (moderately rich); C (middle class); D (moderately poor); and E (very poor). Approximately 7 to 11 percent of Filipinos are regarded as the "ABC crowd," 58 to 73 percent as class D and 18 to 32 percent as class E. Thus, around 90 percent of the population define themselves as poor, which represents the highly unequal and skewed distribution of income, not just the low economic development, in the Philippines. A survey conducted in 2001 in the Philippines confirms that the poor are much more prone to vote-selling than the middle and upper classes. Among the respondents who were offered money for votes, 68 percent of class D and 75 percent of class E people accepted the offer, compared to 38 percent of the ABC crowd (Schaffer 2007). Thus, a high proportion of the poor, as well as a high propensity of the poor to sell votes, contributes to the continuation of clientelism in the Philippines.

In Korea and Taiwan, land reform, growth with equity, rapid urbanization and expansion of education were all factors that reduced the size of the population prone to clientelism. In the Philippines, however, high inequality has remained due to the failure of land reform, and it translates into a large proportion of poor people who are susceptible to clientelism. In addition, the weakness of programmatic party politics has reinforced clientelistic voting behavior. Because parties were originally indistinguishable and politicians frequently switched party affiliations, voters came to be more concerned about the particularistic benefits provided by individual politicians. Clientelistic voting behavior also reinforced the clientelistic competition among politicians, thus creating a vicious cycle. High inequality increased both the prevalence and persistence of clientelism in the Philippines. The age of democracy or change of governing parties has had no effect on clientelism in this country.

It is interesting to note that inequality seemed to have some impact on clientelism even under authoritarian regimes. While Presidents Park Chung-hee and Chun Doo-hwan in Korea and Chiang Kai-shek and Chiang Ching-kuo in Taiwan did not compete with powerful political-economic elites, Marcos had to deal with political-economic elite families who dominated both provincial and local politics. He had to buy off a large proportion of the opposition with promises of patronage, although he concentrated favors to his family members and close cronies. For example, in the 1984 legislative elections, powerful opposition clans in eight provinces successfully defeated the ruling Kilusang Bagong Lipunan (KBL) candidates using their own family-based political machines and financial resources (Thompson 1995: 129). The existence of powerful opposition clans forced him to further intensify the mobilization of clientelistic resources. Thus, inequality and the existence of a powerful political-economic elite likely increased clientelism even during a dictatorship.

The consequences of clientelism

We have seen that clientelism has involved vote-buying practices in all three countries. However, the corrupt effect of clientelism has not been limited to electoral corruption. Clientelism has increased political corruption during the policy-making process as well, because clientelistic politicians have needed to recoup their huge election expenses. Furthermore, clientelistic politicians have had no incentives for effective anti-corruption reform, so their anti-corruption promises have been mere rhetoric, and anti-corruption measures have not been rigorously enforced. Clientelism has been more prevalent and persistent in the Philippines than in Korea and Taiwan, and political corruption has also been more endemic in the Philippines. There have been many corruption scandals involving high-level politicians in all three countries, but the most important difference has been that those corrupt politicians were punished by voters and prosecuted in Korea and Taiwan, but not in the Philippines.

Early period of electoral democracy in the Philippines and Korea

In the Philippines, electoral clientelism inevitably produced and was maintained by political corruption, and corruption was a recurrent political issue throughout the post-independence history. Philippine politics were centered on creating and dividing rents among the ruling elite. Shortly after import and exchange controls were introduced in 1949, congressmen acted as brokers for firm owners applying for import and foreign exchange licenses (Montinola 2012). These congressmen were called "ten percenters," referring to the typical commission from the brokerage. One scholar of Philippine politics lamented in 1959: "Business is born, and flourishes or fails, not so much in the market place as in the halls of the legislature or in the administrative offices of government" (McHale 1959: 217).

Corruption scandals occurred repeatedly, but high-level officials were rarely punished. Since all members of the party, from the president, senators and representatives, down to petty local politicians, formed a pyramid of clientelistic relationships, and the clientelistic system could not work without state patronage and corruption, anti-corruption measures could not be pursued with vigor. Indeed, any anti-corruption reforms introduced by various administrations proved to be ineffective. Magsaysay's executive order creating a commission to investigate complaints against bureaucrats was hampered by the failure of Congress to appropriate sufficient funds for implementation. Anti-corruption legislation in 1960 under President Garcia had little effect. President Macapagal created in 1962 a Presidential Anti-Graft Committee, but the committee's 1964 annual report stated that it had "miserably failed to send to jail a single public crook" (Montinola 1999).

Clientelistic politics in Korea also encouraged political corruption. Since the control of clientelistic resources was traditionally concentrated among the president or top leadership of the ruling party, unlike in the Philippines, political corruption was also concentrated among the presidents and top leadership of the ruling party. As the popularity of the first president, Syngman Rhee, plummeted and his reliance on clientelistic mobilization increased, major corruption scandals broke out during every presidential election year. The government dispensed favors to the incipient *chaebol* in return for illegal political donations. Since the running of Park Chung-hee's Democratic Republican Party during the presidential and legislative elections of 1963 cost a huge amount of money, it was not surprising that "four big scandals" and the "three flour scandals" broke out or that these scandals were political financing schemes for the DRP. During the early years of Park's rule, foreign sources of funds, such as illicit contributions from Japanese firms and US companies, were important (Clifford 1998: 92–3; Woo 1991: 107). Over time, the party increased fundraising from domestic *chaebol* by receiving standard kickbacks in return for allocating underpriced bank credit and foreign loans with government guarantee (Woo 1991: 108; Kim and Park 1968).

Since opposition parties attacked the corruption of the ruling party via programmatic mobilization, the authoritarian rulers often had to promise to implement anti-corruption reform. Anti-corruption was a key demand of the Student Revolution in 1960. Special legislation to punish illicit profiteers was passed by the parliament, but its implementation was interrupted by the military coup in 1961. Park Chung-hee's civilian government during the electoral democracy (1963 to 1972) showed no rigor in anti-corruption enforcement. Since Park's DRP heavily relied on clientelistic strategies, it is not surprising that there were no thorough investigations of major corruption scandals (Cumings 2005: 369; Kim 1975: 253).

In summary, political corruption was endemic and anti-corruption enforcement was weak in both the Philippines and Korea during the early period of electoral democracy. The main difference was that political corruption was more decentralized in the Philippines, while it was more centralized in Korea. This was because clientelistic networks and resources were more decentralized in the former and centralized in the latter.

Authoritarian period in the three countries

In the Philippines, Marcos's martial law regime did not reduce corruption in spite of his anti-corruption pledge. Before martial law, corruption was tempered to a certain extent by democratic constraints, such as exposure by the media and opposition parties. Under martial law, however, corruption was centralized and restraints on Marcos's accumulation of wealth were removed. Unlike Korean and Taiwanese dictators, Marcos was not constrained by external threats either. He shared an endless bounty of profits derived from government-sponsored contracts and concessions with his wife, Imelda, as well as his relatives and selected cronies. The Marcoses became the richest couple in the Philippines and among the wealthiest in the world, amassing a fortune estimated between $5 and $10 billion (Quimpo 2009). In 1978, Marcos established the Office of the Ombudsman, known as Tanodbayan, and a special anti-graft court called Sandiganbayan. He often boasted about these anti-corruption agencies whenever a foreign journalist asked about the corruption of his regime (Balgos 1998). However, they were hardly independent from the president and were therefore unable to constrain the corruption undertaken by him and his cronies.

In Korea, the military junta led by Park Chung-hee in 1961 pledged to curb corruption, but, as in the Philippines under Marcos, was not successful. The junta initially demonstrated rigorous anti-corruption enforcement with its arrest of prominent businessmen in charge of illicit profiteering and its purge of corrupt politicians and bureaucrats. But the junta soon weakened its anti-corruption drive with the release of the illicit profiteers, and Park's regime itself became corrupt. Park's centralized political corruption did not diminish after his declaration of *Yushin* in 1972. The annual contributions by the top *chaebol* to Park are known to have increased, reaching 500 to 600 million won (about 1.7 to 2.5 billion won in 2000 constant prices) during the late *Yushin* period (Oh and Sim 1995: 253). After seizing power through another military coup in 1980, Chun Doo-hwan launched a "purification campaign" to root out corruption and various social vices in an effort to compensate for his legitimacy deficit. The campaign soon became an object of public dismay as countless scandals involving the president's extended family surfaced (Clifford 1998: 193–6). When Chun was prosecuted for charges of corruption and mutiny, he justified his illegal fundraising from the *chaebol* as legitimate political funds rather than bribes. Out of 950 billion won he had raised through slush funds during his presidency, he claimed that he had contributed 251.5 billion won to various foundations and used 567.5 billion won to support the operation of the ruling Democratic Justice Party and various pro-government organizations and to finance various electoral campaigns (Park 1996). Although Chun was also found to have taken home 160 billion won, his illegal fundraising was driven in large part by the need for clientelistic resources.

Taiwan enjoyed a relatively good reputation with regard to corruption during its long authoritarian period. The KMT's defeat on the mainland taught Chiang Kai-shek a few bitter lessons. Moreover, the February 28 incident made the reform of the party and the administration all the more urgent. As soon as the nationalist government relocated to Taiwan, Chiang launched an extensive reform of the KMT. The party admitted past errors, purged corrupt or disloyal officials, and strengthened discipline and indoctrination to reinvigorate the party (Gold 1986: 59). The reform was made possible because the Chiang regime was no longer beholden to the powerful private interests in the mainland and clientelist politics was largely confined to the local level.

The KMT regime tolerated a certain degree of corruption at the local level because it had to reward local factions with local economic monopolies and local government contracts (Fell 2005b). As the size of the businesses led by local faction leaders grew, and their political influence increased with partial electoral opening at the national level, political corruption inevitably reached the national level. During the 1980s, economic and political scandals exposed the ruling party officials' complicity in corrupt business dealings. In 1985, a political scandal in the bankruptcy of the Tenth Credit Cooperative run by a local factional leader, the Cai family, ignited island-wide anger (Wu 2005b: 260–1).

The clean image of the KMT party-state during the authoritarian era may have been exaggerated because of its strict control over the media, as well as the huge party assets. The KMT took advantage of its dominant position to accumulate a vast real estate and business empire, investing in over 100 companies, including media enterprises. It became the fifth largest business group in Taiwan and the richest political party in the world. Because of the profits from its business empire, the KMT was able to outspend its rivals in election campaigns. It was also able to employ thousands of party cadres in its central and local headquarters and community service centers throughout the island (Fell 2005a).

Comparison of the three countries during the authoritarian period shows that the confinement of clientelism in local politics enabled Taiwan to limit corruption at the local level. In Korea and the Philippines, political corruption did not decline during the authoritarian period because of continued clientelism and removal of democratic constraints.

The democratic period since the late 1980s

In the Philippines, democratization failed to reduce political corruption. In fact, the return of oligarchic democracy and endemic clientelism encouraged political corruption. The presidents' and politicians' reliance on clientelistic networks and huge amounts of campaign funds made them vulnerable to corrupt demands. Aquino (1986 to 1992) herself was considered a clean leader, but she was unable to clean up corruption. Ramos (1992 to 1998) made some progress in increasing transparency, but pork barrel politics became worse during his presidency.

Subsequently, President Estrada (1998 to 2000) was implicated in a multi-million peso *jueteng* (illegal gambling) racket, and he was forced to resign by "people power II" in January 2001. Transparency International included Estrada, along with Marcos, in its list of the world's top ten corrupt leaders of the contemporary era (Quimpo 2009). President Gloria Macapagal Arroyo, the daughter of former president Macapagal, who assumed the presidency after Estrada's fall, soon turned out to be no less corrupt than Estrada. Within Arroyo's first year in office, several big scandals hit the headlines. The scope of corruption scandals and the amount of money involved in them far exceeded those of Estrada. In 2005, the president's husband, son and brother-in-law were accused of being involved in racketeering for *jueteng* – the same multi-million peso illegal numbers game that had caused Estrada's fall. The president, together with her husband and the election commission chief, was implicated in the $329 million NBN-ZTE deal, in which $130 million was reportedly earmarked in kickbacks. According to a survey conducted in 2007, Filipinos believed that Arroyo was the "most corrupt" among the five Filipino presidents over the past twenty-one years, surpassing even Marcos and Estrada (Social Weather Stations 2008).

Filipinos' high expectations for accountable democratic governments were repeatedly betrayed by successive administrations. Figure 5.2 shows that people's disappointment in corruption control started soon after democratic transition, according to the Social Weather Stations' surveys. In spite of poor economic performance and political instability, Filipinos gave generous appraisal of their governments' overall performances: from 1989 to 2009, the percentage satisfied was, on average, 6.6 percent higher than the percentage dissatisfied among the survey respondents. During the same period, however, the average percentage satisfied with anti-corruption performance was 18.7 percent lower than the average percentage dissatisfied.

As anti-corruption has remained a key political agenda for every administration, the Philippines has maintained a considerable stockpile of anti-corruption laws and one of the largest groups of anti-corruption agencies and audit institutions: seventeen agencies led by the Office of the Ombudsman and the special anti-corruption court, Sandiganbayan. The problem is not the lack of anti-corruption laws and agencies: it lies in the lack of genuine political will to fight against corruption and in subpar enforcement. A study shows that out of nearly 80,000 cases of

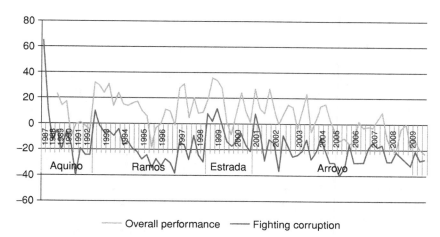

Figure 5.2 Net satisfaction of Filipinos with the national administration's overall performance and fight against graft and corruption, 1987–2009
Note: Net satisfaction refers to "the percentage satisfied minus the percentage dissatisfied" among the survey respondents.
Source: Social Weather Stations (www.sws.org.ph/).

corruption, bribery and other issues brought to the Ombudsman and Sandiganbayan from 1979 to 2006, only twenty-seven meaningful convictions were handed down in as many years (Tuazon 2008).

In addition, the Philippine voters repeatedly proved unable to punish corrupt politicians at polls. Seizing the popular mood to commemorate the integrity of Cory Aquino upon her death in 2009, a reform movement coalesced around the presidential candidacy of Benigno Aquino III. His electoral victory in 2010 seemed to indicate some hope for reform. However, Filipinos chose to elect Joseph Estrada's running mate, Jejomar Binay, as vice-president instead of Aquino III's running mate. Estrada came second in the presidential race, garnering 26 percent of the vote, despite his conviction and subsequent pardon. Even more disturbing were the elections of Imelda Marcos, Gloria Arroyo, a rapist, a cult group leader and a warlord as members of the House. Ferdinand Marcos Jr. was elected as a member of the Senate, and Imee Marcos, the late dictator's daughter, was elected as governor of Ilocos Norte. These politicians had no problem employing clientelism in order to obtain sufficient votes. Regression analysis showed that corruption charges had no significant effect on the vote share of senatorial candidates in the 2010 elections (Reyes 2012).

In Korea, political corruption seems to have declined over time as clientelism has declined and programmatic politics have increased. This trend corresponds with corrupt politicians having been prosecuted and punished at polls. During the early years of democratic transition, however, political corruption in Korea became decentralized and more widespread as clientelism became more endemic. The expensive presidential and legislative campaigns of 1987 to 1988 and 1992 dramatically increased the demand for illicit funds, and numerous corruption scandals occurred. The *chaebol*'s informal donation to the president continued under President Roh Tae-woo. In addition, the *chaebol* and many private interests often had to provide informal political funds or bribes to the members of the National Assembly, including opposition members, as the policy-making power of the law-makers increased. Roh cancelled his pledge to introduce a real-name financial transaction system, which would have made it difficult for him to hide his corrupt transactions with the *chaebol*. Later, he was found to have managed huge slush funds in borrowed-name accounts. He was convicted for taking bribes, or illegal contributions of at least 450 billion won, and for taking home 230 billion won (Mo 2009).

President Kim Young-sam launched an aggressive anti-corruption campaign. He introduced the long-delayed real-name transaction system and other anti-corruption reforms. Many prominent politicians of his own party were prosecuted on charges of corruption. The anti-corruption drive peaked with the prosecution of two former presidents, Chun and Roh, in 1995. But his dilemma was ultimately revealed when his son and close aides were found to be involved in the management of illegal campaign funds for the 1996 legislative elections and several large-scale corruption scandals, including the Hanbo group scandal. Kim Young-sam was unable to sever collusive ties between the ruling party and the *chaebol*. A series of *chaebol* failures, which started with the collapse of the Hanbo group and the advent of the financial crisis, caused him to retire with disgrace. Still, his anti-corruption reforms laid the foundation for further reforms under subsequent presidents.

Two successive liberal governments in Korea that had relied less on clientelistic mobilization were able to make substantial improvements in reducing political corruption. Whereas Kim Dae-jung's accomplishment was more focused on the supply side of corruption (i.e. economic reforms), Roh Moo-hyun made progress in political reform, or the demand side. Kim Dae-jung was less constrained by *chaebol* influence than his predecessors had been; he was also faced with the grave financial crisis that the public blamed on the *chaebol* and on high-level corruption. In response to this, Kim Dae-jung implemented sweeping reform of the *chaebol* and financial institutions; this was the kind of reform which Kim Young-sam was unable to implement. The economic reform weakened the collusive links of government-*chaebol*-banks and increased the transparency of *chaebol* management. In addition, the thorough investigation and prosecution of illegal campaign funds for the 2002 presidential election under President Roh made an important impact on the behavior of politicians, political parties and the *chaebol*.

Thanks to a series of reforms under Kim Young-sam, Kim Dae-jung and Roh Moo-hyun, *chaebol*'s routine practices of annually delivering billions of won to the president have disappeared. As clientelistic practices like vote-buying have declined considerably, large-scale corruption between the *chaebol* and the ruling party has also decreased. But political corruption scandals, albeit on a smaller scale compared with the past, still recur continuously. Many prominent politicians in both the ruling and opposition parties, including those with a reformist reputation, have been prosecuted and convicted. Even Kim Dae-jung's and Roh Moo-hyun's reputations were tainted because of their family members' involvement in corruption scandals. On the one hand, politicians found it challenging to completely abandon the old practices of clientelism and involvement in corruption. On the other, the prosecution was increasingly strict in enforcement. Prosecution of Kim's sons during his presidency demonstrated the independence of the prosecution. Investigation of Roh and his family members after his presidency led to Roh's suicide. Although the prosecution has been accused of politicization, it has become evident that no politician is immune from punishment for corruption.

In addition, the voters' punishment of corrupt politicians at the polls played an important role in reducing political corruption. The civil society organizations' campaigns against "unfit candidates" during the 2000 National Assembly elections had a notable impact on corruption reduction. A broad coalition of civil society organizations issued a list of unfit candidates and campaigned against their election. The blacklisted candidates included both pro-government and opposition politicians who had been involved in bribery and corruption scandals, violation of election laws and military coups. Fifty-nine out of eighty-six blacklisted candidates were not elected. This successful blacklist campaign pressured the political parties to exclude corrupt politicians from future nomination of candidacy in the subsequent elections.

In Taiwan, democratization initially increased political corruption with the spread of clientelistic politics at the national level, but political corruption appears to have eventually declined. Corrupt politicians are now punished in correspondence with the decline of clientelism and the development of programmatic competition.

As the KMT's reliance on clientelistic mobilization increased with democratization, political corruption also increased. In the early 1990s, major scandals of corruption and shady financial deals involving KMT politicians and government officials were exposed. Factional links with organized crime, involvement in land speculation and correspondence with illegal businesses, such as gambling houses and brothels, were also exposed (Fell 2005a). As the realization dawned on citizens that gangsters and business leaders were very much politically linked, however, public criticism of "black-gold politics" intensified (Chin 2003).

The DPP criticized the KMT's close association to black-gold politics with the following slogan: "Plutocrats rule nation [sic], and gangsters rule counties" (Kuo 1995). The KMT government was forced to show the public its commitment to crack down on black-gold politics. Minister of Justice Ma Ying-jeou then encouraged prosecutors to investigate corruption. Ambitious prosecution of vote-buying during the 1994 elections for speakers and vice-speakers of County Assemblies was shocking. A total of 257 assemblymen in sixteen out of twenty-one County Assemblies were prosecuted. Among them, 190 belonged to the KMT, seven the DPP and sixty were independents (Wang 2004a: 129–30). Chen Shui-bian's victory in the 2000 presidential election was considerably aided by the KMT's corrupt image and the Democratic Progressive Party's effective campaign against "black-gold politics." During the first television debate in 2000, Chen appealed to the voters with the anti-black-gold message: "Since the end of martial law the KMT has relied on gangsters and money politics to maintain its power. So hoping for the KMT to tackle 'black gold' is like dying charcoal white, it is impossible. Only if Abian[4] is elected can the danger of 'black gold' be dealt with" (*China Times*, February 21, 2000, quoted in Fell 2005a).

Ironically, however, the Chen Shui-bian government (2000 to 2008) was implicated in many corruption scandals. Recurring corruption scandals around Chen's closest aides and family members during his presidency tainted the DPP's reputation. The DPP came to be regarded by a majority of the public as more corrupt than the KMT, and anti-corruption became a KMT weapon against the DPP. In 2008, KMT candidate Ma Ying-jeou, long noted as a clean politician, was elected as president (Copper 2009).

Although Chen tarnished the DPP's image, it is notable that prosecutors demonstrated their political independence by indicting the president's family members, including the First Lady. They even stated that they had evidence to charge the president himself, were it not for the

---

[4] Abian is Chen Shui-bian's preferred nickname.

Table 5.3 *Perceived political corruption*

	Philippines	Korea	Taiwan
Irregular payment in government policy-making	2.7	4.4	5.3
Prevalence of illegal political donations	2.2	3.7	4.0
Policy consequences of legal political donations	2.6	3.9	4.1
Political corruption (average of above three)	2.5	4.0	4.5
Public trust in politicians	1.7	2.7	3.0

Source: World Economic Forum, Executive Opinion Surveys (2000–2009).
Notes: Response to each question ranges from 1 (most corrupt) to 7 (least corrupt). The values for the questions about political corruption are averages for 2002, 2003, 2004 and 2006. The values for public trust of politicians are averages for 2000–2009.

immunity conferred by his office. Chen was formally indicted after finishing his term, and received a sentence of 17.5 years in prison and a fine of NT$154 million (US$5.05 million). His wife, Wu Shu-chen, was also sentenced to eleven years' imprisonment (Quah 2011: 155). Chen's disgraceful exit disappointed many DPP supporters. However, it would have been unimaginable for rigorous prosecution of corruption and judicial independence to have existed under Chen's Philippine presidency. The fact that neither high-level political corruption nor petty electoral corruption is exempt from anti-corruption prosecution indicates that anti-corruption reform and the rule of law are working in Taiwan.

In summary, prevalent and persistent clientelism in the Philippines has caused endemic political corruption, and corrupt politicians are seldom punished by the prosecution or by the voters. In Korea and Taiwan, effective anti-corruption reforms and vigilant prosecution of corrupt politicians have been implemented in tandem with the development of programmatic politics and the decline of clientelism. Not surprisingly, Filipinos have extremely high perceptions of political corruption and are highly cynical about their politicians, according to the World Economic Forum's Executive Opinion Surveys (2000 to 2009), as Table 5.3 indicates. Koreans and Taiwanese also have low trust in politicians, but their perceptions of political corruption are lower, and their trust in politicians is higher than that of the Filipinos. Between Korea and Taiwan, the perceived political corruption is a little higher and trust in politicians is slightly lower in Korea than in Taiwan.

6   Bureaucracy, patronage and bureaucratic corruption

I have proposed that inequality increases clientelistic politics and leads to increased bureaucratic corruption. It does this through increased patronage in bureaucratic recruitment and promotion. Weberian bureaucracy, in particular meritocratic recruitment, is closely associated with lower corruption and higher economic growth (Dahlström *et al.* 2012; Evans and Rauch 1999; Rauch and Evans 2000). Bureaucracies with prevalent patronage appointments tend to have high levels of corruption. Hence, bureaucratic structure should be treated as an intervening variable.

Where clientelism is prevalent, the meritocratic recruitment of bureaucrats is hindered by political pressures for patronage jobs. Thus, clientelism creates adverse selection problems not only for politicians, but also for bureaucrats. Politicians with appointment authorities, such as the president, governors and mayors who have been elected via clientelistic competition, are more likely to use bureaucratic appointments for clientelistic purposes than those who have been elected through programmatic competition. In addition, other politicians, such as members of the parliament, have a variety of means to influence those who have appointment authorities, and clientelistic politicians will try to influence bureaucratic recruitment and promotion for clientelistic purposes. In addition, bureaucrats who have acquired their jobs through patronage are also likely to seek promotion via patronage. This increases their incentives to engage in corruption in order to support and reward their patrons. Therefore, clientelism is likely to increase bureaucratic corruption during policy implementation process as well as political corruption during the policy implementation process.

In the previous chapter, I showed that in the highly unequal Philippines, the dominance of political-economic elite families and the presence of a large proportion of poor people led to extensive and persistent practices of political clientelism. I also demonstrated that political clientelim has been declining in Korea and Taiwan. While the previous chapter focused on vote-buying, corrupt forms of pork barrel politics and high-level political corruption, this chapter will examine how clientelism has affected bureaucratic recruitment and promotion and therefore bureaucratic corruption. Based on my theoretical expectation, Korea and Taiwan should have developed meritocracy in bureaucratic recruitment and promotion, but in the Philippines, patronage should have persisted or even increased over time due to the clientelistic provision of jobs in the bureaucracy.

Indeed, as I will show in this chapter, the bureaucracy in the Philippines has suffered from extensive practices of patronage appointments, while Korea and Taiwan have enjoyed a reputation of a meritocratic and competent bureaucracy. According to Evans and Rauch's (1999) "Weberianness" data for thirty-five countries over the period of 1970 to 1990, the Philippines had a low score of six. Korea and Taiwan, on the other hand, were among the top developing countries with scores of thirteen and twelve. The Philippines had lower scores in both meritocratic recruitment and internal promotion than Korea and Taiwan (Table 8.4). At the time of independence, however, the Philippines inherited a better bureaucracy from the colonial period than Korea and Taiwan did. The Philippines had established a meritocratic principle early during the US colonial period. In fact, the Korean government sent its bureaucrats to the Philippines to learn more advanced public administration up until the 1960s (Doner *et al.* 2005: 336; Lee 1996: 63).

This chapter will show that different levels of political clientelism caused by different levels of inequality have produced different bureaucratic structures across the three countries. Rampant clientelism and penetration by the wealthy elite increased patronage over time in the Philippines. On the other hand, meritocracy developed over time in Korea and Taiwan. In these countries, political and economic elites were separate, and political clientelism was less extensive than in the Philippines. Not surprisingly, the differences in bureaucratic structure have had a direct impact on the levels of bureaucratic corruption.

Development of patronage in the Philippine bureaucracy

In contrast to the autonomous and meritocratic bureaucracies in Korea and Taiwan, the Philippine bureaucracy is generally considered weak and incompetent, dominated by patronage appointments and political interference. Indeed, the patronage-riddled bureaucracy is a defining element of the "weak state" of the Philippines (Hutchcroft 1998; Kang 2002; Montinola 2012). It is notable, however, that the Philippines had established a meritocratic principle early during the US colonial period and that Filipino bureaucrats had been much better educated than their counterparts in Korea and Taiwan. The problem with the Philippine bureaucracy after independence was that meritocracy became increasingly replaced by patronage. Over time, rampant clientelism and penetration by the elite increased patronage appointments in the Philippines, and the bureaucracy lost autonomy from both societal influence and political interference.

The Philippine civil service system formally follows the pattern of that of the United States. During the American colonial period, a merit system in the government was institutionalized. Civil service positions required passing the civil service examination. This practice did not exist under the feudal, subjective and politicized practices of the Spanish colonial regime. Public Law No. 5, also known as the Act for the Establishment and Maintenance of Our Efficient and Honest Civil Service in the Philippine Island, established the Philippine civil service system in 1900. The 1935 Philippine Constitution established the merit system as the basis for employment in the government (Mangahas and Sonco II 2011).

Corpuz (1957: 223) claims that practice of the spoils system had been largely unknown in the Philippines during the Commonwealth period. Hayden (1942) notes that President Quezon's executive order "Prohibiting and Restricting the Practice of Nepotism" in 1937 indicated the presence of personal, family and political influence in the advancement of Philippine civil servants. But he found that the democratic principle of promotion by merit was essentially preserved and that most of the higher officials reached the peak of their career without the aid of outside influence (de la Torre 1986: 84–7).

Article XI of the post-war constitution stipulated that appointment to the civil service be based on merit alone, "to be determined as far as practicable by competitive examination." Civil servants and members of the military were prohibited from engaging in partisan political activity and were not to be removed or suspended "except for cause as provided by law" (Wurfel 1988: 78). With the birth of the two-party system, however, the bureaucracy was vulnerable to party politics. The triumph of the Liberal Party in 1946 was followed by a distribution of the spoils. Politicians did, however, still respect the security of tenure for classified employees as a general rule. For that reason, in 1946, the spoils consisted only of vacant and newly classified service positions. The Liberal regime (1946 to 1953) was characterized by bureaucratic appointment and promotion for political reasons. In 1950, a US mission to survey Philippine conditions noted in its report: "The present system, although designed to be based on merit, does not function in this way" (Corpuz 1957: 225–7).

By the early years of independence, the pattern had been set. Bureaucratic directors and division chiefs received appropriations from the legislature in exchange for appointing friends, relatives and strategic constituents of congressmen. According to David Wurfel (1988: 79): "The Philippine bureaucracy was almost entirely subordinate to political direction, for good or ill. The landed elite exerted influence, through congressmen, on bureaucratic appointments and promotions. Bureaucrats were also beset by their own family, friends, and neighbors for favored treatment."

The Bureau of Civil Service had apparently degenerated into something like a "diploma mill." The civil service examinations did not accurately test the competence of those who obtained civil service eligibility. In fact, most people who passed the examinations were often unfit to take a job in government. Moreover, obtaining civil service eligibility through examination did not guarantee employment in the bureaucracy. An article in a weekly magazine in 1958 stated: "the Bureau (of Civil Service) is nothing more than a testing body; it is impotent against the maneuverings of politicians and influence peddlers who have the final say on who to name to an existing vacancy." In the article, a congressman was quoted as saying that "(in order to dictate or use his influence on the Bureau of Civil Service or department heads to take in his protégés) all he has to do is become a member, or a chairman, of a committee under whose jurisdiction the bureau or department falls." The congressman could then use his power to withhold or approve the appropriation requests of the bureau. Or he could ask other committee members to do the same. A bureau or department head often had to create new positions or vacancies for congressional protégés to receive desired appropriations. Some protégés were included in the government payroll without doing anything: "They would just go to the office twice a month to collect their undeserved salaries" (de la Torre 1986: 107–8).

The prevalence of political clientelism in post-war politics increased the demand for patronage jobs in the government. In particular, the provision of patronage jobs was crucial for the re-election of house representatives, while it was less critical for senators. For representatives, patronage was the "main business of politics." Congressmen spent most of their time running an employment agency. "Long lines of hopeful constituents appeared every day at their offices, waiting for a letter of recommendation or a personal phone call to a government department" (Wurfel 1988: 85).

As the demand for patronage posts increased, competition intensified about available jobs among congressmen, between the Nationalist and Liberal Parties, and between the Congress and the Office of the President. In particular, the first-term representatives had great difficulty in helping their clients to get a job. The situation became so chaotic that in 1958, the president and the Congress worked out a "50–50 agreement," whereby half of the available bureaucratic posts would be filled by presidential appointees and half by appointees of the House of Representatives. The scandalous arrangement collapsed because of public outcry and objection from the Senate, but a similar scheme was attempted again in 1967 (Francisco and de Guzman 1963; Kang 2002: 77; Wurfel 1988: 84).

There were a series of attempts to reform the bureaucracy. In 1950, the Quirino administration created an economic survey mission, otherwise known as the Bell Mission, staffed with US experts. The mission recommended far-reaching reforms to the Philippine civil service, including improved recruitment, examinations, training and higher salaries. President Magsaysay established the "Presidential Complaints and Action Commission" in 1953 to receive and investigate complaints about bureaucratic abuses from all sources. He also created the President's Committee on Civil Service, which drafted a new Civil Service bill and placed it before Congress in 1955 (de la Torre 1986: 97–102). Four years later, the Civil Service Act of 1959 was enacted. As the first integral law on Philippine bureaucracy, it introduced personnel policies, such as promotion based on a system of ranking positions – a performance appraisal system to improve employee performance. It also introduced a more participative approach to management and interaction with employees (Mangahas and Sonco II 2011).

The problem was in the enormous "gulf between formal arrangements and informal practices in public personnel administration" (Heady 1957, cited from Wurfel 1988: 78–9). Although bureaucratic recruitment was supposed to be based on open competitive examinations, a majority of government officials obtained information about their government job opportunities in private rather than through public announcements. In a survey of 127 higher civil servants in 1958, Gregorio Francisco (1960: 134) found that 50.4 percent of the sample had learned of their first government job through friends or relatives and by making personal inquiries in the agencies. Only 21.6 percent answered that they had found out about their jobs through the Bureau of Civil Service. Moreover, comparison of the younger (age 45 or younger) and older (over 45 years old) cohorts shows a trend of increasing reliance on friends or relatives (from 13.3 percent among the older cohort to 33.3 percent among the younger cohort). This comparison also shows a decreasing reliance on official information from the Bureau of Civil Service (from 25.5 percent among the older cohort to 7.5 percent among the younger cohort). The same survey also indicates an "upward trend" of patronage appointments. The percentage of those who had entered the civil service through the competitive civil service examination declined from 37.7 percent among the older cohort to 26.0 percent among the younger cohort. Altogether, 57.1 percent of the respondents entered the civil service without taking the examination, and 54.8 percent had no civil service eligibility upon entrance (Francisco 1960: 140–1).

The problem with the Philippine bureaucracy was not in the training and competence of the civil servants. They were highly trained, with 95.2 percent having college degrees and 19.1 percent having higher degrees (Francisco 1960: 95). The real problem was increasing patronage in the recruitment and promotion. According to Wurfel (1988: 80), "more than eighty percent of national government employees in 1964 had entered the civil service without competitive examination and with only a temporary appointment." The pressure for patronage appointments is also seen in the ever-growing size of the public sector. In the 1960s and 1970s, public sector investment averaged 2 percent of GNP, compared with 5.1 percent in Korea. In 1962, however, the government accounted for 83.3 percent of employment in the organized segment of the services sector (Kang 2002: 77). Typically, surges came shortly before presidential election campaigns. The increasing size of the Philippine bureaucracy prevented adequate salary increases, which encouraged many low-level bureaucrats with below living wages to accept bribes (Wurfel 1988: 80). President Garcia is known to have acknowledged the problem of inflated bureaucracy due to patronage appointments. The president talked about a governor who had 2,500 employees when he only needed 500 in order to run the department efficiently. "These men were put here mainly by three speakers of the House of Representatives. And out of those three, two of them are still very much alive" (Chanco 1961: 71).

In provincial and local governments, elite families came to dominate not only elective offices, but also appointive ones. Case studies of political-economic elite families show that provincial and municipal governments were often filled by family members or close associates of governors and mayors. Even the appointment of local judges was sponsored by powerful families, and these judges then paid homage to their sponsors. In the city of Danao, for example, the Durano family controlled all the public posts ranging from mayor to school janitors (Cullinane 1993: 171–2, 203).

When Marcos declared martial law in 1972, he pledged to reform the bureaucracy, which was dominated at the time by a corrupt oligarchic democracy. The Integrated Reorganization Plan (IRP) of 1972 promised the most extensive attempt at administrative reform in the country's history. The IRP sought to introduce structural changes, such as decentralization, standardization and reduction of the bureaucracy; it also introduced reforms to strengthen the merit system and to professionalize the civil service system (ADB 2005). Indeed, several ministries were run by American-trained technocrats. The technocrats served as contacts to the International Monetary Fund (IMF) and foreign banks, whose loans subsidized the regime. When technocrats tried to limit government corruption and abuse of power, however, they were overruled or forced out of office. Executive Secretary Alejandro Melchor was fired in 1975 when he tried to reform the military, and National Economic Development Authority head Gerardo Sicat was dismissed in 1981 because of his over-enthusiasm for the free market. When Finance Minister Cesar Virata revoked the coconut levy in 1981, Marcos, under pressure from Cojuangco, restored the tax (Thompson 1995: 55–6). While the bureaucracy appeared to increase autonomy and capacity under martial law, cronies close to Marcos were able to circumvent almost any policy implemented by the bureaucrats (Hutchcroft 2011: 563–4; Kang 2002: 84). Marcos undermined the autonomy of other state institutions, primarily the military and secondarily the bureaucracy. Marcos used his authority to promote generals in order to ensure that they would remain personally loyal to him. Marcos also undermined the independence of the judiciary. Even during the democratic era, lower-level judges had been vulnerable to pressures from local politicians. Under martial law, the entire judiciary was vulnerable to Marcos's power to arbitrarily dismiss any judge. "The court submitted to the regime to the point that Chief Justice Enrique Fernando held a parasol over Imelda Marcos during a public gathering" (Thompson 1995: 54–5).

The technocrats were important for international reasons, but they were insignificant as a domestic source of innovation or reform. Although putatively giving power to technocrats – especially in bargaining with the IMF and the World Bank – Marcos actually ignored their advice and disbursed dispensations to his cronies (Haggard 1990b; Kang 2002: 82). By dissolving the Congress, Marcos removed one major source of patronage. However, patronage did not disappear, but it was concentrated on Marcos. He awarded his family members and cronies high government positions that they used for personal profit. Imelda Marcos was appointed governor of Metro Manila in 1975 and minister of human settlements in 1977 (Wurfel 1988: 241). Her ministry, commonly called a "government within a government," was the "largest patronage machine in the country." Imelda's favorite brother, Benjamin Kokoy Romualdez, controlled the Bureau of Customs, the General Auditing Commission and the Bureau of Internal Revenue. Imelda's sister, Alita Martel, was the "franchise holder" of the Central Bank and the Ministry of Agriculture.

The president's brother, Pacifico Marcos, led the Medicare Commission, and even his elderly mother exercised control of the Rice and Corn Administration (Thompson 1995: 52–3). With technocrats weakened and many ministries dominated by the First Couple's relatives, bureaucratic competence declined and corruption increased.

The new democratic era did not produce much improvement in terms of meritocratic and autonomous bureaucracy. The 1987 Constitution provides the framework for the professionalization of the Philippine bureaucracy after the fall of the Marcos dictatorship (Mangahas and Sonco II 2011). However, the civil service system remains vulnerable to the political influence of clientelism. Appointments and promotions to senior and other key career positions are still influenced by patronage politics. Local governments are extremely politicized. Revival of the old practices of patronage appointment began with the resumption of political clientelism under President Aquino. Although the Aquino administration introduced a new wave of administrative reforms, it was largely a failure. In the name of downsizing the bloated government, thousands of civil servants were laid off. Later, however, most vacancies were filled by new political appointees, many of them from the private sector. This revived the tradition of creating new positions to accommodate political appointees. The proliferation of political appointees during the Aquino administration compromised the merit and career system of the civil service (ADB 2005: 11).

Today, the Office of the President has legitimate authority to make some 5,000 to 6,000 appointments to the upper level of the bureaucracy (i.e. secretaries, undersecretaries, assistant secretaries and directors) and to more junior levels in certain agencies. Appointees are sometimes drawn from the ranks of the career civil service, although very often they are brought in from outside the permanent service. Legislators (members of the Senate and the Lower House) can also legitimately influence appointments at the highest level through the Commission on Appointments (Hodder 2009). The Philippines is known as the only country where political appointees in the public bureaucracy extend down to the director level, according to a World Bank study (quoted in ADB 2005: 32). President Estrada is known to have handsomely rewarded his campaign donors with appointments to Cabinet portfolios, government corporations and financial institutions. Out of the sixty individuals and seven organizations that are known to have donated to his presidential campaign, more than half were awarded such appointments and contracts and other favors during his presidency. Many campaign donors to President Arroyo enjoyed the same privilege. For example, Pancho Villaraza, a co-founder of the Carpio Villaraza Cruz Law Firm and a generous donor to Arroyo's 2004 presidential campaign, was able to place his senior partners in various cabinet and high-level government positions (Mangahas 2010a).

In addition, both the Office of the President and the legislature exert informal influence over national, regional and local governments. The Office of the President may simply override legal provisions to fix the number of upper-level posts and create a new position. The president may also exert influence through political appointees and through existing appointments in the career service, including heads of agencies and local governments. Indeed, local governments are so politicized that it is common knowledge that "you cannot be appointed in local government if you do not know the appointing authority or, at least, if you do not have any [political] recommendation . . . And even once in place, the civil servant's position is not secure: when the new mayor [comes], he just tells them 'resign or I'll file a case against you,'" according to an official at the Civil Service Commission (Hodder 2009). Civil servants in the Philippines know that a senator or house representative may appoint an anonymous constituent to lodge a formal complaint with the ombudsman against them. Civil servants also recognize that legislators may launch an investigation against a department or to reduce a department's funding. Pressure is sometimes applied directly: officials are "approached by politicians with the intention of shaping decisions either on disciplinary cases, promotions, appointments, and other personnel matters, or on the direction of spending and programs." Pressure is also applied through the Office of the President via intermediaries in the House. On some occasions, a legislator's influence may even be strong enough to persuade the president to create an upper-level post within a department against the wishes of its secretary (Hodder 2009).

It is difficult to correctly assess the flow of political appointments throughout the years, but the number of incumbent undersecretaries and assistant secretaries in excess of the maximum prescribed by law may serve as a proxy measure. Those presidents who were elected through clientelistic competition have needed to satisfy certain clientelistic needs through political appointments. As of December 2007, out of twenty-four departments, thirteen had excess undersecretaries or assistant secretaries, bringing the number of incumbents to 222 when only 131 were prescribed. This is an excess of eighty-one incumbents, or 62 percent. Moreover, out of the 222 incumbents, around 56 percent were without Career Executive Service (CES) eligibility, and thus were technically ineligible to occupy their respective positions. Overall, appointments of CES officials are often authorized disregarding CES eligibility rules. Evidence indicates that the share of CES *eligibles* occupying CES positions has been declining, which implies that political appointments have been increasing. The highly politicized CES has been a key constraint in professionalizing the entire bureaucracy (Mangahas and Sonco II 2011; Monsod 2008/2009).

There were attempts for reform, but they were merely token gestures. In 2004, under pressure for reform, President Arroyo abolished eighty positions in the Office of the President. She requested that Congress pass a law enabling her to do away with excess personnel in the government. In 2006, Arroyo directed Budget Secretary Rolando Andaya Jr. to filter through the entire government bureaucracy and to purge "ghost employees" (Baum 2011: 103). However, little has changed with the ever-increasing practice of patronage in the Philippine bureaucracy. Highly clientelistic politics, upon which all the politicians rely heavily, have proven to be a major obstacle to the implementation of any serious reform. Clientelistic politics have seriously challenged the removal of patronage and the introduction of meritocracy in the bureaucracy.

Development of meritocracy in Korean bureaucracy

It is conventional wisdom that Korea's meritocratic bureaucracy was the core of the developmental state. But previous studies have not given accurate descriptions as to how Korea established such a Weberian type of bureaucracy. It was often claimed that the bureaucracy suffered from rampant patronage and corruption under Syngman Rhee (1948 to 1960), but that Park Chung-hee (1961–79) established a meritocratic and autonomous bureaucracy (Cheng et al. 1998; Evans 1995; Kim 1987). This implies that Park Chung-hee's developmental leadership played a crucial role in creating meritocracy in Korea's bureaucracy. Citing Byung-kook Kim's (1987) earlier work, Peter Evans (1995: 51–2) noted:

Under Rhee Syngman, the civil service exam was largely bypassed. Only about 4 percent of those filling higher entry-level positions came in via the civil service exam. Nor were those who entered the higher civil service able to count on making their way up through the ranks via a standard process of internal promotion. Instead, higher ranks were filled primarily on the basis of "special appointments" (Kim 1987: 101– 2). Under Park, the proportion of higher entry-level positions filled with *Haengsi* examinees quintupled, and internal promotion became the principal means of filling the ranks above them (Kim 1987: 101–8).

Byung-kook Kim's (1987) comparative study of bureaucracies in Korea and Mexico presented evidence that Korea's bureaucracy under Rhee was extremely clientelistic, but that it became very meritocratic under

Table 6.1 *Modes of new recruitment at the Grade III-B level in Korea, 1948–1995*

Period	Haengsi	Special
1948–52	4.7	95.3
1953–59	48.3	51.7
1964	38.3	61.7
1965	35.6	64.4
1966–73	55.0	45.0
1977–79	65.2	34.8
1980–87	64.6	35.4
1988–95	70.4	29.6

Sources: Ahn (1978); Bark (1966); Ju and Kim (2006); Ministry of Government (1977–95).

Park. In contrast to his argument, I find evidence that Korea's meritocratic bureaucracy was not established overnight, but developed gradually over time. In this regard, previous developmental state literature has erroneously contrasted Syngman Rhee's reliance on patronage with Park's establishment of meritocracy in bureaucratic recruitment. Kim (1987) uses the proportion of *Haengsi* (the higher civil service examination) examinees in higher entry-level (Grade III-B, equivalent to today's Grade 5, or section chief) positions as a measure of meritocracy, and he treats special recruitment as patronage appointment. He argues that the proportion of higher entry-level positions filled with *Haengsi* examinees quintupled from 4.1 percent under Rhee to 20.6 percent under Park (Kim 1987: 101). Since internal promotions represented 65.3 and 68.5 percent of Grade III-B appointments during the Rhee and Park periods respectively, this implies that the proportion of *Haengsi* recruits among the new recruits increased from 11.8 percent under Rhee to 65.4 percent under Park.

However, this finding is incorrect and misleading. Kim (1987) compares the average *Haengsi* proportion for the whole period of Rhee's presidency (1948 to 1960) and that for the later period (1977 to 1979), not the entire period of Park's rule (1961 to 1979). It turns out that the proportion of meritocratic appointments changed drastically between the early and late periods of both Rhee and Park. As Table 6.1 shows, new appointments at the Grade III-B level were increasingly recruited through highly competitive *Haengsi* rather than special appointments. While *Haengsi* represented only a small fraction of new recruits during the first few years of state building (4.7 percent during 1948 to 1952), the proportion of *Haengsi* among the new recruits increased steeply during the later years of the Rhee period (48.3 percent during 1953 to 1959). This proportion continued to rise throughout the Park and post-Park period, except for a slight decline during the early Park years. The proportion of *Haengsi* recruits at the Grade III-B level during the whole period of President Rhee (1948 to 1959) was 15.0 percent, according to Yong-Sik Ahn's (1978) statistics on annual recruits and the Ministry of Government's (1977) statistics on successful *Haengsi* candidates.[1]

The extremely high proportion (95.3 percent) of special appointments and low proportion (4.7 percent) of *Haengsi* recruits during the early years of President Rhee (1948 to 1952) should be understood in the context of state-building. When the South Korean state was established in 1948, it needed to recruit a large number of civil servants. It seemed inevitable to recruit the bulk of these civil servants from the pool of Korean officials previously serving in the American Military Government (1945 to 1948), many of whom had worked for the Japanese colonial government. Given urgent time constraints to fill a large number of positions, it was unrealistic to recruit so many officials through civil service examinations and to provide them all with training. The pool of university-educated workers was also too small to embark on a rapid expansion of *Haengsi* during the early years of state-building, as David Kang (2002: 69) points out. During the late years of Rhee (1953 to 1959), the proportion of *Haengsi* recruits rose to almost a half. This is not because the number of Haengsi recruits increased rapidly, but, on the contrary, because the total number of new recruits declined steeply after the first few years of new state-building. Thus, it is unfair to conclude that the Rhee regime did not respect the merit principle and subjected the bureaucracy to patronage based on the average proportion of special recruits during his entire presidency.

The Park regime seems to have discounted the establishment of meritocracy in order to secure the loyalty of the military by rewarding them with bureaucratic posts and to control the bureaucracy through military-turned-bureaucrats. While the proportion of *Haengsi* recruits continued to increase through the Park (1961 to 1979), Chun Doo-hwan (1980 to 1987) and post-authoritarian periods (1988 to 1995), there was a slight drop during the early Park period (38.3 percent in 1964 and 35.6 percent in 1965), compared to the later period of Rhee (48.3 percent during 1953 to 1959). This reflects a sizable number of Grade III-B and higher-level

---

[1] My calculation for the proportion of *Haengsi* in the new recruits during the Rhee period (15.0 percent) slightly varies from Byung-kook Kim's 11.8 percent (1987).

position appointments given to ex-military members. While the military junta criticized the special recruitment practices during the Rhee and Chang administrations, they soon employed the same practices.

The relative frequency of internal promotions versus special appointments can be interpreted as reflecting meritocracy versus patronage. Regarding the relative proportion of internal promotions and special appointments for higher levels than Grade III-B, Byung-kook Kim (1987) and Peter Evans (1995) noted that the proportion of special appointments decreased and that the proportion of internal promotions increased between the entire period of Rhee (1948 to 1960) and the late period of Park (1977 to 1979). This comparison is again problematic, because in the early years of new state-building, it would have been impossible to fill most of the higher positions through internal promotion, as such promotions require several years of internal experience. While the average proportions of internal promotions for Grade II (director general) and Grade III-A (director) during the whole period of Rhee (1948 to 1960) were 47.1 and 60.2 percent respectively, the same proportions in 1960 were 78.9 and 79.6 percent respectively (Bark 1961: 206; Kang 2002: 70–1). These proportions further increased to 93.2 percent and 91.9 percent by 1977–1979 (Kang 2002: 71; Kim 1987: 101). If we interpret the increase of internal promotion and reduction of special appointments at higher levels of bureaucracy as an improvement in meritocracy, this improvement was made gradually over time. But it is possible that a large part of the increase in internal promotion simply reflects the maturity of the bureaucracy. As David Kang (2002: 69–71) points out, the number of bureaucrats eligible for internal promotion (i.e. who have served at least the minimum required number of years) has increased.

Special recruitment of public officials was often subject to patronage and political interference. However, not all special recruits were patronage-driven. For example, Hahn-been Lee, Director of the Bureau of the Budget, Ministry of Finance from 1958 to 1961, often recruited college graduates and those completing American training programs in addition to those who passed the *Haengsi*. This cadre fed into the Economic Planning Board when it was established in 1961 (Kang 2002: 69–70). Although he relied extensively on special recruitments, it was far from patronage. In fact, he himself entered the civil service through special appointment after graduating from Harvard's School of Government with a Master's Degree in 1951. His application materials along with a Harvard professor's letter of recommendation were sufficient to secure him a job without taking *Haengsi* (Lee 1996: 47).

Although it is challenging to determine how frequently special recruitment was subject to patronage, there were plentiful complaints about nepotism, favoritism and patronage in bureaucratic recruitment and promotion not only throughout the 1950s, but also during the 1960s (Bark 1961; Lee 1968; Yi 1966). During the democratic Chang administration, there was discussion of allowing each member of the National Assembly to recommend two eligible candidates to the state bureaucracy. Although this discussion was criticized by the public and was never implemented because of the military coup, it shows that there was substantial demand for patronage jobs by politicians (*Hanguk Hyeokmyeong Jaepansa* 1962). National Assembly members found it difficult to help their relatives and constituents acquire jobs in the central and local governments because of the shortage of available patronage positions.

Table 6.2 presents the trend for recruitment of Grade III-B civil servants at the Ministry of Commerce and Industry; this trend is consistent with that for the whole bureaucracy presented in Table 6.1. The proportion of *Haengsi* recruits generally increased over time, from 1 percent in 1948 to 1955 to 29 percent in 1956 to 1960 to 52 percent in 1976 to 1979. It shows a slight decline to 20 percent in 1961 to 1965, which coincided with the 21 percent of special appointments from the ex-military. Although the proportion of the ex-military decreased in the late 1960s and the early 1970s, it rose again in the 1977 to 1979 period. This last change reflects the institutionalization of special recruitment from the military, which was officially introduced in 1977 and commonly called *Yushin samuguan*. *Yushin* refers to Park's authoritarian regime (1972 to 1979), and *samuguan* refers to Grade III-B officials. The *Yushin samuguan* system continued to operate during Chun's regime until it was abolished in 1988 after the democratic transition (Bark 1998; Ju and Kim 2006: 262).

The overall performance of the Park Chung-hee regime in establishing a meritocratic bureaucracy is mixed. On the one hand, the regime reduced the overall proportion of special recruits and increased the proportion of meritocratic recruitment through competitive civil service examinations. On the other hand, it increased special recruitment of the ex-military, especially during its early and late years. In addition, there were complaints about preferential treatment for the workers from Youngnam, Park's home region, and discrimination against people from the Honam region. Thus, Park compromised the meritocratic principle with favoritism because he was simultaneously concerned about the professionalization of the bureaucracy and securing the loyalty of bureaucrats (Ha and Kang 2011).

Table 6.2 *The trend of recruitment of Grade III-B civil servants at the Ministry of Commerce and Industry*

Recruitment	1948–55		1956–60		1961–65		1966–70		1971–75		1976–79		Subtotal	
	N	%	N	%	N	%	N	%	N	%	N	%	N	%
Civil service exam	1	1%	4	29%	18	20%	22	46%	54	61%	36	52%	135	36%
Ex-military	1	1%	–	–	19	21%	3	6%	2	2%	12	17%	37	10%
Transfer	30	44%	1	7%	16	18%	11	23%	18	20%	14	20%	90	24%
Special recruits	36	53%	9	64%	37	41%	12	25%	15	17%	7	10%	116	31%
Total	68	100%	14	100%	90	100%	48	100%	89	100%	69	100%	378	100%

Source: Ha and Kang (2011).

When Park seized power through a military coup in 1961, one of his rationales was to eradicate corruption. The military junta criticized the practices of patronage appointment in the civil service during the Rhee and Chang years and claimed that they were creating professional bureaucracy by establishing the principles of meritocratic recruitment and career civil service. The military junta led by Park purged tens of thousands of civil servants; most of the older generation officials who had served in the Japanese colonial bureaucracy either retired or were purged. This meant that the main resistance to meritocracy within the bureaucracy was removed. Most of the remaining officials were younger and better educated. Those who entered the bureaucracy via *Haengsi* during the 1950s rapidly advanced to higher positions, and they became the core of economic ministries, such as the Economic Planning Board. Park's regime placed emphasis on economic development in order to compensate for a legitimacy deficit, as the Chang Myon government (1960 to 1961) had declared the "Economy First" policy in response to popular demand after the Student Revolution in 1960. Park's obsession with economic development required respect for competency and meritocracy.

However, Park was equally obsessed with the security of his regime and hence with the loyalty of his subordinates in the military, the bureaucracy and the party. In order to secure loyalty, Park dispensed patronage to trusted military officers and distributed them into every organization. Those bureaucrats whose loyalty to the regime was not completely trusted found their career path jeopardized. For example, Hahn-been Lee, who had contributed to the creation of the Economic Planning Board (EPB) as well as the budget reform, had to eventually quit the civil service after his remarks were suspected by the regime as disloyal (Lee 1996). Although Park claimed that he established a professional bureaucracy, the KCIA's interference in bureaucratic promotion and personnel administration was ubiquitous. Local government officials and the police were also mobilized for electoral purposes at the expense of political neutrality (Kim 1975).

Park's combination of meritocracy and patronage was termed a "bifurcated bureaucracy" by some scholars (Cheng *et al.* 1998; Kang 2002). Analysis of the career backgrounds of ministers and vice-ministers during Park's rule showed that many ministries were heavily staffed with ex-military officials. On the contrary, the core economic ministries, such as the EPB, Ministry of Finance, and Ministry of Commerce and Industry, had relatively little military infiltration. According to Kang (2002: 87), Park created a bifurcated bureaucracy, directing patronage appointments to domestic "service" ministries while maintaining the professionalism of the "fiscal" ministries. Table 6.2 shows that patronage appointments

Table 6.3 *Number of successful applicants in civil service exams*

Year	Grade III-B	Grade IV-B	Grade V-B	Year	Grade III-B	Grade IV-B	Grade V-B
1949	5	32		1965	28	1,033	6,372
1950				1966	50	193	3,418
1951	38	38		1967	24	214	10,391
1952	16	61		1968	45	664	4,673
1953	33	44		1969	55	509	3,878
1954	13	87		1970	65	24	2,863
1955	58	61		1971	188	58	2,359
1956	11	56		1972	88	100	771
1957	7	18		1973	212		2,037
1958	27	44		1974	115	205	4,120
1959	36	54		1975	201	154	2,723
1960	20	106	2,066	1976	73	446	4,651
1961	72	107	1,643	1977	186	531	3,975
1962	38	57	2,413	1978	250	693	3,992
1963	39	236	5,535	1979	248	551	1,365
1964	24	121	3,014	1980	187	395	1,473

Source: Ministry of Government, Republic of Korea (1981).

of the ex-military during the Park period were not confined to minister and vice-minister levels, but a substantial number of ex-military were appointed to higher entry-level positions at the Ministry of Commerce and Industry. This number reached about 30 percent of the recruits through higher civil service examination.

So far, we have focused on the patterns of bureaucratic recruitment at the Grade III-B level, the highest level for which civil service examinations have been administered. While previous developmental state literature has neglected the patterns of recruitment at lower levels, we also need to examine the development of meritocratic recruitment at the Grade IV-B (today's Grade 7) and Grade V-B (today's Grade 9) levels. A significant development in this regard took place after the Student Revolution; civil service examinations for Grade V-B (lowest level) were first administered in 1960. The short-lived democratic government led by Prime Minister Chang Myon (1960 to 1961) responded to university student pressures by attempting to absorb the students through civil service examinations (Lee 1996: 111–12). It was important to recruit a large number of lower-level civil servants at Grade V-B through open and competitive examination, considering that a large number of those who entered the civil service at the lowest level were promoted in a relatively short time period during the 1950s and 1960s. Table 6.3 presents the number of successful applicants in civil service exams at Grades III-B, IV-B and V-B, from 1949 to 1980. The table underscores the importance of introducing the civil service examination for Grade V-B. Until 1959, civil service examinations were restricted to the recruitment of a small number of highly coveted elite bureaucrats at Grades III-B and IV-B. Starting in 1960 after the Student Revolution, civil service examinations became widely accessible to thousands of youths every year, opening up the wide road to the bureaucracy.

The above discussion suggests that too much credit has been given to Park by previous developmental state literature with regard to the establishment of meritocratic bureaucracy in Korea. The overall picture displays the gradual development of meritocracy throughout the later years of Rhee (1953 to 1960), democratic Chang (1960 to 1961), Park (1961 to 1979) and post-Park periods. Meritocracy further developed after the democratic transition in 1987. The special recruitment system for the ex-military officers was abolished in 1988, and the proportion of *Haengsi* recruits at the Grade 5 level surpassed 70 percent (see Table 6.1). In addition, a series of reforms were implemented to advance professional bureaucracy. Some of these reforms included the assurance of political neutrality, the legalization of public unions and the introduction of parliamentary hearings for the appointment of ministers. The rigidity of the closed system has recently become a major concern, and an open position system has thus been introduced for 20 percent of bureau-director positions. This reform is intended to diversify employment channels for senior officials and to enhance innovative and versatile leadership and expertise (Ju and Kim 2006).

In August 2010, the Ministry of Foreign Affairs and Trade (MOFAT) recruited a Grade 5 (higher-entry level) official through special open recruitment, and it was revealed that the only successful applicant was the daughter of the Minister of MOFAT. It was suspected that the qualification specifications for the job were adjusted to fit her credentials. In a few days of stormy criticisms from thousands of netizens, the minister's daughter withdrew her job application and the minister himself had to resign (Hong 2010). A few high-level officials involved in the hiring process were sanctioned. Moreover, the government's plan to increase special open recruitment and to reduce recruitment through higher diplomatic examination had to be suspended (Son 2010).

This episode illustrates that special recruitment can be misused, but also that Koreans do not tolerate nepotism that violates the principle of meritocratic recruitment in the bureaucracy. Over the last decade, a major theme in the Korean civil service reform has been to introduce and expand the open position system and special open recruitment. This originated over increasing concern that Korea's too-rigid system of meritocratic recruitment had weaknesses in recruiting officials with specialized expertise. But the case of the minister's daughter reminded Koreans that expanding special open recruitment could be faulty.

Development of meritocracy in the Taiwanese bureaucracy

Taiwan's competent and meritocratic bureaucracy is considered the key to its highly performing developmental state. In particular, the development of economic bureaucracy in the 1950s and 1960s was very important for the sustained economic growth with equity in Taiwan. Like in Korea and Japan, civil servants are respected and civil service examinations are highly competitive. In Taiwan, the Examination Yuan (branch), one of the five Yuan (executive, legislative, judicial, examination and control) of the central government, is responsible for the examinations and management of all civil service personnel. In the spirit of the five-power Constitution, the Examination Yuan exercises authority independently and, at least in theory, enjoys equal status with the other four central government branches. This demonstrates how much importance is attached to the personnel administration for the civil service.

Taiwan's autonomous and meritocratic bureaucracy, however, was not created overnight: its historical evolution has in fact been a struggle for open access and open competition. The Nationalist (KMT) government in mainland China was notoriously corrupt, and patronage was rampant in bureaucratic recruitment. The KMT government in Taiwan was initially dominated by the military and security forces, and the bureaucracy was far from autonomous. Also, bureaucratic recruitment through open competitive examinations was limited, and some special examinations were reserved for military officers and loyal party members who were predominantly mainlanders. Clearly, the Examination Yuan contributed to expanding meritocratic recruitment of bureaucrats over time in Taiwan. The percentage of government employees who had passed civil service examinations steadily increased from 10.8 percent in 1954 to 45.3 percent in 1980 (Clark 2000). It took a long time to build a meritocratic bureaucracy based on civil service examinations in Taiwan.

The Examination Yuan was established in 1930 to take charge of holding national examinations, recruiting public functionaries and running the personnel system. It was largely regarded as an empty, unimportant organization, whose efforts did little to change the KMT regime's weak, corrupt and ineffective state bureaucracy during its tenure on the mainland of China. Taiwanese ministries usually viewed the Examination Yuan as a mere provider of "qualifying examinations" rather than of binding "appointment examinations." Since the civil service examinees never constituted more than perhaps 1 percent of the total civil servants in the Nationalist government on the mainland, the examinations chiefly served as an idealistic symbol (Strauss 1994).

Even though the Nationalist government's examination and personnel system was partially consolidated in the mid-1930s, personal ties and old boys' networks of various sorts continued to be the primary source of entry into the bureaucracy. The examination successes of 1931 and 1933 were very bright young men in their mid to late 20s who had attended the better public and private universities in China. By 1932, some from the 1931 *gaokao* (higher civil service examination) had still not been assigned a position, some had already received arbitrary dismissal from their jobs and others had not yet been accorded the recommended appointment status to which they were entitled. Some fifteen dissatisfied 1931 examinees wrote a joint letter of protest to the Examination Yuan, in which they expressed their grievances and requested job security together with immediate conferral of the recommended appointment ranking. In 1935, the same group wrote another letter, citing the prevalence of non-examinee appointments in the ministries, and urged the Examination Yuan to ensure that those who had passed the exams be appointed before anyone else. The examination system did not become the main channel of recruitment into the civil service until the mid-1960s in Taiwan (Strauss 1994).

The role of the Examination Yuan in personnel administration has been strengthened over time since the Nationalist government relocated to Taiwan. Under the Examination Yuan, the Ministry of Examination administers national examinations for civil servants and professional and technical personnel. It has administered senior (higher) and junior (ordinary) examinations, special examinations, professional and technical examinations. The senior and junior examinations are administered corresponding to senior ranks (from grades 10 to 14) and junior ranks (from grades 6 to 9), and they are very competitive. Special examinations are held whenever successful candidates in senior and junior examinations are inadequate in number or fail to meet the demand of the government agencies. During the authoritarian era, some special examinations were reserved for military officers and other privileged people. These closed examinations were relatively easy to pass (Su 2010). In addition, the Ministry of Examination administered "screening of qualifications," which was applicable to political officials appointed by the President, elected officials and military officers converted to civil servants.

The percentage of government employees who passed the civil service examination steadily increased. Since 1950, senior and junior examinations have been given annually in Taipei. Up to 1983, more than 17,000 candidates passed senior examinations and more than 30,000 candidates passed junior examinations (Examination Yuan 1984). In 1954, the percentage of government employees who passed the civil service examination was only 10.8 percent. This indicates that nearly 90 percent of the civil servants were either inherited from the colonial government or were former mainlander bureaucrats. But the percentage of bureaucrats recruited through the civil service examination gradually rose to 25.8 percent in 1962, to 35.5 percent in 1972, to 45.3 percent in 1980. Most of the new recruits were college graduates, so the percentage of government employees with college education increased accordingly, from 38.2 percent in 1962 to 58 percent in 1972 (Clark 2000). The university system in Taiwan supplied a steady stream of graduates to fill positions at the government bureaucracy (Ho 1987).

Traditionally, mainlanders dominated not only the Nationalist Party (KMT), but also the administrative positions in the Executive Yuan, while the Taiwanese dominated the local governments. The mainlander-dominated KMT maintained its power through penetration into the bureaucracy, military and legislative institutions. Many mainlanders were in government service before they arrived in Taiwan, so the situation partly reflected the ROC's peculiar history (Tien 1989: 121). In addition, the civil service examination system was initially biased in favor of mainlanders. Selection in the senior and junior examinations held between 1950 and 1961 was based on a provincial quota. This made it easier for mainlanders to pass the examinations and to become government employees because they would be the only eligible candidates to fill mainland provincial quotas. Special examinations for veterans before 1982 had very high pass rates, which increased the overall ethnic bias toward mainlanders. In 1954, about 65 percent of the provincial government employees were Taiwanese, but only 39 percent of the middle-rank officers and 23 percent of the high-rank officers were Taiwanese (Kuo 1995: 40). Thus, a large group of mainland Chinese bureaucrats who took refuge on the island were occupying a majority of high- and middle-level bureaucracy both at the central and provincial government. Most of the middle-level Taiwanese bureaucrats were those who had been trained by the Japanese during the colonial period. In the 1950s and 1960s, they were concentrated in the provincial government (Ho 1987).

During the 1950s, the military and security forces occupied the bulk of the KMT positions at the Central Executive Committee, which constituted the core of the national political elite. Chiang Kai-shek's regime was then obsessed with the aim of recovering mainland China and – more realistically – defending the island from the military threat from communist China. It also indicates the weak power of the bureaucracy during the 1950s and early 1960s. The party and the military dominated the bureaucracy. As the regime placed increasing emphasis on industrialization and economic development, however, the career civil servants began to rise to the top of the political system. The number of bureaucrats in the KMT Central Executive Committee gradually increased, and bureaucrats became the largest group by the early 1980s. Thus, a pattern of party and military leaders dominating the bureaucracy reversed to a pattern of career civil servants not just rising to the ministerial positions within the bureaucracy, but also becoming a dominant force within the party. This reflects the increasing autonomy and power of the bureaucracy within the regime (Wu 1987: 184).

The development of the economic bureaucracy in the 1950s and 1960s was particularly important to Taiwan's sustained economic growth. The Council on Economic Planning and Development (CEPD) and the Industrial Development Bureau of the Ministry of Economic Affairs (IDB) played key roles in economic planning. Fortunately, there were some economic bureaucracies with considerable managerial experience within the KMT regime on the mainland. The National Resources Commission (NRC), founded in 1932 to oversee state-owned enterprises (SOEs), was an island of relatively meritocratic recruitment within the mainland regime. NRC alumni eventually came to play a major role in managing industrial policy in Taiwan (Evans 1995: 55). The pool of NRC technocrats provided eight out of fourteen ministers of economic affairs (Wade 1990: 272–3).

Although many of the first generation of economic technocrats joined the government through the NRC, the expansion of the economic bureaucracy in Taiwan generated demand for new staff. Initially, most recruits came via direct hiring from elite universities, particularly the National Taiwan University. Because of the bureaucratic independence of the early economic agencies, they were able to bypass the civil service examination process. Although direct hires continued until 1986, more new recruits came through the civil service examination process, as the economic agencies were increasingly incorporated into the formal bureaucratic structure (Cheng et al. 1998).

Since bureaucratic appointments to high-level positions were initially limted to mainlanders, the bureaucratic career path was not as attractive in Taiwan as in Korea. Moreover, the civil service examination process was partly tarnished by political exceptionalism, including "backdoor" examinations for KMT party elites and retired military officers and special provincial quotas for descendants of mainlanders. Consequently, passing the higher civil service examination in Taiwan did not confer the same degree of prestige as it did in Korea. However, entry into the economic bureaucracies was more selective and prestigious than that for the general public administration. Direct hiring from elite universities, such as the National Taiwan University, meant that candidates had already passed through a rigorous screening process. In addition, "there was no 'backdoor' entry into the economic agencies for party cadres or retired military personnel, nor any special quotas for mainlanders" (Cheng *et al.* 1998).

With the Taiwanization drive initiated by Chiang Ching-kuo from 1972, discrimination against the Taiwanese diminished, and the proportion of Taiwanese in the administrative bureaucracy increased over time. A 1983 random survey of 504 section chiefs and lower-level administrative functionaries in the Executive Yuan indicated that about 61 percent of those aged 49 and younger were Taiwanese, whereas mainlanders constituted 87.7 percent of those over 50. The survey also revealed that 404, or 80 percent, of the 504 civil servants were KMT members. Thus, even with the trend of Taiwanization, bureaucratic appointment was still closely connected to KMT membership (Tien 1989: 124).

With the advent of democratization, meritocracy developed further, and backdoor practices for the military and the loyal members of the KMT virtually disappeared. Civil service examinations today are open to the public and are generally considered to be fair. Now, the sources of criticism and dissatisfaction with the selection process have more to do with substantive rather than procedural justice. For example, most civil service examinations only employ written tests, which require memorizing tedious facts and abstract theories rather than the realistic application of job content. There is also criticism on the closed employment system for senior-ranked civil servants, whose appointments are confined to the internal labor market in the bureaucracy. Another important issue is the political neutrality of the civil service. Under the long period of KMT rule, there was never a clear distinction between political appointees and senior civil servants, and there was confusion between governmental accountability and party responsibility. The enactment of the Civil Service Administrative Neutrality Act in 2009 is expected to help to ensure the political neutrality of the professional bureaucracy (Su 2010).

The above description of Taiwanese bureaucratic evolution shows that the development of meritocracy took a long time and that there were considerable conflicts between the political pressures for patronage and the demand for meritocracy.

Causes of meritocracy and patronage

Comparison of the post-war development of bureaucracies in the three countries shows the following clearly contrasting patterns: increasing patronage in the Philippines and gradual development of meritocracy in Korea and Taiwan. Of course, patronage was not rare, and there are still complaints about patronage appointments and promotions in Korea and Taiwan. A recent scandal about the special recruitment of a minister's daughter in Korea mentioned above is such an example. However, that the minister had to resign over public outrage within a few days of this coming to light is something that cannot be expected in the Philippines, where such abuses are common and no one is held accountable.

Some of the data presented in the country narratives permit comparison of the extent of meritocracy versus patronage across the three countries. According to a survey of higher civil servants in 1958 in the Philippines, the percentage of those who had entered the civil service through the competitive civil service examination declined from 37.7 percent among the older cohort to 26.0 percent among the younger cohort (Francisco 1960). Another study showed that more than 80 percent of civil servants in 1964 had entered the civil service without sitting the competitive examination (Wurfel 1988: 80). These indicate the declining trend of meritocratic recruitment via civil service examinations. But in Korea, the proportion of *Haengsi* (higher civil service examination) examinees among the new recruits at the higher entry level increased from 4.7 percent in 1948 to 1952 to 48.3 percent in 1953 to 1959, to 55 percent in 1966 to 1973, to 65.2 percent in 1977 to 1979, to 70.4 percent in 1988 to 1995. In Taiwan, the percentage of government employees who had passed civil service examinations steadily increased from 10.8 percent in 1954, to 25.8 percent in 1962, to 35.5 percent in 1972, to 45.3 percent in 1980 (Clark 2000).[2]

The narratives I have provided in this chapter support my hypothesis on the critical role of the success or failure of land reform and its impact on political clientelism. The historical experience of the Philippine bureaucracy suggests that the domination of the landed oligarchy in both political and economic arenas, combined with the prevalence of electoral clientelism, continuously produced pressures for patronage. Due to the

---

[2] These figures seem to indicate that civil service examinations played a much larger role in Korea than in Taiwan. Note, however, that the figures for Korea represent *flow* variables (the proportion of *Haengsi* examinees among the new recruits *for a certain period*), while those for Taiwan represent *stock* variables (the proportion of those who had entered civil service via higher civil service examination *at a given time*), and hence these figures are not directly comparable.

failure of land reform, the landed elite in the Philippines was not only able to diversify into industry, commerce and finance, but also penetrate into politics and bureaucracy. The strong landlord families often influenced bureaucratic appointment and promotion through congressmen, governors, mayors and even the president. Relatives of legislators who are close to the president have often secured valued, high-level posts (Hodder 2009). Political parties have been shifting coalitions of elite families, and presidents have formed a clientelistic relationship with them. The existence of 62 percent of excess undersecretaries or assistant secretaries can be understood in this context.

The prevalence of political clientelism in post-war politics increased demand for patronage jobs in the government. For congressmen, patronage was the main business of politics. Marcos's martial law regime initially appeared to reduce patronage and to increase the role of competent technocrats. However, the dictator dispensed patronage appointments to his family members and close cronies. With the revival of traditional clientelistic politics after the fall of the Marcos regime, patronage appointments and promotions in the bureaucracy also resurfaced. Continued domination of political-economic elite families enables them to help their relatives and friends obtain high-level positions even without eligibility, and to provide their supporters with patronage jobs at the lower level of bureaucracy. Clientelism is still prevalent in Philippine politics and, for politicians, provision of patronage jobs is not only a way of rewarding their supporters, but also a means of raising political funds (Hodder 2009). Thus, politicians do not have strong incentives to improve meritocracy.

On the other hand, successful land reform played an important role in developing meritocratic bureaucracy in Korea and Taiwan. Land reform dissolved the landed elite and thereby helped to remove patronage pressures from the powerful elite. It also reduced rural poverty and thereby clientelistic politics, and it contributed to the rapid expansion of education, thereby increasing pressures for meritocratic recruitment of civil servants. Many scholars noted that land reform in Korea and Taiwan opened space for state autonomy by insulating the bureaucracy from powerful societal interests (Amsden 1989; Cumings 1984; Evans 1995; Lie 1998; Minns 2001; Rodrik 1995). However, the previous literature ignored the impact of land reform on bureaucratic recruitment and promotion, or the problem of adverse selection of bureaucrats. Instead, previous literature mostly attributed Confucian tradition and/or Japanese colonial legacy to the development of meritocratic and autonomous bureaucracy in Korea and Taiwan. Let us examine these explanations briefly.

Many scholars emphasized the influence of a Confucian tradition of bureaucracy in China and Korea (Cumings 1984; Evans 1995; Kim

1987; Lie 1998; Luedde-Neurath 1988; Woo-Cumings 1995). A competitive civil service examination system was introduced over 1,000 years ago in China and Korea. The public servant recruitment system in China dates back to the Tang Dynasty (618 to 906), which organized a regular system of civil service examinations. There were ups and downs, however, in the use of competitive civil service examinations in Chinese history. In certain periods, the government used to sell degrees or offices for money. Even for those who sought office by the regular path, there were instances of bribing examination officials (Meskill 1963: ix–x). Notably, the role of the civil service examination system in bureaucratic recruitment was insignificant during the Nationalist government in mainland China under Chiang Kai-shek's leadership. It is puzzling that the same Examination Yuan under Chiang Kai-shek's rule failed to create a meritocratic bureaucracy on the mainland, but succeeded after being defeated by the communists and relocating to the island of Taiwan.

In Korea, competitive examination for civil servant recruitment was first introduced in 958 during the Koryo Dynasty (918 to 1392). The Chosun Dynasty (1392 to 1910) further developed the *Gwageo*, or civil service examinations, and out of 352 top officials from 1392 to 1600 who served in the three-member State Council, the highest policy-making institution, 304 (86.4 percent) entered the government via *Gwageo* (Lee and Jung 2010). In the late Chosun period, however, the sale of offices and various types of cheating in civil service examinations became increasingly common (Lee 2000). Thus, there were fluctuations in the use of competitive civil service examinations in Korean history. The Confucian-bureaucratic tradition cannot sufficiently explain the development of meritocracy in Taiwan and Korea, although it might have been one of the enabling factors. This suggests that historical tradition is not necessarily a defining factor.

Some scholars have also mentioned the positive effect of Japanese colonial bureaucracy on the establishment of meritocratic bureaucracy in Korea and Taiwan. It should be noted, however, that American colonial bureaucracy perhaps had a more positive impact on meritocracy in the Philippines than the Japanese influence on Korean and Taiwanese bureaucracy. It is also notable that the positive influence of the Japanese legacy, if any, was particularly limited in Korea, because few Koreans had occupied high-level positions in the colonial bureaucracy. In addition, former Japanese colonial bureaucrats had a negative influence on the development of meritocracy because they did not want a rapid expansion of meritocratic recruitment through civil service examinations, as this could reduce their opportunities for promotion and even threaten their positions. It is also notable that the American Military Government (1945 to 1948) in Korea did not have a positive influence, either. The AMG, which was often called the "interpreters' government," relied on the special recruitment of English-speaking Koreans, especially those affiliated with the Korean Democratic Party, for the upper levels of the bureaucracy and the low and middle levels of the colonial bureaucracy. Although the AMG officially pronounced the principle of meritocratic recruitment, it administered only one civil service examination without open announcement (Ahn 2001; Ju and Kim 2006).

The role of Confucian tradition and colonial legacy in the development of meritocracy in Korea and Taiwan was limited. So, how did land reform contribute to the gradual development of meritocracy in Korea and Taiwan? I offer two explanations: first, by limiting the extent of political clientelism; and second, by contributing to the rapid expansion of education and increase in pressures for meritocracy.

First, political clientelism was limited to a certain extent in Korea and Taiwan because of successful land reform. With the dissolution of the landed elite and the separation of political and economic elites in these countries, clientelistic politics were limited. Likewise, the provision of patronage jobs in bureaucracy was less extensive than that in the Philippines. In Korea, the clientelistic use of state resources, including patronage jobs, was mostly concentrated on the top political leadership. In addition, relatively low levels of poverty and unemployment, due to land reform and labor-intensive industrialization, produced a relatively low demand for patronage jobs. In Taiwan, electoral clientelism was initially confined to local politics. Since local executives exercised little control over local administrative bureaucrats, as well as limited autonomy in policy-making, there was little scope for patronage appointments and promotions (Tan 2000). Typically, a mayor could bring only one aide into his office (Kuo 1995: 116–17). Mayors have been allowed to make political appointments of one vice-mayor and a few top local administrators only since 1994. This was the year when local autonomy was expanded in the context of democratization (Tan 2000). The rise of clientelistic politics at the national level after democratization could have led to an increase of patronage in bureaucracy. However, the decline of clientelism coupled with the rise of programmatic politics, as well as increased public demand for meritocracy, helped to limit the practices of patronage.

Second, land reform contributed to the rapid expansion of education, particularly college education, and the corresponding increase in pressures for democracy and fairness were a major drive for meritocracy in both countries. In Korea, discussions about civil service reform during the 1950s and 1960s show that the pressures for meritocracy came mainly from college students and professors. They often complained that the number of recruits through civil service examinations was too small. They thought that the resistance to their demand for expansion of the civil service examination system came from the old bureaucrats who had served under the Japanese colonial bureaucracy (Bark 1966; Lee 1968). Rapid expansion of education in general, and higher education in particular, increased pressures for democracy and meritocracy. The April 19 Student Revolution of 1960 further increased pressure for civil service reform (Bark 1980). In Taiwan, the KMT regime wanted to maintain patronage for loyal party cadres and the military, but the regime could not ignore the resentment of the Taiwanese who wanted to have a level playing field. The pressure for meritocracy increased with the expansion of education and with the subsequent arrival of democratization. In particular, opportunities for higher education were no longer restricted to the upper classes in Korea and Taiwan after land reform. Hence, the expansion of higher education institutionalized meritocracy as a norm in these countries.

Consequences of meritocracy and patronage

What were the consequences of meritocracy and patronage in these countries? Patronage itself can be considered a form of corruption. More importantly, however, patronage encourages other types of corruption, particularly bureaucratic corruption. In the Philippines, many patronage jobs were temporary positions, so continued employment was often tied to an employee's continuous support of his patrons as well as the intermediaries between him and his patrons. Employees often employed corruption as one way of directly rewarding their patrons and intermediaries, or as a means of preparing bribes or gifts for them. A vicious cycle of corruption persisted: bloated bureaucracy resulted from a large number of patronage jobs, making it difficult to increase the salaries of bureaucrats. Likewise, inadequate salaries gave bureaucrats further incentives for corruption. The prevalence of patronage appointments also increased patronage promotions. Civil servants often had to bribe their bureaucratic superiors and politician patrons to receive preferential treatment in promotion. In particular, those bureaucrats placed in sensitive agencies, such as the Bureau of Customs, the Bureau of Internal Revenue, the Department of Public Works and Highways, and the Bureau of Immigration, were often expected to raise illicit campaign contributions for their patron politicians. The bureaucrats employed by patronage were also vulnerable to their patrons' request for favors in policy implementation. Therefore, policy decisions were often skewed to benefit the patron politicians and their clients, who were usually big businesses (Hodder 2009).

Corrupt practices encouraged by patronage appointments and promotions were not rare in Korea, Taiwan or the Philippines. But differences in the prevalence of meritocracy and patronage translated into each country experiencing bureaucratic corruption to a different extent. In the Philippines, bureaucratic corruption has continued to persist in a widespread fashion, and there is still no sign of decline. In Korea and Taiwan, the gradual development of meritocratic bureaucracy has led to the gradual decline of bureaucratic corruption.

The Philippine state, with persistent practices of patronage in bureaucratic recruitment and promotion, failed to reduce bureaucratic corruption. In a 1971 survey of Philippine bureaucrats, two-thirds of respondents admitted widespread corruption in the bureaucracy (Montinola 1999). Bureaucratic corruption also seems to have increased over the last three decades. The annual number of complaints received by the Office of the Ombudsman, known as Tanodbayan, can be used as a proxy measure of bureaucratic corruption. The office was established by Marcos in 1978 and has continued to exist according to the 1987 Constitution. The Tanodbayan receives and investigates complaints in relation to public office. It then files and prosecutes criminal, civil and administrative cases before the judicial court. Not every complaint received by the Office of the Ombudsman is necessarily a corruption case, but this number can still be used as a proxy measure of corruption prevalence. While this form of statistics is not comparable across countries due to the wide variation in institutional features and country-specific factors, it can be useful with regard to observing a trend over time within a country. Since the proportion of the cases in which high-level politicians are involved is very small, this number will mostly reflect the frequency of bureaucratic corruption rather than political corruption.[3]

Figure 6.1 shows that the annual number of complaints received by the Office of the Ombudsman has generally increased over time, from around 4,000 in the early years of democratic transition to over 10,000 in recent years. The increasing number of complaints may partly reflect the enhanced effectiveness of the institution and the reduced fear of filing complaints, especially during the early years of the post-Marcos

---

[3] A special anti-graft court called Sandiganbayan was also established in 1978 and has continued to exist according to the 1987 Constitution. The number of cases filed at the Sandiganbayan may also be used as a measure of corruption frequency, but the jurisdiction of the court has changed frequently over time. For example, its jurisdiction has been confined to public officials of grade 27 or higher since 1995, so the numbers of filed cases before and after 1995 are not comparable.

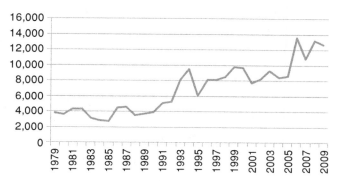

Figure 6.1 Number of complaints received by the Office of the Ombudsman, 1979–2009
Source: Office of the Ombudsman, the Philippines.

democratic period. However, the fact that the number has been continuously growing for over twenty years after democratic transition reflects a continuous, if not increasing, high-level abuse of power by public officials.

Available survey evidence also indicates a continuous, or even increasing, high level of bureaucratic corruption. The Social Weather Stations have conducted enterprise surveys on the experience of bribe-solicitations from public officials. The percentage of respondents who have experienced solicitation of bribery during the past year increased from 58 percent in 2006 to 61 percent in 2007 to 71 percent in 2008, and decreased to 60 percent in 2009, averaging 62.5 percent during the four years. It is impossible to say whether bribe-solicitations are increasing or decreasing, but the percentage is very high. So, it is understandable that business people in the Philippines claim that corruption is the number one obstacle to doing business. In the same enterprise surveys, between 45 and 54 percent of the respondents replied: "Most companies in my line of business give bribes to win public sector contracts." The responses ranged from 54 percent in 2005, to 46 percent in 2006, 48 percent in 2007, 45 percent in 2008 and 48 percent in 2009. Social Weather Station has also conducted surveys of the general public on topics inclusive of corruption. According to the surveys (Mangahas 2010b), the percentage of the general public who say "there is a lot of corruption in the public sector" has increased during the last decade (from 42 percent in 2001 to 56 percent in 2009).

Unlike in the Philippines, bureaucratic corruption declined over time in Korea with the development of a meritocratic bureaucracy. Table 6.4

Table 6.4 *Number of public officials indicted on corruption charges by presidency in Korea*

	Bribery	Embezzle	Sum	Ratio A*	Ratio B**
Rhee (1948–60)***	60	152	211	36.8%	0.20%
Park (1961–72)****	73	157	230	17.2%	0.12%
Park (1973–79)	120	72	192	16.1%	0.06%
Chun (1980–87)	116	43	159	14.3%	0.04%
Roh TW (1988–92)	82	25	107	5.4%	0.02%
Kim YS (1993–97)	319	111	430	5.1%	0.04%
Kim DJ (1998–2002)	350	86	436	5.4%	0.04%
Roh MH (2003–07)	141	60	200	3.6%	0.02%

Notes: "Bribery" and "Embezzle" denote the average annual number of public officials indicted for bribery and embezzlement, respectively.
"Sum" denotes the sum of "Bribery" and "Embezzle."
  * Ratio A: Ratio of number of public officials indicted for corruption to number of public officials indicted for any crime.
 ** Ratio B: Ratio of number of public officials indicted for corruption to number of people (officials plus civilians) indicted for any crime.
*** Data available for 1954 and 1957 only.
**** Data available for 1964 and 1966–72 only.
Sources: Prosecution Yearbook (for 1966–2007), Korea Statistics Yearbook (for 1954, 1957 and 1964).

shows that the annual number of public officials indicted for corruption (i.e. the sum of bribery and embezzlement) was roughly constant around 200 from the 1950s through to the 2000s, except for a slight decline in the 1980s and a surge in the 1990s during Kim Young-sam's (1993 to 1997) and Kim Dae-jung's (1998 to 2002) presidencies. As I noted earlier, these numbers may reflect the rigor and effectiveness of the prosecution, as well as the frequency of corruption.[4] Hence, it is important to control for the overall effectiveness of prosecution.

We can control for the effectiveness of prosecution in two ways. The ratio of public officials indicted for corruption to public officials indicted for any crime (Ratio A) has steadily declined from 36.8 percent in the 1950s under President Rhee, to 17.2 percent in the 1960s and 16.1 percent in the 1970s under President Park, to 14.3 percent in the

---

[4] The surge in prosecution during Kim Young-sam's and Kim Dae-jung's presidencies probably reflects the intensified crack-down on corruption. The ratio of the number of public officials who were indicted for corruption charges to the number of public officials who were indicted for any criminal charges (Ratio A) did not increase during the two Kims' administrations. This fact confirms that the increase in the prosecution of corrupt officials was not due to increased corruption, but due to intensified prosecution of any misconduct of public officials.

early 1980s under President Chun, and to 3.6 percent in the 2000s under President Roh Moo-hyun (2003 to 2007). In the 1950s, if a public official were indicted, the probability that the cause for indictment was a charge of corruption would have been more than one in three. If a public official were indicted in the early 1980s, the probability of him having been accused of corruption would have been around one in seven. In the 2000s, that probability would be only one in thirty.

The ratio of public officials indicted for corruption to all people indicted for any crime (Ratio B) has also steadily declined over time, from 0.2 percent in the 1950s to 0.04 percent in the early 1980s, to 0.02 percent in the 2000s. Both ratios decreased by a factor of ten. This indicates that the prevalence of corruption in the bureaucracy has substantially diminished over time. Since the number of politicians indicted for corruption represents a tiny portion of the number of total public officials indicted for corruption, the statistics in this table can be interpreted as representing bureaucratic corruption. It is notable that the development of meritocracy (Table 6.1) and the reduction in the relative frequency of bureaucrats prosecuted for corruption (Table 6.4) are highly correlated. The improvement in bureaucratic corruption has occurred gradually over time, in tandem with the gradual improvement in meritocracy. In particular, there was a quite rapid decline in bureaucratic corruption during the first few decades of state-building.

There is evidence that improvement in bureaucratic corruption has continued in Korea, even after the democratic transition, with the decline of clientelistic politics and further development of a meritocratic bureaucracy. Table 6.5 displays a couple of indicators for bureaucratic corruption in Korea between 1992 and 2008. The surveys of public perceptions on corruption conducted by the Korean Institute of Public Administration (KIPA) show that the percentage of people who assess the integrity of public officials as "low" has decreased considerably over the last two decades after the democratic transition, from 58 percent in 1992, to 39 percent in 2001, to 24 percent in 2007. Furthermore, the percentage of public servants who were punished for corruption charges out of all the public servants who received disciplinary actions has generally declined from around 15 percent in the 1990s, to around 10 percent in the early 2000s, to around 5 percent in the late 2000s. These data consistently suggest that bureaucratic corruption has been substantially decreasing.

The decline in bureaucratic corruption is also observed in Taiwan. Figure 6.2 displays the trend of the proportion of people prosecuted for corruption out of the total prosecuted for any crime in Taiwan. The figure shows a steep fall during the 1950s and 1960s. In the early 1950s, around 4 percent of prosecution in Taiwan was due to corruption charges. That

Table 6.5 *Trends of bureaucratic corruption in Korea, 1992–2008*

	1992	1996	1997	1998	1999	2000	2001	2002	2003	2004	2005	2006	2007	2008
KIPA perceived corruption	58	–	–	–	–	–	39	–	–	–	–	–	24	–
% sanctioned for bribery	16.1	12.7	17.5	16.0	15.7	14.6	10.6	11.6	8.2	11.0	8.0	5.3	5.3	3.8

Source: You (2009).

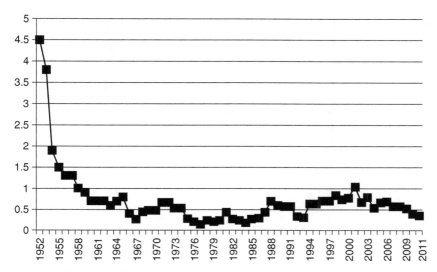

Figure 6.2 The percentage of people prosecuted for corruption out of the total people prosecuted for any crime in Taiwan, 1952–2011
Source: Ministry of Justice (1952–85; 1986–2011), Republic of China.

percentage dropped to below 1 percent by the 1960s. The high proportion of corruption prosecution in the early years must reflect the vigorous anti-corruption drive of the KMT regime. However, the subsequent drop in the prosecution of corruption cannot be explained by lax enforcement. When Chiang Ching-kuo stepped up the anti-corruption drive in the 1970s, the proportion of corruption prosecution slightly increased, but it still remained well under 1 percent. Since prosecution of politicians was rare before the democratic transition, this should be interpreted as the decline in bureaucratic corruption during the first few decades of state-building in Taiwan. It is notable that the improvement in bureaucratic corruption took place in tandem with the improvement in meritocratic recruitment in bureaucracy.

Figure 6.2 shows some increase in the prosecution of corruption during the 1990s and early 2000s, reflecting both increased clientelism and more vigorous prosecution after democratic transition. However, there is evidence that bureaucratic corruption has actually been declining, while prosecution of corruption has become increasingly stricter, especially towards high-level officials. In particular, prosecution of high-level officials has increased steeply since the announcement of the anti-black-gold action plan immediately after President Chen's inauguration in 2000.

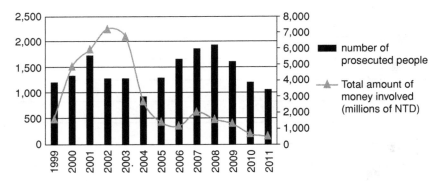

Figure 6.3 Corruption and malfeasance, number of people and amount involved, 1999–2011
Source: Ministry of Justice, Agency Against Corruption (法務部 廉政 署), Republic of China.

Comparison of the prosecution of corrupt officials for two ninety-four-month periods, pre- and post-anti-black-gold action plan, shows that the number of high-level officials prosecuted for corruption increased by 55 percent, while the number of middle-level officials increased by 15 percent and the number of low-level officials decreased by 8 percent (Ministry of Justice 2009).

The total amount of money involved in corruption has been decreasing since 2002, although the number of prosecuted people for corruption has not decreased (Figure 6.3). This indicates an increasingly vigilant prosecution of corruption in spite of declining corruption. Surveys of public perceptions of bureaucratic corruption also show a trend of decreasing corruption. The Taiwan Integrity Survey that has been conducted by the Ministry of Justice since 1997 shows that the perceived level of bureaucratic corruption (i.e. via civil servants) has slightly decreased, while the perceived level of political corruption (i.e. via cabinet ministers and legislators) has slightly increased since the early 2000s, or during Chen's term.

All the evidence from the three countries shows that bureaucratic corruption has not declined in the Philippines, while it declined over time with the improvement in meritocracy in Korea and Taiwan. So, it is understandable that the average percentage of people whose family members have given or accepted a bribe in the last year from 2004 to 2010 was 17.5 percent in the Philippines, while it was only 2.9 percent in Korea and 3.3 percent in Taiwan, according to the Transparency International's

Global Corruption Barometer surveys. If the same survey had been conducted a few decades ago or in the early years of independence, the differences between the Philippines and the other two countries would have been smaller.

In addition to bureaucratic corruption, bureaucratic competence and autonomy have also been greatly influenced by meritocracy and patronage. In Korea and Taiwan, the civil service has been able to attract the "best and brightest" through highly competitive civil service examinations. Bureaucratic autonomy is maintained from both societal pressures and inappropriate political interference. In the Philippines, however, the civil service is generally not a very attractive career choice. Aside from the low compensation, concerns about the recruitment process and promotion prospects discourage the best and brightest from taking the civil service examinations (Mangahas and Sonco II 2011). Within the bureaucracy, resentments build up among permanent civil servants against political appointees and an atmosphere of cynicism is created. The belief that so many other civil servants have the support of political backers encourages civil servants to also seek political support. Thus, bureaucratic autonomy is weak and policy decisions are often improperly altered due to political interference (Hodder 2009).

7 Industrial policy, capture and corporate corruption

Corruption typically involves public officials and private actors. It is often assumed that the corrupt officials are perpetrators, while the private actors are victims of bribe-demanding officials. Most studies on corruption have focused on the demand side of corruption, while ignoring the supply side. However, entrepreneurs often actively initiate corrupt transactions with government agents (Ufere *et al.* 2012). Thus, more attention needs to be given to the supply side of corruption (Wu 2005a).

The previous two chapters have focused on the demand side of corruption, or the corrupt incentives for clientelistic politicians and bureaucrats. We have observed why and how the combination of inequality and elections increases incentives for politicians to employ clientelism and patronage and thereby increases political and bureaucratic corruption. This chapter will consider the supply side of corruption. I will examine how income inequality and wealth concentration increase incentives and capacity for the wealthy elite to pursue rent-seeking and corruption.

I argued in Chapter 2 that economic inequality, or concentration of wealth, increases the probability of state capture by powerful private interests, especially in democracies. Higher inequality will lead to higher redistributive pressures, which will in turn give the few wealthy people more incentives and capacity to capture the state in order to prioritize their interests. In the absence of capture, high inequality should lead to high levels of redistribution, but the wealthy will likely buy political influence and employ corruption to minimize taxation and redistribution, and to seek further rents. This will allow elites to protect monopoly, circumvent costly regulations and secure preferential treatment. Although state capture can theoretically occur without corruption (i.e. through legal campaign contributions), capture by private interests typically involves corruption. This corruption is often seen in the exchange of governmental favors and illegal political donations or bribes.

In addition, capture by the elite will spread corruption to the entire private sector. As large firms and business groups have great incentives and abilities for capture under high redistributive pressures, smaller firms are also drawn to corruption. While the former is likely to exert greater political influence through both legal lobbying and extralegal means, the latter will be compelled to rely more on extralegal means, such as bribery and illegal political donations. Small firms will do this in order to compensate for their smaller influence, which cannot be obtained through legal lobbying alone.

Under low levels of inequality, or in the absence of a powerful economic elite, the private interests may not have sufficient capacity to capture the state. Incentives for the private sector to capture the state will be weaker because redistributive pressures will be weaker than those under high levels of inequality. In addition, there will be a large middle class that can monitor and raise awareness about the signs of rent-seeking and capture. Thus, state autonomy is likely strengthened under low levels of inequality. In the absence of capture, the state is more likely to implement coherent economic policies, discouraging excessive rent-seeking and corruption by the private sector actors.

Although "captured democracy" is more likely at higher levels of wealth concentration, the likelihood of capture will also be affected by the politics and structure of the state. Clientelistic politics will make politicians more dependent on campaign contributions, both legal and illegal, from the business, and hence more vulnerable to capture. It is also possible that the rich elite strategically help the politicians to use clientelistic mobilization as a means of capturing democratic politics (Acemoglu *et al.* 2011). Also, patronage-ridden bureaucracy is more likely to be vulnerable to capture than meritocratic bureaucracy.

This chapter will explore how different levels of income inequality and wealth concentration have affected rent-seeking and capture in the three countries. I will examine government-business relations, focusing on the degree of state autonomy and capture, and their effects on rent-seeking and corruption in economic policy-making and implementation. The chapter will examine economic policies that affect business interests, focusing on industrial policies that create and distribute rents to particular sectors, industries and firms. Autonomous states will adopt coherent industrial policies and administer them impartially to curb rent-seeking and corruption. Captured states, on the other hand, will introduce incoherent policies and/or administer them inconsistently in order to award rents to the captors. I will explore how different degrees of economic concentration produced different types of government-business relations in the three countries. I will also explore how the latter has influenced rent-seeking and corruption via coherent/incoherent formulation and administration of industrial policy.

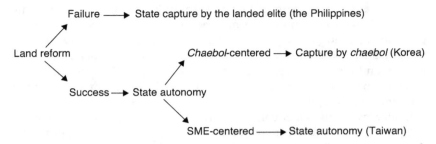

Figure 7.1 Land reform, industrial policy and capture

In the highly unequal Philippines, we should expect that widespread clientelism should lead to high levels of rent-seeking and capture there. Indeed, the Philippine state lost autonomy and was captured by powerful economic interests. In contrast, Korea and Taiwan, which both maintained low levels of inequality, enjoyed high degrees of state autonomy. The absence of a powerful economic elite and the establishment of meritocratic bureaucracy enabled the formation of developmental states. However, Korea and Taiwan diverged over time. The Korean government chose *chaebol*, or family conglomerates, as the primary engine of industrialization, while the Taiwanese government tried to restrict the growth of indigenous large businesses, allowing small and medium-sized enterprises (SMEs) to flourish instead. As a result, the *chaebol* grew over time and the Korean state became increasingly captured by these powerful conglomerates, especially during the first decade of post-democratic transition. The differences in economic concentration by conglomerates in the three countries had an impact on the politics of industrial policy, and thereby rent-seeking and corruption. Figure 7.1 depicts the different trajectories of these countries. The following three sections will trace the historical experiences of these countries regarding government-business relations and industrial policy. The final two sections will then discuss the causes and consequences of state autonomy and capture.

Business–government relations and industrial policy in the Philippines

When the Philippines acquired full independence from the United States in 1946, the national economy was primarily based on agriculture, and the political system was dominated by the landed oligarchy. The Congress failed to legislate for significant land reform, and high inequality in wealth and income was maintained. The powerful landed elite diversified into commerce, industry, finance and politics. The weak Philippine state was largely captured by diversified family conglomerates and was unable to formulate or implement a coherent policy of economic development. In addition to the repeated blocking of land reform efforts, the powerful elite interests sought to maximize rents from the allocation of foreign exchange and selective credit, monopoly protection and evasion of taxes. Import and exchange controls during the import-substituting industrialization period were incoherent. Moreover, export-oriented industrialization was delayed and never fully implemented due to resistance from the import-substituting interests. Liberalization reforms before and after the democratic transition of 1986 failed to curb economic concentration and rent-seeking despite the rhetoric of anti-oligarchy reform. Thus, the Philippines was (pre-1972) and is (post-1986) a typical case of "captured democracy."

Captured democracy (1946 to 1972)

In the Philippines, democratic elections enabled the landed oligarchy to dominate national politics in addition to local politics. The patron-client relationship between landlords and tenants could easily be utilized for mobilization of votes, and the typical legislator was a member of a wealthy landlord family (Abueva 1965). Dante Simbulan's 1965 study of 169 politically dominant families from 1946 to 1963 shows that only eleven of these families did not have land as their socioeconomic base of power (Simbulan 2005 [1965]). Most of these families also had business interests (Rivera 1994: 51; Simbulan 2005 [1965]: 305–22). Stauffer (1966) found that the proportion of House representatives with a very wealthy family background increased from 21.5 percent in 1946 to 49.9 percent in 1962, and the same proportion for senators increased from 45.8 to 70.8 percent over the same period. The landed elite also dominated local politics. Most mayors were landowners, and even the local court judges were usually landowners or closely connected to them. In many municipalities, important positions were filled by landlord-mayors' family members or close associates (Putzel 1992: 146, 162).

Unlike in Korea and Taiwan, where the landed class was completely dissolved and a new entrepreneurial class emerged in an egalitarian context, the Philippine landed elite remained powerful enough to block or water down any land reform attempts. Indeed, repeated failure of land reform was a manifestation of "captured democracy." Moreover, many of the large landlords evolved into diversified family conglomerates by expanding into industry, finance and commerce. They often sponsored family members, relatives or close friends in politics and used their political influence to benefit their business interests.

The Philippine government's economic policy-making was heavily influenced by the landed and business interests, and hence it was hard to craft and implement coherent economic policies. Faced with particularistic demands of powerful elite interests, the weak state could not implement a coherent industrial policy (Haggard 1994). The landowning elite's diversification into industry was facilitated by the import-substituting industrialization policy. Import-substitution industrialization was initially stimulated by import and exchange controls imposed in response to the balance-of-payments crises in the late 1940s (Haggard 1990b). Since the official exchange rates were around 35 to 45 percent lower than black market rates from 1954 to 1961, those who were allocated scarce foreign exchange enjoyed sizable rents. Rent-seeking entrepreneurs flooded the halls of the central bank in search of dollar allocations that would give them windfall profits in producing for a protected domestic market. Seizing this opportunity, the landed oligarchy invested in import-substituting industries and became the dominant segment of the post-war manufacturing class. Out of eighty-seven families who controlled the top 120 manufacturing companies from 1964 to 1986, twenty-three families with substantial landholdings controlled forty leading manufacturing firms in the same period. Sixteen of these families were also major exporters of agricultural produce, mineral resources, and logs and lumber (Rivera 1994: 44–52). Most of these families were also involved in politics (Coronel 2007).

Corruption and favoritism in the administration of import and exchange controls advantaged entrepreneurs with strong political connections (Doronila 1992: 54). Given the weak capacity of the state apparatus and the strong political influence of the landed-industrial elite, the controls were far less a tool of state industrial policy than an "object of oligarchic plunder" (Hutchcroft 1998: 72–5). While only 9 percent of those who started their manufacturing enterprises before 1945 had upper-class fathers, this had risen to 51 percent for those who began after 1950 (Wurfel 1988: 69).

The beneficiaries of the import and exchange controls had little obligation to contribute to larger developmental goals, and the system was frequently abused. Some industrialists requested a foreign exchange license to support manufacturing ventures and then diverted the proceeds to import finished goods (Hutchcroft 2011). The protection and subsidies given to import-substituting industrialists tended to remain permanent. This was different in Korea and Taiwan, where protection was typically reduced over time and industrialists were exposed to domestic and international competition after some period of protection. The Philippine industrialists were powerful enough to obtain continuous protection in different forms, even after the exchange controls system was dismantled.

By the late 1950s, the Philippine economy encountered the "exhaustion of the easy phase" of the import-substitution industrialization (ISI) strategy. The Philippines had difficulty with the transition to an export-oriented industrialization (EOI) strategy, however, largely due to the entrenched interests of import substitution industries. Upon his inauguration in 1962, President Macapagal dismantled exchange controls. His main rationale was to curb corruption that had been encouraged by the controls system. However, the external pressures from the US government, IMF and World Bank seem to have played an important role in bringing about the policy change (Bello *et al.* 1982: 128–30; Doronila 1992: 64–6). Decontrol and devaluation of the early 1960s could have been coupled with export-oriented industrialization, but that did not happen. The "traditional" export sector (i.e. sugar, coconut, logs and copper) gained most from the devaluation. But there was no surge of "new" exports or development of export-oriented industries (Power and Sicat 1971). On the other hand, decontrol of exchange rates was accompanied by tariff protection and tax incentives for import-substituting industries (Crowther 1986: 344).

The passage of the Investment Incentives Act of 1967 was ostensibly based on the strategy of export-led industrialization (Doronila 1992: 69–70). However, incentives were geared mainly toward production for the domestic market, assisting import-dependent manufacturing firms and inhibiting the fuller development of the export sector (Medalla 1998). Even with the enactment of the Export Processing Zone Act of 1969 and Export Incentives Act of 1970, meaningful implementation of export-oriented industrialization strategy was not taking place.

Another important area into which the landed oligarchy found an opportunity to diversify was the financial sector. While the landed elites diversified into industrial ventures during the 1950s, they diversified into financial ventures in the 1960s. Unlike in Korea and Taiwan, where the government owned and controlled the commercial banks, nearly all major families in the Philippines took advantage of incentives to establish new private banks. In the early 1950s, the banking sector was dominated by foreign and government banks, but private banks became more central over time. In particular, the number of private commercial banks increased rapidly during the early 1960s, from thirteen in 1960 to thirty-three in 1965. Whereas in Korea and Taiwan the government used the banks to provide the firms with financial incentives for coherent implementation of industrial policy, the outcome in the Philippines was exactly the opposite. In essence, government resources were made available to the family-based banks, and their owners could freely milk the loan portfolios for the benefit of diversified family conglomerates (Hutchcroft 2011). A major source of rents for the family-controlled commercial banks related to loans from the Central Bank. Since real discount rates (the rate at which the Central Bank made loans to commercial and government-owned banks) were often negative, the Central Bank was subsidizing the banks and their borrowers through its rediscount facility (Montinola 2012). The dominance of landed-industrial-financial family conglomerates and the weak supervisory capacity of the Central Bank led to serious abuses as well as bank failures. Prominent cases of bank failures show some important patterns, such as the milking of bank loans to support related family enterprises, the Central Bank's weak capacity to prosecute bank owners for abuses because of political pressures, and even capture of the courts by the powerful private interests (Hutchcroft 1998: 95–101).

The strong power of the landlords and the diversified family conglomerates together with the weakness of the state were reflected in the political economy of taxation. High income inequality should have led to progressive taxes and transfers in the absence of capture by the rich elite. Indeed, marginal income tax rates were high, but collection rates were very low. The corporate tax code was riddled with special exemptions (Haggard 1990b: 228). A study of tax burden by income class revealed the regressive nature of the Philippine taxation system. In 1960, families with an annual income of less than 500 pesos paid 23 percent of their income in taxes, mostly indirectly, whereas families with income between 5,000 and 10,000 pesos paid less than 15 percent. Evasion in higher brackets was extremely widespread, rendering the accuracy of any figures suspect. "Potential taxpayers in the upper brackets found it easy to buy their way out of a heavy assessment, either by bribing the tax collector or by making a campaign contribution to his patron, usually in Congress" (Wurfel 1988: 56).

The Philippine state lacked any clear vision for economic development, and the weak state was continuously captured by the powerful rent-seeking oligarchic interests. Import and exchange controls as well as credit subsidies were major sources of rents for the oligarchic elites in the pre-martial law period of captured democracy. The landed elite transformed into more diversified conglomerates based on commerce, industry, finance and land. In addition to the highly skewed distribution of land, the ownership of business corporations was even more heavily concentrated. Of 1,511 corporations with assets of over half a million pesos in the early 1970s, 5 percent of the stockholding families controlled 60.7 percent of the assets; the top 10 percent controlled 77.6 percent. The top fifty corporations in income earned 78 percent of the total income out of the top 1,000 in 1970 (Wurfel 1988, 55–6). Unlike the Korean *chaebol* and Taiwanese business groups, most major Philippine family conglomerates clustered their firms around a commercial bank, which provided the affiliated firms with financing. In addition, interlocking seats on the boards of multiple firms and banks gave a small group of individuals control over a large number of corporations. In this manner, a family could create a diversified group, remaining behind the scenes (Kang 2002: 136).

Predatory regime and the failed EOI (1972 to 1986)

There was both change and continuity in the nature of business-government relations after the declaration of martial law. When Marcos declared martial law to "save the country from an oligarchy that appropriated for itself all power and bounty" (Marcos 1974: 6) in 1972, some economists welcomed the move in spite of its authoritarian nature. The first director of the National Economic Development Authority (NEDA), economist Gerardo P. Sicat, defended martial law as a progressive "revolution from the top." Martial law would arrest the "social cancer" of the "false democracy" dominated by the oligarchy. Robert Stauffer argued that the declaration of martial law was a prerequisite for a new, more outward-oriented development strategy (Haggard 1990b). With the declaration of martial law, the relationship between the state and the traditional oligarchy shifted in favor of the state. Thus, captured democracy of the pre-martial law era turned into a predatory authoritarian regime. Despite Marcos's pledge of anti-oligarchy reform, however, the oligarchic structure of the economy did not change under the martial law regime. Only the composition of the oligarchy changed, with the rise of a number of new conglomerates controlled by Marcos's cronies. Family conglomerates continued to expand in the import-substitution industry sector as well as the newly promoted EOI sector. The state resources were plundered by the powerful oligarchy, in particular Marcos's cronies, and the weak state bureaucracy did not have coherent development strategies (Hutchcroft 1991).

In fact, continuity in economic policy turned out to be greater between the pre- and post-martial law periods than Sicat and Stauffer had expected. The promised land reform did not materialize, except for the partial implementation mainly targeted toward Marcos's political enemies (see Chapter 4 for details). An export-oriented industrialization strategy became the official economic policy of the country under the

martial law regime (Ofreneo 1984), but EOI was not coherently implemented. There was renewed emphasis and promotion of exports, but at
the same time continued protection of ISI firms (de Dios and Hutchcroft
2003). In fact, the number of quantitative restrictions on imports doubled from 1970 to 1980 (World Bank 1993). Import-substituting interests were strongly supportive of the martial law regime (Haggard 1990b).
In particular, the non-landed capitalists who were more dependent on
state resources than the landed capitalists developed close ties with the
Marcos regime and advocated for continued protection for ISI industries.

The introduction of EOI was largely a result of pressures from the
World Bank and IMF. The government's commitment to export promotion was limited, and export-processing zones remained as enclaves
within an inward-oriented economy. The ratio of total exports to GDP
increased only marginally from 13.1 percent in 1972 to 16.4 percent in
1980 (World Bank 1987). Moreover, the failed EOI was a major con-
tributor to the country's snowballing foreign debt problem that exploded
in the early 1980s (Bello et al. 1982: 156). The provision of export subsidies rewarded the already established family conglomerates as well as
Marcos's cronies, lacking clear and consistent criteria based on export
performance. Thus, the non-traditional export sector became just one
more avenue of diversification for the major family conglomerates to
pursue (Hutchcroft 2011).

Return of captured democracy and liberalization reforms (1986 to present)

The political dominance by the economic elite continued even after the
democratic transition of 1986. The May 1987 congressional elections
produced a return of the traditional elite. Consistent with the results
of previous Philippine elections, between one-half and three-quarters of
the congressmen were landowners (Riedinger 1995: 115). A number
of political families had their roots in hacienda wealth, and 58 percent
of the members of the 9th House (1992 to 1995) were still agricultural
landowners. The percentage of agricultural landowners decreased to 39
percent in the 12th House (2001 to 2004), but most post-Marcos representatives had multiple business interests. Approximately half of the representatives were involved in property development and real estate. One-
third of legislators were in trading, nearly a quarter in manufacturing, and
a quarter in the restaurant, travel and leisure business. Only a small percentage of representatives had no business interests. Overall, post-Marcos
congressmen tend to be richer than pre-Marcos legislators. Comparison of the socioeconomic status of House representatives in 1962 and

1992 shows that the percentage of representatives from the upper class increased from 27.6 percent in 1962 to 44 percent in 1992. On the other hand, the percentages of those in the upper middle class (from 62.1 to 49.2 percent) and lower middle class (from 10.3 to 6.6 percent) decreased during the same period, according to Coronel (2004b).

Democratization brought popular demand for progressive socioeconomic reforms, including land reform, but the large landlords and the diversified family conglomerates that dominated the Philippine economy had no problem with exerting political influence through their kin and friends in Congress. Although President Aquino (1986 to 1992) pledged to carry out "genuine" agrarian reform, the Comprehensive Agrarian Reform Law of 1988 enacted by the landowner-dominated Congress was below the expectations of peasants. Under the new law, the landowner retention limit was set to 5 hectares, but there were exceptions to the limit. The law guaranteed full market compensation to landlords, in a combination of cash and bonds. The law would be implemented over a period of ten years. While it would initially cover just the public lands and large private holdings, it would leave the majority of lands until the end of the program (Putzel 1992: 272–5; Riedinger 1995: 139–76).

Economic liberalization reform has been implemented by democratic governments often with the rhetoric of anti-oligarchic reform. However, the oligarchic family conglomerates still dominate the Philippine economy, and most economic sectors still lack competition, encouraging collusion and corrupt rent-seeking. In fact, liberalization reform started in the early 1980s. By the end of 1970s, the failure of EOI and crony abuse became apparent. The World Bank and IMF responded by applying pressure for major liberalizing reform in trade and finance. Gradual tariff reduction and the relaxation of quantitative restrictions were set as conditions for a series of structural adjustment loans granted by the World Bank beginning in 1980. The Marcos regime had to accept liberalization measures imposed by the Bretton Woods institutions, and the democratic governments of Aquino and Ramos continued to implement liberalization. Protectionist trade policy was liberalized substantially during the 1980s and 1990s. Effective protection rates steadily declined from 49 percent in 1985 to 29 percent in 1990 to 6 percent in 2004 (Aldaba 2005). Financial liberalization in the early 1980s included gradual liberalization of interest rates and deregulation on a range of financial operations. Further financial reforms took place under democratic governments. While proponents of liberalizing reform argued that liberalization would lead to increased efficiency in resource allocation and ameliorate the dominance of the oligarchy, the outcome of liberalization reform has not been very encouraging. The country's economy still suffers from high inequality and poverty, and its economic growth has been lower than its Southeast Asian neighbors. In 2006, the poverty incidence was 32.9 percent for the population and 26.9 percent for families at the official poverty line (Canlas *et al.* 2009).

A series of financial reforms failed to increase competition in the banking sector that had been long dominated by a few large commercial banks. The Ramos government rehabilitated the weakened Central Bank. A new central bank, Bangko Sentral ng Pilipinas (BSP), was created in 1993, but it did little to resolve the weakness of supervisory capacity. Reforms during the early 1990s included the deregulation of entry for new domestic banks as well as the easing of restriction on the entry of foreign banks. As a result, the number of commercial banks expanded from thirty-two in 1993 to forty-seven in 1996 (Hutchcroft 1998: 218). However, the asset share of the five largest commercial banks that had stayed around 50 percent until 1993 declined to about 37 percent in 1997, but this trend was reversed, reaching around 50 percent again by 2000. The mergers and acquisitions in the late 1990s resulted in increasing concentration, and the oligopolistic structure of the banking sector has not changed (Milo 2002; Pasadilla and Milo 2005).

A particularly robust liberalization reform, the General Banking Law of 2000, proved unable to change the oligopolistic structure of the financial sector in the Philippines because of the strong lobby from those being regulated. After the East Asian financial crisis highlighted the importance of prudent regulations, additional reform was introduced with the enactment of this new law (RA 8791). The limits on loans to directors, officers, stockholders and related interests (DOSRI loans) were tightened, by requiring them to be approved by a majority of directors of the bank. The new law also required inclusion of two independent directors in a bank's board. However, the ownership ceilings became less restrictive, now limited to 40 percent up from the previous 20 percent limit (Milo 2002). It is questionable whether a 40 percent limit will be enough to prevent the banks from being effectively controlled by a single family conglomerate or an alliance of such conglomerates. In contrast, the ownership limit for banks is 9 percent in Korea and 15 percent in Taiwan. In the Philippines, family conglomerates are typically organized around a commercial bank, which provides the affiliated firms with loans. Of the top ten private banks in 1986, six were controlled by landed-capitalist families (Rivera 1994). At the time of the East Asian financial crisis, some commentators argued that the Philippines escaped the crisis because of the robust financial system due to its earlier reforms. The truth, however, lies in the lack of capital inflow due to the country's unattractiveness to foreign investors, which made the Philippines less vulnerable than its neighbors to sudden capital outflow that could cause a currency crisis (Hicken 2008). Today, the inefficient financial sector in the Philippines is still regarded as one of the weaknesses for development.[1]

One of the major problems in economic governance in the Philippines is the weak tax collection and accumulated fiscal deficits, which benefit the most powerful and wealthy families. Of the ten companies that registered the largest tax-exempt projects with the Board of Investment (BOI), seven are owned, controlled or run by some of the Philippines' best-known family-based conglomerates (i.e. the Lopezes, Ayalas, Gokongweis and Cojuangcos). Not one of the top ten is just an exporter, and all cater to domestic customers in the oligopolistic markets dominated by just a few players. Congress, beholden to the large, rich corporations, has been unable to fix the tax system. Instead, some provisions of the Comprehensive Tax Reform Law of 1997 allowed significant exemptions to large corporations and high-income individuals. These loopholes further contributed to the decline in the tax collection (Canlas et al. 2009: 61). The fiscal incentive system to promote investments for export-oriented industrialization has been seriously abused since the Marcos years. The democratic governments have been unable to fix it, and the abuse has been increasing. According to a report by the Philippine Center for Investigative Journalism (PCIJ) (Landingin 2006), the amount of tax and duty exemptions granted under various fiscal incentives laws increased, reaching 47.9 percent of the national government revenue, or 7 percent of GDP in 2003. It is estimated that up to 90 percent of the tax and duty exemptions granted by the BOI are "redundant," as these have gone to companies selling goods and services to domestic customers rather than the export market. According to former economic planning secretary Felipe Medalla, each of his three attempts to limit tax and duty exemptions between 1986 and 1999 failed. Although another bill was proposed by a senator to fix the fiscal incentives system in July 2006 right after the publication of the PCIJ report, the bill is still pending as of February 2013 in the Senate without any deliberation (Senate of the Philippines website).

Privatization of government monopoly often led to the privatization of monopoly rents in the absence of genuine competition. Powerful conglomerates also frequently lobbied the government to delay or limit the

[1] The World Economic Forum's *Financial Development Report* ranked the Philippines fiftieth out of fifty-seven countries in 2010 and forty-fourth out of sixty countries in 2011, while it ranked Korea twenty-fourth and eighteenth in 2010 and 2011, respectively. Taiwan was not included in the report. The World Bank's *Doing Business* report in 2012 gave the Philippines a 126th place out of 183 countries in "getting credit" rank, while Korea was placed eighth and Taiwan sixty-seventh.

deregulation of entry and to curb effective competition. Liberalization reform, such as the privatization of state-owned enterprises and the deregulation of entry, has been implemented in many economic sectors since the 1980s. However, deregulation has failed to produce competitive markets in most sectors of the economy. The domestic manufacturing sector as well as the key service sector still remain largely oligopolistic, resulting in high price-cost margins. Overall, economic liberalization during the last three decades has neither reduced wealth concentration by diversified family conglomerates nor enhanced market competition.

Business-government relations and industrial policy in Korea

The complete dissolution of the landed elite and the absence of powerful industrial capitalists provided favorable conditions for state autonomy in Korea. In addition, the gradual development of a meritocratic bureaucracy further enhanced state autonomy as well as state capacity. Thus, Korea was able to establish a developmental state, and its industrial policy was relatively coherent in the absence of a strong economic elite. However, Park Chung-hee's industrialization strategy favored large conglomerates, and economic concentration increased over time. As a result, Korea's industrial policy became increasingly more subject to capture by the *chaebol*, especially after democratic transition in 1987. The Korean state restored its autonomy in the aftermath of the East Asian financial crisis of 1997 and implemented sweeping reforms to tame the *chaebol*, but the *chaebol*'s political influence and economic domination have recently become a major public concern once again.

State autonomy and a shift from ISI to EOI

Unlike in the Philippines, the landed elite were unable to block land reform legislation, largely because of the communist threat from North Korea, as well as popular demand for redistribution of agrarian land. The leveling effect of land reform was further intensified by the Korean War (1950 to 1953), as it destroyed a substantial share of industrial and commercial properties. Most landlords not only lost land, but were also unable to transform themselves into industrial capitalists. Although family conglomerates, or *chaebol*, were gradually formed, their political influence was weak. Therefore, there was no powerful economic elite that could capture the state.

Korea's industrial policy was focused on import substitution during the 1950s, which provided many *chaebols* with an initial base for control.

Chronic balance-of-payments difficulties and President Rhee's desire to build up a self-sufficient national economy led to an import substitution industrialization strategy (Haggard 1990a). The Korean government maintained import restrictions and highly overvalued exchange rates. The allocation of import quotas that accompanied foreign exchange allocation entailed substantial rent. Importers received windfall gains and prospered; some of the Korean *chaebol* were formed during this period as major recipients of this rent. In addition, the sale of vested properties, formerly Japanese-owned industrial properties taken over by the American Military Government and subsequently transferred to the Rhee government, allocation of aid goods and access to bank loans were major instruments of industrial policy (Woo 1991: 59). The sale of vested properties favored politically well-connected people as well as interim plant managers. The Rhee government set the price of the properties at 25 to 30 percent of the market value and offered the new owners generous installment plans. In return for their windfall gains, the new owners of these properties provided kickbacks to Rhee's Liberal Party. Vested properties provided the initial base for many *chaebols* (Lim 2003: 42). As a result, a new class of industrial capitalists was emerging, but many Koreans viewed them negatively as "illicit profiteers" who colluded with the government.

Korea's shift to export-oriented industrialization strategy in the 1960s was primarily caused by external pressures. The first five-year economic development plan (1962 to 1966), which had first been drafted during the late Rhee years, was amended under the short-lived Chang Myon administration (1960 to 1961) and finalized under Park Chung-hee's military rule in 1961. It did not envision an EOI strategy, but instead emphasized a "self-reliant national economy" through ISI strategy (Lie 1998: 55–6). Declining aid commitments and increasing pressures for policy reform from the United States forced Park to move toward an export promotion strategy (Haggard 1990a: 69–70). Unlike in the Philippines, there was no resistance to the shift to EOI strategy from the weak private sector. The ISI firms and *chaebol* in Korea in the 1960s did not have much political influence. The Korean state enjoyed nearly complete autonomy in economic policy-making despite the existence of corrupt exchanges between the government and the businesses.

The EOI strategy involved both macro-level and micro-level reforms that further decreased the potential for elite capture. At the level of macroeconomic policy, devaluation of Korean currency and interest-rate reform were important (Haggard 1990a: 70). At the micro-level, various interventions were devised and implemented to promote investment and exports. The government strengthened its control over the financial system by nationalizing commercial banks and by subordinating the Bank of Korea to a position underneath the government. The government used credit allocation as the major policy instrument. Despite the interest rate reform, bank interest rates were still substantially lower than market rates, and the allocation of underpriced bank credit produced substantial rent. In particular, the interest rate on export loans was heavily subsidized. When the interest rate on general loans increased to 26 percent in 1965, the export loan rate remained at 6.5 percent (Cho 1997).

Foreign capital also helped to strengthen the state in Korea at this time. In order to compensate for the shortage of domestic capital and declining foreign aid, the government normalized its relations with Japan in 1965 and allowed state-owned banks to guarantee foreign borrowing by the private sector. Each foreign loan had to be approved and allocated by the government, and foreign loans were used selectively to support industrial policy goals. By providing export industries with domestic credit as well as foreign loan guarantees, the government formed a risk partnership with the business, sharing investment risks of the private sector (Lim 2003). However, the Park government's partnership with the business was not based on an equal standing. The business sector was too weak to wield power, and the government was in a commanding position.

While the rents associated with foreign exchange allocation were all but eliminated, the rents associated with domestic credit allocation and foreign loans were substantial (Cho 1997). The Park regime needed political funds to maintain its political machines. It became a common practice that recipients of foreign loans with low interest rates paid a commission of 10 to 15 percent in illicit political contributions to Park's Democratic Republican Party (Woo 1991: 108). It is notable that the military junta's anti-corruption rhetoric was quickly weakened to forge a partnership with the business elite for industrialization and economic development. Cultivating good relationships with the president became a golden road for business expansion under Park Chung-hee and subsequent presidents. Chung Joo-young of Hyundai and Kim Wu-joong of Daewoo had close personal links with Park Chung-hee and received extensive support (Moran 1999). On the other hand, Samhak, a major distillery and one of the largest Korean conglomerates in the late 1960s, faced misfortune because the owner backed Kim Dae-jung in the 1971 presidential election. After the election, Samhak was convicted of tax evasion and forced into bankruptcy (Lie 1998: 90–1).

However, there were substantial differences in the importance of rent-seeking and corruption between import substitution and export-oriented industrialization strategies (You 2012b). Under an import substitution policy, government protection and favors were decisive for the profitability of businesses. Under an export-oriented policy, however, firms had to compete in foreign markets. Although various forms of favors and subsidies helped the firms to compete in foreign markets, productivity and competitiveness became increasingly important. In order to promote exports, the government disciplined the firms with favors based on export performance rather than clientelistic criteria. For example, the short-term export credit system was streamlined as early as 1960, with the automatic approval of loans to those with an export letter of credit (Choi 1993). Park tolerated a certain degree of corruption in order to mobilize clientelistic resources, but he nevertheless maintained autonomy in formulating and implementing coherent industrial policy.

Park's strategy of chaebol-centered HCI

Although the Park regime maintained state autonomy vis-à-vis the private sector, Park favored large firms and *chaebol* as an engine of industrialization. For him, modernization and industrialization meant emulating Japan, including the pre-war "*zaibatsu*," or family conglomerates. His authoritarian regime, or *Yushin* system (1972 to 1979), was modeled on the *Meiji Ishin*, or Meiji Restoration (1860) of Japan, and he openly expressed his admiration for its leaders (Moran 1999). (Note that the Korean *Yushin* and Japanese *Ishin* share the same Chinese charaters, 維新, as Korean *chaebol* and Japanese *zaibatsu* do, 財閥.) Many *chaebol* groups began to form in the 1950s. At this time, they were not yet large business groups, but instead just family-owned firms, typically involved in the production of light manufactures (Lim 2012). The Park regime only supported the *chaebol* groups that had begun to grow under the patronage of the Rhee regime if they supplied the Park regime with both export performance and unofficial political contributions. As a result, the *chaebol* expanded rapidly, while most SMEs had difficulty in getting bank loans and had to rely on the curb market.

The rise of a new industry in the 1970s helped the *chaebol* to expand their size. While the initial EOI centered on labor-intensive light industries, a new urgency for industrial upgrading was added in the early 1970s with a partial withdrawal of the US troops from Korea after President Nixon's announcement of the Guam Doctrine. President Park determined that Korea must develop heavy and chemical industries (HCI) in order to manufacture its own weapons (Lim 2012). The HCI drive of the 1970s further helped the *chaebol* to expand their size. President Park personally sanctioned major investment projects and selected private business people who would undertake them (Choi 1993). Because of the high investment risks, even the major *chaebol* groups were initially reluctant to participate in the HCI, but Park's extraordinary commitment to turn the HCI into a "privileged sector" reduced the risks, and the *chaebol* saw a real opportunity to prosper under the state's generous subsidies and protection. As a result, the ten largest *chaebol* grew very rapidly during the 1970s at a rate five to nine times faster than the economy as a whole. In particular, the Hyundai group increased its total assets by eighteen times, and the Daewoo group by forty-eight times between 1971 and 1980. These groups saw average annual growth rates of 38 and 53.7 percent respectively (Kim 1997).

Although the Korean state initially enjoyed a commanding position in the formulation and implementation of industrial policies such as the EOI and HCI drive, the government found itself increasingly interdependent on the relationship with the *chaebol*. Park's *chaebol*-centered industrialization strategy was not a result of the *chaebol*'s lobby, but rather was based on his own desire to emulate Japan's industrialization and the demand for a large fixed investment of HCI. The incipient *chaebol*'s share of the national economy was small when Park seized power, and the level of economic concentration was still relatively low until the early 1970s in comparison with other developing countries (Jones and Sakong 1980: 261–9). As the *chaebol* grew over time, however, Park and subsequent regimes often had to accommodate their demands for bail-out when they were in crisis. This was when the logic of "too big to fail" came to be established.

When big businesses faced the threat of financial insolvency in 1972,[2] the Federation of Korean Industrialists (FKI), the lobbying arm of the *chaebol*, petitioned President Park to bail them out. Park issued an Emergency Decree for Economic Stability and Growth, which transformed curb market loans into bank loans. These loans had to be repaid over five years at lower interest rates, with a grace period of three years during which curb market loans were to be frozen. To bail out the overleveraged *chaebol*, the Emergency Decree shifted the burden to small savers, simply ignoring their property rights. Out of 209,896 persons who registered as creditors, 70 percent were small lenders with assets in the market below 1 million won, or $2,890 (Woo 1991: 109–15; Kim and Im 2001). The 1972 bail-out of big businesses signaled that the state would be unable to let big businesses fail.

Park encouraged businesses to organize business associations in order to simplify the control of individual firms. Business associations were,

[2] Because of the IMF pressure after the first debt crisis of 1969, Park had to implement tough stabilization policies. As a result, the *chaebol* could not obtain bank loans as easily as before and had to substantially rely on the high-interest curb market.

on the one hand, valuable and reliable sources of information for state officials and thus facilitated collaboration between the state and business (Evans 1995; Schneider and Maxfield 1997). They also served as a conduit of raising official funds, like the National Security Fund, as well as unofficial political funds. For example, the FKI used to allocate to the *chaebol* specific amounts of political donations and contributions for the National Security Fund (Oh and Sim 1995). Business associations and the *chaebol* became increasingly powerful over time, and senior government officials often moved to corporate think tanks or to leadership positions in business associations (Perkins 2000). Korea's developmental state never degenerated into a hopeless degree of capture and corruption, largely thanks to the meritocratic bureaucracy and the discipline provided by the export markets. However, the growing power of the *chaebol* and consequent collusion between government and business became increasingly large concerns.

The HCI drive helped to build the foundation of many Korean leading industries such as steel, shipbuilding, machinery, electronics, automobiles and petrochemicals, although it also encouraged the *chaebol*'s overinvestment. Thanks to preferential policy loans, more than 77 percent of total manufacturing investment during 1976 to 1978 was undertaken in the HCI. By the end of 1978, the outstanding balance of various policy loans for the HCI constituted 92.8 percent of total loans to the manufacturing sector (Choi 1993). The Park Chung-hee government had to call off the HCI drive and adopt a comprehensive stabilization program in April 1979 at the verge of a debt crisis (Lim 2012; Stern *et al.* 1995). The measures for price stabilization and economic liberalization announced by Park signaled the decline of the developmental state.

The practices of government intervention and indirect control by private interests continued through reforms by the Chun Doo-hwan government (1980 to 1987) (Hahm 2003). This government adopted macroeconomic stabilization measures to fight inflation. It began to liberalize the economy, abolishing direct price controls and privatizing the commercial banks. It also opened trade and investment in response to pressure from the Reagan administration. The underlying theme of the overarching push for liberalization reform was the transition to an economy in which the private sector and the price system would play a greater role in the allocation of resources (Kim 1997; Lim 2012). Another significant move was Chun's attempt to gain popular support by cracking down on the *chaebol* after having seized power through a military coup and a bloody suppression of the pro-democracy movement. He initially attempted to prosecute big businesses on charges of illicit wealth accumulation, but he soon accepted the pledges of loyalty from the *chaebol* in return for dropping the corruption charges – exactly as Park had done in 1961. In September 1980, Chun's new government announced sweeping reforms to reduce business concentration, such as the forced sale of the *chaebol*'s "idle" real estate and non-essential subsidiaries and tight credit control over big business. In the same vein, the Monopoly Regulation and Fair Trade Act (MRFTA) was enacted in April 1981. Special emphasis was placed on preventing *chaebol* concentration through cross-investment and cross-subsidization among the subsidiaries. Chun presented the MRFTA as a symbol of political commitment to ensuring fairness, as well as improving economic efficiency, promoting consumer welfare and protecting small producers (Lim 2012; Moon 1994).

Despite the liberalization reform and the introduction of the MRFTA, there was little progress in reducing economic concentration during Chun's presidency. Between 1981 and 1988, the ten largest *chaebol* increased their total assets substantially: Daewoo by 3.3 times, Samsung by 4.8 times, Lucky-Gold Star by 3.9 times, and even Hyundai (which did not fare well under Chun's regime) by 2.7 times in real terms (Kim 1997). Chun's financial liberalization was also far from genuine liberalization and gave the *chaebol* new opportunities to expand their influence in the financial sector. Privatization of commercial banks did not end government intervention in the banking sector, and this intervention was still seen in the appointment of chief executives and indirect controls over credit allocation. While the government tried to ameliorate the problem of loan concentration and required the commercial banks to increase the share of loans to SMEs, non-bank financial institutions (NBFIs) emerged as alternative financing sources for *chaebol*. While the principle of separation of banking and commerce was strictly applied to commercial banks, limiting any individual or corporation's ownership to 8 percent of total shares, there was no such restriction to the ownership of NBFIs. Moreover, financial supervision over NBFIs was weak (Hahm 2003; Moon 1994).

Democratization and capture by the chaebol

The democratic transition of 1987 brought about a new political environment, in which increasing public demand for reducing the concentration of wealth and growing political influence of the *chaebol* collided. The Roh Tae-woo administration (1988 to 2002), a minority government with the opposition parties holding the majority seats in the National Assembly, had to respond to the public's grave concerns about the dominance of the *chaebol*, proclaiming a tough anti-big-business line. The government announced the introduction of the "public concept" of land ownership, which would limit land ownership by big business. It also introduced a comprehensive land tax system to prevent real estate speculation by the *chaebol* and the wealthy. Lastly, the government pursued measures to reduce business concentration by limiting credit flows to big business and restricting the scope for horizontal corporate expansion (Moon 1994).

However, the anti-*chaebol* campaign did not last long. The powerful *chaebol* staged a careful but formidable counter-offensive. Koo Ja-kyung, chairman of both the Lucky-Gold Star and the FKI, warned politicians of both the ruling and opposition sides of potential retaliation through the selective use of political contributions (Moon 1994). In a case of open defiance, Kim Wu-joong, Chairman of Daewoo – one of the four largest *chaebol*, forced the government to provide emergency financing at the brink of the bankruptcy of Daewoo Shipbuilding in 1988. Upon Kim's urge, the National Assembly amended the law on the Korea Development Bank to raise the bank's authorized capital, which could then be used to refinance Daewoo's debt (Kim 1997: 196–7). This episode illustrates the changed politics of economic policy: the government had to respond to growing public criticism of *chaebol*'s dominance, but the growing political and economic influence of the *chaebol* made any genuine reform of the *chaebol* difficult. Intensified clientelistic politics and the politicians' reliance on the *chaebol*'s contributions further increased the *chaebol*'s political influence. The democratic political process was largely captured by the *chaebol*, and Korea was often dubbed the "*Chaebol Republic*" (Kim 1997).

After Roh succeeded in forming a grand conservative coalition in the early 1990s by merging his party with two opposition parties, he reshuffled the economic cabinet and shifted to a pro-business line that was effectively pro-*chaebol*. The new economic team announced a series of measures to boost the corporate sector, such as scrapping of the "public concept" of land ownership, relaxation of real estate taxes, weakening of labor laws and postponement of the "real name" financial transaction system. Although the Roh Tae-woo government did not entirely abandon the rhetoric of *chaebol* reform and the policy of economic deconcentration, its policy of encouraging the top thirty *chaebol* to specialize in core businesses failed miserably (Moon 1994; Kim 2003).

The early presidency of President Kim Young-sam (1993 to 1997), who had been a long-time opposition leader until the three-party merger of 1990, gave renewed hope for a decline in capture by the *chaebol*. Some of his significant anti-corruption reforms, including the introduction of the "real name financial transaction system" in his first year of presidency, generated expectations for further reform of the corporate and financial sectors. However, his conservative political base as well as his heavy reliance on the *chaebol*'s generous contributions for his presidential campaign made it hard to push for significant reform of the *chaebol*-centered economy. His new *chaebol* policy of "sectoral specialization" constituted an extension of Roh's previous policy of specialization by "core businesses." Even the minimal restrictions on the entry into non-core sectors soon collapsed. When Samsung lobbied to establish an integrated passenger car plant in Pusan, Kim Young-sam's regional base, he approved it over initial objection from the bureaucrats (Kim 2003). His attempt for financial reform also failed miserably. He belatedly established a Presidential Commission on Financial Reform in January 1997, but thirteen of its thirty members were drawn from big business. The Commission predictably failed to produce comprehensive reform proposals, and even some minimal proposals of the Commission subsequently failed to survive the legislative process (Kim 2003).

Economic concentration by the *chaebol* increased further during the 1980s and 1990s despite various measures undertaken to reduce it: the sales, value added (revenue less outside purchases (of materials and services)) and assets of the thirty largest *chaebol* reached 45, 41 and 50 percent, respectively, of the entire manufacturing sector by 1995 (Cho 1997). *Chaebol*-centered industrialization also increased the inequality of income distribution. The *Gini* Index for income rose with the phenomenal growth of *chaebol* during the 1970s, fell slightly in the 1980s, but rose again in the 1990s. Inequality was probably rising more rapidly than indicated by the official income statistics. While the *Gini* Index based on official income statistics was 33.6 in 1988, it was as high as 38.6 including capital gains from land, and 41.2 including capital gains from shares as well as land, according to Lee (1991).

Economic liberalization and political democratization weakened government control, while market-based discipline was still weak, and expectations for government protection against large bankruptcies remained strong. Confident that they were too big and influential to fail, the *chaebol* discounted downside risks and aggressively expanded their businesses through debt financing. The average debt to equity ratio of the top thirty *chaebol* reached an astounding 519 percent in 1997 (Lim 2012). One important consequence of the financial liberalization was the explosive growth of the non-bank financial institutions, many of which were controlled by various *chaebol* groups. As a result, the allocation of financial resources came increasingly under the control of the *chaebol* groups. Although the NBFIs accounted for 29.1 percent of total deposits and 36.7 percent of total loans in 1980, they accounted for 72.2 percent of total deposits and 63.5 percent of total loans by 1995. Moreover, the Kim Young-sam government's accelerated financial and capital market liberalization without prudent regulations, in the name of "globalization policy," further provided the *chaebol* with new opportunities to raise funds from abroad. The ensuing build-up of short-term external debt made the Korean economy an easy victim to the Asian financial crisis (You 2010).

A series of massive *chaebol* group bankruptcies, such as Hanbo, Jinro and Kia, took place in 1997. Bank balance sheets, which had been already suffering from many non-performing loans, deteriorated further. However, the institutional mechanisms to handle large bankruptcies were totally inadequate, and the government aggravated the problems by "suspension of default," which rendered the Korean economy vulnerable to the contagion of the East Asian financial crisis (You 2010).

Democratic autonomy or capture?

President Kim Dae-jung (1998 to 2002), elected in the midst of a financial crisis in December 1997, committed himself to a vigorous reform program designed to weaken the domination of the *chaebol*. Kim Dae-jung's relatively weak connection with the *chaebol*, his progressive political support base, external pressures from the IMF and the United States, and the severity of this crisis all contributed to his pursuit of sweeping reforms (Kim 2000b; Mo and Moon 2003). The weakened position of the *chaebol* – which the public claimed was the cause of the crisis – together with a newly formed reform coalition between the liberal government, organized labor and civil society organizations, both prevented state capture by the *chaebol* and provided a space for "democratic autonomy." The goal of Kim's reform was to create a "democratic market economy" or a dual transition from a still partly authoritarian political system to a full democracy and from a monopolistic economic system dominated by the *chaebol* to a competitive market economy (Kalinowski 2009).

Kim Dae-jung's government sought comprehensive reforms, including external liberalization and domestic structural reforms in the financial, corporate, labor and public sectors, designed to enhance transparency and accountability in corporate management among the *chaebol*. Kim Dae-jung declared the end of government-business collusion, or crony capitalism. Financial reform included the expansion of deposit insurance, consolidated financial supervisory functions and strengthened asset management criteria for financial institutions in line with international standards. Kim's reforms also included measures to expand the social safety net (for example, the expansion of unemployment insurance and public assistance for the poor) (You 2010). Many of the institutional reforms were in fact carried over from the earlier reform plans that

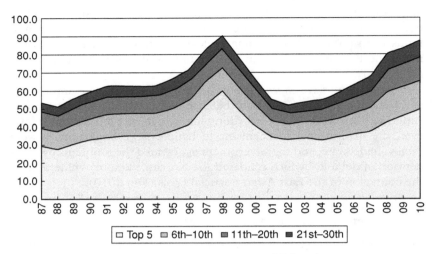

Figure 7.2 The trend of *chaebol*-asset-to-GDP ratio
Source: Kim (2011b).

had failed to materialize. The reforms sought to address market failures and enhance market discipline in the corporate and financial sectors (You 2010). In contrast to the approach taken by past governments, there has been a marked shift in emphasis from industrial policy to competition policy. The government today increasingly relies on market mechanism rather than "the rule of government officials" (Lim 2012). Over the two years in the aftermath of the crisis, the Kim Dae-jung government achieved impressive results. It cleaned up massive non-performing loans and adopted institutional reforms to reduce moral hazards, improve corporate governance, promote competition, install prudent regulations in the financial sector and strengthen the social safety net. With sixteen out of the thirty largest *chaebol* groups disappearing during the restructuring process, the market discipline was immensely strengthened, and the firms greatly improved their debt to equity ratio. In particular, the demise of Daewoo, one of the top *chaebol* groups, was a strong signal to the market of the end of the "Too Big To Fail" policy perspective. Korea effectively used the crisis as an opportunity to make the transition to a "democratic (or, competitive and transparent) market economy" (Lim 2011; You 2010).

Apparently, the sweeping reforms have contributed to reducing *chaebol* concentration, at least for several years. Figure 7.2 shows that the asset to GDP ratio of the top thirty *chaebols* gradually increased before the financial crisis, but then decreased sharply from 90 percent in 1998 to 52 percent in 2002. However, the trend was reversed and it has risen again since then, reaching 88 percent in 2010. The resurge of *chaebol* concentration has been associated with the weakening of the *chaebol* reform.

Largely due to resistance from the *chaebol*, the reform program has been continuously weakened. The most contentious issue was restriction on cross-shareholding, which was designed to prevent *chaebol* families from controlling all affiliates when they held little equity in these firms. But the pro-*chaebol* forces argued that the regulation was responsible for declining investment (You 2010). The Kim Dae-jung government failed to improve the *chaebol*'s ownership structure. The problem with separation of ownership and control has worsened over time: shares held by controlling families decreased over time, but shares held by affiliates increased, enabling the *chaebol* families to maintain their control. The ensuing government led by Roh Moo-hyun (2003 to 2008) continued to relax the restriction on cross-shareholding. In the end, the regulation was lifted altogether under the professedly business-friendly Lee Myung-bak government (2008 to 2012). In addition, the former *chaebol* CEO Lee Myung-bak's conservative government implemented tax cuts for the rich and large corporations, weakened the separation of financial and industrial capital, and relaxed other regulations relating to the *chaebol* (You 2010). The failure of the progressive Roh Moo-hyun government to advance *chaebol* reform was somewhat ironic, although the pro-*chaebol* stance of the conservative Lee Myung-bak government is more understandable. Critics argue that the Roh government was not immune from capture by the *chaebol* on the economic policy front (Kalinowski 2009).

The continuing domination of the *chaebol* and their influence still poses serious concerns regarding capture. Economic reforms in the aftermath of the 1997 financial crisis, together with political reforms that curtailed clientelistic politics, certainly contributed to improving corporate governance and somewhat decreasing *chaebol* concentration, and thereby reduced the serious danger of elite capture. However, some critics argue that the re-emergence of the *chaebol* undermined state autonomy and Korea has entered the "second *Chaebol* Republic" under the Lee Myung-bak government (Kalinowski 2009).

Business-government relations and industrial policy in Taiwan

Sweeping land reform in 1949 to 1953 laid the foundation for Taiwan's state autonomy and economic growth with equity. With the dissolution of the landlord class, there were no powerful private interests that could exert strong influence on the government. The fact that political leadership of the KMT came from the mainland, while businesses were mostly run by indigenous people, also contributed to the insulation of the state from private interests. The state autonomy was further strengthened with the reform of the KMT, containment of clientelistic politics at the local level and gradual development of meritocratic bureaucracy. Unlike the Korean government, which promoted the growth of the *chaebol* and large enterprises, the Taiwanese government did not encourage the growth of large businesses, but promoted an SME-centered economy. With democratization and politicization of economic policymaking, state autonomy experienced temporary erosion. However, Taiwan's democracy was largely able to avoid capture by private interests.

Authoritarian state autonomy and industrial policy

As in Korea, Taiwan's adoption of import-substituting strategy was largely caused by external constraints. A serious balance-of-payments crisis compelled the KMT government to introduce strict import controls, together with a multiple exchange rate system in 1951 (Haggard 1990a: 85). The official exchange rates were substantially overvalued. The black market exchange rates with the US dollar were 15 to 70 percent higher than the official rates, which led to lucrative windfalls from importing and import-substituting activities. The government established quotas for the allocation of foreign exchange by commodity categories. Import applications were many times greater than the amount of foreign exchange available. During 1951 to 1953, for example, the authorities permitted only 20 percent of the requested amount (Wade 1990: 77–8).

Taiwan's ISI differed significantly from that of Korea in two areas: maintenance of a state-owned sector and adherence to monetary conservatism. First, Taiwan made creating and maintaining a strong state-owned sector a greater priority. This choice was largely motivated by political and ideological reasons. The KMT leadership feared that private-sector growth would inevitably strengthen the native Taiwanese, who then might use their economic power for political ends. Moreover, the KMT leadership also fostered an anti-big capitalist conviction, believing the capture of the Nationalist government by vested interests of large industrialists and landlords to be one of the main causes of their mainland defeat. Rather than turning Japanese properties over to the private sector as its American advisors recommended, the KMT retained control, generating one of the largest state-owned sectors in the non-communist world (Evans 1995: 55; Haggard 1990a: 88; Wade 1990: 302). The KMT used state-owned enterprises (SOEs) as key instruments of industrial development. Taiwan's state-owned sector accounted for over half of all industrial production in the 1950s, and, after falling off a little in the 1960s, its share rose again in the 1970s (Evans 1995: 55). Second, Taiwan adhered to monetary conservatism, unlike Korea (Kim and Im 2001). The disastrous political consequences of hyperinflation on the mainland made the KMT elites receptive to US advice for a conservative macro-economic policy. The KMT regime gave the central bank strong power relative to spending ministries such as the industrial planning authorities (Cheng 1993).

Taiwan's ISI was not captured by the entrepreneurs it had created, unlike ISI in the Philippines. Instead, the KMT regime progressively exposed its "greenhouse capitalists" to the rigors of the competitive market. It reduced protection over time and did not allow the creation of "rental havens." The strong and autonomous state, which was made possible by a powerful bureaucratic apparatus, was able to discipline the private entrepreneurs (Evans 1995: 57). Chiang Kai-shek delegated substantial decision-making authority and new policy instruments to the technocrats.

An absence of ISI capture did not mean the absence of corruption. Since the import and exchange controls produced huge amounts of rent, it was natural that rent-seeking opportunities bred corrupt exchanges between entrepreneurs and officials. At local and provincial levels, the two most common processes that were prone to corruption were tax assessment and the securing of licenses and permits (Cole 1967: 651–2). Fortunately, however, the authoritarian regime and its economic bureaucracy were largely immune from capture by the weak private sector. Corrupt practices were relatively rare at high levels in the central administration, although they were more widespread at the local level. As clientelistic politics developed at the local level, local oligopolies were often formed that were connected to local factions. However, containment of clientelistic politics at the local level enabled Taiwan to better control rent-seeking and corruption involving the central government and political elite during the ISI period than Korea and the Philippines.

The challenges related to the exhaustion of import-substitution and the balance-of-payments led to the replacement of ISI with EOI strategy. Recognizing that the trade and exchange-rate control created corruption and inefficiency, and contributed to the balance-of-payments problems, technocrats argued for liberalization. American advisors also played an important role in the export-oriented industrial policy reform of 1958 to 1960 (Gold 1986: 72; Haggard 1990a: 90–2). The 1958 to 1960 economic reform, which culminated in the enactment of the Statute for the Encouragement of Investment in 1960, reduced the price distortions that had discriminated against exports. The Bank of Taiwan launched an export-loan program, and firms were granted credit lines on the basis of past export performance and future plans (Haggard 1990a: 94).

Unlike Korea, where large firms and *chaebol* were the major engines of EOI, SMEs played a more dominant role in Taiwan's EOI. SMEs contributed about 70 percent of Taiwan's total exports at the peak in the late 1970s and early 1980s, while the ten largest *chaebol* accounted for about 70 percent of total exports in the early 1980s in Korea. SMEs also exported nearly 70 percent of their total output during the same period in Taiwan (Wu 2004). The difference in industrial structure between Korea and Taiwan was largely caused by the state's different policy toward large enterprises. While the Korean state forged an alliance with business groups for industrialization, the Taiwanese state distanced itself from business, reflecting the KMT regime's anti-big capitalist sentiments and concerns about the political potential of native Taiwanese economic power. Although government intervention in credit allocation such as export financing continued throughout the period of EOI, the degree of intervention in Taiwan was less than in Korea. Export financing was not particularistic, but universal (i.e. not industry- or firm-specific) and automatic (i.e. extended to any firm with export-shipping documents). However, the amount of concessional credit was less than in Korea (Cheng 1993; Shea 1994).

The state became increasingly vigilant against large enterprises from the 1970s when they began to develop into business groups. Legal restrictions and regulations were imposed to discourage conglomerate development. The KMT regime's anti-big business orientation was not disturbed by the policy of industrial upgrading launched in the 1970s. Unlike in Korea, where most of the heavy and chemical industries were undertaken by *chaebol* firms with government support, SOEs undertook these projects with policy loans from the Development Fund. In the name of "backward integration," the state intentionally strengthened the SOEs in upstream industries. This prevented the large enterprises from becoming vertically integrated conglomerates. Such restrictions had consequences on the size of the business groups. Compared to their Japanese and South Korean counterparts, the leading business groups in Taiwan were less vertically integrated and much smaller in size (Wu 2004).

Premier Chiang Ching-kuo explicitly endorsed special treatment for the SMEs. The government established the Credit Guarantee Fund for Small and Medium Businesses in 1974, and the Small and Medium Enterprise Bank was created in 1976. Political leaders thought that the SMEs could counterbalance the influence of the large enterprises (Cheng 1993; Wu 2005b: 191–3, 289). The government's policy of favoring

SMEs was also reflected in the promotion of the information industry during the 1970s and 1980s. Inspired by Korean efforts to develop industrial technology at all costs, the Taiwanese government established the Industrial Technology Research Institute (ITRI) in 1973. Initially, the private sector in Taiwan showed little interest in the semiconductor project. Until the late 1980s, all long-term projects of the ITRI were initiated by the state. The method of technology transfer favored smaller rather than larger firms, unlike in Korea, where technology was transferred from research institutes directly to the large private conglomerates. State incentives encouraged the creation of small and medium-sized high-tech firms. In 1980, the state created the Xinzhu Science Park, which became the main base for Taiwan's high-tech industry. The firms within the park were entitled to a wide range of benefits, from tax cuts to low-interest loans to government investment. The government also provided financial incentives by introducing the American practice of venture capitalism. A major strategy was to invite Chinese graduates of American universities to return to Taiwan to head up these firms. As a result, Taiwan has numerous small design houses and manufacturing firms rather than the vertically integrated conglomerates that dominate the high-tech industries of Japan and Korea (Wu 2005b: 265–74).

In general, relations between the KMT state and private entrepreneurs were distant compared to the close ties between the Korean state and the *chaebol*. Unlike in Japan and Korea, there is no tradition of *amakudari* from the public to the private sector, although many senior bureaucrats previously worked for a period of time in either state- or party-owned enterprises, and many of them re-enter the public enterprise sector upon retirement. Unlike official Korean tolerance for symbiotic government-business relations, such intimate interaction was suspected by the KMT regime as collusion. Economic planners typically maintained an aloof posture toward the private sector and allowed minimal direct business input during the policy-making process. According to a former minister of finance, President Chiang Ching-kuo's strict "ten commandments" for government officials required that any public official attending a social engagement that included private business people was to report it to the government's Bureau of Personnel (Fields 1997; Wade 1990).

As in Korea, Taiwan's private sector is intensely organized through a network of state-corporatist business associations. Economic policy-makers used the industrial associations to gather data on production capabilities, conduct industrial surveys, disseminate business information, negotiate overcapacity production reductions, solicit policy inputs and implement government policy initiatives such as export quotas. However, Taiwan's business associations had much less power than their

Korean counterparts. They did not provide significant inputs into policy-making until the early 1980s. They functioned largely as a mechanism for mobilizing and controlling the business sector and as a channel for the government to relay its policies to business (Chu 1994; Fields 1997; Gold 1986: 71).

Behind the corporatist arrangements, a complex web of clientelistic networks developed over time, particularly at the local level. The local factions largely captured the economic rents created by local government procurements and regulations. They held an economic stake in local oligopolies, such as public transportation, credit unions, farm produce cartels, construction, public utilities and certain illicit economic activities. At the national level, rents were mostly accrued to state-owned and party-owned enterprises. However, some politically well-connected mainlander firms and prominent Taiwanese families developed close personal ties with the party central leadership (Chu 1994).

Relatively thin clientelistic networks at the national level meant that rent-seeking and corruption was less prevalent. With the gradual electoral opening and Taiwanization at the national level, however, some business elites like the Tsai family attempted to expand their political influence in economic policy-making. The Tsais, petty merchants by origin, came to take the management of the Tenth Credit Co-op (TCC) in 1957. The Tsai family established Cathay Life Insurance in 1962 and Cathay Credit in the 1970s. By the early 1980s, they had become one of the richest families in Taiwan. The family began to make political investments in the late 1970s. They successfully sent two members in a row to the Legislative Yuan under the KMT ticket and established close personal ties with high officials in the Ministry of Finance. The Tsai family member of the Legislative Yuan brought together twelve other members with business backgrounds to form the "Thirteen Brothers" in 1983. This group pushed for a revision of the Bank Act to allow credit companies to become involved in bank-related business, but the revision was blocked by senior legislators. The TCC then collapsed in 1985 when the real estate market turned sluggish and the corporate debt of Cathay Plastics accumulated. It was revealed that the TCC's funds had been illegally diverted to support the family-owned enterprises, as well as real estate speculation. The insolvency of the TCC and Cathay Plastics triggered a chain reaction, causing an island-wide financial crisis. As a result of the TCC scandal, a good score of top officials at the Ministry of Finance were censured, and two ministers resigned (Cheng 1993; Wu 2005b: 260–1). The rise and fall of the Tsai family illustrates the emerging business penetration into politics and policy-making, but it also shows that the Taiwanese state was not to be easily captured.

Table 7.1 *Business group sales share in major sectors, 1983 (%)*

Sector	Top 50 *chaebol* in Korea	Top 96 groups in Taiwan
Mining	10.6%	0.0%
Manufacturing	45.4%	19.0%
Construction	66.0%	5.6%
Transport and storage	23.1%	1.8%

Source: Feenstra and Hamilton (2006: 55).

A comparison of the business group sales share in 1983 shows a striking difference in the degree of market concentration by conglomerates between Korea and Taiwan. Table 7.1 indicates that the top ninety-six business groups in Taiwan accounted for only 19 percent of total sales in the manufacturing sector in 1983, and the non-affiliated companies, mostly SMEs, enjoyed the remaining 81 percent of the combined market share. The figure for the top fifty *chaebol* in Korea was 45.4 percent, which shows a very high market concentration. In the construction sector, the business group sales share was only 5.6 percent in Taiwan, while it was 66 percent in Korea (Feenstra and Hamilton 2006: 55).

Liberalization, democratization and challenges to state autonomy

Economic liberalization and political democratization that started in the mid-1980s brought about substantial changes in the previous top-down government-business relations in Taiwan. Trade and financial liberalization and deregulation strengthened the private sector in its relationship with the government, and business groups expanded over time. Democratization further helped to increase business influence in policy-making.

Liberalization of trade and financial regimes was primarily caused by increasing pressures from the United States, Taiwan's number one trading partner. Taiwan's long-established protectionist trade policies, such as mandatory export-ratio requirements, domestic content requirements and export subsidies, were gradually phased out. The Central Bank was forced to ease its control over foreign exchange, resulting in a 48 percent appreciation of the New Taiwan dollar against the US dollar between 1986 and 1988 (Chu 1994). Financial liberalization involved deregulation of interest rates, liberalization of capital outflow, and opening of new security houses and private banks. Unlike Korea, however, Taiwan did not liberalize capital inflow. Throughout the 1990s, Taiwan's Central

Bank of China (CBC) kept a vigilant eye on transnational capital flows and maintained emergency powers of intervention (Wu 2007). The Taiwanese government also strengthened prudential regulations on private financial institutions after the TCC scandal (Cheng 1993). As a result, Taiwan was less vulnerable than Korea to the East Asian financial crisis of 1997. Taiwan's private sector was not as indebted as its Korean counterpart. Because of Taiwan's conservative monetary policy and lack of development coalition, or a risk partnership, between the state and big business, even the large firms and business groups in Taiwan did not dare to make risky investments relying on over-borrowing. All of these factors helped the Taiwanese economy to weather the East Asian financial crisis, although it was later adversely affected by the political uncertainty caused by the first-ever change of governing party and subsequent tensions in cross-strait relations.

When the banking sector was opened to the private sector in the early 1990s, all nineteen applicants for new bank licenses were affiliated with big businesses, and the Ministry of Finance turned down only four applications. The share of a single corporate investor was limited to 5 percent, with that of a diversified business group limited to 15 percent (Chu 1994). The high rate of approval implies a policy of avoiding the concentration of big capital (Cheng 1993). However, the establishment of sixteen new banks created an "over-banking" problem, leading to excessive competition and aggressive banking practices. These outcomes thereby deteriorated the banks' asset quality and led to the rise of Taiwan's traditionally low ratio of non-performing loans over time. In addition, the need to create financial institutions capable of international competition led the Taiwanese government to request mandatory mergers to reach economies of scale in 2004 (Wu 2007).

The entry of private enterprises into service sectors such as telecommunications and public utilities when they were liberalized in the late 1980s facilitated the rapid expansion of family-owned business groups. State-owned enterprises, the traditional vehicle for the development of capital-intensive sectors, came to be seen as increasingly inadequate for high-tech sectors (Chu 1994). Deregulation of the telecommunications industry beginning in the early 1990s, together with the opening of the wireless telecommunications service to the private sector in 1996, provided new opportunities for diversification for the business groups. In 1996, a total of forty-two applications competing for eight licenses from seventeen consortia were submitted. Most of the seventeen applicant consortia were alliances of multiple family-owned groups and foreign partners. The Ministry of Transportation and Telecommunications awarded eight licenses to six applicants, and the six newly incorporated providers

Table 7.2 *Economic significance of the top 100 Taiwanese business groups,*
1973–2002

Economic significance	1973	1977	1981	1986	1990	1994	1998	2002
Number of member firms	724	651	719	746	815	1,021	1,362	2,419
Group sales/GDP (%)	32.4	28.8	28.6	29.4	39.2	41.5	54.3	85.4
Share in total employment (%)	5.1	5.2	4.8	4.3	4.8	5.2	7.9	9.5

Sources: Chung and Mahmood (2006; 2010).

sparked fierce competition to win customers. By 2000, besides the
state-operated Chunghwa Telecom, three major providers came to share
out the market: Taiwan Cellular, Far EasTone Telecom and KG Telecom. All three of these private telecom companies were primarily owned
by celebrated Taiwanese business groups. These three providers intensified competition until 2003, when Far EasTone announced a merger
with the operations of KG Telecom.

As liberalization of the financial and telecommunications industry
illustrates, liberalization allowed business groups to diversify and expand
their businesses. As a result, the economic significance of business
groups increased. Table 7.2 shows the increasing trend of the economic
significance of the top 100 business groups in Taiwan. The ratio of
total group sales to national GDP remained at around 30 percent until
1986, but it has increased rapidly since then, reaching 85 percent in
2002.[3] The employment share of business groups also rose from 4.3
percent in 1986 to 9.5 percent in 2002. Although Taiwanese business
groups have expanded their size, they are still relatively small compared
to Korean *chaebol* groups. Furthermore, very few Taiwanese groups,
except for Acer, have been able to develop a global brand name (Chung
and Mahmood 2010).

The ownership structure of business groups in Taiwan resembles that
of *chaebol* in Korea. Between 1988 and 1998, family ownership dropped
from 23 to 4 percent, but affiliate ownership rose from 35 to 53 percent.
In fact, many of the ultimate owners of group affiliates were private holding companies and investment companies that were controlled
by the family. Thus, the pyramidal structure of business groups provides controlling families with opportunities to expropriate minority

---

[3] A better indicator for economic significance would be a ratio of total value added, rather
than sales, of the business groups to national GDP, but the figures for value added are
not available. Also, there may be an overestimation of total sales of business groups due
to the possible double counting of foreign and domestic sales (Kawakami 2007).

shareholders, as seen in Korean *chaebol*. However, the structure of the control and management of Taiwanese business groups is different from that of Korean *chaebol*. In Taiwan, family-controlled holding companies, or investment companies, are not necessarily involved in the decision-making and administration of the whole group. Unlike the group head-quarters of the Korean *chaebol* that rule all group affiliates, the main function of the top organization here is to hold the shares of the affiliated firms. The overall planning of the whole group relies on a set of socially related top executives, and the proportion of family members in the inner circle of the top 100 groups declined from 61 percent in 1981 to 53 percent in 1998 (Chung and Mahmood 2010).

Economic liberalization and the subsequent expansion of business groups helped to increase the political influence of the private sector. The newly available option of overseas relocation and foreign investment further strengthened the bargaining position of the business vis- à-vis the state (Chu 1994). Moreover, economic liberalization was accompanied by political democratization that began with the lifting of martial law in 1987. The expansion of electoral politics and the growing importance of the legislature provided the business elite with new opportunities to buy political influence. Clientelism and corruption that had long grown in local politics spread to national politics. Large businesses suddenly became the most sought-after sponsors for politicians (Chu 1994). This represents a shift away from the era when political leaders harbored fundamental distrust of the big capitalists and tried to curb the expansion of large enterprises. Thirty-eight of the 101 popularly elected members of the Legislative Yuan of 1989 to 1992 had publicly known ties with at least one business group. New and less well-established firms were typically the most enthusiastic sponsors of elected politicians. Established business groups, which had already built up clientelistic networks with party and bureaucratic leaders, were less enthusiastic sponsors. Business groups with a regional base also invested heavily in the elections for county magistrates and city mayors. Of the twenty-four magistrates and mayors elected in 1989, eighteen received financial support from one business group or another (Chu 1994).

The increasing influence of business within the KMT and the legislature during the early years of democratic transition contributed to a shift in the prevailing policy directions of the economic ministries. Traditional *dirigiste* thinking came to be replaced by a more liberal and pro-business approach, and there was a strong drive for economic liberalization with numerous deregulatory initiatives. The Legislative Yuan became an arena for horse-trading among economic officials, party officials and law-makers, who often acted as surrogates for special business interests. Economic officials ran into tough legislative battles over important economic and financial regulations. For instance, when the Ministry of Finance sought to strengthen a security transaction tax in order to cool the overheated stock market, it encountered fierce opposition from the parliamentary representatives of the brokerage firms. After initially proposing to raise the tax rate from 0.3 to 1.5 percent, the Ministry finally agreed to a compromise of 0.6 percent following mediation by the party's central secretariat (Chu 1994). The growing political influence of the business elite and the parliament also eroded the autonomy of the state's economic bureaucracy. The enforcement of anti-trust laws was weak, and critics argued that the loose enforcement, in effect, served to legalize or even encourage collusive behavior as orchestrated by conglomerates. According to the statistics published by the government's Fair Trade Commission, between 1992 and 1997, the government approved forty-nine and rejected only seven applications for collusive behavior, while it approved 2,093 yet rejected only one application for mergers (Kuo 2000).

There was, however, a limit to money politics and business influence. On balance, the economic bureaucracy was still the steering force behind upcoming economic policies. Many of the deregulatory reforms were not simply policy concessions to the private sector, but initiations directed by the economic bureaucracy. For example, when the Banking Law went into revision to deregulate the banking sector, the Ministry of Finance prepared provisions for the dispersal of new bank ownership. This survived intact, limiting the share of a single corporate investor and that of a diversified business group to 5 and 15 percent, respectively. The only major concession made to law-makers in the final version of the bill was a 50 percent reduction in the minimum capital requirement, from NT$20 to NT$10 billion. The Fair Trade Law and other important economic pieces of legislation promoted by the economic bureaucracy were also successfully enacted during the late 1980s and early 1990s (Chu 1994).

Moreover, money politics and rising business influence alarmed the public to the extent that there was a backlash against the so-called "black-gold politics." The opposition DPP attacked the KMT for its involvement in black-gold politics, and the KMT suffered from the charge in the polls. The politicians increasingly realized that revealing ties with business would alienate them from the middle-class voters. Also, the lobbying capacity of Taiwan's big business was not that strong, compared to the Korean *chaebol*. The business community lacked independent think tanks that could scrutinize government proposals, initiate new policy proposals or counter-proposals, and serve as policy advocates on behalf of the private sector (Chu 1994). All of these factors served to prevent state capture by the private sector, and money politics and corruption gradually decreased after their initial rise during the early period of democratization. Overall, it appears that the concerns about capture in Taiwan are less than in Korea because there exists a lower degree of economic concentration and a weaker influence of business groups.

The causes of state autonomy and capture

The history of business-government relations and economic policy in the three countries shows that weak states, such as the Philippines, are vulnerable to capture by oligarchic interests, and are thus unable to formulate and implement coherent economic policies. As Hutchcroft (1998: 57) states, "the Philippines is not plagued by the overpowering strength of a predatory state but rather by the overpowering strength of a predatory oligarchy." In other words, "the oligarchy was a plunderer rather than plundered by the state." The basic characteristics of the oligarchic democracy, or captured democracy, of the pre-martial law era have not changed much during the post-Marcos era. In contrast, the strong states in Korea and Taiwan largely maintained autonomy from the private interests and were able to design and implement coherent economic policies. Unlike the Philippines, Korea and Taiwan made a swift transition from ISI to EOI without significant resistance from ISI industrialists, and they both incentivized the private firms to invest in EOI by rewarding them according to objective criteria of export performances. However, the Korean state increasingly lost autonomy and came to be captured by the powerful *chaebol*, especially after the democratic transition of 1987. The Korean state restored autonomy during the aftermath of the East Asian financial crisis of 1997 and implemented a sweeping reform of the *chaebol* and financial sector. The *chaebol* have since regained influence during recent years, and capture is still an ongoing concern. In contrast, the Taiwanese state has largely avoided capture, even after the democratic transition.

What caused the differences across these three countries in their level of vulnerability to capture? I have argued that high income inequality and wealth concentration causes elite capture. Different degrees of capture in these countries must have been caused by different degrees of income inequality or wealth concentration. I further argued that a high level of inequality due to the failure of land reform in the Philippines led to state capture by the powerful private interests, while low levels of inequality due to successful land reform in Korea and Taiwan provided favorable conditions for state autonomy in those countries. I have also indicated that the Korean state's choice of *chaebol*-centered industrialization strategy led to increasing power of the *chaebol* over time, which

Table 7.3 *How concentrated is family control?*

| Country | Average number of firms per family | % of total value of listed corporate assets Controlled by families (1996) | | | |
		No. 1 family	Top 5 families	Top 10 families	Top 15 families
Hong Kong	2.36	6.5	26.2	32.1	34.4
Indonesia	4.09	16.6	40.7	57.7	61.7
Japan	1.04	0.5	1.8	2.4	2.8
Korea	**2.07**	**11.4**	**29.7**	**36.8**	**38.4**
Malaysia	1.97	7.4	17.3	24.8	28.3
Philippines	**2.68**	**17.1**	**42.8**	**52.5**	**55.1**
Singapore	1.26	6.4	19.5	26.6	29.9
Taiwan	**1.17**	**4.0**	**14.5**	**18.4**	**20.1**
Thailand	1.68	9.4	32.2	46.2	53.3

Source: Claessens *et al.* (2000).

in turn resulted in increasing capture. I have acknowledged that capture reinforces inequality. Without capture, a democracy could not maintain high inequality because of the redistributive demand from the median voter and a large proportion of the population being poor. But capture enables the elite to minimize redistribution and to further obtain rents from the state, and thereby high inequality is maintained.

Data on income inequality and economic concentration support my argument. The Philippines has maintained a much higher level of income inequality than Korea and Taiwan, as I presented in Chapter 3 (see Figure 3.5). Also, there is evidence that economic concentration by family conglomerates has been the highest in the Philippines, followed by Korea, and the lowest in Taiwan. According to a study of East Asian corporations by Claessens *et al.* (2000), the top ten families in the Philippines were controlling 52.5 percent of the total value of listed corporate assets as of 1996, while that percentage was 36.8 percent for Korea and 18.4 percent for Taiwan. This measure is indicative of the degree of economic concentration. The Philippines was among the most concentrated economies in East Asia, and Taiwan was among the least concentrated, as Table 7.3 indicates.

However, the possibility of bidirectional causal relationships mandates that we examine the possibility of capture causing inequality rather than inequality causing capture in the historical experiences of the three countries. I have already addressed this question with regard to land reform in Chapter 4. In the Philippines, it seems that bidirectional causal relationships worked continuously. High inequality and the existence of the powerful landed elite led to state capture and failure of land reform. The failure of land reform helped to maintain high inequality, which in turn led to the continuous state capture by the landed oligarchy. In Korea and Taiwan, external communist threats weakened the influence of the landed class and led to sweeping land reform. The land reform permanently dissolved the landed elite and produced a relatively equal distribution of wealth and income, which in turn opened the space for state autonomy. Thus, external factors were primarily responsible for the success or failure of land reform, which produced different levels of inequality, which in turn led to state autonomy or capture.

Accordingly, a crucial question is about Korea's *chaebol*-centered industrialization policy versus Taiwan's SME-centered policy. Was the *chaebol*-favoring policy introduced in Korea because the state was captured by the *chaebol*? Or was the policy chosen by the autonomous Korean state, but the *chaebol*'s growth and increasing power subsequently led to state capture? The evidence is more consistent with the latter explanation than with the former. Korea's autonomous state chose to promote the *chaebol*, but their growth and increasing economic concentration led to their capture of the state capture over time.

In Korea, Park Chung-hee's *chaebol*-favored industrialization strategy was not a result of the *chaebol*'s lobby, but rather was based on his own desire to emulate Japan's industrialization. Park's HCI drive further strengthened the need to favor the *chaebol*, because of the demand for a large fixed investment of HCI. The incipient *chaebol*'s share of the national economy was small when Park seized power, and Park's economic policy formulation and implementation was initially autonomous. Although many *chaebols* began to form in the 1950s, they were not yet large business groups, but instead family-owned firms (Lim 2012). The level of economic concentration was still relatively low until the 1970s, although business concentration was rapidly growing in Korea at that time (Jones and Sakong 1980: 261–9). Thus, Park's choice of *chaebol*-favoring strategy was not caused by capture, but by his own preferences. However, the growth of the *chaebol* inevitably increased their political influence over time, and the Korean state was increasingly captured by them until the financial crisis of 1997.

In contrast, in Taiwan, Chiang Kai-shek and Chiang Ching-kuo harbored anti-big business conviction and promoted SOEs and SMEs, while discouraging the development of large corporations. During the early years of democratic transition, however, the KMT leadership not only sought financial contributions from businesses, but also encouraged the direct participation in politics by business leaders. These actions sparked alarming signs of business influence in policy-making and public criticism over "gold politics" grew. The KMT reacted by recruiting business people for legislative candidates, and the legislature asserted independence from business influence. Taiwan's big business groups were not as powerful as their Korean counterparts. Taiwan's state was hence less vulnerable to capture.

I also previously asserted that clientelistic politics and patronage-ridden bureaucracy would be more prone to capture than programmatic politics and meritocratic bureaucracy. Historical evidence supports this argument. Highly clientelistic politics in the Philippines have made the politicians, including the presidents, vulnerable to the rent-seeking demands of large campaign contributors. Lucio Tan, a former Marcos crony and one of the largest contributors to Estrada's presidential campaign, provides an example of business capture of the policy process. He obtained ownership of the Philippine Airlines (PAL), which monopolized the international air services (Austria 2002). President Estrada returned his favors, and this included a delay in the liberalization of international air services and the further shielding of some lucrative international routes from competition with foreign airlines. Estrada also acquitted Tan from the biggest tax evasion case, and Tan eventually gained the majority control of the privatized Philippine National Bank, the biggest commercial bank in the nation (Bello *et al.* 2004: 243–53). Thus, Lucio Tan, who had prospered under Marcos, was able to enjoy special privileges as Estrada's crony, and his business group continues to flourish even after Estrada's fall. This story shows that clientelistic politicians like Estrada are prone to capture by big businesses.

In contrast, Korea and Taiwan have not only established meritocratic bureaucracy, but have also developed programmatic politics to a considerable extent. Hence, the Korean and Taiwanese states have been less vulnerable to capture by the private interests for some time now. When both countries experienced the rise of clientelism and money politics during the early years of democratic transition, however, they also experienced a considerable degree of capture. Unlike the Philippines, both countries were able to again assert state autonomy because of the traditionally meritocratic bureaucracy and the development of programmatic politics. In Taiwan, the KMT leadership quickly distanced itself from the big businesses when their money politics became severely criticized by the public. In Korea, the *chaebol*'s influence was greater than that of its Taiwanese counterpart, but the change of political leadership during the aftermath of the financial crisis produced democratic state autonomy. The transfer of power to the liberal opposition meant the development of programmatic politics. The popular demand for *chaebol* reform made the position of the *chaebol* weak. Additionally, the new political leadership was less clientelistic than its predecessors. Although state capture by the *chaebol* is a continuing concern in Korea, programmatic politics and a meritocratic bureaucracy will certainly lessen the degree of capture, compared with the Philippines. At the same time, however, Korea's reform was recently stalled and partly reversed under the conservative Lee Myung-bak government. This was largely due to resistance from the powerful *chaebol*. Korea is more vulnerable to elite capture than Taiwan due to higher economic concentration by the *chaebol*.

The impact of state capture on corporate governance and corruption

What were the consequences of differing degrees of capture in the three countries? In the historical narratives, we have seen that state capture by the powerful elite led to incoherence of the economic policy. This resulted in the persistence of income inequality and economic concentration, oligopolistic market structure and poor corporate governance. It also resulted in the prevalence of corruption and rent-seeking in the private sector – not just the big corporations and conglomerates, but all firms regardless of size. Since state capture has been the most pronounced in the Philippines, followed by Korea, these consequences have been the most visible in the Philippines, followed by Korea, and the least visible in Taiwan.

An important consequence of economic concentration and state capture can be found in the oligopolistic market structure that exists in the Philippines. The three countries all embarked on economic liberalization at some time in the 1980s, and one of the goals was to promote market competition by removing protection from both foreign and domestic competition. However, liberalization reforms such as trade and financial liberalization, privatization and deregulation did not necessarily enhance market competition. In the Philippines, privatization often replaced government monopoly with private monopoly, and deregulation failed to enhance competition. Family conglomerates were able to exert influence to protect their monopoly. According to Aldaba (2008), the four-firm concentration ratio for the whole manufacturing sector actually increased from 71 percent in 1988 to 74 percent in 1994 and further to 81 percent in 1998. This is contrasted with Taiwan, where the ratio decreased from 38 percent in 1981 to 31 percent in 1991 (Bhattacharya and Chen 2009). While economic liberalization increased competition in Taiwan, it did not in the Philippines. In Korea, the four-firm concentration ratio in 1998 ranged from 32 percent for chemical industry, 57 percent for textiles, 68 percent for machinery, 69 percent for electronics and 70 percent

Table 7.4 *CG Watch's corporate governance ranks and scores, 2007 and 2010*

Country	2007		2010	
	Rank	Score	Rank	Score
Singapore	2	65	1	67
Hong Kong	1	67	2	65
Japan	5	52	3	57
Taiwan	4	54	4	55
Thailand	8	47	4	55
Malaysia	6	49	6	52
India	3	56	7	49
China	9	45	7	49
Korea	6	49	9	45
Indonesia	11	37	10	40
Philippines	10	41	11	37

Sources: CG Watch (2007; 2010).

for automobiles (Alakent and Lee 2010). Thus, the average four-firm concentration ratio in Korea must be much higher than that in Taiwan. High industrial concentration and capture by the *chaebol* in Korea seem to have maintained considerable degrees of an oligopolistic market structure in many important manufacturing sectors. However, Korean markets were more competitive than those in the Philippines, where almost 90 percent of manufacturing industries had a high concentration ratio of between 70 and 100 percent in 1998 (Aldaba 2008).

This suggests that the effect of liberalization on enhancing competition differed depending on the degree of economic concentration and the ability of the dominant market players to influence and capture the regulatory authorities. This also indicates that the importance of monopoly rents, vis-à-vis innovation rents, is extremely high in the Philippines, still substantial in Korea, but relatively minor in Taiwan. While Korean *chaebols* such as Samsung, Hyundai and LG have proven their competitiveness in global markets, they can still extract substantial monopoly rents from domestic consumers. The oligopolistic market structures in the Philippines and Korea seem to continuously provide the family conglomerates with substantial rents.

High economic concentration and capture in the Philippines and Korea have prohibited the development of transparent corporate governance. Table 7.4 shows CG Watch's corporate governance ranks and scores of eleven Asian countries in 2007 and 2010. Taiwan has maintained a relatively good standing: the fourth place out of eleven. The Philippines has shown the worst performance, the tenth place in 2007 and the eleventh in 2010. Korea was in the middle group in 2007 at sixth place, but it deteriorated to ninth in 2010. Although post-financial crisis reform in Korea substantially improved transparency in corporate governance and the financial sector, corporate governance has markedly deteriorated during the *chaebol*-friendly Lee Myung-bak administration, considerably offsetting the progress made under the two previous liberal governments (CG Watch 2010; World Economic Forum 2011). The weak corporate governance in Korea poses serious concerns to the future of the country's political economy.

Carney and Child (2013) highlight the problems of opaque corporate governance in their study of shifts in ownership and control in East Asian corporations between 1996 and 2008. They found that the prevalence of opaque ownership vehicles was very high in the Philippines, and the percentage of publicly traded corporations controlled by a family has increased between 1996 and 2008 in the Philippines and Korea. They examined data for the 200 largest corporations by market capitalization for each country at the end of 2008, including both financial and non-financial institutions. The proportion of firms for which the largest owner could not be discerned due to the use of trust accounts, nominee accounts or holding companies was as high as 42.7 percent in the Philippines, the highest among the nine East Asian countries they surveyed. The same percentage was 20.5 percent for Korea and 17.7 percent for Taiwan. Thus, the Philippine firms had the most opaque ownership structure.

Carney and Child (2013) also looked at changes to the control of publicly traded companies in these countries.[4] The percentage of family-controlled corporations in 2008 was 76.5 percent in the Philippines, up from 44.6 percent in 1996. The percentage increased in Korea from 26.3 percent in 1996 to 35.8 percent in 2008, while the percentage declined in Taiwan from 48.2 percent in 1996 to 4.7 percent in 2008. The proportion of widely held firms in Taiwan increased during the same period from 26.2 to 75.1 percent. Considering that they were unable to determine the largest owner for more than 40 percent of firms in the Philippines, the proportion of family-controlled firms in the country may be even higher than 76.5 percent. Their analysis shows the continuing, and increasing, dominance of elite families in the Philippine economy. It also suggests

---

[4] Carney and Child (2013) examined the ultimate control of firms at two cut-off levels: 10 and 20 percent of voting rights. I present their results based on a 20 percent cut-off level. If a family controls more than 20 percent of voting rights and no one else has a larger control than the family, the firm is considered to be family-controlled.

that the dominance of family-controlled large corporations in the Korean economy is growing, while it is declining in the Taiwanese economy.

Finally, state capture increases the prevalence of corruption and rent-seeking among firms of all sizes. Since the largest conglomerates may be able to exert considerable influence via connections and legal means, they may use illegal means less than smaller conglomerates and firms. But when the most powerful interests can substantially influence the laws and rules to their advantage, less powerful actors have to rely on corruption even more. Marie dela Rama's (2012) ethnographic study of corporate governance and corruption describes the ethical dilemmas faced by Philippine entrepreneurs. She quotes examples of remarks made by private-sector interviewees as follows:

It is a weak state controlled and manipulated by rent-seeking elites that would lean on government so they can extract monopoly and profits ... the culture of rent-seeking is to capture politicians – to capture the decision making. (private sector 6)

Corruption is pervasive not only in the public sector but also in the private sector. Doing business with private corporations, you also have to give kickbacks. Not to all of them but a number. For example, the [sector my business is in] is a duopoly. There is no proper regulation for the regulatory authorities [to oversee it]. For purchasing they ask you for kickbacks. Even banking executives ask for kickbacks for giving loans. That's the environment. (private sector 5)

One sign of elite capture is weakness in enforcing rules about corporate abuse. In the Philippines, this is most clearly manifested in the weak supervisory power of the Central Bank. Although the weak Central Bank tried to clean up the banking system, it was unable to stop collusive practices among the banks or to apply legal sanctions in a uniform and consistent manner. The Central Bank regulators were often intimidated by lawsuits from the private banks as the "supervisors were sued by the supervised" (Hutchcroft 1998: 202–3). Congress weakened the supervisory capacity of the BSP, the new central bank, by strengthening the already strict bank secrecy law, which made it extremely difficult for supervisors to examine suspicious deposit transactions (Hutchcroft 1998: 211). The country's bank secrecy laws are considered "among the strictest in the world in the face of the global trend toward transparency," and a major obstacle to transparent governance and anti-corruption mechanisms, according to former US ambassadors to Manila (Swinnen and Ubac 2012). The pervasive abuses and lack of prosecution are not confined to the banking sector. In over six decades of stock trading in Manila, no individual has ever faced prosecution for insider trading or price manipulation, while there is evidence that family conglomerates frequently trade on their private information (Roche 2005: 228–9). Thus, the problem is not just pervasiveness of corporate corruption, but the lack of prosecution for corrupt businessmen.

In Korea, increasing *chaebol* concentration and opaqueness of corporate governance resulted in an enormous amount of corporate corruption. The case of Hanbo Steel Company is illustrative. Providing astronomical sums of political contributions to the nation's most powerful politicians, including 60 billion won (about US$76 million) of Kim Young-sam's 1992 presidential campaign fund, Hanbo's founder-chairman Chung Tae-soo managed to secure a total of 5.7 trillion won (about US$6.7 billion) in bank loans before his empire eventually crumbled under the weight of snowballing debts (You 2010). The investigation of illegal presidential campaign funds in 2002 shows an interesting pattern. The amount of *chaebol* groups' illegal contributions to the conservative opposition candidate, Lee Hoi-chang, was much greater than those contributions to the liberal ruling party's candidate, Roh Moo-hyun. For example, Samsung group gave Lee 34 billion won (about US$34 million), or more than ten times its contribution of 3 billion won (about US$ 3 million) to Roh. This clearly indicates that the *chaebol* groups were trying to influence the presidential election (Mo 2009).

Most *chaebol* groups also exercise influence through elaborate lobbying programs, apparently including illegal methods. The Samsung group, the largest *chaebol* group, is considered to be the most sophisticated on this front. In 2005, a set of audio tapes recorded by the National Information Service was exposed, in which the chairman of Joongang Ilbo, a major daily, and his brother-in-law, chairman Lee Kun-hee of Samsung, were discussing the amount of money with which to bribe various politicians and prosecutors. However, the prosecution ignored this clear evidence of corruption on the ground that the tapes were a product of illegal eavesdropping. In 2007, a former high-ranking in-house lawyer of Samsung blew the whistle concerning the group's large slush funds, confessing that he himself gave cash-filled envelopes regularly to government officials and prosecutors. A special prosecutor was appointed to investigate the case, but the investigation was less than thorough, and the courts were lenient toward the largest *chaebol* (You 2010). While the courts have tended to give out quite strict sentences to corrupt politicians and bureaucrats, they have seldom given prison terms to corrupt business leaders.

Capture by the *chaebol* seems to operate on multiple levels, including the executive, legislature and the judiciary. The economic bureaucracy, especially its upper echelons, tends to advocate pro-*chaebol* policies. In

2005, it was revealed that the bureaucrats in charge of creating an effective enforcement mechanism for the regulation on equity holdings by *chaebol*-affiliated financial companies, which Samsung was violating, drafted legislation based on feedback from a law firm that was hired by Samsung. The *chaebol's* political influence also derives from their influence over the mass media through direct ownership of some media outlets and through advertisement expenditures (You 2010).

In Taiwan, the degree of business concentration and capture was relatively low, but corporate corruption was not absent. After democratization, business groups tried to establish ties with legislators, providing sizable sums of campaign contributions. Business groups with a regional base also invested heavily in the elections for county magistrates and city mayors (Chu 1994). Some of these conglomerates further invested in the mass media sector; these investments could have been used for political purposes at the time of election (Kuo 2000). In one notorious case, it was known that a top business group, through the exercise of "purse power," once enjoyed majority control over the Finance Committee in the Legislative Yuan (Tien and Chu 1996).

Certainly, economic policy-making has become more politicized in Taiwan, and the political influence of business has increased. Business lobby and kickbacks play a role in various policy decisions about potentially lucrative business opportunities. For example, during the process of privatization and conglomeration of banks in 2004, the major financial holding companies mobilized legislators and used connections to high officials in the presidential office, even to the first family, to gain the upper hand. A series of scandals involving influence peddling, kickbacks and backdoor deals were exposed (Wu 2007). However, there has been no such large-scale corporate attempt to capture the entire state apparatus through systematic lobbying and bribing of key officials in various branches of government as was seen in Samsung's slush fund scandal. The scope and frequency of corporate corruption in Taiwan are generally regarded as less than those in Korea and the Philippines.

8   Cross-national evidence for generalizability

Previous chapters have explored how different levels of inequality have affected electoral clientelism, bureaucratic patronage and elite capture through comparative historical analysis. The diverging historical experiences of the three East Asian countries which shared similar initial conditions at the time of independence after World War II provide convincing evidence in support of my theoretical arguments and theory-based hypotheses. However, it is still by no means certain whether these findings are generalizable beyond the three countries studied. One cannot rule out the possibility of some unobservable factors unique to the East Asian context.

While cross-country quantitative study has disadvantages in terms of unearthing causal directions and mechanisms, it can be an effective method of drawing more generalizable findings by using data collected from large numbers of countries across the world. Although the lack of reliable longitudinal data on corruption limits the ability of quantitative analysis, the use of adequate instrumental variables can help to address the problem of endogeneity. Furthermore, the availability of recently created data on clientelism and patronage for a large number of countries, combined with data on capture (albeit for a more limited number of countries), makes it possible to conduct some rudimentary test of causal mechanisms.

There are numerous cross-national analyses of the causes of corruption, but the results often differ depending on the data and methodology. In particular, the reliability and accuracy of cross-national measures of corruption has been a subject of controversy. Therefore, it is important to understand the issues in measuring corruption, together with the pros and cons of various available data on corruption, as was discussed in some length in Chapter 3. Due to the high correlation between CPI or CCI scores for the earliest available year and the latest year, and the reliability issues regarding the ICRG index discussed in Chapter 3, I will not conduct panel data analysis. Since no single measure of corruption is perfect, I use a variety of available data, including measures of both perceived and experienced corruption. The problem of endogeneity is addressed by employing instrumental variables.

The results of various quantitative analyses provide substantial evidence for both the main hypotheses and the causal mechanism hypotheses of this book. Thus, this chapter is complementary to the previous chapters, and builds a strong case for generalizability.

Data

In my analysis of cross-national patterns of corruption and inequality across levels of democracy, I rely on the large data set compiled by the Quality of Government Institute at the University of Gothenburg (Teorell *et al.* 2011). The QoG Standard Data Set provides data on a range of indicators of government quality, including many political, economic, social and geographic variables. I use its cross-section data for circa 2002 (version 6 Apr 11). I supplement it with some additional data on corruption, inequality and instrumental variables from other sources.

As measures of corruption, I use the CPI, CCI, ICRG, TI's Global Corruption Barometer (GCB) surveys and the World Economic Forum's Executive Opinion Surveys. Since data on some important variables are unavailable for years after 2002 in the data set, I use the average values of CPI and CCI for the five-year period between 2002 and 2006 instead of single-year data. Since the levels of corruption for most countries change little for a five-year period (the correlation between CPI 2002 and CPI 2006 is 0.96, and the equivalent for CCI is 0.94), and short-term variations may contain more measurement errors than real changes, averaging will help to reduce measurement error. The CPI scores can range between zero (most corrupt) and ten (least corrupt), and a higher value counterintuitively represents a lower level of corruption. The CCI scores have a mean of zero and a standard deviation of one, and a higher value represents a better control of corruption, or a lower level of corruption.

Next, I use the ICRG indicator for quality of government (ICRG_QoG), which is the mean value for the ICRG variables "Corruption", "Law and Order" and "Bureaucracy Quality," scaled zero to one. Higher values indicate a higher quality of government. The QoG data set does not provide data for component variables because the PRS Group makes them available for purchase only.[1] I also use data on

---

[1] The component variables can be purchased at www.countrydata.com. Law and Order measures the strength and impartiality of the legal system, as well as popular observance of the law. Bureaucratic quality measures the strength and expertise to govern without drastic changes in policy or interruptions in government services. High quality bureaucracy

experience with bribery from TI's Global Corruption Barometer (GCB) surveys (GCB_Bribery) as a measure of petty bureaucratic corruption. GCB_Bribery is the percentage of respondents whose family member has paid a bribe to any public officials during the last year, averaged for every survey done for each country from 2004 to 2010/2011. As measures for political corruption and corporate corruption, I use data from the World Economic Forum's Executive Opinion Surveys. Three questions ask about the extent of irregular payments in government policy-making, the prevalence of illegal political donations and the policy consequences of legal political donations. I use the average value for these responses to represent political corruption. These questions were asked in 2002, 2003, 2004 and 2006. Corporate corruption is denoted by the average evaluation of the corporate ethics displayed in firms in the country, compared with other countries in the world, averaged for 2003 and 2006. The response values for the questions on political and corporate corruption range between one (among the worst in the world) and seven (among the best in the world).

In addition to the measurement challenges discussed regarding corruption, there are many issues with regard to conceptualization and measurement for the two key explanatory variables – democracy and economic inequality.[2] In order to robustly identify the effect of democracy and inequality on corruption, I use several measures of democracy and economic inequality. As a measure of democracy as a dichotomous variable (democracy versus dictatorship), I use data created by Cheibub et al. (2010).[3] I also constructed a three-category measure of democracy: *liberal democracy*, *illiberal electoral democracy* and *dictatorship*. *Liberal democracies* are countries which the Freedom House assigns "Free" status.[4] *Illiberal electoral democracies* are countries wherein multiple parties

---

tends to be somewhat autonomous from political pressure and to have an established mechanism for recruitment and training (QoG Standard Dataset Codebook 2011).

[2] Regarding the issues in conceptualizing and measuring democracy, see Munck and Verkuilen (2002). Regarding the issues in measuring income inequality, see Deininger and Squire (1996).

[3] Coded 1 if democracy, 0 otherwise. "A regime is considered a democracy if the executive and the legislature is directly or indirectly elected by popular vote, multiple parties are allowed, there is de facto existence of multiple parties outside of regime front, there are multiple parties within the legislature, and there has been no consolidation of incumbent advantage (e.g. unconstitutional closing of the lower house or extension of incumbent's term by postponing of subsequent elections). Transition years are coded as the regime that emerges in that year" (QoG Standard Dataset Codebook 2011).

[4] Freedom House labels countries "Free," "Partly Free" or "Not Free" according to the average of their political rights and civil liberties scores. "Free" countries should have an average score between 1 and 2.5. Both political rights and civil liberties scores range between 1 (most free) and 7 (least free).

win seats in the legislature, and multiple parties compete in the executive elections based on Beck et al.'s (2001) database of political institutions,[5] but which do not qualify as "Free" countries according to the Freedom House. *Dictatorships* are countries that fall short of illiberal electoral democracy. As measures of democracy as a continuous variable, I use the Polity IV Combined Score (Marshall and Jaggers 2002) and the Freedom House's political rights score.[6] The Combined Polity Score ranges between −10 (strongly autocratic) and +10 (strongly democratic). I converted the Freedom House's score (between one and seven) so that a higher score may represent a more free society. I also use the Freedom House's index of Press Freedom, which ranges from zero (least free) to 100 (most free).[7] Finally, I use "Years of electoral democracy" from data created by Treisman (2007). This variable denotes the number of consecutive years since 1930 the country had been an electoral democracy as of 2000, as classified by Beck et al. (2001).[8]

As a measure of income inequality, I primarily use the "Estimated Household Income Inequality" from data provided by the University of Texas Inequality Project (Galbraith and Kum 2004; Galbraith 2009). Galbraith and Kum (2004) estimate *gini* coefficients for gross income inequality through an equation whereby income *gini* in the Deininger and Squire (1996) high quality data set is regressed on a measure of manufacturing pay inequality. They argue that this measure has better comparability both across countries and over time. I also use the *Gini* Index of income inequality from the World Income Inequality Database compiled

---

[5] Electoral democracies are defined as countries that score at least 6 in both the legislative index of political competitiveness and the executive index of political competitiveness in the database of political institutions constructed by Beck et al. (2001).

[6] "Political rights enable people to participate freely in the political process, including the right to vote freely for distinct alternatives in legitimate elections, compete for public office, join political parties and organizations, and elect representatives who have a decisive impact on public policies and are accountable to the electorate" (QoG Standard Dataset Codebook 2011).

[7] The press freedom index is computed by adding three (four) component ratings: Laws and regulations, Political pressures and controls, and Economic Influences (and Repressive actions). Until 2000, "Repressive actions" was a fourth component of the index, but since 2001, such violations within the respective "Political pressures" and "Economic influences" categories are treated as cases of actual political or economic pressure on the content of information (QoG Standard Dataset Codebook 2011). The original score ranges from 0 (most free) to 100 (least free), but I converted it so that a higher score represents a more free press.

[8] Treisman's (2007) definition of electoral democracy is slightly different from mine (see n. 4). He defines electoral democracies as those with a score of 6 or higher on Beck et al.'s (2001) Executive Index of Electoral Competitiveness (QoG Standard Dataset Codebook 2011). Thus, he does not consider the Legislative Index of Electoral Competitiveness in his definition of electoral democracy.

by the United Nations University (UNU-WIDER, version WIID2c). The *Gini* Index varies theoretically from zero (perfectly equal distribution of income) to 100 (the society's total income accrues to only one person/household unit).[9]

In order to test sub-hypotheses on the causal mechanisms, I require cross-national measures of political clientelism, patronage in bureaucracy and state capture by the private sector. Until recently, studies of clientelism have been constrained by the lack of reliable cross-national data. Fortunately, I was able to obtain Herbert Kitschelt's (2013) new data set on the democratic accountability and linkages, which is based on expert surveys of eighty-eight countries about various features of clientelistic and programmatic politics. The surveys were conducted in 2008 and 2009, and members of the Duke Democracy Project, including Singer (2009), have presented some papers using the data.[10] For patronage versus meritocracy in bureaucracy, there exist two available cross-national data sets. Rauch and Evans (2000) constructed data on bureaucratic structure for thirty-five developing countries. Recently, the Quality of Government Institute created another data set on bureaucratic structure for 105 countries around the world, based on a web survey of country experts (Teorell *et al.* 2011). I use their index of professionalization of bureaucracy, which ranges between one and seven, and a higher value indicates a more professionalized and less politicized public administration.[11] Regarding state capture, currently available cross-national data exists for only twenty-two transition economies, which was created by Hellman *et al.* (2000). Their "capture economy index" is based on the 1999 Business Environment and Enterprise Performance Survey (BEEPS) data on how much firms' business is affected by the sale of parliamentary votes on laws and presidential decrees to private interests, the sale of court decisions and illicit political contributions by private interests, etc.

---

[9] *Gini* coefficients for income inequality can be based on different definitions of income, such as gross and net income. Hence, cross-national comparison should be conducted with care. The UTIP data for estimated household income inequality is based on gross income, but the UNU-WIDER data are based on a variety of income and population concepts.

[10] The full data set of the Democratic Accountability and Linkages Project has not been released as of June 2013, but it will be released soon.

[11] Teorell *et al.*'s (2011) professionalization index is based on the following four questions: When recruiting public sector employees, do the skills and merits of the applicants decide who gets the job? When recruiting public sector employees, do the political connections of the applicants decide who gets the job? Does the top political leadership hire and fire senior public officials? Are senior public officials recruited from within the ranks of the public sector?

Instrumental variables

For regression analysis, I first employ ordinary least squares (OLS) regressions. I then use instrumental variable regressions in order to address the concerns of reverse causality in the relationship between inequality and corruption (Gupta *et al.* 2002; Li *et al.* 2000), as well as measurement error. Specifically, OLS regressions may overestimate the effect of inequality because of reverse causality. Hence, I need some instrumental variables that are strongly correlated with inequality, but are not directly correlated with corruption, other than indirectly through inequality. Furthermore, economic development is known to be influenced by corruption (Mauro 1995; Kaufmann and Kraay 2002), so OLS regressions may overestimate the effect of economic development on the control of corruption. Since inequality and economic development are correlated with each other, overestimation of economic development effect could lead to underestimation of inequality effect. Hence, per capita income as an indicator of economic development also needs to be instrumented.

Another problem is the large measurement error in income inequality. It is well known that income inequality is poorly measured in comparison to aggregate income. The measurement error in an independent variable renders the estimated OLS effect biased toward zero if the measurement error is uncorrelated with the dependent variable or the unobserved explanatory variable. This is called attenuation bias (Wooldridge 2000: 294–6). A relatively precise measure of per capita income and an imprecise measure of income inequality can cause the OLS-estimated effect for per capita income to be overestimated and that for inequality to be underestimated. Instrumental variables can help to alleviate the bias caused by measurement error in inequality.

I use two instruments for inequality. First, I use "mature cohort size" as an instrument for inequality, following You and Khagram (2005). Higgins and Williamson (1999) show that "mature cohort size" (ratio of the population 40 to 59 years old to the population 15 to 69 years old) is a powerful predictor of inequality, both across countries and within the United States. Because "fat cohorts" tend to get low rewards, when these fat cohorts lie at the top of the age-earnings curve (or when the mature cohort is fat), earnings inequality is reduced. When the fat cohorts are old or young adults, earnings inequality is augmented. In addition, I use "wheat to sugar ratio" as another instrument for inequality, following Easterly (2007). Engerman and Sokoloff (1997) argued that factor endowments such as the exogenous suitability of land for wheat versus sugar cane were a central determinant of inequality across the Americas. Easterly (2007) shows that the wheat to sugar ratio, defined as the log of [(1 + share of arable land suitable for wheat)/(1 + share of arable land suitable for sugar cane)], is a powerful predictor of inequality across countries. The data for these instrumental variables are taken from You and Khagram (2005) and Easterly (2007).

As instruments for per capita income, I use "distance from the equator" (calculated as the absolute value of latitude) and the "prevalence of malaria index." Distance from the equator is strongly correlated with the level of economic development, but latitude is unlikely to be directly correlated with corruption.[12] Gallup and Sachs (2000) demonstrated that malaria prevalence is a strong determinant of economic development, but that malaria is very geographically specific and minimally affected by economic development.

Cross-national evidence

Let me start by comparing three types of political regimes (liberal democracies, illiberal electoral democracies and dictatorships) across three levels of inequality (low, medium and high) to see if there are systematic differences in the levels of corruption. Table 8.1 displays the average CPI (Corruption Perceptions Index, average for 2002 to 2006), or perceived freedom from corruption, by political regime type and income inequality (both for 2002 or closest year available). Here, the measure of income inequality was taken from the University of Texas Inequality Project (UTIP) data for estimated household income inequality (in the *Gini* Index), and high-inequality and low-inequality countries are those for which the *Gini* Index is at least a half standard deviation higher or lower than the mean. Recall that a higher value of CPI denotes a lower level of corruption. The number of countries in each cell is in parenthesis.

The average CPI for sixty-eight liberal democracies (5.47) is much higher than that for fifty-six illiberal electoral democracies (2.73), as well as that for thirty-seven dictatorships (3.27). It is notable, however, that illiberal electoral democracies are perceived to be slightly more corrupt than dictatorships. Perhaps the introduction of elections without full democratization does increase perceived corruption rather than reduce it. Regardless, the effect of democracy on corruption seems to vary depending on the level of inequality. Among the countries with low inequality, liberal democracies (average CPI = 6.84) tend to be much less corrupt

---

[12] Treisman (2007) used "distance from the equator" as an instrument for economic development.

Table 8.1 *Perceived freedom from corruption (CPI) by income inequality and regime type*

Regime type Inequality	Liberal CPI (N)	Electoral CPI (N)	Dictatorships CPI (N)	Unknown CPI (N)	Total CPI (N)
Low	6.84	4.24	3.63	4	6.21
(*Gini* < 41.5)	(30)	(6)	(2)	(1)	(39)
Medium	4.63	2.6	3.07	–	3.46
(*Gini* 41.5–48.2)	(23)	(26)	(12)		(61)
High	2.98	2.64	3.87	2.1	3.14
(*Gini* > 48.2)	(8)	(16)	(14)	(1)	(39)
Unknown	5.19	2.19	2.53	5.82	3.48
(*Gini* missing)	(7)	(8)	(9)	(3)	(27)
Total	5.47	2.73	3.27	4.71	4.03
	(68)	(56)	(37)	(5)	(166)

than illiberal electoral democracies (average CPI = 4.24) and dictatorships (average CPI = 3.63). Thus, liberal democracy seems to make a big difference among the low-inequality countries. At low levels of inequality, the effect of illiberal electoral democracy is uncertain.[13]

Among the countries with medium inequality, liberal democracies (average CPI = 4.63) tend to be substantially less corrupt than illiberal electoral democracies (average CPI = 2.60) and dictatorships (average CPI = 3.07), but illiberal electoral democracies are slightly more corrupt than dictatorships. Although liberal democracy has a significantly positive effect on controlling corruption among the medium-inequality countries, illiberal electoral democracy seems to have a slightly negative effect.

Among the high-inequality countries, both liberal democracies (average CPI = 2.98) and illiberal electoral democracies (average CPI = 2.64) are slightly more corrupt than dictatorships (average CPI = 3.87). Democracy seems to have a negative effect on controlling corruption among the high-inequality countries. The table suggests that the effect of democracy on controlling corruption varies depending on the level of inequality, being positive and large at low levels of inequality, but slightly negative at high levels of inequality. In particular, illiberal electoral democracy is associated with higher corruption among the medium- and high-inequality countries. The overall pattern is consistent

[13] Although electoral democracies (N = 6) are on average slightly less corrupt than dictatorships (N = 2) among the low-inequality countries, we cannot be certain about that because of the small sample size.

with the main hypothesis (H1) that the effect of democracy on reducing corruption is negatively associated with the level of inequality.

We can read the table in another way. The average CPI for thirty-nine low-inequality countries (6.21) is much higher than that for sixty-one medium-inequality countries (3.46), which in turn is slightly higher than that for thirty-nine high-inequality countries (3.14). Thus, countries with low levels of income inequality tend to be perceived as significantly less corrupt. But the correlation between inequality and corruption seems to vary depending on the political regime type. Within liberal democracies, the average CPI for countries with low income inequality is 6.84, that for countries with medium inequality is 4.63 and that for countries with high inequality is 2.98. Thus, higher inequality is significantly associated with higher corruption among liberal democracies. Within illiberal electoral democracies, the average CPI for countries with low income inequality is 4.24, that for countries with medium inequality is 2.60 and that for countries with high inequality is 2.64. Thus, high and medium inequality do not make a difference among illiberal electoral democracies, and only low inequality seems to be associated with low corruption. Among dictatorships, the average CPI for the countries with low inequality (3.63), that for countries with medium inequality (3.07) and that for countries with high inequality (3.87) are not very different from each other. Thus, inequality does not show any relationship with corruption among dictatorships. The overall pattern shows that higher inequality tends to be strongly associated with higher corruption in liberal democracies and weakly correlated in illiberal electoral democracies, but that inequality does not matter in dictatorships, consistent with hypothesis 2 (H2).

Conducting the most straightforward empirical analysis yields similar results. Using various measures of democracy, Table 8.2 presents the results of OLS regressions of corruption on democracy, income inequality (*Gini* Index measured by UTIP) and the level of economic development (natural logarithm of per capita GDP from Heston *et al.* (2009)). The table shows that income inequality is significantly negative and economic development is significantly positive for perceived freedom from corruption (CPI), but the significance of the democracy effect depends on the measure of democracy. Cheibub *et al.*'s (2010) measure of democracy as a dichotomous variable (democracy or dictatorship) and Polity IV combined score as a continuous variable (-10 to $+10$) are statistically insignificant, when income inequality and economic development are accounted for. However, the three-category measure of democracy (liberal democracy = 2, illiberal electoral democracy = 1 and dictatorship = 0), Freedom House's political rights score (1 to 7) and freedom of the press index (1 to 100), and consecutive years of electoral democracy

(0 to 70) are significantly associated with higher CPI (lower levels of perceived corruption), controlling for income inequality and economic development. When I added an interaction term between democracy and income inequality, the interaction term was significantly negative regardless of the democracy measure. This indicates that democracy is more strongly associated with freedom from corruption at lower levels of inequality, consistent with the main hypothesis (H1). This also indicates that in democracies (or in more democratic countries or older democracies), inequality is more strongly associated with corruption. In particular, column four presents direct evidence supporting hypothesis 2 (H2) that the effect of inequality on corruption in *liberal democracies* is higher than that in *illiberal electoral democracies*, which in turn is higher than that in *dictatorships*. The interaction term between democracy and per capita income is also significant. The democracy effect on control of corruption seems to be higher in richer countries, as well as in more equal countries.

These results are robust to changes in the measures of corruption used. Table 8.3 displays the same patterns as columns eleven and twelve in Table 8.2 (with consecutive years of electoral democracy and UTIP's estimated household income inequality as the key independent variables), using various measures of corruption (Control of Corruption Indicator, ICRG_QoG, GCB_Bribery, political corruption and corporate corruption) as the dependent variable. Older democracies, more equal countries and richer countries are significantly less corrupt, regardless of the measure of corruption. The only exception is that the duration of democracy is not significantly associated with perceived political corruption. These results provide partial evidence for the sub-hypotheses (H1.1 to H1.3) that inequality increases political corruption, bureaucratic corruption and corporate corruption, especially in democracies. In addition, the interaction term between the age of electoral democracy and income inequality is significantly negative for most measures of corruption, except for experience of bribery from TI's Global Barometer Survey (GCB_Bribery).[14] This indicates that the effect of democracy duration varies depending on the level of income inequality. Specifically, the effect of democratic longevity turns out to be positive for perceived freedom from political corruption at low levels of income inequality ($gini < 41.7$), but it becomes negative as inequality increases more highly. Thus, perceived political corruption, as well as other types of corruption, tends to

---

[14] The signs of the coefficients in regressions of bribery (regressions three and eight) are opposite to those in other regression results because a higher value of bribery represents a higher level of corruption, contrary to other measures of corruption.

Table 8.2 *Effects of democracy and income inequality on CPI, using various measures of democracy*

Measure of democracy	Democracy dummy		Liberal/electoral democracy		Polity	Score
	(1)	(2)	(3)	(4)	(5)	(6)
Democracy	0.0169	-3.7123	0.2921*	-1.9011	0.0142	-0.1426***
	(0.2385)	(2.4286)	(0.1598)	(1.7241)	(0.0195)	(0.1656)
Income inequality	-0.0857***	-0.0205	-0.0790***	0.0257	-0.0801***	-0.0312*
	(0.0186)	(0.0257)	(0.0177)	(0.0256)	(0.0193)	(0.0185)
Democracy × Inequality		-0.0600*		-0.0561**		-0.0064**
		(0.0345)		(0.0231)		(0.0027)
Per capita income	1.1399***	0.7626***	1.1138***	0.5041***	1.0970***	0.9296***
	(0.0987)	(0.1388)	(0.0989)	(0.1392)	(0.0977)	(0.1154)
Democracy × Income		0.7542***		0.5380***		0.0516***
		(0.2111)		(0.1189)		(0.0136)
Constant	-2.0156	-1.9372	-2.4390*	-2.0872	-1.9459	-2.9244**
	(1.2879)	(1.2322)	(1.2704)	(1.4464)	(1.2800)	(1.0559)
N	137	137	135	135	129	129
R-squared	0.6316	0.6827	0.6475	0.7152	0.6205	0.6732

Measure of democracy	FH political rights		FH press freedom		Years of electoral democracy	
	(7)	(8)	(9)	(10)	(11)	(12)
Democracy	0.1481**	-1.0860*	0.0222***	-0.0848	0.0345***	-0.0137
	(0.0616)	(0.6215)	(0.0056)	(0.0587)	(0.0061)	(0.0655)
Income inequality	-0.0735***	0.0121	-0.0617***	0.0369	-0.0601***	0.0006
	(0.0172)	(0.0287)	(0.0159)	(0.0409)	(0.0146)	(0.0148)

	(1)	(2)	(3)	(4)	(5)	(6)
Democracy × Inequality		−0.0153*		−0.0014*		−0.0027***
		(0.0085)		(0.0008)		(0.0006)
Per capita income	1.0494***	0.1497	0.9737***	0.0616	0.8596***	0.6721***
	(0.1024)	(0.2138)	(0.1043)	(0.2383)	(0.1069)	(0.0961)
Democracy × Income		0.2154***		0.0185***		0.0160***
		(0.0453)		(0.0041)		(0.0050)
Constant	−2.3015	0.7195	−2.8276**	0.7494	−1.3861	−2.2999**
	(1.1980)	(2.2114)	(1.1441)	(2.7160)	(1.2178)	(1.1387)
N	137	137	137	137	135	135
R-squared	0.6462	0.6793	0.6718	0.7130	0.7226	0.7976

Notes: Robust standard errors are in parentheses. *, ** and *** denote significance at the level of 10, 5 and 1 percent respectively. The same applies to subsequent tables.

Table 8.3 *OLS regressions of corruption, using various measures of corruption*

	CCI	ICRG	Bribery	Political	Corporate
Measure of corruption	(1)	(2)	(3)	(4)	(5)
Years of democracy	0.0146***	0.0025***	−0.0107***	0.0049	0.0141***
	(0.0026)	(0.0006)	(0.0033)	(0.0042)	(0.0027)
Income inequality	−0.0298***	−0.0078***	0.0539***	−0.0234*	−0.0227***
	(0.0080)	(0.0014)	(0.0092)	(0.0125)	(0.0084)
Per capita income	0.4231***	0.0863***	−0.4947***	0.3353***	0.3504***
	(0.0550)	(0.0100)	(0.0675)	(0.0997)	(0.0574)
Constant	−2.6398***	0.0604	4.8116***	1.9770*	1.8622***
	(0.6917)	(0.1179)	(0.8164)	(1.1753)	(0.6858)
N	140	119	97	113	113
R-squared	0.7084	0.7145	0.7904	0.3488	0.6733
With interaction effect:	(6)	(7)	(8)	(9)	(10)
Years of democracy	−0.0170	−0.0082	0.0110	0.0598	0.0468
	(0.0441)	(0.0083)	(0.0556)	(0.0505)	(0.0317)
Income inequality	−0.0115	−0.0044***	0.0512***	0.0265*	0.0062
	(0.0076)	(0.0012)	(0.0113)	(0.0161)	(0.0090)
Democracy × Inequality	−0.0007*	−0.0001	0.0000	−0.0025***	−0.0014***
	(0.0004)	(0.0001)	(0.0005)	(0.0005)	(0.0003)
Per capita income	0.3553***	0.0654***	−0.4721***	0.2387**	0.2955***
	(0.0549)	(0.0109)	(0.0693)	(0.0959)	(0.0545)
Democracy × Income	0.0063**	0.0015**	−0.0023	0.0046	0.0026
	(0.0031)	(0.0007)	(0.0043)	(0.0038)	(0.0024)
Constant	−2.8070***	0.1038	4.7218***	0.7182	1.1266*
	(0.6662)	(0.1145)	(0.8769)	(1.2826)	(0.6086)
N	140	119	97	113	113
R-squared	0.7453	0.7529	0.7920	0.5244	0.7367

decrease over time in low-inequality democracies, but all types tend to increase over time in high-inequality countries. Note that the interaction term between the age of democracy and per capita income is also significant for the Control of Corruption Indicator and ICRG index of Quality of Government, but it is not significant for GCB experience of bribery, political corruption and corporate corruption.

Thus far, the OLS results show that democracy is strongly associated with lower corruption and that inequality is strongly associated with higher corruption, and they have demonstrated this having used a variety of measures for democracy and corruption. In order to address the concerns about reverse causality and measurement error, I employ

instrumental variables for inequality and economic development, as I
noted above. Table 8.4 presents the results of the instrumental variable
regressions in comparison with OLS results, using consecutive years of
electoral democracy as the measure of democracy and CPI as the dependent variable. Two measures of income inequality (UTIP and UNU-
WIDER) are used, and they are instrumented by "mature cohort size"
and "wheat-sugar ratio." Per capita income is instrumented by "distance
from the equator" (absolute value of latitude) and "malaria index." All
of the instrumental variable regressions pass the over-identification test,
implying that we cannot reject the hypothesis that these instruments are
uncorrelated with the error term of the second stage regressions.

The instrumental regression results align with the previous finding that
income inequality is significantly and strongly associated with corruption.
However, per capita income loses significance as a predictor of corruption. Comparison of OLS and IV regression results shows that coefficients for inequality are larger in magnitude from IV regressions than
from OLS regressions, while coefficients for per capita income are smaller
from IV regressions. When the UTIP measure of gross income inequality is used, the coefficient for inequality is -0.0601 from OLS regression
(model 1) and -0.2901 from IV regression (model 2). Although the coefficient for per capita income was large (0.8596) and highly significant
from the OLS regression (model 1), it effectively becomes nil (-0.0840)
from the IV regression (model 2). The IV regression indicates that a one
standard deviation (6.7) increase in UTIP income *gini* is associated with
a 0.86 standard deviation (1.94) decrease in CPI, while the effect of per
capita income is nil.[15] With the UNU-WIDER measure of inequality,
the coefficient for inequality is much larger in magnitude from the IV
regression (-0.1014 in model 6) than from the OLS regression (-0.0326
in model 5). But the coefficient for per capita income from IV regression
(0.3196) is much smaller than that from OLS regression (0.8461).[16]
These results suggest that OLS regressions overestimated the effect of
economic development because of reverse causality and underestimated
the effect of inequality because of measurement error. Also, the IV results
are consistent with the finding of Kaufmann and Kraay (2002) that

---

[15] Precisely speaking, the IV regression (model 2) indicates that a one standard deviation
(1.2) increase in natural logarithm of GDP per capita is associated with a statistically
insignificant 0.04 standard deviation (0.1) decrease in CPI.

[16] According to the IV regression (model 6), a one standard deviation (10.2) increase in
WIDER income *gini* is associated with a 0.47 standard deviation (1.03) decrease in CPI,
while a one standard deviation (1.2) increase in natural logarithm of GDP per capita
is associated with a statistically insignificant 0.16 standard deviation (0.38) increase in
CPI.

Table 8.4 *Effects of democracy and income inequality on CPI, using instrumental variables*

Measure of inequality	UTIP estimated income *gini* (2002)			
	(1) OLS	(2) IV	(3) OLS	(4) IV
Years of democracy	0.0345***	0.0405***	−0.0137	0.2840
	(0.0061)	(0.0125)	(0.0655)	(0.2569)
Income inequality	−0.0601***	−0.2901***	0.0006	−0.1165
	(0.0146)	(0.0818)	(0.0148)	(0.1018)
Democracy × Inequality			−0.0027***	−0.0046
			(0.0006)	(0.0029)
Per capita income	0.8596***	−0.0840	0.6721***	0.2976
	(0.1069)	(0.3749)	(0.0961)	(0.2988)
Democracy × Income			0.0160***	−0.0060
			(0.0050)	(0.0154)
Constant	−1.3861	16.7450***	−2.2999**	5.8783
	(1.2178)	(6.2146)	(1.1387)	(6.6508)
N	135	95	135	95
R-squared	0.7226	0.4852	0.7865	0.7001
Over-id test p-value		0.7958		0.9223

Measure of inequality	UNU-WIDER income *gini* (2002)			
	(5) OLS	(6) IV	(7) OLS	(8) IV
Years of democracy	0.0441***	0.0558***	−0.1142*	0.0175
	(0.0066)	(0.0084)	(0.0612)	(0.1251)
Income inequality	−0.0326***	−0.1014***	0.0053	−0.0101
	(0.0108)	(0.0231)	(0.0118)	(0.0240)
Democracy × Inequality			−0.0012**	−0.0019**
			(0.0005)	(0.0009)
Per capita income	0.8461***	0.3196	0.6207***	0.4657***
	(0.1325)	(0.2168)	(0.1177)	(0.1439)
Democracy × Income			0.0204***	0.0105
			(0.0049)	(0.0103)
Constant	−2.8749**	4.2154*	−2.2691*	−0.4912
	(1.3064)	(2.4671)	(1.1727)	(1.6639)
N	141	110	141	110
R-squared	0.7649	0.7014	0.8200	0.8164
Over-id test p-value		0.8754		0.4064

Note: Income inequality was instrumented by "mature cohort size" and "wheat-sugar ratio." Per capita income was instrumented by "distance from the equator" (absolute value of latitude) and "malaria index." Interaction terms are instrumented by interaction terms between the age of democracy and these instruments.

causation runs exclusively from corruption to economic underdevelopment, not from economic underdevelopment to corruption. Note that the coefficients for democracy are also slightly higher from IV regressions than from OLS regressions.

Comparison of OLS and IV estimates of interaction terms also shows an interesting pattern. The coefficients for interaction terms between democracy and inequality are larger in magnitude when instruments are used, but the coefficients for interaction terms between democracy and income become smaller with the use of instrumental variables. When the UTIP measure of inequality is used, the coefficient for the interaction term between democracy and inequality is larger in magnitude from the IV regression (−0.0046 in model 4) than from the OLS regression (−0.0027 in model 3). But the coefficient for the interaction term between democracy and per capita income is smaller from the IV regression (−0.0060 in model 4) than from the OLS regression (0.0160 in model 3). Although the interaction term between democracy and inequality is not significant at the 10 percent level in the IV regression, it is close to significance with a p-value of 0.119. This indicates that ten additional years of democracy is associated with a 0.9 point increase in CPI on average for a low-inequality country with a UTIP *gini* of thirty, but the age of democracy has no effect on CPI for a high-inequality country with a UTIP *gini* of fifty.[17] When the WIDER measure of inequality is used, the coefficient for the interaction term between democracy and inequality from the IV regression (−0.0019 in model 8) is larger in magnitude than that from the OLS regression (−0.0012 in model 7). But the coefficient for the interaction term between democracy and per capita income from the IV regression (0.0105 in model 8) is smaller than that from the OLS regression (0.0204 in model 7). While the interaction term between democracy and per capita income loses significance in IV regression, the interaction term between democracy and inequality is highly significant. Thus, instrumental variable regressions indicate that the effect of democracy on control of corruption does not significantly depend on the level of economic development, but significantly depends on the level of inequality.

Next, I conducted a series of robustness checks, controlling for various causes of corruption as identified in the extant literature. The results of these tests show that the significance of both duration of democracy and income inequality survives any control that is introduced. This stands true whether CPI or GCB_Bribery are used as the dependent

---

[17] UTIP *gini* has a mean of 44.9 and a standard deviation of 6.7 in the sample of 146 countries. The minimum is 28.96 and the maximum is 64.25.

variable. But many of these causal factors turn out to be insignificant for corruption when duration of democracy, income inequality and economic development are accounted for. For example, various measures of presidential versus parliamentary and electoral systems (i.e. plurality versus proportional representation, closed list versus open list and district magnitude) turned out to be insignificant once duration of democracy, income inequality and economic development were accounted for.[18] Interestingly, the "proportion of women in parliament" was significant even when the duration of democracy, inequality and per capita income were taken into account.[19] Economic freedom was significantly associated with freedom from corruption (higher CPI), and both the number of procedures and time required to start a new business were negatively associated with freedom from corruption (lower CPI). However, the cost of starting a new business was not significant.[20] Trade openness and ethno-linguistic fractionalization were insignificant once the duration of democracy, income inequality and economic development were accounted for.[21]

Next, let me test the three sub-hypotheses (MH1 to MH3) on the causal mechanisms through which inequality inhibits the democratic accountability mechanisms. I have proposed that inequality increases clientelism in elections and thereby political corruption, patronage in bureaucratic recruitment and thereby bureaucratic corruption, state capture by the private sector and thereby corporate corruption, and the difficulty and ineffectiveness of anti-corruption reforms.

In order to more rigorously test the mechanism hypothesis on clientelism, I first examine whether inequality has a causal effect on clientelism. Table 8.5 presents the results. The OLS and IV regressions (columns 1 and 2) both show that inequality has a highly significant effect on clientelism, but economic development (per capita income) loses significance in IV regression. When I introduced interaction terms

---

[18] Regime type (presidential, assembly-elected presidential or parliamentary system), mean district magnitude, plurality or proportional representation (for the House seats) and closed lists (or open lists for proportional representation) from the Beck et al.'s (2001) Database of Political Institutions, as compiled in the QoG Standard Dataset, were used.

[19] "Women in parliament" from both the IPU data and World Development Indicators data was significant.

[20] Both the Fraser Institute's "economic freedom of the world index" and the Heritage Foundation's "business freedom index" were significant. The data for the number of procedures, time and cost required to start a new business are from Djankov et al. (2002).

[21] I experimented with three measures of trade openness: total trade as a percentage of GDP from the Penn World Table (version 6.3), measures from the World Development Indicators data and trade freedom from the Heritage Foundation. All of these measures of trade openness were insignificant.

Table 8.5 *The OLS and IV regressions of clientelism*

	(1)	(2) IV	(3)	(4) IV	(5)	(6)	(7)
Poverty (below $2/day) Secondary enrollment					-0.0070 (0.0026)***		
Urban population (%)						-0.0024 (0.0027)	-0.0016 (0.0043)
Years of democracy	-0.0078 (0.0024)***	-0.0067 (0.0046)	-0.0125 (0.0356)	0.0825 (0.1253)	0.0055 (0.0033)	-0.0074 (0.0023)***	-0.0074 (0.0023)***
Income inequality	0.0412 (0.0105)***	0.1095 (0.0325)***	0.0093 (0.0112)	0.0602 (0.0522)	0.0226 (0.0076)***	0.0419 (0.0104)***	0.0439 (0.0107)***
Democracy × Inequality			0.0010 (0.0003)***	0.0000 (0.0012)			
Per capita income	-0.2127 (0.0712)***	0.0264 (0.1706)	-0.1787 (0.0763)**	-0.0306 (0.1829)	-0.4389 (0.1064)***	-0.1390 (0.0876)	-0.1739 (0.0937)*
Democracy × Income			-0.0034 (0.0027)	-0.0089 (0.0087)			
Constant	3.3502 (0.9594)***	-1.7922 (2.6536)	4.3537 (0.9686)***	0.7743 (3.6787)	6.1224 (1.0836)***	2.8414 (0.9086)***	2.9706 (1.0126)***
N	70	70	70	70	54	78	78
R-squared	0.6788	0.4405	0.7398	0.6750	0.4250	0.6627	0.6601

(column 3), the interaction term between the duration of democracy and inequality is highly significant, but the interaction between democracy and per capita income is not significant. This suggests that the effect of age of democracy on clientelism does not depend on economic development, but on income inequality, although economic development has an independent effect on clientelism regardless of democratic duration. The IV regression with interaction terms produce all of the insignificant coefficients due to large standard errors. I also introduced poverty (percentage population living on less than $2.00 a day), education (secondary school enrollment) and urbanization (percentage urban population) as controls, considering that these were suggested as factors affecting the extent of clientelism.[22] All of these factors have high, simple correlations with clientelism. But as Table 8.5 shows, only poverty maintains significance when democracy, inequality and economic development are accounted for. However, income inequality remains highly significant for clientelism regardless of the factor being controlled for. In particular, income inequality is still significantly associated with clientelism even when both poverty and per capita income are controlled for.[23] Duration of democracy is still significant when education or urbanization is controlled for, but it loses significance when poverty is included. Also, per capita income loses significance when education is controlled for. Overall, the results presented in Table 8.5 indicate a strong causal effect of inequality on clientelism.

Next, I test whether the effect of inequality on corruption runs through clientelism. Table 8.6 shows how the coefficients for inequality from OLS regressions of CPI and political corruption change when clientelism is included. Note that clientelism is significant for both CPI and "political corruption," consistent with Singer (2009). The coefficients for inequality become smaller in magnitude (from –0.0849 in column 1 to –0.0289 in column 2; from –0.0592 in column 5 to –0.0361 in column 6) and less significant when clientelism is introduced. The coefficients for interaction term between democracy and inequality also become smaller in magnitude and less significant (from column 3 to column 4, and from column 7 to column 8) when clientelism is introduced. These results indicate that the effect of inequality on CPI and political corruption runs at least partially through clientelism, considering inequality has a strong causal effect on clientelism.

---

[22] The data for urban population and population living on less than $2.00 a day are from the World Bank's World Development Indicators data, and secondary education enrollment is from the UNESCO data. These data have also been compiled in the QoG data set.

[23] Poverty (population living on less than $2.00 a day) and economic development (natural log of per capita GDP) are strongly correlated with each other at r = 0.85.

Table 8.6 *The effect of inequality and clientelism on corruption*

Dependent variable	Corruption Perceptions Index				Political		Corruption	
	(1)	(2)	(3)	(4)	(5)	(6)	(7)	(8)
Clientelism		-1.3292		-0.9440		-0.5748		-0.3390
		(0.2844)***		(0.3112)***		(0.1586)***		(0.1816)*
Years of democracy	0.0391	0.0267	-0.0185	-0.0250	0.0178	0.0127	0.0345	0.0305
	(0.0079)***	(0.0082)***	(0.0867)	(0.0845)	(0.0038)***	(0.0040)***	(0.0499)	(0.0504)
Income inequality	-0.0849	-0.0289	-0.0072	0.0036	-0.0592	-0.0361	-0.0090	-0.0062
	(0.0226)***	(0.0240)	(0.0278)	(0.0315)	(0.0131)***	(0.0131)***	(0.0166)	(0.0177)
Democracy × Inequality			-0.0023	-0.0014			-0.0017	-0.0013
			(0.0008)***	(0.0008)*			(0.0005)***	(0.0005)**
Per capita income	0.8899	0.6806	0.7354	0.6175	0.0462	-0.0533	0.0211	-0.0285
	(0.2210)***	(0.1868)***	(0.2423)***	(0.2245)***	(0.1095)	(0.1001)	(0.1182)	(0.1190)
Democracy × Income			0.0151	0.0112			0.0049	0.0036
			(0.0069)**	(0.0066)*			(0.0040)	(0.0039)
Constant	-0.9356	2.8857	-2.6674	0.9469	5.5557	7.3227	3.7391	5.1378
	(2.5497)	(2.1707)	(2.9221)	(2.8286)	(1.3369)***	(1.2266)***	(1.5085)**	(1.6818)***
N	78	78	78	78	79	79	79	79
R-squared	0.7828	0.8352	0.8314	0.8523	0.5709	0.6326	0.6571	0.6743

Next, I test the hypothesis on causal mechanism through merito-cratic bureaucracy; inequality increases patronage through clientelism and patronage increases bureaucratic corruption. Table 8.7 shows that income inequality is significantly negatively associated with "professional bureaucracy" (Dahlström *et al.*'s (2012) data), or the absence of patron-age. This, in turn, is strongly associated with lower overall corruption (CPI) and bureaucratic corruption (percentage of respondents whose family members have bribed public officials during the last year). The reduction of the coefficient for inequality from column 1 to column 2 sug-gests that the effect of inequality on patronage runs partially through clientelism. Furthermore, there is some evidence that the effects of inequality on CPI and GCB_Bribery run through clientelism and patron-age (columns 3 to 5 and 6 to 8). Unfortunately, IV regressions for the models presented in Table 8.7 produced all insignificant coefficients due to large standard errors. Although I have not fully solved the endogeneity issue here, the overall pattern from the OLS regressions supports the second mechanism hypothesis on patronage in bureaucracy.

Since the data on "capture economy index" is available for only twenty-two transition economies, it was not possible to rigorously test the mechanism hypothesis through capture. Table 8.8 presents evidence that inequality is significantly associated with capture across the transi-tion countries, but that income per capita is not (column 1). Although both capture and inequality are significantly correlated with both CPI and "corporate corruption," capture is no longer significant for CPI or "corporate corruption" when inequality is included. This prohibits us from concluding that the effects of inequality on CPI and corporate cor-ruption run partially through capture. The small sample size and lack of representativeness of the sample further prevent us from drawing any form of conclusion. But the data still suggest that inequality significantly increases the risk of elite capture.

Finally, I find strong evidence that inequality and corruption mutu-ally reinforce each other in a vicious or virtuous circle when I com-pare the correlation between inequality and corruption by duration of democracy. Figure 8.1 displays four separate scatter plots of income inequality (*gini* on X axis) and corruption (CPI on Y axis) by the age of electoral democracy. The countries in the first box (duration = 0) are dictatorships; those in the second box have been electoral democracies for ten or fewer years; those in the third box (duration = 2) between eleven and thirty years; those in the fourth box (duration = 3) over thirty years. Among dictatorships, there is no significant relationship between inequality and corruption. Among electoral democracies, the relation-ship between inequality and corruption tends to become stronger as

Table 8.7 *The effect of inequality on bureaucracy and corruption*

Dependent variable	Professional		Corruption Perceptions Index				GCB–Bribery	
	(1)	(2)	(3)	(4)	(5)	(6)	(7)	(8)
Professional bureaucracy					0.8880			−0.3924
					(0.2546)***			(0.1378)***
Clientelism		−1.2923		−3.0727	−1.9251		1.2115	0.7054
		(0.2412)***		(0.3362)***	(0.4253)***		(0.2133)***	(0.2508)***
Inequality	−0.0551	0.0494	−0.2444	0.0042	−0.0397	0.1057	0.0079	0.0266
	(0.0242)**	(0.0384)	(0.0583)***	(0.0416)	(0.0318)	(0.0247)***	(0.0223)	(0.0158)
Constant	6.5424	5.7182	15.5136	13.5542	8.4765	−2.4581	−1.6989	0.5793
	(0.9389)***	(1.0876)***	(2.3474)***	(1.2281)***	(1.9536)***	(0.9835)**	(0.6188)***	(1.1204)
N	39	39	39	39	39	39	39	39
R-squared	0.0959	0.4595	0.3489	0.7293	0.8082	0.3230	0.6210	0.6968

Table 8.8 *The effect of inequality on capture and corruption*

Dependent variable	Capture	Corruption Perceptions Index			Corporate corruption		
	(1)	(2)	(3)	(4)	(5)	(6)	(7)
Capture		−0.0485 (0.0205)**		−0.0187 (0.0174)	−0.0206 (0.0099)*		−0.0057 (0.0115)
Inequality	0.7174 (0.2420)***		−0.0955 (0.0186)***	−0.0830 (0.0218)***		−0.0334 (0.0113)***	−0.0285 (0.0130)**
Income per capita	0.8139 (5.3997)						
Constant	−13.6538 (54.1748)	4.4483 (0.5746)***	6.9238 (0.7873)***	6.8379 (0.7719)***	4.2709 (0.2047)***	5.0357 (0.3746)***	4.9801 (0.3729)***
N	22	21	21	21	20	20	20
R-squared	0.2674	0.2063	0.4308	0.4541	0.2384	0.3821	0.3921

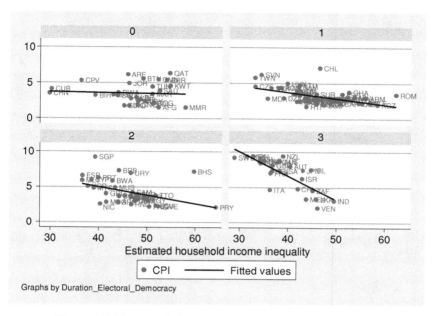

Figure 8.1 The association between inequality and corruption, by duration of democracy
Note: Duration of electoral democracy variable takes the value of 0 for dictatorships, 1 for countries with up to ten consecutive years of electoral democracy, 2 for countries with between eleven and thirty consecutive years of electoral democracy and 3 for countries with more than thirty consecutive years of electoral democracy. Each box displays the scatter plots of estimated household income inequality for 2002 from UTIP data on the X axis and average CPI for 2002 to 2006 on the Y axis.

the age of democracy increases. The fitted line gets steeper in the scatter plots for older democracies. In particular, among the countries with more than thirty years of electoral democracy, those countries tend to be concentrated toward the top left (low inequality and low corruption) or the bottom right (high inequality and high corruption) of the fitted line. This seems to support the theory that countries converge into either of the two equilibria as the age of democracy increases, either in a virtuous circle of low inequality and low corruption or in a vicious circle of high inequality and high corruption.

A similar pattern appears when I compare the correlation between inequality and clientelism by the duration of democracy. Figure 8.2 displays four separate scatter plots of income inequality on the X axis and

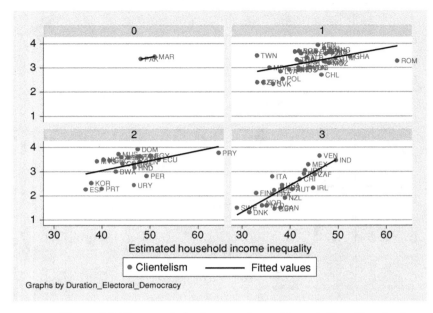

Figure 8.2 The association between inequality and clientelism, by duration of democracy

clientelism on the Y axis by the age of electoral democracy. The figure strongly suggests that only those countries with low inequality tend to reduce clientelism in the long term.

In summary, through a variety of quantitative analysis presented above, I provide convincing cross-national evidence supporting the main hypothesis (H1) that the causal effect of democracy on reducing corruption decreases with inequality, while successfully addressing the issues of endogeneity using instrumental variables. The age of democracy is significant for control of corruption, but the effect of democratic experience on corruption control also depends on the level of inequality. I also provide supporting evidence for the related hypothesis (H2) that the effect of inequality on corruption in liberal democracies is higher than that in illiberal electoral democracies, which is in turn higher than that in dictatorships. In addition, I find evidence that inequality and corruption mutually reinforce each other, in a vicious or virtuous circle, in democracies.

Interestingly, both the effect of inequality on corruption and the interaction effect between democracy and inequality are estimated much larger by IV regressions than by OLS regressions. However, both the effect of economic development and the interaction effect between democracy and economic development become insignificant in IV regressions, while they are strong and significant in OLS regressions. This suggests that the effect of economic development on corruption control is overestimated by OLS regressions, perhaps due to reverse causation, but the effect of inequality is underestimated by OLS regressions, perhaps due to the large measurement error in inequality. This also implies that the effect of democracy on corruption control depends on the degree of economic inequality rather than on the level of economic development.

Regarding the causal mechanisms through which inequality affects corruption, I find strong evidence that high inequality causes persistence of clientelism, which in turn is associated with higher political corruption. I find evidence that inequality is associated with the prevalence of patronage in bureaucracy, and thereby with bureaucratic corruption. I also find some partial evidence that inequality is associated with capture and corporate corruption at least within the sample of twenty-two transition economies.

9   Conclusion

Despite the long-standing observation that corruption and inequality are related, the mechanisms linking the two have not been completely understood (Chong and Gradstein 2007; Johnston 1989). Previous empirical studies have suggested reciprocal causal relationships, i.e. causal effects both "from corruption to inequality" (Gupta *et al.* 2002; Li *et al.* 2000; Rothstein 2011) and "from inequality to corruption" (Uslaner 2008; You and Khagram 2005; You 2006). This book's focus has been about the latter. I have attempted to explain why and how economic inequality tends to increase corruption, especially in democracies. I have argued that economic inequality increases incentives for the political and economic elite to rely on clientelism, patronage and capture. I have also argued that large impoverished populations in highly unequal societies are prone to clientelistic exchanges with politicians. These arguments have been supported through comparative historical analysis of the three East Asian countries and cross-national quantitative methods that address endogeneity problems. This chapter will summarize the key findings, discuss policy implications and illuminate the theoretical and empirical implications for the broader comparative politics and political economy literatures.

Key findings

I conducted a comparative historical analysis of the three East Asian countries – Korea, Taiwan and the Philippines – which had similar initial conditions at the time of independence. In these three case countries, the success and failure of land reform produced different levels of inequality; moreover, I addressed the endogeneity problem by showing that land reform was primarily determined by exogenous factors such as the external communist threat and US pressures. I found that the differences in inequality due to the success (in Korea and Taiwan) or failure (in the Philippines) of land reform have had a profound effect on corruption in these countries.

In the Philippines, failed land reform has maintained high inequality and led to the persistence of clientelism, corruption of the bureaucracy, and capture of the policy-making and implementation processes. These problems were evident throughout the early period of democracy and the later post-Marcos democratic era. Authoritarian elections were no less clientelistic than democratic elections, and Filipinos' expectations for post-Marcos democratic reform were met with disappointment. Meritocratic recruitment of civil servants has been increasingly replaced by patronage appointments as clientelistic competition has intensified. Clientelistic politicians have often promised to clean up corruption, but the reform measures have proved largely ineffective. Corrupt public officials have seldom been prosecuted, and voters have largely been unable to punish corrupt politicians at the polls because of endemic practices of clientelism on the part of all political parties. The Philippine state has never been able to formulate and implement coherent industrial policy due to capture by the powerful landed-industrial-financial family conglomerates, which in turn has bred corruption across both the private and public sectors. The persistent clientelism and capture have constrained the anti-corruption efforts of any Philippine administration, and corruption ratings have continuously deteriorated since the late 1990s.

In contrast, sweeping land reform in Korea and Taiwan created relatively egalitarian societies, producing favorable conditions for limiting clientelism, patronage and elite capture. Expansion of education led to increased pressures for meritocracy, and clientelism was somewhat limited due to the separation of the political and economic elites and by relatively low levels of absolute poverty accompanied by the growing size of the educated middle class in urban areas. The gradual development of meritocratic bureaucracy was accompanied by the decline of bureaucratic corruption. Although clientelistic practices such as vote buying were endemic during the early years of democratic rule, programmatic competition developed gradually over time. There was some progress in corruption control both during the authoritarian (or formally democratic) period and during the democratic period in Korea and Taiwan.

In Korea, clientelism was less prevalent than in the Philippines and programmatic politics developed to a certain extent in urban areas during both the early period of formal democracy and under the authoritarian elections as well. During the long authoritarian era in Taiwan, clientelism was largely confined to the local level in the absence of national elections. Immediately following the democratic transition in the late 1980s and early 1990s, however, clientelism and vote buying intensified in both Korea and Taiwan. In particular, expansion of clientelism at the national level in Taiwan led to the phenomenon of "black-gold" politics, or involvement of rich businessmen and organized crime in the political system. Unlike in the Philippines, however, both Korea and Taiwan have been able to curb clientelism with strict prosecution of vote-buying practices and voters' punishment of corrupt politicians at the polls. The decline of clientelism has been accompanied and reinforced by the gradual development of programmatic party politics in both countries.

While both Korea and Taiwan enjoyed high state autonomy in the absence of an influential economic elite after their respective land reform efforts, the subsequent *chaebol*-centered industrialization led to increasing economic concentration and policy capture by powerful business interests in Korea. This explains Korea's historically higher level of corruption than that of Taiwan. In the aftermath of the East Asian financial crisis, Korea was able to implement sweeping corporate and financial reforms to increase transparency and deter collusive practices. While the reform was successful in improving corporate governance and breaking collusion between government and the *chaebol* at least temporarily, corporate governance as well as corruption ratings have begun to deteriorate again in recent years.

The cross-national analysis in Chapter 8 complements the comparative historical investigation, providing evidence for generalizability. It shows that inequality is significantly associated with corruption in democracies, controlling for economic development and other causes of corruption. The partial correlation between inequality and corruption gets stronger as democracies mature, implying both a vicious circle of high inequality and high corruption and a virtuous circle of low inequality and low corruption. Instrumental variables regression results show an even stronger effect of inequality and an interaction effect of democracy and inequality on corruption than do OLS regressions, while the effects of economic development and its interaction with democracy get smaller and even insignificant when instrumental variables are employed. These results suggest that the effectiveness of democratic control of corruption depends on the level of inequality rather than the level of economic development, even after controlling for the duration of democracy in the analysis. In addition, there is substantial cross-national evidence about the causal pathways from inequality to corruption. Inequality is significantly associated with clientelism, patronage and capture, which in turn are significantly associated with political, bureaucratic and corporate corruption, respectively.

Contributions to the study of corruption

The theoretical framework, methodology and empirical findings of this book have significant implications for the study of corruption.

First, this book refutes the view that good institutions are a derivative from economic prosperity and that policy should focus on encouraging economic growth, because once a country becomes rich enough, corruption will begin to decline. Both my cross-national quantitative analysis and comparative historical analysis of the three countries indicate, however, that inequality has a more important and significant effect on corruption than the level of economic development, as measured by per capita income. The effect of democracy on corruption also depends more on inequality than on economic development. The Philippine democracy did not function better than the Korean democracy even when the former was richer – but crucially more unequal – in the 1950s and 1960s. In particular, the instrumental variables regression results suggest that OLS regressions overestimate the effect of economic development on corruption. The overestimation can be due to reverse causality combined with an omitted variable bias. This happens because corruption hinders economic development and inequality has been typically omitted in most cross-national studies of corruption. Even when inequality was included, the inequality effect has not been adequately captured due to a large measurement error in inequality, and hence economic development might have been overestimated (Husted 1999; Paldam 2002; You and Khagram 2005). In addition, there may be systemic bias in the cross-national measures of perceived corruption in favor of rich countries, which will result in an overestimation of the income effect. Thus, the widely held belief that economic development is the most important determinant of corruption needs to be questioned and more scrutiny is required. As Kaufmann and Kraay (2002) argued, economic development is more a consequence rather than a cause of control of corruption.

Second, this book contributes to the understanding of corruption by systematically linking the problem with clientelism and capture. While the literature on clientelism has been burgeoning recently and it has become largely regarded as a corrupt feature of electoral mobilization, there have not been many attempts to link clientelism and corruption in cross-national or comparative studies (Singer 2009). I have emphasized that the problem of adverse selection of the agent (politicians and bureaucrats) is no less important than the problem of agency loss in understanding and tackling corruption. I have posited that clientelism will lead to the adverse selection of both politicians and bureaucrats, which will in turn increase agency loss in the form of political and bureaucratic corruption. I have presented cross-national evidence that inequality increases clientelism, that clientelism increases patronage, and that clientelism and patronage increase political and bureaucratic corruption. The historical experiences of the three countries provide further evidence for these mechanisms.

While capture was interpreted as a major feature of corruption in some studies (Hellman *et al.* 2000) and the concept of "captured democracy" was proposed by some scholars (Acemoglu and Robinson 2008), there was no systematic attempt to explain democratic variations in corruption with capture. I have posited that elite capture is a major threat to unequal democracies using a principal-agent-client model of corruption, in which the client (the wealthy elite) initiates corruption and captures the agent (politicians and bureaucrats). While I have presented only weak cross-national evidence because of limited data, the comparative historical analysis of the three countries provides convincing evidence for this mechanism. High inequality in the Philippines has led to persistent elite capture; Korea and Taiwan were able to curtail it by foremost addressing the problem of inequality through land reform. In the case of Korea, however, increasing economic concentration in the following decades increased the risk of state capture by the *chaebol*.

Third, this book has demonstrated how comparative historical analysis can be employed to study corruption. I have used a structured comparison of the three "most similar" case countries that share comparable characteristics except for corruption, democracy and inequality, based on Mill's method of difference. I have also conducted process tracing of the historical experiences of these countries in order to identify the sequencing of changes in the key independent and dependent variables. In undertaking structured comparison and process tracing of the three countries, I have paid special attention to how politicians, voters and businesses acted with regard to electoral mobilization, voting behavior and rent-seeking activities, and how inequality affected their motivations. By combining these methodologies, I have been able to identify the causal direction from inequality to corruption and several causal mechanisms that link inequality and corruption. In this regard, this book may inspire more scholars in the field to use comparative historical investigation.

Policy implications for young democracies

While inequality creates unfavorable conditions to curb clientelism and capture in democracies, my investigation shows that it is not impossible to implement significant redistributive and anti-corruption reform, even when inequality is high. Not only authoritarian Taiwan but also democratic South Korea implemented far-reaching land reform in the early post-independence period. Although external factors such as a communist threat from the north played an important role in the legislation of land reform in South Korea, domestic politics also played a significant role. South Korea implemented a sweeping reform of corporate governance of *chaebol* and the financial sector when the *chaebol* concentration was high. While the reform was aided by international pressures as well as the urgency of the crisis, the transfer of power to the opposition and formation of a reform coalition between a new government and civil society organizations also played a significant role.

For young democracies in the developing world that are struggling to control corruption, my research findings provide two broad policy implications. Successful anti-corruption reform requires not only an attack on corruption per se, but attention to economic inequality. The research also suggests that anti-corruption efforts need to go beyond the narrow focus on the problem of agency loss and also need to address the behaviors that are "softer" forms of corruption that lead to more explicit corruption further down the line: elite capture, clientelistic practices such as vote buying and patronage appointments in the bureaucracy. Furthermore, effective anti-corruption reform will likely help to alleviate inequality, perhaps by increasing support for redistribution (Rothstein 2011; Svallfors 2012). Thus, curbing corruption and reducing inequality may mutually reinforce each other in a virtuous cycle, breaking the vicious cycle of inequality and corruption. Allow me to discuss the policy implications with illustrations from the three case countries of this study.

First, it may sound obvious that anti-corruption reform requires attention to inequality. This book has provided cross-national and historical evidence that inequality affects corruption and that inequality and corruption reinforce each other, especially in democracies. To escape the vicious cycle of high inequality and high corruption, the implementation of effective redistributive measures and the adequate provision of public goods could have beneficial effects in developing countries not only because of their direct effects on the incomes and well-being of the poor, but also through their effects on corruption. Growing inequality in many countries, both developed and developing, shows that the mere trickle-down effects of growth fall very short of addressing the problems of inequality and poverty. Governments need to be proactive and prioritize the fight against current trends toward inequality.

One critique of such a redistributive agenda is that it is associated with larger states and that large governments are more likely to be corrupt.

However, empirical studies show that a larger government size is not associated with a higher level of corruption (Gerring and Thacker 2005; Friedman *et al.* 2000; La Porta *et al.* 1999). Indeed, the large governments of Scandinavian countries have both the lowest levels of inequality and corruption in the world. Substantial anti-corruption reform may have antedated the development of welfare states in these countries (Rothstein 2011: 111–18), but it seems that at least the comprehensive welfare states that successfully reduced inequality and poverty have also provided favorable conditions to limit clientelism, patronage and capture, which in turn have contributed to further reducing corruption and/or maintaining low levels of corruption.

In this regard, the Philippines requires particularly strong policies to curb inequality and poverty. When President Aquino III unveiled his "Good Governance and Anti-Corruption" (GACC) plan for 2012 to 2016, some NGOs raised concerns that his plan is based on too simple an idea that simply curbing corruption will reduce poverty, and fails to address the "problems of social inequities and economic and political marginalization of many Filipinos" (CenPEG 2012). Although anti-corruption may partly contribute to reducing poverty, anti-corruption measures cannot replace anti-poverty measures. Anti-corruption efforts should be supplemented by anti-inequality and anti-poverty programs. Of course, growing inequality needs to be addressed in Korea and Taiwan as well.

The importance of tackling inequality as an aspect of anti-corruption strategies has implications for more libertarian approaches to corruption control. Some of the corruption researchers tended to focus narrowly on corruption as agency loss, ignoring the problems of adverse selection of politicians and bureaucrats and state capture by the wealthy elite. The narrow focus on corrupt incentives for public officials led to a neo-liberal policy prescription for anti-corruption: "if you want to cut corruption, cut government" (Becker 1995). Thus, deregulation, privatization and minimization of bureaucratic discretion were often proposed as remedies. However, these prescriptions have not always proven to be successful. Many developing and transition economies saw privatization processes riddled with rampant corruption (Bello *et al.* 2004; Black *et al.* 2000; Hellman *et al.* 2000). Even in the United States, the skyrocketing CEO compensation, which was supposed to align the interests of CEOs with those of shareholders, not only increased income inequality, but also stimulated corporate corruption (You and Khagram 2005).

Second, anti-corruption efforts should go beyond the narrow focus on the problem of agency loss and encompass broad approaches to curb elite capture, clientelism and patronage. One insight of my theory is that the relationship between inequality and corruption is not deterministic, but that inequality increases incentives for the elite to rely on capture, clientelism and patronage. The implication of this theory is that changing these incentives in the system can help to circumvent the relationship between inequality and corruption.

In this regard, anti-corruption reform should address the problem of elite capture of policy processes, which in turn requires greater transparency in government. The role of free media and civil society is critically important in monitoring and exposing undue influence of powerful actors in legislative and bureaucratic processes. The role of NGOs, including independent think tanks, is important in analyzing the impact of existing and proposed policies on the benefits and costs both to those with special interests and the general public. Any policies that protect monopolies and illegitimate rents for the privileged should be exposed. Free and open access to public information is a necessary condition for the civil society to effectively monitor the policy-making and policy implementation processes. Monitoring of corporate governance and corporate corruption is also important. Hence, transparency requirements should be rigorously applied to the private sector, especially large conglomerates, as well as the public sector.

The Philippines requires particularly strong efforts to curb state capture by the elite. While Aquino III's GACC plan includes reform measures such as the integration of digitalized and publicly accessible government databases, particularly on budget and engagement of NGOs in social audit, critics argue that the reform efforts will not be effective without "the passage of the Freedom of Information bill minus its major restrictions or conditions, strengthening of the whistleblower's act and the witness protection program, and supporting anti-dynasty bills" (CenPEG 2012).

In Korea, some of the progress made by the post-financial crisis reform was reversed during the business-friendly Lee Myung-bak government. A particularly worrisome development was the deterioration of corporate governance coupled with increasing economic concentration by the largest *chaebol*. David Kang's (2002) concerns about crony capitalism in Korea as well as in the Philippines seems to be still valid. In this regard, the Park Geun-hye administration (2013 to 2018) that pledged to fight for "economic democracy" during the presidential campaign needs to effectively address the issues of corporate governance and unfair trade practices of the *chaebol*.

Anti-corruption reforms will not be effective if clientelistic politics are prevalent, since clientelistic politicians lack incentives for rigorous enforcement of anti-corruption measures and are likely to rely on diversion of state as well as private resources illicitly provided by the wealthy elite. Hence, it is important to curb clientelistic practices such as vote buying in elections. Rigorous prosecution of vote-buying cases and anti-vote-selling educational campaigns should be pursued in tandem. It is also important to develop programmatic politics. Various efforts to promote programmatic competition are needed, including the reform of the electoral system and measures to better inform the public about issues. There should be strict enforcement of campaign finance regulations and transparency of campaign contributions and expenses, while making these regulations reasonable. Excessive regulations of campaign finance and election campaigning will encourage various attempts to circumvent them, via cheating and corruption, and make strict and impartial enforcement impossible. After all, politicians and political parties will choose between clientelistic and programmatic strategies depending on the expected benefits (vote gains) and costs (risks of prosecution and removal from elected office). It follows that measures to increase the expected costs of clientelistic competition and the expected benefits of programmatic completion should be pursued together.

Curbing clientelism such as vote buying is also an important agenda for the Philippines. Active prosecution of vote buying accompanied by extensive voter education campaigns will be critical to increase the costs of vote-buying strategies. The laws on political donation disclosure and campaign spending limits that have not been enforced to date should be rigorously implemented. The electoral system for the Senate that encourages clientelistic competition needs to be reformed. Taiwan also needs to put more efforts into eliminating vote-buying practices in rural areas. Reform of the SNTV electoral system for local elections may help to reduce clientelistic competition in rural areas.

In addition, successful anti-corruption reform requires establishing a meritocratic and professional bureaucracy, foremost by eliminating patronage appointments in the civil service. Anti-corruption agencies and NGOs need to expand their work to monitoring and surveying the mode of recruitment and promotion at the central and local government levels. Since it is easier to survey the prevalence of patronage appointments than the frequency of corrupt acts, this will be a promising approach in fighting against bureaucratic corruption.

The Philippines requires rigorous efforts to curb patronage in central and local government agencies and to better implement civil service examinations. The Civil Service Commission needs to be strengthened, there should be a mechanism to ensure that only those eligible for the Career Executive Service (CES) occupy CES positions. The role of the media and civil society organizations is also important here.

The above two broad approaches can help guide policy-makers and activists to design comprehensive anti-corruption strategies, especially for young democracies. In many countries, the establishment of new anti-corruption agencies and various anti-corruption legislations have turned out to be ineffective. Indeed, the findings of this book suggest that this kind of narrow approach to anti-corruption reform can be futile unless inequality and poverty are adequately addressed, and unless some effective measures to directly tackle clientelism, patronage and capture are employed.

Implications on broader literature in comparative politics and political economy

In addition to the contributions to the study of corruption, the findings of this book have broader theoretical and empirical implications on some important topics in comparative politics and political economy.

First, corruption may be an important channel through which inequality adversely affects economic development (You and Khagram 2005). Many cross-national quantitative studies and some comparative historical studies have found a negative effect of inequality on economic growth (Alesina and Rodrik 1994; Benabou 1996; Deininger and Squire 1998; Easterly 2007; Engerman and Sokoloff 1997; Perotti 1996; Persson and Tabelini 1994). Various explanations about causal pathways from high inequality to low growth have been proposed, including redistributive politics, political instability, investment in human capital and institutions (World Bank 2006). Easterly (2007) showed some evidence that inequality leads to underdevelopment through "low institutional quality," including high corruption. This book supports this causal path from inequality to corruption to underdevelopment, considering that corruption deters investment and growth (Lambsdorff 2005; Mauro 1995).

In particular, the findings of this book shed new light on the origin of developmental states in Korea and Taiwan. The developmental state literature has emphasized the role of the meritocratic and professional bureaucracy in maintaining autonomy and designing and implementing coherent industrial policy. However, the literature has generally been largely unsuccessful in explaining what enabled these countries to establish a developmental state with a meritocratic bureaucracy. The significant role of land reform in promoting the development of meritocratic bureaucracy in Korea and Taiwan suggests that this was a critically important factor leading to the establishment of developmental states. It may not be mere coincidence that Japan also benefited from land reform implemented by the US occupation after World War II. In addition, my findings suggest that Korea's developmental state was not created overnight by Park Chung-hee as previous literature suggested, but its foundation was made much earlier with the land reform (You 2012b).

Second, capture and clientelism may explain the negative effect of inequality on redistribution and the persistence of inequality in democracies. The Meltzer-Richard (1981) model predicts that higher market income inequality should lead to higher redistribution in democracies, based on the median voter theorem. In fact, higher levels of market income inequality are not associated with higher levels of redistribution across industrialized democracies (Iversen and Soskice 2006). This puzzle may be explained by the effect of inequality on capture and clientelism, because both of these undermine redistribution. In captured democracies, the redistributive demand of the poor and the median voter will not translate into government policies because the wealthy elite capture the policy processes (Acemoglu and Robinson 2008). Under clientelistic politics, programmatic parties that can represent the interests of the poor cannot develop and the poor voters support a perverse system dominated by clientelistic politicians "that keeps them poor" (Diaz-Cayeros et al. 2011: 4). Thus, higher market income inequality does not lead to higher redistribution, which could lower inequality over time. This explains the reinforcing relationship between inequality and corruption and the persistence of inequality observed in many democracies, contrary to the Meltzer-Richard (1981) model (Acemoglu and Robinson 2008; You and Khagram 2005).

Third, the mutually reinforcing relationship between inequality and corruption may be extended further to the "inequality-corruption-low trust" trap (Rothstein 2011; Uslaner 2008; You 2012a). Uslaner (2008) argues that high inequality leads to low trust, high corruption, and then to more inequality, while Rothstein (2011) suggests that causal chains run from corruption to social trust to redistribution and inequality. My own study shows that inequality and corruption erode social trust, but there may also be a reciprocal causal effect of social trust on inequality and corruption (You 2012a). Although it is very difficult to find out exact causal relationships between these three variables, it seems that inequality, corruption and low social trust reinforce each other in a vicious cycle. Considering that social trust helps to overcome collective action problems and lower transaction costs, there is room to further study the relationships between inequality, corruption, social trust and various indicators of human development.

Fourth, this book complements the recent political economy literature that attempts to explain both political development and economic development with an integrated approach. In particular, the findings of this book are in line with Acemoglu and Robinson's (2008) model of "captured democracy," Acemoglu et al.'s (2011) theory of patronage politics, and North et al.'s (2009) framework of distinguishing between "limited access orders" and "open access orders" in interpreting political and economic development together. Under a captured democracy in Acemoglu and Robinson (2008), de jure political power of the masses is offset by de facto political power of the elite. Investments by the elite in de facto political power create corruption. Under patronage politics in Acemoglu et al. (2011), bureaucrats support the rich, who set lower taxes, but also provide rents to bureaucrats. Their model shows that the rich-bureaucrats coalition of patronage politics is more likely to arise at higher levels of income inequality. My empirical findings show that these models are quite plausible in the real world.

North et al. (2009) posit that in limited access order societies, access to valuable rights and activities are limited to the privileged few who have violence potential and these privileges create rents. The dominant coalition is maintained by the distribution of rents among the powerful groups and individuals. In open access order societies, access to political and economic rights and organizational activities are open to everyone, and open competition in political and economic arenas is the driving force for development. In addition, their "theory of double balance" implies that societies tend to have both open access polity and open access economy or both limited access polity and limited access economy. If open access polity is introduced in a limited access economy, the society may make a transition to an open access order in both polity and economy or the formally open access polity may retreat to a limited access polity (authoritarian reversal) or function like a limited access polity.

One interpretation of this work is that clientelism and capture make the formally open access polity, or democracy, function like a limited access polity, in which privileges and associated rents are preserved. Clientelism distributes part of the rents to the poor voters, but the price of these particularistic benefits to the poor is maintaining the limited access polity that helps to maintain the limited access economy that keeps them poor. Capture enables the wealthy elite to preserve and increase rents based on privileges. Comparing the three countries shows that the Philippines is locked in a limited access order, while Korea and Taiwan have been making a transition to open access orders (Montinola 2012; You 2012b). The limited access economy that is dominated by landed-industrial-financial family conglomerates in the Philippines constrains the functioning of formally open access polity through endemic clientelism and elite capture. Economic inequality facilitates and increases clientelism and capture, which maintains political inequality.

Finally, let me conclude by re-emphasizing that my research findings should not be interpreted in a pessimistic manner. The link between inequality and corruption that I have pursued here could be given a highly pessimistic interpretation. Inequality is slow-moving and difficult to reverse; if we have to tackle inequality in order to affect corruption, we may be waiting for a long time. But despite the daunting challenges, I have also shown how reformist governments have exploited opportunities to push forward redistribution that has positive effects not only on corruption, but also on economic development. Seeing the fights against corruption and inequality as linked opens up a different political approach to corruption than those prevailing today, especially neo-liberal approaches that emphasize the need for small government. Importantly, my research findings suggest that it is possible to break the vicious cycle of high inequality and high corruption and move toward a low-inequality and low-corruption equilibrium.

Bibliography

Abueva, Jose Veloso 1965. "Social Backgrounds and Recruitment of Legislators and Administrators in the Philippines." *Philippine Journal of Public Administration* 9.1: 10–29.

——— 1970. "Administrative Culture and Behavior and Middle Civil Servants in the Philippines," in Edward W. Weidner (ed.), *Development Administration in Asia*. Durham, NC: Duke University Press, 132–86.

Acemoglu, Daron and J. Robinson 2008. "Persistence of Power, Elites, and Institutions." *American Economic Review* 98.1: 267–93.

Acemoglu, Daron, Davide Ticchi and Andrea Vindigni 2011. "Emergence and Persistence of Inefficient States." *Journal of the European Economic Association* 9.2: 177–208.

Ades, Alberto and Rafael Di Tella 1999. "Rents, Competition and Corruption." *American Economic Review* 89: 982–94.

Adsera, A., Carles Boix and Mark Payne 2003. "Are You Being Served? Political Accountability and the Quality of Government." *Journal of Law, Economics & Organization* 19.2: 445–90.

Ahn, Yong-sik (안용식) 1978. "한국 고급공무원의 모빌리티에 관한 연구 (A Study of Mobility of Korean Higher Civil Servants)." Ph.D. thesis, Yonsei University, Seoul, Korea.

——— 2001. 한국 관료 연구 (*A Study of Korean Civil Servants*). Seoul, Korea: 대영문화사 (Daeyoungmunhwasa).

Alakent, Ekin and Seung-hyun Lee 2010. "Do Institutionalized Traditions Matter During Crisis? Employee Downsizing in Korean Manufacturing Organizations." *Journal of Management Studies* 47.3: 509–32.

Aldaba, Rafaelita M. 2005. "The Impact of Market Reforms on Competition, Structure and Performance of the Philippine Economy." Philippine Institute for Development Studies Discussion Paper Series No. 2005–24.

Aldaba, Rafaelita M. 2008. "Assessing Competition in Philippine Markets." Philippine Institute for Development Studies Discussion Paper Series No. 2008–23.

Alesina, Alberto F. and Dani Rodrik. 1994. "Distributive Politics and Economic Growth." *Quarterly Journal of Economics* 109: 465–90.

Alt, J. E. and D. D. Lassen 2003. "The Political Economy of Institutions and Corruption in American States." *Journal of Theoretical Politics* 15.3: 341–65.

Amsden, A. 1989. *Asia's Next Giant: South Korea and Late Industrialization*. New York: Oxford University Press.

Apergis, Nicholas, James E. Payne and Oguzhan C. Dincer 2010. "The Relationship between Corruption and Income Inequality in U.S. States: Evidence from a Panel Cointegration and Error Correction Model." *Public Choice* 145: 125–35.

Asian Development Bank (ADB) 2005. "Country Governance Assessment: Philippines." Manila, Philippines: Asian Development Bank.

Austria, Myrna S. 2002. "The State of Competition and Market Structure of the Philippine Air Transport Industry," in Erlinda M. Medalla (ed.), *Toward a National Competition Policy for the Philippines*. Makati, Philippines: Philippine Institute for Development Studies, 189–252.

Bäck, Hanna and Axel Hadenius 2008. "Democracy and State Capacity: Exploring a J-Shaped Relationship." *Governance* 21.1: 1–24.

Balgos, Cecile C. A. 1998. "Ombudsman," in Sheila Coronel (ed.), *Pork and Other Perks: Corruption and Governance in the Philippines*. Quezon City, Philippines: Philippine Center for Investigative Journalism, 244–71.

Ban, Sung Hwan, Pal Yong Moon and Dwight H. Perkins 1980. *Rural Development: Studies in the Modernization of the Republic of Korea, 1945–1975*. Cambridge, MA: Harvard University Press.

Banfield, Edward C. 1958. *The Moral Basis of a Backward Society*. Chicago, IL: Free Press.

Bardhan, Pranab 2005. *Scarcity, Conflicts, and Cooperation: Essays in the Political and Institutional Economics of Development*. Cambridge, MA: The MIT Press.

Bark, Dong Suh (박동서) 1961. 한국 관료제도의 역사적 전개 (*The Historical Development of the Korean Bureaucratic System*). Seoul, Korea: 한국연구도서관 (Korea Research Library).

    1966. "신규채용과 승진: 인사행정상의문제점 (New Recruitments and Promotions: Problems in Personnel Administration)." 사법행정 (*Judicial Administration*) 7.7: 9–11.

    1980. "Major Causes of Administrative Development in Korea." 행정논총 (*Korea Journal of Public Administration*) 18.1: 103–11.

    1998. "고급 공무원의 성분 변화 (Changes in Social Background of the Higher Civil Servants)." 행정논총 (*Korea Journal of Public Administration*) 30.1: 181–201.

Barro, R. J. and J. W. Lee 2001. "International Data on Educational Attainment: Updates and Implications." *Oxford Economic Papers New Series* 53.3: 541–63.

Baum, Jeeyang Rhee 2011. *Responsive Democracy: Increasing State Accountability in East Asia*. Ann Arbor, MI: University of Michigan Press.

Beck, T., G. Clarke, A. Groff, P. Keefer and P. Walsh 2001. "New Tools in Comparative Political Economy: The Database of Political Institutions." *World Bank Economic Review* 15.1: 165–76.

Becker, Gary S. 1995. "If You Want to Cut Corruption, Cut Government." *Business Week* 3454: 26.

Bello, Walden, David Kinley and Elaine Elinson 1982. *Development Debacle: The World Bank in the Philippines*. San Francisco, CA: Institute for Food and Development Policy; Oakland, CA: Philippine Solidarity Network.

Bello, Walden, Herbert Docena, Marissa de Guzman and Marylou Malig 2004. *The Anti-Development State: The Political Economy of Permanent Crisis in the Philippines*. Diliman, Quezon City, Philippines: University of the Philippines.

Benabou, Ronald 1996. "Inequality and Growth." *NBER Macroeconomics Annual* 11: 11–92.

Bentzen, Jeanet Sinding 2012. "How Bad is Corruption? Cross-Country Evidence of the Impact of Corruption on Economic Prosperity." *Review of Development Economics* 16.1: 167–84.

Bhattacharya, Mita and Jong-rong Chen 2009. "Market Dynamics and Dichotomy: Evidence from Taiwanese Manufacturing." *Applied Economics* 41.17: 2169–79.

Black, Bernard, Reinier Kraakman and Anna Tarassova 2000. "Russian Privatization and Corporate Governance: What Went Wrong?" *Stanford Law Review* 52: 1731–808.

Bloom, D. E., P. H. Craig and P. N. Malaney 2001. *Study of Rural Asia: Volume 4. The Quality of Life in Rural Asia*. Oxford; New York: Oxford University Press.

Bosco, Joseph 1994. "Faction Versus Ideology: Mobilization Strategies in Taiwan's Elections." *The China Quarterly* 137: 28–62.

Botero, Juan, Alejandro Ponce and Andrei Shleifer 2012. "Education and the Quality of Government." NBER Working Paper No. 18119. Available at www.nber.org/papers/w18119.

Brunetti, A. and B. Weder 2003. "A Free Press is Bad News for Corruption." *Journal of Public Economics* 87.7–8: 1801–24.

Brusco, V., M. Nazareno and S. C. Stokes 2004. "Vote Buying in Argentina." *Latin American Research Review* 39.2: 66–88.

Calvo, Ernesto and Maria Victoria Murillo 2004. "Who Delivers? Partisan Clients in the Argentine Electoral Market." *American Journal of Political Science* 48.4: 742–57.

Campos, José Edgardo and Hilton L. Root 1996. *The Key to the Asian Miracle: Making Shared Growth Credible*. Washington, DC: Brookings Institution.

Canlas, D., M. E. Khan and J. Zhuang 2009. "Critical Constraints to Growth and Poverty Reduction," in D. Canlas, M. E. Khan and J. Zhuang (eds.), *Diagnosing the Philippine Economy: Toward Inclusive Growth*. London; New York: Anthem Press; and Manila, Philippines: Asian Development Bank, 33–97.

Carey, J. M. and M. S. Shugart 1995. "Incentives to Cultivate a Personal Vote: A Rank Ordering of Electoral Formulas." *Electoral Studies* 14.4: 417–39.

Carney, Richard W. and Travers Barclay Child 2013. "Changes to the Ownership and Control of East Asian Corporations between 1996 and 2008: The Primacy of Politics." *Journal of Financial Economics* 107.2: 494–513.

CenPEG 2012. "Nowhere to Go: Will Aquino's Anti-Corruption Reform Work?" *Policy Study, Publication, and Advocacy (PSPA) Issue Analysis No. 2* Center for People Empowerment in Governance, Philippines.

CG Watch 2007, 2010. "CG Watch: Corporate Governance in Asia." CLSA Asia-Pacific Markets. Available at: www.acga-asia.org.

Chanco, Mario P. 1961. *The Anatomy of Corruption*. Manila, Philippines: Manor News Corporation.

Chang, Eric C. C. and Miriam A. Golden 2007. "Electoral Systems, District Magnitude and Corruption." *British Journal of Political Science* 37: 115–37.

Chang, Eric C. C., Miriam A. Golden and Seth J. Hill 2010. "Legislative Malfeasance and Political Accountability." *World Politics* 62.2: 177.

Charron, Nicholas and Victor Lapuente 2010. "Does Democracy Produce Quality of Government?" *European Journal of Political Research* 49.4: 443–70.

Cheibub, Jose Antonio, Jennifer Gandhi and James Raymond Vreeland 2010. "Democracy and Dictatorship Revisited." *Public Choice* 143.1–2: 67–101.

Chen, Ming-tong 2012. "Taiwan in 2011: Focus on Crucial Presidential Election." *Asian Survey* 52.1: 72–80.

Cheng, Chen 1961. *Land Reform in Taiwan*. Taipei, Taiwan: China Pub. Co.

Cheng, Tun-jen 1993. "Guarding the Commanding Heights: The State as Banker in Taiwan," in Stephan Haggard, C. H. Lee and S. Maxfield (eds.), *The Politics of Finance in Developing Countries* (Ithaca, NY: Cornell University Press), 55–92.

Cheng, Tun-jen, Stephan Haggard and David Kang 1998. "Institutions and Growth in Korea and Taiwan: The Bureaucracy." *Journal of Development Studies* 34.6: 87–111.

Chiang, Sang-hwan 1984, 1985. "농지개혁 과정에 관한 실증적 연구: 충남 근흥면의 실태조사를 중심으로, 상,하 (An Empirical Study of the Process of Land Reform: Focusing on the Case Study of Geunheung-myon, Seosan-gun, Chungnam, I, II)." 경제사학 (*Studies in Economic History*) 8 (1984): 195–272; 9 (1985): 13–90.

Chin, Ko-lin 2003. *Heijin: Organized Crime, Business, and Politics in Taiwan*. Armonk, NY: M. E. Sharpe.

Cho, Yoon Je 1997. "Government Intervention, Rent Distribution, and Industrialization of Korea," in Masahiko Aoki, H. K. Kim and M. Okuno-Fujiwara (eds.), *The Role of Government in East Asian Economic Development: Comparative Institutional Analysis* (New York: Oxford University Press), 208–32.

Choi, Byung-sun 1993. "Financial Policy and Big Business in Korea: The Perils of Financial Regulation," in Stephan Haggard, C. H. Lee and S. Maxfield (eds.), *The Politics of Finance in Developing Countries* (Ithaca, NY: Cornell University Press), 23–54.

Chong, Alberto and Mark Gradstein 2007. "Inequality and Institutions." *Review of Economics and Statistics* 89.3: 454–65.

Chu, Yun-han 1994. "The Realignment of Business-Government Relations and Regime Transition in Taiwan," in Andrew MacIntyre (ed.), *Business and Government in Industrialising Asia*. Ithaca, NY: Cornell University Press, 113–41.

Chung, Byung-joon (정병준) 2003. "한국 농지개혁 재검토: 완료시점, 추진동력, 성격 (A Reinvestigation of Korean Agrarian Land Reform: Completed Date, Driving Force, and Characteristics)." 역사비평 (*Critique of History*) 65: 117–57.

Chung, Chi-nien and Ishtiaq P. Mahmood 2006. "Taiwanese Business Groups: Steady Growth in Institutional Transition," in Sea-jin Chang (ed.), *Business*

Groups in East Asia: Financial Crisis, Restructuring and New Growth. Oxford University Press, 70–93.

Chung, Chi-nien and Ishtiaq P. Mahmood 2010. "Business Groups in Taiwan," in Asli M. Colpan, Takashi Hikino and James R. Lincoln (eds.), *The Oxford Handbook of Business Groups.* Oxford University Press (online version).

Claessens, Stijn, Simeon Djankov and Larry H. P. Lang 2000. "The Separation of Ownership and Control in East Asian Corporations." *Journal of Financial Economics* 58: 81–112.

Clark, C. 2000. "Democracy, Bureaucracy, and State Capacity in Taiwan." *International Journal of Public Administration* 23.10: 1833–53.

Clifford, Mark L. 1998. *Troubled Tiger: Businessmen, Bureaucrats, and Generals in South Korea.* Armonk, NY: M. E. Sharpe.

Cole, A. 1967. "Political Roles of Taiwanese Enterprisers." *Asian Survey* 7: 645–54.

Copper, J. F. 2009. "The Devolution of Taiwan's Democracy during the Chen Shui-bian Era." *Journal of Contemporary China* 18.60: 463–78.

Coronel, Sheila S. (ed.) 1998. *Pork and Other Perks: Corruption and Governance in the Philippines.* Quezon City, Philippines: Philippine Center for Investigative Journalism.

    2004a. "Born to Rule: Dynasty," in Sheila S. Coronel, B. B. Cruz, L. Rimban and Y. T. Chua 2004. *The Rulemakers: How the Wealthy and Well-Born Dominate Congress.* Quezon City, Philippines: Philippine Center for Investigative Journalism, 44–117.

    2004b. "Houses of Privilege," in Sheila S. Coronel, B. B. Cruz, L. Rimban and Y. T. Chua 2004. *The Rulemakers: How the Wealthy and Well-Born Dominate Congress.* Quezon City, Philippines: Philippine Center for Investigative Journalism, 3–43.

    2007. "The Seven Ms of Dynasty Building." Philippines Center for Investigative Journalism. Available at http://pcij.org/stories/the-seven-ms-of-dynasty-building/.

Coronel, Sheila S., B. B. Cruz, L. Rimban and Y. T. Chua 2004. *The Rulemakers: How the Wealthy and Well-Born Dominate Congress.* Quezon City, Philippines: Philippine Center for Investigative Journalism.

Corpuz, Onofre D. 1957. *The Bureaucracy in the Philippines.* Quezon City, Philippines: University of the Philippines.

Crowther, William 1986. "Philippine Authoritarianism and the International Economy." *Comparative Politics* 18.3: 339–56.

Cullinane, Michael 1993. "Patron as Client: Warlord Politics and the Duranos of Danao," in Alfred W. McCoy (ed.), *An Anarchy of Families: State and Family in the Philippines.* Madison, WI: University of Wisconsin, Center for Southeast Asian Studies, in cooperation with Ateneo de Manila University Press, 163–242.

Cumings, Bruce 1984. "The Origins and Development of the Northeast Asian Political Economy: Industrial Sectors, Product Cycles and Political Consequences." *International Organization* 38.1: 1–40.

    2005. *Korea's Place in the Sun: A Modern History.* New York: Norton (updated edn).

Dahlström, Carl, Jan Teorell and Victor Lapuente 2012. "The Merit of Merito-cratization: Politics, Bureaucracy, and the Institutional Deterrents of Cor-ruption." *Political Research Quarterly* 65.3: 658–70.

de Castro, Isagani 1998. "Campaign Kitty," in Sheila S. Coronel (ed.), *Pork and Other Perks: Corruption and Governance in the Philippines*. Quezon City, Philippines: Philippine Center for Investigative Journalism, 216–43.

de Dios, Emmanuel S. and Paul D. Hutchcroft 2003. "Political Economy," in A. M. Balisacan and Hal Hill (eds.), *The Philippine Economy: Develop-ment, Policies, and Challenges* (Oxford; New York: Oxford University Press), 45–75.

de la Torre, Visitacion R. 1986. *History of the Philippine Civil Service*. Quezon City, Philippines: New Day Publishers.

Debs, Alexandre and Gretchen Helmket 2010. "Inequality under Democracy: Explaining the Left Decade in Latin America." *Quarterly Journal of Political Science* 5.3: 209–41.

Deininger, Klaus and Lyn Squire 1996. "A New Data Set Measuring Income Inequality." *World Bank Economic Review* 10: 565–91.

1998. "New Ways of Looking at Old Issues: Inequality and Growth." *Journal of Development Economics* 57.2: 259–87.

dela Rama, Marie 2012. "Corporate Governance and Corruption: Ethical Dilem-mas of Asian Business Groups." *Journal of Business Ethics* 109.4: 501–19.

Diaz-Cayeros, Alberto, Federico Estévez and Beatriz Magaloni 2011. *Strategies of Vote Buying: Democracy, Clientelism and Poverty Relief in Mexico*. Unpublished book manuscript.

Dincer, Oguzhan C. and Burak Gunalp 2012. "Corruption and Income Inequal-ity in the United States." *Contemporary Economic Policy* 30.2: 283–92.

Djankov, S., A. Shleifer, F. Lopez-de-Silanes and R. La Porta 2002. "The Reg-ulation of Entry." *Quarterly Journal of Economics* 117: 1–37.

Donchev, Dilyan and Gergely Ujhelyi 2009. "What Do Corruption Indices Mea-sure?" Available at SSRN: http://ssrn.com/abstract=1124066 or http://dx.doi.org/10.2139/ssrn.1124066.

Doner, Richard F., Bryan K. Ritchie and Dan Slater 2005. "Systemic Vulnerabil-ity and the Origins of Developmental States: Northeast and Southeast Asia in Comparative Perspective." *International Organization* 59.Spring: 327–61.

Doronila, A. 1992. *The State, Economic Transformation, and Political Change in the Philippines, 1946–1972*. Singapore: Oxford University Press.

Easterly, W. 2007. "Inequality Does Cause Underdevelopment: Insights from a New Instrument." *Journal of Development Economics* 84: 755–76.

Eichengreen, Barry 2010. *The Korean Economy: Coping with Maturity*. Unpub-lished book manuscript.

Engerman, Stanley L. and Kenneth L. Sokoloff. 1997. "Factor Endow-ments, Institutions, and Differential Paths of Growth among New World Economies: A View from Economic Historians of the United States," in Stephen Haber (ed.), *How Latin America Fell Behind*. Stanford, CA: Stanford University Press, 260–304.

Evans, Peter 1995. *Embedded Autonomy: States and Industrial Transformation*. Princeton, NJ: Princeton University Press.

Evans, Peter and James Rauch 1999. "Bureaucracy and Growth: A Cross-National Analysis of the Effects of 'Weberian' State Structures on Economic Growth." *American Sociological Review* 64: 748–65.

Examination Yuan 1984. *The Chinese Civil Service Examination System: A Historical Review*. Examination Yuan Secretariat, Republic of China.

Feenstra, Robert C. and Gary G. Hamilton 2006. *Emergent Economies, Divergent Paths: Economic Organization and International Trade in South Korea and Taiwan*. New York: Cambridge University Press.

Fei, J. C. H., G. Ranis and S. W. Y. Kuo 1979. *Growth with Equity: The Taiwan Case*. Washington, DC: IBRD/World Bank.

Fell, Dafydd 2005a. "Political and Media Liberalization and Political Corruption in Taiwan." *China Quarterly* 184: 875–93.

   2005b. *Party Politics in Taiwan: Party Change and the Democratic Evolution of Taiwan, 1991–2004*. London and New York: Routledge.

   2006. "Democratisation of Candidate Selection in Taiwanese Political Parties." *Journal of Electoral Studies* 13.2: 167–98.

Fields, Karl 1997. "Strong States and Business Organization in Korea and Taiwan," in S. Maxfield and B. R. Schneider (eds.), *Business and the State in Developing Countries*. Ithaca, NY: Cornell University Press, 122–51.

Fogel, Kathy 2006. "Oligarchic Family Control, Social Economic Outcomes, and the Quality of Government." *Journal of International Business Studies* 37.5: 603–22.

Francisco, Gregorio A. Jr. 1960. "Career Development of Filipino Higher Civil Servants." *Philippine Journal of Public Administration* 4.1: 1–18.

Francisco, Gregorio A. Jr. and Raul P. de Guzman 1963. "The 50–50 Agreement," in Raul P. de Guzman (ed.), *Patterns in Decision Making: Case Studies in Philippine Public Administration* (Manila, Philippines: Graduate School of Public Administration, University of the Philippines), 93–102.

Frankema, E. H. P. 2006. *The Colonial Origins of Inequality: The Causes and Consequences of Land Distribution*. Unpublished manuscript.

Friedman, Eric, Daniel Kaufmann, Pablo Zoido-Lobaton and Simon Johnson 2000. "Dodging the Grabbing Hand: The Determinants of Unofficial Activity in 69 Countries." *Journal of Public Economics* 76: 459–93.

Fukuyama, F. 1995. *Trust: The Social Virtues and the Creation of Prosperity*. New York: Free Press.

Galbraith, James 2009. "Inequality, Unemployment and Growth: New Measures for Old Controversies." *Journal of Economic Inequality* 7: 189–206.

Galbraith, James and Hyunsub Kum 2004. "Estimating the Inequality of Household Incomes: A Statistical Approach to the Creation of a Dense and Consistent Global Data Set." UTIP Working Paper No. 22. Available at http://utip.gov.utexas.edu/papers/utip_22rv5.pdf.

Gallin, Bernard 1961. "Hsin Hsing: A Taiwanese Agricultural Village." Ph.D. thesis, Cornell University.

Gallup, John L. and Jeffrey D. Sachs 2000. "The Economic Burden of Malaria." *American Journal of Tropical Medicine and Hygiene* 64: 85–96.

Gandhi, Jennifer and Ellen Lust-Okar 2009. "Elections under Authoritarianism." *Annual Review of Political Science* 12: 403–22.

Gayn, Mark 1954. "What Price Rhee? Profile of a Despot." *Nation* March 13: 214–17.

Geddes, Barbara 1994. *Politician's Dilemma: Building State Capacity in Latin America.* Berkeley, CA: University of California Press.

Gerring, John 2007. *Case Study Research: Principles and Practices.* New York: Cambridge University Press.

Gerring, John and Strom C. Thacker 2005. "Do Neoliberal Policies Deter Political Corruption?" *International Organization* 59.1: 233–54.

2004. "Political Institutions and Corruption: The Role of Unitarism and Parliamentarism." *British Journal of Political Science* 34.2: 295–330.

Glaeser, E. L. and R. E. Saks 2006. "Corruption in America." *Journal of Public Economics* 90.6–7: 1053–72.

Gold, Thomas B. 1986. *State and Society in the Taiwan Miracle.* Armonk, NY: M. E. Sharpe.

Gupta, Sanjeev, Hamid R. Davoodi and Rosa Alonso-Terme 2002. "Does Corruption Affect Income Inequality and Poverty?" *Economics of Governance* 3: 23–45.

Ha, Yong-chool and Myung-koo Kang 2011. "Creating a Capable Bureaucracy with Loyalists: The Internal Dynamics of the South Korean Developmental State, 1948–1979." *Comparative Political Studies* 44.1: 78–108.

Haggard, S., W. Lim and E. Kim (eds.) 2003. *Economic Crisis and Corporate Restructuring in Korea.* Cambridge University Press.

Haggard, Stephan 1990a. *Pathways from the Periphery: The Newly Industrializing Countries in the International System.* Ithaca, NY: Cornell University Press.

1990b. "The Political Economy of the Philippine Debt Crisis," in J. M. Nelson (ed.), *Economic Crisis and Policy Choice: The Politics of Adjustment in the Third World.* Princeton, NJ: Princeton University Press, 215–55.

1994. "Business, Politics and Policy in Northeast and Southeast Asia," in Andrew MacIntyre (ed.), *Business and Government in Industrialising Asia.* Ithaca, NY: Cornell University Press, 268–301.

Haggard, Stephan and Robert R. Kaufman 2008. *Development, Democracy, and Welfare States: Latin America, East Asia, and Eastern Europe.* Princeton University Press.

Hahm, Joon-ho 2003. "The Government, the Chaebol and Financial Institutions before the Economic Crisis," in S. Haggard, W. Lim and E. Kim (eds.), *Economic Crisis and Corporate Restructuring in Korea.* Cambridge University Press, 79–101.

Halkos, George Emm and Nickolaos G. Tzeremes 2010. "Corruption and Economic Efficiency: Panel Data Evidence." *Global Economic Review* 39.4: 441–54.

Ham, Han Hee (함한희) 1991. "해방 이후의 농지개혁과 궁삼면 농민의 사회경제적 지위 및 그 변화 (Post-liberation Land Reform and Changes in Socioeconomic Statuses of Peasants in Gungsam Village)." *Korean Anthropology* (한국문화인류학) 23: 21–62.

Han, Sungjoo 1974. *The Failure of Democracy in South Korea.* Berkeley, CA: University of California Press.

Hanguk Hyeokmyeong Jaepansa Pyeonchanwiwonhoi (한국혁명재판사 편찬위원회). 1962. 한국혁명재판사 (*A History of a Revolution in Korea*). 한국혁명재판사 편찬위원회.

Hayden, Joseph Ralston 1942. *Philippines: A Study in National Development*. New York: Macmillan Co.

Hazri, Herizal 2006. "Taiwan Legislative Election 2004: Report of International Observation Mission." Bangkok, Thailand: Asian Network for Free Elections (ANFREL). Available at: http://anfrel.org/download/2004_taiwan.pdf.

Heady, Ferrel 1957. "The Philippine Administrative System: Fusion of East and West," in William J. Siffin (ed.), *Toward a Comparative Study of Public Administration* (Bloomington, IN: Indiana University Press), 253–77.

Heidenheimer, A. J. 1963. "Comparative Party Finance: Notes on Practices and Toward a Theory." *Journal of Politics* 25.4: 790–811.

Hellman, Joel S., Daniel Kaufmann and Geraint Jones 2000. "Seize the State, Seize the Day: State Capture, Corruption, and Influence in Transition." *World Bank Policy Research Working Paper No. 2444*. Washington, DC: World Bank.

Hellmann, Olli 2011. *Political Parties and Electoral Strategy: The Development of Party Organization in East Asia*. New York: Palgrave Macmillan.

Henderson, Gregory 1968. *Korea: The Politics of the Vortex*. Cambridge, MA: Harvard University Press.

Heston, A., B. Aten and R. Summers 2009. *Penn World Table Version 6.3*. Center for International Comparisons of Production, Income, and Prices at the University of Pennsylvania (CICUP). Available at: https://pwt.sas.upenn.edu/php_site/pwt_index.php.

Hicken, Allen 2007. "How Do Rules and Institutions Encourage Vote Buying?" in Frederic C. Schaffer (ed.), *Elections for Sale: The Causes and Consequences of Vote Buying* (Boulder, CL: Lynne Rienner Publishers, Inc.), 47–60.

2008. "Politics of Economic Recovery in Thailand and the Philippines," in Andrew MacIntyre, T. J. Pempel and John Ravenhill (eds.), *Crisis as Catalyst: Asia's Dynamic Political Economy*. Ithaca, NY: Cornell University Press, 206–30.

2011. "Clientelism." *Annual Review of Political Science* 14: 289–310.

Higgins, Matthew and Jeffrey G. Williamson 1999. "Explaining Inequality the World Round: Cohort Size, Kuznets Curves, and Openness." *NBER Working Paper 7224*. Cambridge, MA: National Bureau of Economic Research.

Ho, Samuel P. S. 1978. *Economic Development of Taiwan, 1860–1970*. New Haven, CT: Yale University Press.

1987. "Economics, Economic Bureaucracy, and Taiwan's Economic Development." *Pacific Affairs* 60.2: 226–47.

Hodder, R. 2009. "Political Interference in the Philippine Civil Service." *Environment and Planning C: Government & Policy* 27.5: 766–82.

Hollyer, James R. and Leonard Wantchekon 2012. "Corruption in Autocracies." Available at SSRN: http://ssrn.com/abstract=1861464.

Hong, Song-chan (홍성찬) 2001. "농지개혁 전후의 대지주 동향 (Responses of the Landlords before and after the Land Reform)," in Song-Chan Hong (홍성찬) (ed.), 농지개혁 연구 (*Studies of Agrarian Land Reform*). Seoul, Korea: Yonsei University Press.

Hong, Sung-chul (홍성철) 2010. "유명환 장관 딸 특채파문 전모 (Full Story about the Special Recruitment of Minister Yoo Myung-hwan's Daughter)". 일요신문 (*Sunday Newspaper*), September 6, 2010.

Huntington, Samuel P. 1968. *Political Order in Changing Societies*. New Haven, CT: Yale University Press.

Husted, Bryan W. 1999. "Wealth, Culture, and Corruption." *Journal of International Business Studies* 30: 339–60.

Hutchcroft, Paul D. 1991. "Oligarchs and Cronies in the Philippine State: The Politics of Patrimonial Plunder." *World Politics* 43:3: 414–50.

1994. "Booty Capitalism: Business-Government Relations in the Philippines," in Andrew MacIntyre (ed.), *Business and Government in Industrialising Asia*. Ithaca, NY: Cornell University Press, 216–43.

1998. *Booty Capitalism: The Politics of Banking in the Philippines*. Ithaca, NY: Cornell University Press.

2011. "Reflections on a Reverse Image: South Korea under Park Chung Hee and the Philippines under Ferdinand Marcos," in Byung-kook Kim and Ezra F. Vogel (eds.), *The Park Chung Hee Era: The Transformation of South Korea* (Cambridge, MA: Harvard University Press), 542–72.

Iversen, Torben and David Soskice 2006. "Electoral Systems and the Politics of Coalitions: Why Some Democracies Redistribute More than Others." *American Political Science Review* 100.2: 165–81.

Iwasaki, Mum and Taku Suzuki 2007. "Transition strategy, Corporate Exploitation, and State Capture: An Empirical Analysis of the Former Soviet States." *Communist and Post-Communist Studies* 40.4: 393–422.

Jacobs, J. Bruce 2008. *Local Politics in Rural Taiwan under Dictatorship and Democracy*. Norwalk, CT: EastBridge.

Johnson, C. 1987. "Institutions and Economic Performance in South Korea and Taiwan," in F. Deyo (ed.), *The Political Economy of the New Asian Industrialism*. Ithaca, NY: Cornell University Press, 136–56.

Johnson, Noel D., Courtney L. LaFountain and Steven Yamarik 2011. "Corruption is Bad for Growth (Even in the United States)." *Public Choice* 147: 377–93.

Johnston, Michael 1989. "Corruption, Inequality, and Change," in P. Ward (ed.), *Corruption, Development and Inequality* (London and New York: Routledge), 13–37.

2008. "Japan, Korea, the Philippines, China: Four Syndromes of Corruption." *Crime, Law and Social Change* 49.3: 205–23.

Jones, Leroy and Il Sakong 1980. *Government, Business, and Entrepreneurship in Economic Development: The Korean Case*. Cambridge, MA: Harvard University Press.

Ju, Gyung-il (Korean name) and Mi-na Kim (Korean name) 2006. *(Understanding of Personnel Administration System in Korean Bureaucracy)*. Seoul, Korea: Gyongsewon.

Kalinowski, Thomas 2009. "The Politics of Market Reforms: Korea's Path from Chaebol Republic to Market Democracy and Back." *Contemporary Politics* 15.3: 287–304.

Kang, David C. 2002. *Crony Capitalism: Corruption and Development in South Korea and the Philippines*. Cambridge University Press.

2003. "Regional Politics and Democratic Consolidation," in Samuel S. Kim (ed.), *Korea's Democratization*. Cambridge University Press, 161–80.

Kasuya, Yuko 2009. *Presidential Bandwagon: Parties and Party Systems in the Philippines*. Pasig City, Philippines: Anvil Pub.

Kaufmann, Daniel and Aart Kraay 2002. "Growth without Governance." World Bank Policy Research Working Paper No. 2928.

Kaufmann, Daniel., A. Kraay and M. Mastruzzi 2010. "The Worldwide Governance Indicators: Methodology and Analytical Issues." *World Bank Policy Research Working Paper No. 5430*. Washington, DC: World Bank.

Kawakami, Momoko 2007. "The Rise of Taiwanese Family-Owned Business Groups in the Telecommunications Industry," in Alex E. Fernández Jilberto and Barbara Hogenboom (eds.), *Big Business and Economic Development: Conglomerates and Economic Groups in Developing Countries and Transition Economies under Globalisation*. London; New York: Routledge, 86–108.

Kawanaka, Takeshi 2007. "Who Eats the Most?: Quantitative Analysis of Pork Barrel Distributions in the Philippines." Institute of Developing Economies Discussion Paper No. 126. Available at: https://ir.ide.go.jp/dspace/bitstream/2344/633/3/ARRIDE_Discussion_No.126_kawanaka.pdf.

Keefer, P. and R. Vlaicu 2008. "Democracy, Credibility and Clientelism." *Journal of Law, Economics & Organization* 24.2: 371–406.

Keefer, Philip 2007. "Clientelism, Credibility, and the Policy Choices of Young Democracies." *American Journal of Political Science* 51.4: 804–21.

Keefer, Philip and Stephen Knack 1997. "Why Don't Poor Countries Catch up? A Cross-National Test of an Institutional Explanation." *Economic Inquiry* 35.3: 590–602.

Kerr, George H. 1965. *Formosa Betrayed*. Boston, MA: Houghton Mifflin.

Khan, Mushtaq H. 2000. "Rents, Efficiency and Growth," in Mushtaq H. Khan and Kwame Sundaram Jomo (eds.), *Rents, Rent-Seeking and Economic Development: Theory and Evidence in Asia*. Cambridge University Press, 21–69.

2006. "Determinants of Corruption in Developing Countries: The Limits of Conventional Economic Analysis," in Susan Rose-Ackerman (ed.), *International Handbook on the Economics of Corruption*. Cheltenham, UK; Northampton, MA: Edward Elgar Publishing, 216–44.

Kim, Byung-kook 1987. "Bringing and Managing Socioeconomic Change: The State in Korea and Mexico." Ph.D. dissertation, Harvard University, Cambridge, MA.

2000a. "Party Politics in South Korea's Democracy: The Crisis of Success," in Larry Jay Diamond and Byung-kook Kim (eds.), *Consolidating Democracy in South Korea*. Boulder, CO: Lynne Rienner Publishers, 53–85.

2003. "The Politics of *Chaebol* Reform, 1980–1997," in S. Haggard, W. Lim and E. Kim (eds.), *Economic Crisis and Corporate Restructuring in Korea*. Cambridge University Press, 53–78.

2011a. "The Leviathan: Economic Bureaucracy under Park," in Kim Byung-kook and Ezra F. Vogel (eds.), *The Park Chung Hee Era: The Transformation of South Korea*. Cambridge, MA: Harvard University Press, 200–32.

Kim, Byung-kook and Hyug-baeg Im 2001. "Crony Capitalism in South Korea, Thailand and Taiwan: Myth and Reality." *Journal of East Asian Studies* 1.2: 5–52.

Kim, Eun Mee 1997. *Big Business, Strong State: Collusion and Conflict in South Korean Development, 1960–1990*. Albany, NY: State University of New York Press.

2000b. "Reforming the Chaebols," in Larry Diamond and Doh Chull Shin (eds.), *Institutional Reform and Democratic Consolidation in Korea*. Stanford, CA: Hoover Institution Press, 171–98.

Kim, Hee Min, Jun Young Choi and Jinman Cho 2008. "Changing Cleavage Structure in New Democracies: An Empirical Analysis of Political Cleavages in Korea." *Electoral Studies* 27.1: 136–50.

Kim, Il-young (김일영) 1995. "농지개혁, 5.30 선거, 그리고 한국전쟁 (Agrarian Land Reform, May 30 Elections, and the Korean War)." 한국과 국제정치 (*Korea and International Politics*) 21: 301–35.

Kim, Jin-bae (김진배) and Chang-rae Park (박창래) 1968. "차관 (Foreign Loans)." 신동아 (*Shindonga*) (December) 76–94.

Kim, Joungwon A. 1975. *Divided Korea: The Politics of Development, 1945–1972*. Cambridge, MA: East Asian Research Center, Harvard University.

Kim, Kyongjae (김경제) 1991. 혁명과 우상: 김형욱 회고록 (*Revolution and Idols: Kim Hyong-uk's Memoir*). Seoul, Korea: 전예원 (Chonyewon).

Kim, Kyung Il (김경일) 1999. 공자를 죽여야 나라가 산다 (*Kill Confucius and the Nation will Prosper*). Seoul, Korea: 바다출판사 (Bada Press).

Kim, Sang-jo 2011b. "Concentration of Economic Power by Korean *Chaebols*: Engines of Growth or Threats to Democracy?" Working paper. Seoul, Korea: Hansung University.

Kim, Sung-ho (김성호) 2009. "이승만과 농지개혁 (Syngman Rhee and Land Reform)." 한국논단 (*Hanguknondan*) 9: 174–77.

Kim, Tae-woo (김태우) 2005. "한국전쟁기 북한의 남한 점령지역 토지개혁 (Land Reform in the Areas Occupied by the North during the Korean War)." 역사비평 (*Historical Critique*) 70: 243–73.

Kim, Wonik 2010. "Does Class Matter? Social Cleavages in South Korea's Electoral Politics in the Era of Neoliberalism." *Review of Political Economy* 22.4: 589–616.

Kim, Young-mo (김영모) 1982. 한국 지배층 연구 (*A Study of the Korean Ruling Class*). Seoul, Korea: 일조각 (Iljogak).

King, Russell 1977. *Land Reform: A World Survey*. Boulder, CO: Westview Press.

Kitschelt, Herbert 2000. "Linkages between Citizens and Politicians in Democratic Polities." *Comparative Political Studies* 33. Aug–Sept: 845–79.

Kitschelt, Herbert 2007. "The Demise of Clientelism in Affluent Capitalist Societies," in Herbert Kitschelt and Steven Wilkinson (eds.), *Patrons, Clients*

and Policies: Patterns of Democratic Accountability and Political Competition.
Cambridge, UK; New York: Cambridge University Press, 298–321.

2013. Dataset of the Democratic Accountability and Linkages Project (DALP).
Duke University. Available at: https://web.duke.edu/democracy/index.html.

Kitschelt, Herbert and Steven Wilkinson (eds.) 2007. *Patrons, Clients, and Policies: Patterns of Democratic Accountability and Political Competition.* New York: Cambridge University Press.

2007. "Citizen-Politician Linkages: An Introduction," in Herbert Kitschelt and Steven Wilkinson (eds.), *Patrons, Clients and Policies: Patterns of Democratic Accountability and Political Competition.* New York: Cambridge University Press, 298–321.

Klitgaard, Robert 1988. *Controlling Corruption.* Berkeley, CA: University of California Press.

Knack, S. 2006. *Measuring Corruption in Eastern Europe and Central Asia: A Critique of the Cross-Country Indicators.* Washington, DC: World Bank.

Koo, Hagen 2007. "The Korean Stratification System: Continuity and Change," in H. R. Kim and B. Song (eds.), *Modern Korean Society: Its Development and Prospect.* Berkeley, CA: Institute of East Asian Studies, 36–62.

Kunicová, J. and S. Rose-Ackerman 2005. "Electoral Rules and Constitutional Structure as Constraints on Corruption." *British Journal of Political Science* 35: 573–606.

Kuo, Cheng-tian 2000. "TWN's Distorted Democracy in Comparative Perspective." *Journal of Asian and African Studies* 35.1: 85–111.

Kuo, Jeng-liang Julian. 1995. "The Reach of the Party-State: Organizing Local Politics in Taiwan." Ph.D. dissertation, Department of Political Science, Yale University.

Kwon, Byung Tak (권병탁). 1984. "농지개혁의 과정과 경제적 기여 (Processes of Farmland Reform and its Economic Contribution in Korea)." 농업정책 연구 (*Korean Journal of Agricultural Policy*) 11.1: 191–207.

Kwon, Hyeok Yong 2008. "A Dynamic Analysis of Partisan Voting: The Issue Salience Effect of Unemployment in South Korea." *Electoral Studies* 27.3: 518–32.

La Porta, Rafael, Andrei Schleifer, Florencio Lopez-de-Silanes and Robert W. Vishny 1999. "The Quality of Government." *Journal of Law, Economics and Organization* 15: 222–79.

Lamba, S. K. and J. S. Tomar. 1986. *Impact of Land Reforms on Rural Development: A Critical Appraisal of India, Republic of China and Some Other Selected Countries.* New Dehli, India: Agricole Publishing Academy.

Lambsdorff, J. G. 2005. "Causes and Consequences of Corruption: What do we Know from a Cross-section of Countries?" Working Paper. University of Passau.

2006. "Measuring Corruption: The Validity and Precision of Subjective Indicators (CPI)," in C. Sampford, A. Shacklock, C. Connors and F. Galtung (eds.), *Measuring Corruption.* Aldershot, UK; Burlington, VT: Ashgate, 101–30.

Lande, C. H. 1965. *Leaders, Factions, and Parties: The Structure of Philippine Politics.* New Haven, CT: Yale University Press.

Landingin, Roel R. 2006. "Incentives for the Rich Harm the Poor." Philippine Center for Investigative Journalism. Available at: http://pcij.org/stories/incentives-for-the-rich-harm-the-poor/.

Lederman, D., N. V. Loayza and R. R. Soares 2005. "Accountability and Corruption: Political Institutions Matter." *Economics and Politics* 17.1: 1–35.

Lee, Hahn-been 1968. *Korea: Time, Change, and Administration*. Honolulu: East-West Center Press.

1996. *Lee Han-been hoigorok: Ilhamyo saenggakhamyo (Lee Han-been's Memoir: Working and Thinking)*. Seoul, Korea: Chosunilbosa.

Lee, Jae-hyung 2006. "Business Corruption, Public Sector Corruption and Growth Rate: Time Series Analysis Using Korean Data." *Applied Economics Letters* 13: 881–5.

Lee, Joung-woo (이정우) 1991. "한국의 부, 자본이득과 소득불평등 (Wealth, Capital Gain, and Income Inequality in Korea)." 경제논집 (*Economic Essays*) 30.3: 327–62.

Lee, Kang-seon (이강선) 2000. "조선왕조 관료채용제도에 관한 연구 (A Study of Bureaucratic Recruitment in Chosun Ddynasty)." 한국행정사학지 (*Korean Administrative History Review*) 9: 21–38.

Lee, Sam Youl and Kwangho Jung 2010. "Public Service Ethics and Anticorruption Efforts in South Korea," in Evan M. Berman, M. Jae Moon and Heungsuk Choi (eds.), *Public Administration in East Asia: Mainland China, Japan, South Korea, and Taiwan*. Boca Raton, FL: CRC Press, 401–26.

Lee, T. H. 1971. *Intersectoral Capital Flows in the Economic Development of Taiwan, 1895–1960*. Ithaca, NY: Cornell University Press.

Lee, Woong-hee (이웅희) and Chin-hyon Kim (김진현) 1964. "정치자금 (Political Funds)." 신동아 (*Shindonga*) September: 108–33.

Lee, Young Jo 1990. "Legitimation, Accumulation, and Exclusionary Authoritarianism: Political Economy of Rapid Industrialization in South Korea and Brazil." Ph.D. thesis, Harvard University.

Leff, Nathaniel 1964. "Economic Development through Bureaucratic Corruption." *American Behavioral Scientist* 8.3: 8–14.

Li, Hongyi, Heng-fu Zou and Lixin C. Xu 2000. "Corruption, Income Distribution, and Growth." *Economics and Politics* 12: 155–82.

Lie, John 1998. *Han Unbound: The Political Economy of South Korea*. Stanford, CA: Stanford University Press.

Lim, Wonhyuk 2003. "The Emergence of the Chaebol and the Origins of the Chaebol Problem," in S. Haggard, W. Lim and E. Kim (eds.), *Economic Crisis and Corporate Restructuring in Korea*. Cambridge University Press, 35–52.

2011. "Joint Discovery and Upgrading of Comparative Advantage: Lessons from Korea's Development Experience," in Shahrokh Fardoust, Yongbeom Kim and Claudia Sepúlveda (eds.), *Postcrisis Growth and Development: A Development Agenda for the G-20*. Washington DC: World Bank, 173–226.

2012. "Chaebol and Industrial Policy in Korea." *Asian Economic Policy Review* 7: 69–86.

Lin, Chia-lung 1998. "Paths to Democracy: Taiwan in Comparative Perspective." Ph.D. dissertation, New Haven, CT: Department of Political Science, Yale University.

Lucas, Robert E. Jr. 1993. "Making a Miracle." *Econometrica* 61.2: 251–72.

Luedde-Neurath, R. 1988. "State Intervention and Export-Oriented Development in South Korea," in Gordon White (ed.), *Developmental States in East Asia*. London: MacMillan.

MacIntyre, Andrew (ed.) 1994. *Business and Government in Industrialising Asia*. Ithaca, NY: Cornell University Press.

Magaloni, Beatriz 2006. *Voting for Autocracy: Hegemonic Party Survival and its Demise in Mexico*. Cambridge University Press.

Mahoney, James 2003. "Strategies of Causal Assessment in Comparative Historical Analysis," in James Mahoney and Dietrich Rueschemeyer (eds.), *Comparative Historical Analysis in the Social Sciences*. Cambridge University Press, 337–72.

Mahoney, James and Dietrich Rueschemeyer 2003. "Comparative-Historical Analysis: Achievements and Agendas," in James Mahoney and Dietrich Rueschemeyer (eds.), *Comparative Historical Analysis in the Social Sciences*. Cambridge University Press, 3–40.

Mangahas, Joel V. and Jose O. Tiu Sonco II 2011. "Civil Service System in the Philippines," in Evan M. Berman (ed.), *Public Administration in Southeast Asia: Thailand, Philippines, Malaysia, Hong Kong, and Macao*. Boca Raton, FL: CRC Press, 421–57.

Mangahas, Malou 2010a. "Poll Expense Reports of Erap, Arroyo, Wanna-Be Presidents Shot Full of Holes." Available at: http://pcij.org/stories/poll-expense-reports-of-erap-arroyo-wanna-be-presidents-shot-full-of-holes/.

Mangahas, Mahar 2010b. "Transparent Accountable Governance: The 2009 SWS Surveys on Corruption." Available at www.sws.org.ph.

Manow, P. 2005. "Politische Korruption und politischer Wettbewerb: Probleme der quantitativen Analyse (Political Corruption and Political Competition: Problems of Quantitative Analysis)." *Dimensionen politischer Korruption, Sonderheft der Politischen Vierteljahresschrift (Dimensions of Political Corruption, Special Issue of Political Quarterly)*. Wiesbaden: VS Verlag für Sozialwissenschaften (VS Publisher of Social Sciences).

Manzetti, Luigi and Carole J. Wilson 2007. "Why Do Corrupt Governments Maintain Public Support?" *Comparative Political Studies* 40.8: 949–70.

Marcos, Ferdinand E. 1974. *The Democratic Revolution in the Philippines*. Englewood Cliffs, NJ: Prentice-Hall International.

Markussen, Thomas 2011. "Inequality and Political Clientelism: Evidence from South India." *Journal of Development Studies* 47.11: 1721–38.

Marshall, M. G. and K. Jaggers 2002. "Polity IV Project: Political Regime Characteristics and Transitions, 1800–2002: Dataset Users Manual." University of Maryland.

Mason, Edward S., David C. Cole, Donald R. Snodgrass, Dwight H. Perkins, Il Sakong, Kwang Suk Kim, Leroy Jones, Mahn Je Kim and Noel F. McGinn 1980. *The Economic and Social Modernization of the Republic of Korea*. Cambridge, MA: Harvard University Press.

Mauro, Paolo 1995. "Corruption and Growth." *Quarterly Journal of Economics* 110: 681–712.

McGinn, Noel F., Donald R. Snodgrass, Shin-bok Kim, Quee-young Kim and Yung-bong Kim 1980. *Education and Development in Korea*. Cambridge, MA: Council on East Asian Studies, Harvard University.

McHale, Thomas R. 1959. "An Econecological Approach to Economic Development." Ph.D. dissertation, Harvard University.

Medalla, Erlinda M. 1998. "Trade and Industrial Policy Beyond 2000: An Assessment of the Philippine Economy." Philippine Institute for Development Studies Discussion Paper Series No. 98–105.

Meltzer, Allan H. and Scott F. Richard 1981. "A Rational Theory of the Size of Government." *Journal of Political Economy* 89: 914–27.

Mendoza, Ronald U., David Yap, Edsel L. Beja and Victor Soriano Venida 2012. "An Empirical Analysis of Political Dynasties in the 15th Philippine Congress." Available at SSRN: http://ssrn.com/abstract=1969605.

Meskill, Johanna M. M. (ed.) 1963. *The Chinese Civil Service: Career Open to Talent?* Boston, MA: Heath.

Milne, R. S. 1968. "Political Finance in Southeast Asia with Particular Reference to the Philippines and Malaysia." *Pacific Affairs* 41.4: 491–510.

Milo, Melanie S. 2002. "Analysis of the State of Competition and Market Structure of the Banking and Insurance Sectors," in Erlinda M. Medalla (ed), *Toward a National Competition Policy for the Philippines*. Makati, Philippines: Philippine Institute for Development Studies, 254–306.

Ministry of Government (총무처) 1977–1995 (various years). 총무처 연보 (*Government Affairs Yearbook*). 총무처 (Ministry of Government), Republic of Korea.

Ministry of Interior, Bureau of Statistics (내무부 통계국) 1954, 1957, 1964. 대한민국 통계연감 (*Statistical Yearbook of Republic of Korea*), 내무부 (Ministry of Interior), Republic of Korea.

Ministry of Justice (法務部), 1952–1985 (various years), 犯罪狀況及其分析 (*Crime Situation and Its Analysis*). 法務部 (Ministry of Justice), Republic of China.

    1986–2011 (various years). 法務統計年報 (*Annual Report of Legal Affairs Statistics*). 法務部 (Ministry of Justice), Republic of China.

Ministry of Justice Investigation Bueau (MJIB) 2011. *Anti-Corruption Yearbook*. Taipei, Taiwan: Ministry of Justice Investigation Bureau, Republic of China.

Minns, John 2001. "Of Miracles and Models: The Rise and Decline of the Developmental State in South Korea." *Third World Quarterly* 22.6: 1025–43.

Mitchell, C. Clyde 1949. "Land Reform in South Korea." *Pacific Affairs* 22.2 (June): 144–54.

Mitton, Todd 2008. "Institutions and Concentration." *Journal of Development Economics* 86.2: 367–94.

Mo, Jongryn 2009. "How Does Democracy Reduce Money Politics?: Competition versus the Rule of Law," in Jongryn Mo and David Brady (eds.), *The Rule of Law in South Korea*. Stanford, CA: Hoover Institution Press, 83–116.

Mo, Jongryn and Chung-in Moon 2003. "Business-Government Relations under Kim Dae-jung," in S. Haggard, W. Lim and E. Kim (eds.), *Economic Crisis and Corporate Restructuring in Korea*. Cambridge University Press, 127–49.

Mo, P. H. 2001. "Corruption and Economic Growth." *Journal of Comparative Economics* 29.1: 66–79.

Mojares, Resil B. 1993. "The Dream Goes On and On: Three Generations of the Osmenas, 1906–1990," in Alfred W. McCoy (ed.), *An Anarchy of Families: State and Family in the Philippines*. Madison, WI: University of Wisconsin, Center for Southeast Asian Studies, in cooperation with Ateneo de Manila University Press, 311–46.

Monsod, Toby C. 2008/2009. "The Philippine Bureaucracy: Incentive Structures and Implications for Performance." HDN Discussion Paper Series. PHDR 4.

Montinola, G. and R. Jackman 2002. "Sources of Corruption: a Cross-Country Study." *British Journal of Political Science* 32: 147–70.

Montinola, Gabriella 1999. "Politicians, Parties, and the Persistence of Weak States: Lessons from the Philippines." *Development and Change* 30: 739–74.

2012. "Change and Continuity in a Limited Access Order: The Philippines," in Douglas C. North, John Wallis, Steven Webb and Barry Weingast (eds.), *In the Shadow of Violence: Politics, Economics, and the Problems of Development*. Cambridge University Press, 149–97.

Moon, Chung-in 1994. "Changing Patterns of Business-Government Relations in South Korea," in Andrew MacIntyre (ed.), *Business and Government in Industrialising Asia*. Ithaca, NY: Cornell University Press, 142–66.

Moon, Woojin 2005. "Decomposition of Regional Voting in South Korea: Ideological Conflicts and Regional Interests." *Party Politics* 11.5: 579–99.

Moran, Jon 1999. "Patterns of Corruption and Development in East Asia." *Third World Quarterly* 20.3: 569–87.

Munck, Gerardo L. and Jay Verkuilen 2002. "Conceptualizing and Measuring Democracy: Evaluating Alternative Indices." *Comparative Political Studies* 35.1: 5–34.

Nemoto, Kuniaki 2009. "Committing to the Party: The Costs of Governance in East Asian Democracies." Ph.D. thesis, University of California, San Diego.

Nielson, Daniel L. and Matthew S. Shugart 1999. "Constitutional Change in Colombia: Policy Adjustment through Institutional Reform." *Comparative Political Studies* 32.3: 313–51.

North, Douglass C., John J. Wallis and Barry R. Weingast 2009. *Violence and Social Orders: A Conceptual Framework for Interpreting Recorded Human History*. New York: Cambridge University Press.

Oberdorfer, Don 2002. *The Two Koreas: A Contemporary History*. New York: Basic Books (revised and updated edn).

Ofreneo, Rene 1984. "Contradictions in Export-Led Industrialization: The Philippine Experience." *Journal of Contemporary Asia* 14.4: 485–95.

Oh, Dae-young (오대영) and Sang-min Sim (심상민) 1995. 한국의 지하경제 (*Underground Economy of Korea*). Seoul, Korea: 미래사 (Miraesa).

Oh, Sung-bae (오성배) 2004. "사립대학 팽창과정 탐색: 해방후 농지개혁기를 중심으로 (Exploration of Private University Expansion Process: Based on Land Reform after the Liberation)." *KEDI* 학술마당 (*KEDI Research Reports*) KD 2004–31–03–03: 1–20.

Paldam, M. 2001. "Corruption and Religion: Adding to the Economic Model." *Kyklos* 54: 383–413.

2002. "The Cross-Country Pattern of Corruption: Economics, Culture, and the Seesaw Dynamics." *European Journal of Political Economy* 18: 215–40.

Palmier, Leslie 1985. *The Control of Bureaucratic Corruption: Case Studies in Asia.* New Delhi: Allied Publishers.

Panizza, U. 2001. "Electoral Rules, Political Systems, and Institutional Quality." *Economics and Politics* 13.3: 311–42.

Park, Bae-gyoon 2003. "Territorialized Party Politics and the Politics of Local Economic Development: State-Led Industrialization and Political Regionalism in South Korea." *Political Geography* 22.8: 811–39.

Park, Cheol Hee 2008. "A Comparative Institutional Analysis of Korean and Japanese Clientelism." *Asian Journal of Political Science* 16.2: 111–29.

Park, Kyoungseok (박경석) 1967. "대통령 국회의원 선거자금 (Presidential and Legislative Campaign Funds)." 신동아 (*Shindonga*) May: 202–14.

Park, Suk Doo (박석두) 1987. "농지개혁과 식민지 지주제의 해체 : 경주 이 씨가 (李氏家) 의 토지경영사례를 중심으로 (Agrarian Land Reform and the Dissolution of Colonial Landlord System: The Case of Gyungjoo Lee Family's Land Management)." 경제사학 (*Studies in Economic History*) 11: 187–281.

Park, Sun-hwa (박선화) 1996. "전씨 비자금 2차공판: 어디에 얼마 썼나 (The Second Trial for Chun's Slush Fund: For What and How Much Did He Spend?)" 서울신문 (*Seoul Shinmun*) 4.16.

Parreno, Earl 1998. "Pork," in Sheila Coronel (ed.), *Pork and Other Perks: Corruption and Governance in the Philippines.* Quezon City, Philippines: Philippine Center for Investigative Journalism, 32–55.

Pasadilla, Gloria and Melanie S. Milo. 2005. "Effect of Liberalization on Banking Competition." Philippine Institute for Development Studies Discussion Paper Series No. 2005–03.

Pellegrini, L. and R. Gerlagh 2004. "Corruption's Effect on Growth and Its Transmission Channels." *Kyklos* 57.3: 429–56.

Pera't Pulitika (PAP) 2008. "Developing Baseline Data on Campaign Spending in the Philippines (Pilot Test: 2007 National and Local Elections." August 27, 2008.

Perkins, Dwight 2000. "Law, Family Ties, and the East Asian Way of Business," in Lawrence E. Harrison and Samuel P. Huntington (eds.), *Culture Matters: How Values Shape Human Progress.* New York: Basic Books, 232–43.

Perotti, Roberto 1996. "Growth, Income Distribution, and Democracy: What the Data Say." *Journal of Economic Growth* 1: 149–88.

Persson, T., G. Tabellini and F. Trebbi 2003. "Electoral Rules and Corruption." *Journal of the European Economic Association* 1.4: 958–89.

Persson, Torsten and Guido Tabellini 1994. "Is Inequality Harmful for Growth?" *American Economic Review* 84: 600–21.

Powelson, John P. and Richard Stock 1990. *The Peasant Betrayed: Agriculture and Land Reform in the Third World*. Washington, DC: Cato Institute.

Power, John H. and Gerardo P. Sicat 1971. *The Philippines: Industrialization and Trade Policies*. New York: Oxford University Press.

Putzel, James 1992. *A Captive Land: The Politics of Agrarian Reform in the Philippines*. London: Catholic Institute for International Relations.

Pye, Lucian W. with Mary W. Pye 1985. *Asian Power and Politics: The Cultural Dimensions of Authority*. Cambridge, MA: Belknap Press.

Quah, Jon S. T. 1999. "Comparing Anti-Corruption Measures in Asian Countries." CAS Research Paper Series No. 13. National University of Singapore.

2003. *Curbing Corruption in Asia: A Comparative Study of Six Countries*. Singapore: Eastern Universities Press.

2011. *Curbing Corruption in Asian Countries: An Impossible Dream?* Bingley, UK: Emerald Group.

Quimpo, Nathan Gilbert 2009. "The Philippines: Predatory Regime, Growing Authoritarian Features." *Pacific Review* 22:3: 335–53.

Quirino, Carlos and Laverne Y. Peralta 1986. *Ramon Durano: The Story of the Foremost Filipino Philanthropist*. Danao: Ramon Durano Foundation.

Ramseyer, J. M. and F. M. Rosenbluth 1993. *Japan's Political Marketplace*. Cambridge, MA: Harvard University Press.

Rauch, James E. and Peter Evans 2000. "Bureaucratic Structure and Bureaucratic Performance in Less Developed Countries." *Journal of Public Economics* 75.1: 49–71.

Reinikka, Ritva and Jakob Svensson 2003. "Using Micro-Surveys to Measure and Explain Corruption." *World Development* 34.2: 359–70.

Reyes, Vincente 2012. "Can Public Financing Overcome Corruption? A View from the Philippines," in Jonathan Mendilow (ed.), *Money, Corruption, and Political Competition in Established and Emerging Democracies*. Lanham, MD: Lexington Books, 145–68.

Riedinger, J. M. 1995. *Agrarian Reform in the Philippines: Democratic Transitions and Redistributive Reform*. Stanford, CA: Stanford University Press.

Rigger, Shelley 1994. "Machine Politics in the New Taiwan: Institutional Reform and Electoral Strategy in the Republic of China on Taiwan." Ph.D. dissertation, Cambridge, MA: Department of Government, Harvard University.

1999. *Politics in Taiwan: Voting for Democracy*. London: Routledge.

Rivera, Temario C. 1994. *Landlords and Capitalists: Class, Family, and State in Philippine Manufacturing*. Diliman, Quezon City, Philippines: U. P. Center for Integrative and Development Studies and University of the Philippines Press.

Robinson, James and Thierry Verdier 2013. "The Political Economy of Clientelism." *Scandinavian Journal of Economics* 115.2: 260–91.

Roche, Julian 2005. *Corporate Governance in Asia*. London and New York: Routledge.

Rodrik, Dani 1995. "Getting Interventions Right: How South Korea and Taiwan Grew Rich." *Economic Policy* 20: 55–107.

Roh, Tae-woo (노태우) 2011. 노태우 회고록: 국가, 민주화, 나의 운명 (*Roh Tae-woo Hoigorok: Gukga, Minjuhwa, Naui Unmyeong*). Seoul, Korea: 조선 뉴스프레스 (Chosun News Press), 1312.

Rose-Ackerman, Susan 1978. *Corruption: A Study in Political Economy*. London; New York: Academic Press.

　　1999. *Corruption and Government: Causes, Consequences and Reform*. Cambridge University Press.

　　2008. "Corruption," in C. K. Rowley and F. G. Schneider (eds.), *Readings in Public Choice and Constitutional Political Economy*. New York: Springer, 551–66.

Rothstein, Bo 2011. *The Quality of Government: Corruption, Social Trust, and Inequality in International Perspective*. University of Chicago Press.

Roy, Denny 2003. *Taiwan: A Political History*. Ithaca, NY: Cornell University Press.

Rueschemeyer, D. and J. D. Stephens 1997. "Comparing Historical Sequences – A Powerful Tool for Causal Analysis." *Comparative Social Research* 16: 55–72.

Schaffer, Frederic Charles 2007. "How Effective is Voter Education?" in F. C. Schaffer (ed.), *Elections for Sale: The Causes and Consequences of Vote Buying*. Boulder, CO: Lynne Rienner Publishers, 161–79.

Schneider, Ben Ross and Sylvia Maxfield 1997. "Business, the State, and Economic Performance in Developing Countries," in S. Maxfield and B. R. Schneider (eds.), *Business and the State in Developing Countries*. Ithaca, NY: Cornell University Press, 3–35.

Schopf, James C. 2004. "Corruption and Democratization in the Republic of Korea: The End of Political Bank Robbery." Ph.D. dissertation, University of California, San Diego.

Scott, James C. 1972. *Comparative Political Corruption*. Englewood Cliffs, NJ: Prentice-Hall.

Seligson, Mitchell A. 2006. "The Measurement and Impact of Corruption Victimization: Survey Evidence from Latin America." *World Development* 34.2: 381–404.

Seo, Joong-seok (서중석) 2008. 대한민국 선거 이야기: 1948 제헌선거에서 2007 대선까지 (*Stories of Elections in Republic of Korea: From the Constitutional Elections of 1948 to the Presidential Election of 2007*). Seoul, Korea: 역사비평 사 (Yeoksa Bipyoungsa).

Seo, Yong-tae (서용태) 2007. "대한민국 헌법 농지개혁 조항 입법화 과정과 귀 결 (The Process and Result of the Legislation of the Land Reform Clause in the Constitution of Rep. of Korea)." 역사와 세계 (*History and World*) 31: 105–42.

Seong, Kyoung-ryung 2008. "Strategic Regionalism and Realignment of Regional Electoral Coalitions: Emergence of a Conservative Government in the 2007 Presidential Election." *Korean Journal of Sociology* 42.8: 1–26.

Shea, Jia-dong 1994. "Taiwan: Development and Structural Change of the Financial System," in Hugh T. Patrick and Yung Chul Park (eds.), *The Financial Development of Japan, Korea, and Taiwan: Growth, Repression, and Liberalization*. New York: Oxford University Press, 222–87.

Shiau, Chyuan-jenq 1996. "Elections and the Changing State-Business Relationship," in Hung-mao Tien (ed.), *Taiwan's Electoral Politics and Democratic Transition: Riding the Third Wave*. New York: M. E. Sharpe, 213–25.

Shim, Ji-yeon (심지연) and Min-jeon Kim (김민전) 2006. 한국정치제도의 진화 경로: 선거, 정당, 정치자금 제도 (*The Evolutionary Path of Political Institutions in Korea: Electoral, Party, and Political Funds Systems*). Seoul, Korea: 백산서당 (Baeksanseodang).

Shin, Byeong-shik (신병식) 1997. "제1공화국 토지개혁의 정치경제 (The Political Economy of Land Reform in the First Republic)." 한국정치학회보 (*Korean Political Science Review*) 31.3: 25–46.

Simbulan, D. 2005 [1965]. *The Modern Principalia: The Historical Evolution of the Philippine Ruling Oligarchy*. Quezon City, Philippines: University of the Philippines Press.

Singer, Matthew 2009. "Buying Voters with Dirty Money: The Relationship between Clientelism and Corruption." Paper prepared for the American Political Science Association Annual Meeting. Toronto, September 3–6, 2009.

Simth, Theodore Reynolds 1970. *East Asian Agrarian Reform: Japan, Republic of Korea, Taiwan, and the Philippines*. Hartford, CT: John C. Lincoln Institute.

Social Weather Stations 2008. "The 2008 SWS survey review." Available at www.sws.org.ph/.

Solt, Frederick 2008. "Economic Inequality and Democratic Political Engagement." *American Journal of Political Science* 52.1: 48–60.

Son, Dae-sun (손대선) 2010. "행안부 행정고시 개편안, 성난 민심에 결국 제동 (Administration and Security Ministry's Civil Service Examination Reform Proposal Stopped by Public Outrage)." 뉴시스 (*Newsis*), September 9, 2010.

Stauffer, R. B. 1966. "Philippine Legislators and their Changing Universe." *Journal of Politics* 28.3: 556–97.

Steinberg, David I. and Myung Shin 2006. "Tensions in South Korean Political Parties in Transition: From Entourage to Ideology?" *Asian Survey* 46.4: 517–37.

Stern, Joseph J., Dwight Perkins, Ji-hong Kim and Jung-ho Yoo 1995. *Industrialization and the State: The Korean Heavy and Chemical Industry Drive*. Cambridge, MA: Harvard Institute for International Development.

Stokes, Susan 2007. "Political Clientelism," in Carles Boix and Susan Stokes (eds.), *The Oxford Handbook of Comparative Politics*. Oxford University Press, 604–27.

Strauss, Julia C. 1994. "Symbol and Reflection of the Reconstituting State: The Examination Yuan in the 1930s." *Modern China* 20.2(Apr): 211–38.

Su, Tsai-tsu 2010. "Civil Service Reforms in Taiwan," in Evan M. Berman, M. Jae Moon and Heungsuk Choi (eds.), *Public Administration in East Asia: Mainland China, Japan, South Korea, and Taiwan*. Boca Raton, FL: CRC Press, 609–26.

Sung, Hung-en 2004. "Democracy and Political Corruption: A Cross-National Comparison." *Crime, Law, and Social Change* 41.2: 179–94.

Supreme Prosecutors' Office (대검찰청) 1966–2009. 검찰연감 (*Prosecution yearbook*). 대검찰청 (Supreme Prosecutors' Office), Republic of Korea.

Svallfors, Stefan 2012. "Does Government Quality Matter? Egalitarianism and Attitudes toTaxes and Welfare Policies in Europe." *Department of Sociology Working Paper*. Umeå, Sweden: Umeå University.

Svensson, J. 2005. "Eight Questions about Corruption." *Journal of Economic Perspectives* 19.3: 19–42.

Swinnen, Lucy and Michael Lim Ubac 2012. "Philippine Bank Secrecy Laws Strictest in the World." *Manila/Philippine Daily Inquirer/Asia News Network*, February 18, 2012.

Tai, Hung Chao 1974. *Land Reform and Politics: A Comparative Analysis*. Berkeley, CA: University of California Press.

Tan, Quingshan 2000. "Democratization and Bureaucratic Restructuring in Taiwan." *Studies in Comparative International Development* 35.2: 48–64.

Taylor, C. L. and D. Jodice 1983. *World Handbook of Political and Social Indicators*. New Haven, CT: Yale University Press (3rd edn).

Taylor, Jay 2009. *The Generalissimo: Chiang Kai-shek and the Struggle for Modern China*. Cambridge, MA: Belknap Press of Harvard University Press.

Teehankee, Julio C. 2007. "And the Clans Play on." Philippine Center for Investigative Journalism. Available at: http://pcij.org/stories/and-the-clans-play-on/.

2009. "Citizen-Party Linkages in the Philippines: Failure to Connect?" in Friedrich Ebert Stiftung (ed.), *Reforming the Philippine Political Party System: Ideas and Initiatives, Debates and Dynamics*. Pasig City, Metro Manila, Philippines: Friedrich Ebert Stiftung.

2010. "Image, Issues, and Machinery: Presidential Campaigns in Post-1986 Philippines", in Yuko Kasuya and Nathan Gilbert Quimpo (eds.), *The Politics of Change in the Philippines*. Pasig City, the Philippines: Anvil.

Teorell, Jan, Marcus Samanni, Sören Holmberg and Bo Rothstein 2011. "The QoG Standard Dataset version 6Apr11." University of Gothenburg: The Quality of Government Institute. Available at: www.qog.pol.gu.se.

Thompson, M. R. 1995. *The Anti-Marcos Struggle: Personalistic Rule and Democratic Transition in the Philippines*. New Haven, CT: Yale University Press.

Tien, Hung-mao 1989. *The Great Transition: Political and Social Change in the Republic of China*. Stanford, CA: Hoover Institution Press, Stanford University.

Tien, Hung-mao and Yun-han Chu 1996. "Building Democracy in Taiwan." *China Quarterly* 148: 1141–70.

Transparency International. Corruption Perceptions Index (CPI) and Global Barometer Survey. Available at: www.transparency.org/.

Treisman, D. 2007. "What Have We Learned about the Causes of Corruption from Ten Years of Cross-national Empirical Research?" *Annual Review of Political Science* 10: 211–44.

Tuazon, Bobby 2008. "Kleptocracy: Using Corruption for Political Power and Private Gain." Quezon City, Philippines: Center for People Empowerment in Governance, University of the Philippines.

Ufere, Nnaoke, Richard Boland and Sheri Perelli 2012. "Merchants of Corruption: How Entrepreneurs Manufacture and Supply Bribes." *World Development* 40.12: 2440–53.

Uslaner, Eric and Bo Rothstein 2012. "Mass Education, State-Building and Equality: Searching for the Roots of Corruption." *QoG Working Paper Series* 2012: 5. Quality of Government Institute, University of Gothenburg.

Uslaner, Eric M. 2008. *Corruption, Inequality, and the Rule of Law: The Bulging Pocket Makes the Easy Life.* Cambridge; New York: Cambridge University Press.

Vanhanen, T. 2003. *Democratization: A Comparative Analysis of 170 Countries.* London: Routledge.

Wade, Robert 1990. *Governing the Market: Economic Theory and the Role of Government in East Asian Industrialization.* Princeton University Press.

Wang, Chin-shou 2004a. "Democratization and the Breakdown of Clientelism in Taiwan, 1987–2001." Ph.D. Thesis, University of North Carolina at Chapel Hill.

Wang, Chin-shou and Charles Kurzman 2007. "Dilemmas of Electoral Clientelism: Taiwan, 1993." *International Political Science Review* 28.2: 225–45.

Wang, Chin-shou (王金壽) 2004b. "瓦解中的地方派系:以屏東為例 (Collapsing Local Factions: The Case of Pingtung)." 台灣社會學 (*Taiwanese Sociology*) 7: 177–207.

Wang, Yi-ting 2012a. "South Korea," in Herbert Kitschelt and Yi-ting Wang (eds.), *Research and Dialogue on Programmatic Parties and Party Systems: Case Study Reports.* Durham, NC: Duke University, 158–91.

2012b. "Taiwan," in Herbert Kitschelt and Yi-ting Wang (eds.), *Research and Dialogue on Programmatic Parties and Party Systems: Case Study Reports.* Durham, NC: Duke University, 192–224.

Wedeman, Andrew 1997. "Looters, Rent-Scrapers, and Dividend Collectors: Corruption and Growth in Zaire, South Korea, and the Philippines." *Journal of Developing Areas* 31(Summer): 457–78.

2012. *Double Paradox: Rapid Growth and Rising Corruption in China.* Ithaca, NY: Cornell University Press.

Wei, S. J. 2000. "How Taxing is Corruption on International Investors?" *Review of Economics and Statistics* 82.1: 1–11.

Weitz-Shapiro, Rebecca 2012. "What Wins Votes: Why Some Politicians Opt Out of Clientelism." *American Journal of Political Science* 56.3: 568–83.

Wong, Kevin Tze Wai 2010. "The Emergence of Class Cleavage in Taiwan in the Twenty-First Century: The Impact of Cross-Strait Economic Integration." *Issues & Studies* 46.2: 127–72.

Woo, Jung-en 1991. *Race to the Swift: State and Finance in Korean Industrialization.* New York: Columbia University Press.

Woo-Cumings, Meredith 1995. "The Korean Bureacratic State: Historical Legacies and Comparative Perspectives," in James Cotton (ed.), *Politics and Policy in the New Korean State: From Roh Tae-woo to Kim Young-sam.* New York: St. Martin's Press, 141–69.

Wooldridge, Jeffrey M. 2000. *Introductory Econometrics: A Modern Approach.* Cincinnati, OH: South-Western College Publishing.

World Bank 1987. *World Development Report 1987*. New York: Oxford University Press.
  1993. *The East Asian Miracle: Economic Growth and Public Policy*. New York: Oxford University Press.
  2006. *World Development Report 2006: Equity and Development*. New York: Oxford University Press.
  2012. *Doing Business in a More Transparent World: Comparing Regulation for Domestic Firms in 183 Economies*. Washington, DC: World Bank.
World Economic Forum 2001–2012. *Global Competitiveness Report*.
  2011. *Financial Development Report*.
World Institute for Development Economics Research of the United Nations University (UNU-WIDER). *World Income Inequality Database (WIID)*, version 2.0C.
Wu, Chung-li 2001. "The Transformation of the Kuomintang's Candidate Selection System." *Party Politics* 7.1: 103.
Wu, Nai-teh 1987. "The Politics of a Regime Patronage System: Mobilization and Control within an Authoritarian Regime." Ph.D. dissertation, Chicago, IL: Department of Political Science, University of Chicago.
Wu, Xun 2005a. "Corporate Governance and Corruption: A Cross-Country Analysis." *Governance* 18.2: 151–70.
Wu, Yiping and Jiangnan Zhu 2011. "Corruption, Anti-Corruption, and Inter-County Income Disparity in China." *Social Science Journal* 48.3: 435–48.
Wu, Yongping 2004. "Rethinking the Taiwanese Developmental State." *China Quarterly* 77: 1–114.
  2005b. *A Political Explanation of Economic Growth: State Survival, Bureaucratic Politics, and Private Enterprises in the Making of Taiwan's Economy, 1950–1985*. Cambridge, MA: Harvard University Asia Center.
Wu, Yu-shan 2007. "Taiwan's Developmental State." *Asian Survey* 47: 977–1001.
Wurfel, David 1988. *Filipino Politics: Development and Decay*. Ithaca, NY: Cornell University Press.
Yang, Martin M. C. 1970. *Socio-Economic Results of Land Reform in Taiwan*. Honolulu: East-West Center Press.
Yi, Munyoung (이문영) 1966. "공무원 부패 이십년사 (Twenty Years of Civil Service Corruption)." 사상계 (*Sasanggye*) 14.3: 159–70.
You, Jong-Il 2010. "Political Economy of Economic Reform in South Korea." Working paper.
  1998. "Income Distribution and Growth in East Asia." *Journal of Development Studies* 34.6: 37–65.
You, Jong-sung 2006. "A Comparative Study of Corruption, Inequality, and Social Trust." Ph.D. dissertation, Harvard University.
  2009. "Is South Korea Succeeding in Controlling Corruption?" Paper prepared for the American Political Science Association Annual Meeting. Toronto, September 3–6, 2009.
  2012a. "Social Trust: Fairness Matters More Than Homogeneity." *Political Psychology* 33.5: 701–21.

2012b. "Transition from a Limited Access Order to an Open Access Order: The Case of South Korea," in Douglas C. North, John Wallis, Steven Webb and Barry Weingast (eds.), *In the Shadow of Violence: Politics, Economics, and the Problems of Development.* Cambridge University Press, 293–327.

You, Jong-sung and Sanjeev Khagram 2005. "A Comparative Study of Inequality and Corruption." *American Sociological Review* 70.1: 136–57.

Zak, P. J. and S. Knack 2001. "Trust and Growth." *Economic Journal* 111.470: 295–321.

Zakaria, Fareed 1994. "Culture Is Destiny: A Conversation with Lee Kuan Yew." *Foreign Affairs* 73.2: 109–26.

Ziblatt, D. 2009. "Shaping Democratic Practice and the Causes of Electoral Fraud: The Case of Nineteenth-Century Germany." *American Political Science Review* 103.1: 1–21.

Index

accountability, i, 1, 6, 9, 18, 21, 22, 24, 30, 33, 61, 65, 95, 101, 162, 197, 224, 236
  democratic accountability mechanisms, 1, 9, 18, 21, 22, 30, 33, 61, 236
  horizontal accountability mechanism, 7
  vertical accountability mechanism, 6, 24
adverse selection, 24, 25, 26, 27, 29, 30, 33, 65, 140, 164, 249, 252
agency loss, 23, 24, 25, 27, 30, 249, 251, 252
anti-corruption reforms. *See under* corruption
anti-oligarchy reform, 179
anti-trust laws, 209
Aquino, 80, 81, 101, 104, 134, 135, 147, 185, 252, 253, 261
  Benigno Aquino, 100
  Benigno Aquino III, 135
  Corazon Aquino, 100
Arroyo, Gloria Macapagal, 134, 135, 147, 149, 273
authoritarian regime, ix, 4, 13, 17, 22, 24, 35, 38, 46, 64, 65, 94, 95, 126, 129
authoritarian rule, 6, 17, 55
  Confucianism's authoritarian features, 10
autonomous state. *See* state autonomy, *See also* state, autonomous

balance-of-payments crises, 180
Bangko Sentral ng Pilipinas, 186
Bank of Korea, 190
Bank of Taiwan, 202
Bell Mission, 144
Binay, Jejomar, 135
black-gold politics, 119, 138, 209
  anti-black gold action plan, 173
block-vote system, 125
Board of Investment, 187

bribery. *See under* corruption
bureaucracy
  autonomous bureaucracies, 91
  bifurcated bureaucracy, 155
  bureaucratic apparatus, 127
  bureaucratic autonomy, 175
  bureaucratic corruption, viii, 8, 9, 12, 19, 20, 23, 25, 27, 29, 30, 34, 35, 36, 42, 44, 45, 53, 54, 62, 65, 93, 140, 141, 167, 168, 169, 171, 172, 173, 174, 175, 176, 222, 229, 236, 240, 245, 247, 249, 250, 254
  bureaucratic patronage, 14, 18, 19, 20, 220
  Confucian tradition, 164
  consequences of meritocracy and patronage, 167
  ghost employees, 149
  internal promotion and career stability, 62
  meritocratic bureaucracy, 19, 60, 141
  meritocratic recruitment, 22, 26, 27, 31, 61, 62, 140, 141, 153, 155, 156, 157, 158, 161, 163, 164, 165, 166, 173
  military-turned-bureaucrats, 151
  patronage appointment, 13, 22, 26, 27, 33, 36, 45, 65, 140, 141, 142, 144, 145, 155, 163, 164, 166, 167, 168, 247, 251, 254
  patronage jobs in, 9, 22, 26, 33, 93, 143, 164, 166
  patronage-ridden bureaucracy, 177, 213
  patronage-riddled bureaucracy, 141
  policy implementation process in, 10
  professional bureaucracy, 62
  professionalization of the bureaucracy, 153
  samuguan, 153
  Weberian bureaucracy, 4, 27, 61, 140
Business Environment and Enterprise Performance Survey, 224

CPSIA information can be obtained
at www.ICGtesting.com
Printed in the USA
LVHW080502271219
641802LV00007B/79/P